THE PLAYS OF IBSEN
Translated from the Norwegian
in Four Volumes by Michael Meyer

"This, one may think, is how Ibsen might have expressed himself in English."
—*The* (London) *Times*

"Meyer does justice, both in scholarship and understanding, to one of the most fascinating creative artists ever to find the chief expression of his gifts in drama."
—*Washington Post*

"Meyer's translations of Ibsen are a major fact in one's general sense of post-war drama. Their vital pace, their unforced insistence on the poetic center of Ibsen's genius, have beaten academic versions from the field."
—George Steiner, *The New Statesman*

"Crisp and cobweb-free, purged of verbal Victoriana."
—Kenneth Tynan

"Michael Meyer's translation gives back to the lines the poetry and dignity . . . which they certainly lack in the translations we have had for so long."
—*The Listener*

"Mr. Meyer's versions should remain definitive for this generation at least."
—*The Times Educational Supplement*

The Plays of Ibsen

Volume I
  A DOLL'S HOUSE
  EMPEROR AND GALILEAN
  JOHN GABRIEL BORKMAN
  WHEN WE DEAD AWAKEN

Volume II
  HEDDA GABLER
  THE PRETENDERS
  BRAND
  THE PILLARS OF SOCIETY

Published by WASHINGTON SQUARE PRESS

Volume III
  GHOSTS
  THE WILD DUCK
  THE MASTER BUILDER
  AN ENEMY OF THE PEOPLE

Volume IV
  PEER GYNT
  ROSMERSHOLM
  THE LADY FROM THE SEA
  LITTLE EYOLF

Coming Soon from WASHINGTON SQUARE PRESS

THE PLAYS OF
IBSEN

VOLUME II

HEDDA GABLER ▪ THE PRETENDERS
BRAND ▪ THE PILLARS OF SOCIETY

Translated from the Norwegian
and Introduced by
Michael Meyer

WASHINGTON SQUARE PRESS
PUBLISHED BY POCKET BOOKS NEW YORK

Hedda Gabler was first published in this translation in 1962 by Rupert Hart-Davis Ltd., subsequently by Methuen & Co. Ltd., in 1967 and in a revised edition by Eyre Methuen Ltd., in 1974. Copyright © Michael Meyer 1962, 1974. Introduction copyright © Michael Meyer 1962, 1974. Revised, 1980.

The Pretenders published in this translation in 1964 by Rupert Hart-Davis. Copyright © Michael Meyer 1964.

Brand was first published in Great Britain by Rupert Hart-Davis Ltd., in 1960. Copyright © Michael Meyer 1960. First published in a paperback edition by Methuen & Co. Ltd., in 1967. Reprinted 1973 by Eyre Methuen Ltd.

The Pillars of Society was first published in this translation in 1963 by Rupert Hart-Davis Ltd. Copyright © Michael Meyer 1963. Introduction copyright © Michael Meyer 1963. Revised, 1980.

A Washington Square Press Publication of
POCKET BOOKS, a division of Simon & Schuster, Inc.
1230 Avenue of the Americas, New York, N.Y. 10020

NOTE ON THE REVISED EDITION

In this edition, I have made certain revisions to the text resulting from successive productions of these translations. Occasionally, an actor or actress or director has come up with a better line than the one I originally wrote, and I have happily made the change. I have also made certain adjustments for American usage where a word or phrase would sound out of place to an American audience.

Michael Meyer
London
1985

CONTENTS

CONTENTS

HENRIK JOHAN IBSEN: A Chronology

1828   Born at Skien in southeast Norway on 20 March, the second child of Knud Ibsen, a merchant, and his wife Marichen, *née* Altenburg.

1834–5 Father becomes ruined. The family moves to Venstœp, a few miles outside Skien.

1844   Ibsen (aged fifteen) becomes assistant to an apothecary at Grimstad, a tiny seaport further down the coast. Stays there for six years in great poverty.

1846   Has an illegitimate son with a servant-girl, Else Sofie Jensdatter.

1849   Writes his first play, *Catiline* (in verse).

1850   Leaves Grimstad to become a student in Christiania (now Oslo). Writes second play, *The Warrior's Barrow.*

1851   Is invited to join Ole Bull's newly formed National Theatre at Bergen. Does so, and stays six years, writing, directing, designing costumes and keeping the accounts.

1852   Visits Copenhagen and Dresden to learn about the theatre. Writes *St. John's Eve,* a romantic comedy in verse and prose.

1853   *St. John's Eve* acted at Bergen. Failure.

1854   Writes *Lady Inger of Œstraat,* an historical tragedy in prose.

ix

1855   *Lady Inger of Œstraat* acted at Bergen. Failure.
        Writes *The Feast at Solhaug,* another romantic
        verse-and-prose comedy.

1856   *The Feast at Solhaug* acted at Bergen. Small suc-
        cess. Meets Suzannah Thoresen. Writes *Olaf
        Liljekrans,* a third verse-and-prose comedy.

1857   *Olaf Liljekrans* acted at Bergen. Failure. Leaves
        Bergen to become artistic manager of the Christi-
        ania Norwegian Theatre. Writes *The Vikings at
        Helgeland,* an historical prose tragedy.

1858   Marries Suzannah Thoresen. *The Vikings at
        Helgeland* staged. Small success.

1859   His only legitimate child, Sigurd, born.

1860-1 Years of poverty and despair. Unable to write.

1862   Writes *Love's Comedy,* a modern verse satire, his
        first play for five years. It is rejected by his own
        theatre, which goes bankrupt.

1863   Ibsen gets part-time job as literary adviser to the
        Danish-controlled Christiania Theatre. Extremely
        poor. Applies unsuccessfully to Government for fi-
        nancial support. Resorts to moneylenders. Writes
        The Pretenders, another historical prose tragedy. Is
        granted a travel stipend by the Government; this is
        augmented by a collection raised by Bjœrnson and
        other friends.

1864   *The Pretenders* staged in Christiania. A success.
        He leaves Norway and settles in Rome. Remains
        resident abroad for the next twenty-seven years.
        Begins *Emperor and Galilean.*

1865   Writes *Brand,* in verse (as a play for reading, not
        acting), in Rome and Ariccia.

1866   *Brand* published. Immense success; Ibsen be-
        comes famous throughout Scandinavia (but it is not
        acted for nineteen years).

1867 Writes *Peer Gynt,* in verse (also to be read, not acted), in Rome, Ischia and Sorrento. It, too, is a great success; but is not staged for seven years.

1868 Moves from Rome and settles in Dresden.

1869 Attends opening of Suez Canal as Norwegian delegate. Completes *The League of Youth,* a modern prose comedy.

1871 Revises his shorter poems and issues them in a volume. His farewell to verse; for the rest of his life he publishes exclusively in prose.

1873 Completes (after nine years) *Emperor and Galilean,* his last historical play. Begins to be known in Germany and England.

1874 Returns briefly to Norway for first time in ten years. The students hold a torchlight procession in his honour.

1875 Leaves Dresden after seven years and settles in Munich. Begins *The Pillars of Society,* the first of his twelve great modern prose dramas.

1876 *Peer Gynt* staged for first time. *The Vikings at Helgeland* is performed in Munich, the first of his plays to be staged outside Scandinavia.

1877 Completes *The Pillars of Society.* This makes him famous in Germany, where it is widely acted.

1878 Returns to Italy for a year.

1879 Writes *A Doll's House* in Rome and Amalfi. It causes an immediate sensation, though a decade elapses before it makes Ibsen internationally famous. Returns for a year to Munich.

1880 Resettles in Italy for a further five years. First performance of an Ibsen play in England (*The Pillars of Society* for a single matinée in London).

1881 Writes *Ghosts* in Rome and Sorrento. Violently attacked; all theatres reject it, and bookshops return it to the publisher.

1882	Writes *An Enemy of the People* in Rome. Cordially received. *Ghosts* receives its first performance (in Chicago).
1884	Writes *The Wild Duck* in Rome and Gossensass. It, and all his subsequent plays, were regarded as obscure and were greeted with varying degrees of bewilderment.
1885	Revisits Norway again, for the first time since 1874. Leaves Rome and resettles in Munich.
1886	Writes *Rosmersholm* in Munich.
1888	Writes *The Lady from the Sea* in Munich.
1889	Meets and becomes infatuated with the eighteen-year-old Emilie Bardach in Gossensass. Does not see her again, but the experience shadows the remainder of his writing. Janet Achurch acts Nora in London, the first major English-speaking production of Ibsen.
1890	Writes *Hedda Gabler* in Munich.
1891	Returns to settle permanently in Norway.
1892	Writes *The Master Builder* in Christiania.
1894	Writes *Little Eyolf* in Christiania.
1896	Writes *John Gabriel Borkman* in Christiania.
1899	Writes *When We Dead Awaken* in Christiania.
1901	First stroke. Partly paralysed.
1903	Second stroke. Left largely helpless.
1906	Dies in Christiania on 23 May, aged seventy-eight.

Hedda Gabler

Introduction

Hedda Gabler occupies a curious, almost anachronistic position in the Ibsen cycle. He wrote it in 1890, between *The Lady from the Sea* and *The Master Builder*, but if one had to date it from internal evidence one would be tempted to place it ten years earlier, as a companion piece to *A Doll's House*, *Ghosts* and *An Enemy of the People*. Like them, it is written very simply and directly; we feel, as in those plays, that he is working within an illuminated circle and not, as in the plays of his final period from *The Lady from the Sea* onwards, that he is exploring the darkness outside that circle. At first sight, again, it appears to differ from these final plays in not being an exercise in self-analysis. This, however, is an illusion, for if we examine *Hedda Gabler* closely we find that it contains one of the most revealing self-portraits he ever painted. The play might, indeed, be subtitled 'Portrait of the Dramatist as a Young Woman'.

The circumstances under which he wrote *Hedda Gabler* were as follows. In the summer of 1889, while holidaying at Gossensass in the Tyrol, Ibsen, then aged sixty-one, had become violently infatuated with an eighteen-year-old Viennese girl named Emilie Bardach. After his return to Munich in September, they wrote to each other continuously for four months; then Ibsen broke off the correspondence, and apart from two brief letters towards the end of the year and a third, seven years later, in acknowledgement of a telegram of congratulations, he did not contact her again. Two years later he was to use this relationship of mutual infatuation as the basis for *The Master Builder,* but the change it wrought on Ibsen was immediate. For years he had deliberately suppressed his own emotional life, an undersized and ugly man resigned to a loveless marriage; but his encounter with Emilie had awoken him to the realization that, as Graham Greene has remarked, fame is a powerful aphrodisiac, and he now entered on a series of romantic relationships with women thirty to forty years his junior. (Indeed, the second of these, with the artist Helene Raff, began while he was still corresponding with Emilie.)

It is unlikely, however, that any of these relationships ever resulted in a physical affair, and this meant that, while immensely enriching his work, they also introduced into it a strong undertone of pessimism. In 1887, in a speech in Stockholm, he had startled his audience by describing himself as an 'optimist', and *The Lady from the Sea,* written in 1888, had reflected this optimism. 'After so many tragedies,' Edmund Gosse had written on its appearance, 'this is a comedy . . . the tone is quite unusually sunny, and without a tinge of pessimism. It is in some respects the reverse of *Rosmersholm,* the bitterness of restrained and balked individuality, which ends in death, being contrasted with the sweetness of emancipated and gratified individuality, which leads to health and peace.' But none of his five subsequent plays could by any possible stretch of the imagination be described as comedies. The mood of *Hedda Gabler, The Master Builder, Little Eyolf, John Gabriel Borkman* and *When We Dead Awaken* is, like that of *Rosmersholm,* 'restrained and balked individuality', and I do not think there can be much doubt that this stems from the realization that for various reasons (fear of scandal, sense of duty towards his wife, consciousness of old age, perhaps the consciousness or fear of physical impotence), he, who had suppressed his emotional life for so long, now had the opportunities to fulfil it, but was unable to take advantage of them. As a result of his meeting with Emilie Bardach a new glory, but also a new darkness, entered into his work.

He began to plan a new play immediately on his return from Gossensass. Only a week after arriving in Munich, on 7 October 1889, he wrote to Emilie: 'A new poem begins to dawn in me. I want to work on it this winter, transmuting into it the glowing inspiration of the summer. But the end may be disappointment. I feel it. It is my way.' A week later, on 15 October, he wrote to her: 'My imagination is ragingly at work, but always straying to where in working hours it should not. I cannot keep down the memories of the summer, neither do I want to. The things we have lived through I live again and again—and still again. To make of them a poem is for the time being impossible. For the time being? Shall I ever succeed in the future? And do I really wish that I could and would so succeed? For the moment, at any rate, I cannot.' However, on 19 November he wrote more cheerfully: 'I am greatly preoccupied with the preparations for my new play. Sit tight at my desk the whole day. Go out only towards evening. I dream and remember and write.'

Unfortunately, we do not know whether the play he was working on at this time was in fact *Hedda Gabler*. Ibsen left eight sets of rough notes dating from around this period; most of them obviously refer to *Hedda Gabler*, but some seem to point towards *The Master Builder* and others towards a third play which he never ultimately wrote, and since these notes are undated we cannot be sure to which of the three projects he was referring in his letters to Emilie. Some scholars think he did not begin to plan *Hedda* until April 1890; others believe he had already conceived it as early as February 1889. At any rate, by the spring of 1890 Ibsen's plans for *Hedda* were sufficiently advanced for him to express the hope that he would have his first draft ready by midsummer, so that he would be able to work on it during his summer holiday in (again) Gossensass. But on 29 June 1890 he wrote to Carl Snoilsky, the Swedish poet (generally assumed to be the original of Rosmer) that the play had not worked out and that he was staying in Munich until he could get the first draft finished. Perhaps he feared Gossensass might awake disturbing memories.

As things turned out, he did not complete the first draft of even Act I until 10 August. On 13 August he began Act 2, but early in September he scrapped this, and on 6 September he began a new draft of this act. Things now went better, for by 7 October he had completed the draft not only of Act 2 but also of Acts 3 and 4. The play was at this stage entitled simply *Hedda,* and the draft in which it exists bears all the appearance of having been made as a fair copy to send to the printer. But he was not satisfied, and rewrote the play thoroughly, introducing into it for the first time many of its most striking and famous features. This revisionary work occupied him until 18 November, and *Hedda Gabler,* as he now entitled it, to underline the fact that she was her father's daughter rather than her husband's wife, was published by Gyldendal of Copenhagen on 16 December 1890, only just in time for the Christmas sales—always an important consideration with Ibsen, who depended on book sales in Scandinavia for a large proportion of his income.*

As with every play he wrote after *A Doll's House* in 1879, excepting only the comparatively light and simple *Enemy of the People,* the public reaction was one of utter bewilderment. Halvdan Koht, in his introduction (1934) to the play in the centenary edition of Ibsen's works, has described how

---

*His plays, though widely staged, were usually put on for a few performances only. For example, it was not until 1925 that any English production of Ibsen achieved a run of fifty performances.

Norway received it. 'Its only message seemed to be despair. No meaning nor purpose, simply a suicide ending an absolutely pointless life. . . . In contemporary criticisms the most common word used to describe the main character is "puzzling", "improbable" or "incredible". Readers got the impression that in the concluding line of the play—"But, good God! People don't do such things!"—Ibsen was making fun of them; for it reminded them that too many of them had said just that about Nora's final action in *A Doll's House*. There were things in *Hedda Gabler* that seemed almost intended to parody *A Doll's House*—for example, Hedda's lie about having destroyed the manuscript to help her husband, or the curious form of "comradeship" between man and woman portrayed here.' Bredo Morgenstierna wrote in *Aftenposten* of 'the obscurity, the eccentric and abnormal psychology, the empty and desolate impression which the whole picture leaves', while Alfred Sinding-Larsen in *Morgenbladet* described Hedda herself as 'a horrid miscarriage of the imagination, a monster in female form to whom no parallel can be found in real life'.

Nor, as with some of his plays (e.g. *Ghosts*), were people much enlightened when *Hedda Gabler* was performed. At the première on 31 January 1891, at the Residenztheater, Munich, the public whistled. Ibsen was present and was much displeased at the declamatory manner of the actress who played Hedda. On 10 February there was a rather better performance at the Lessing Theatre in Berlin, but even here neither the public nor the critics seem to have understood the play. Nor was it a success in Stockholm or Gothenburg, while in Copenhagen on 25 February it was a complete fiasco, being greeted by hissing, whistling and laughter. The following evening it was given in Christiania, also inadequately. The first respectable performance of *Hedda Gabler* was, improbably, in London (20 April 1891), where, although it called forth the usual stream of abuse from the popular newspapers ('What a horrible story! What a hideous play!' wrote Clement Scott in the *Daily Telegraph,* and the *Pictorial World* commented: 'The play is simply a bad escape of moral sewage-gas . . . Hedda's soul is a-crawl with the foulest passions of humanity'), intelligent opinion was considerably impressed. Henry James, who had been puzzled by *Hedda Gabler* on reading it, found the performance gratifyingly illuminating. 'The play on perusal', he wrote (*On the Occasion of Hedda Gabler,* 1891), 'left one comparatively muddled and mystified, fascinated but—in one's intellectual sympathy—snubbed. Acted, it leads that sympathy over the straightest of roads with all the exhilaration of a superior pace.' But he added a gentle rider. 'Much more, I confess, one doesn't get from it; but an hour of refreshing exercise is a reward in itself. . . . Ibsen is various, and *Hedda Gabler* is probably an ironical pleasantry, the artistic exercise of a mind saturated with the vision of human infirmities; saturated, above all, with a sense of the infinitude, for all its mortal savour, of *character,* finding that an endless romance and a perpetual challenge. Can there have been at the source of such a production a mere refinement of conscious power, an enjoyment of difficulty and a preconceived victory over it?'

There are many people who share James's view of *Hedda Gabler* as a brilliant but, for Ibsen, curiously detached, objective, almost brutal 'exercise'—a view which has been greatly fostered by the tendency of actresses to portray Hedda as an evil genius, a kind of suburban Lady Macbeth. The opposite view, that it is one of Ibsen's most 'committed' plays, has been brilliantly argued by Dr. Arne Duve in his wayward but stimulating book *Symbolikken i Henrik Ibsens Skuespill* (Nasjonalforlaget, Oslo, 1945). Dr. Duve suggests that Hedda represents Ibsen's repressed and crippled emotional life. As a young man, he reminds us, Ibsen had been wildly emotional; at eighteen he had fathered an illegitimate child, and at least once during those early years he became a near-alcoholic and is believed to have attempted suicide. Lœvborg and Tesman, Dr. Duve argues, are aspects of Ibsen's own self; Lœvborg is an idealized portrait of himself as he had been in the wild years of his youth, Tesman a *reductio ad absurdum* of what he had chosen to become. Lœvborg stands for Ibsen's emotional self, Tesman for his intellectual self. Ibsen was haunted throughout the latter half of his life by the feeling that he had stifled his emotional self and that only his bourgeois and slightly ludicrous intellectual self had lived on. He had persuaded himself to accept this state of affairs, but the encounter with Emilie Bardach seems to have brought all his old feelings of guilt rushing to the surface. Hedda longs to be like Lœvborg, but lacks the courage; she is repelled by the reality of sex (as Ibsen himself was?) and prefers to experience it vicariously by encouraging Lœvborg to describe his experiences to her. Two emotions are dominant in her, the fear of scandal and the fear of ridicule, and Ibsen himself, though always willing to trail his coat in print, seems also to have been privately dominated by these emotions.

But if *Hedda Gabler* is, in fact, a self-portrait, it is certainly an unconscious one—not that that makes it any the less truthful or valuable; rather the reverse. Ibsen's rough preliminary jottings referred to above make it clear that he *intended* the play as a tragedy of the purposelessness of life, and in particular of the purposelessness imposed on women of his time both by their upbringing and by the social conventions which limited their activities. The following extracts will serve as examples:

'(1) They aren't all created to be mothers.
 (2) They all have a leaning towards sensuality, but are afraid of the scandal.

(3) They realize that life holds a purpose for them, but they cannot find that purpose.'

'Women have no influence on public affairs. So they want to influence individuals spiritually.'

'The great tragedy of life is that so many people have nothing to do but yearn for happiness without ever being able to find it.'

'Men and women don't belong to the same century.'

'There are very few true parents in the world. Most people are brought up by uncles or aunts—neglected or misunderstood or spoiled.'

'The play is to be about "the insuperable"—the longing and striving to defy convention, to defy what people accept (including Hedda).'

'Hedda is typical of women in her position and with her character. One marries Tesman but one titillates one's imagination with Eilert Lœvborg. One leans back in one's chair, closes one's eyes and pictures to oneself his adventures. The enormous difference: Mrs. Elvsted "works to improve him morally", while for Hedda he is merely a subject for cowardly and tantalizing dreams. She lacks the courage to partake actively in such goings-on. Then her confession as to how she really feels. Tied! Don't understand— But to be an object of ridicule! Of ridicule!'

'The daemon in Hedda is that she wants to influence another human being, but once that has happened, she despises him.'

'Lœvborg has leanings towards Bohemianism. Hedda is also attracted to it, but dares not take the jump.'

'It's really a man's life she wants to lead. In all respects. But then scruples intervene. Some inherited—some implanted.'

'Remember I was born the child of an old man. And not merely old. Played-out—or anyway, decrepit. Perhaps that has left its mark.'

'It is a great delusion that one only loves one person.'

'Tesman represents propriety. Hedda represents *ennui*. Mrs. R. [i.e. Mrs. Elvsted] modern nervousness and hysteria. Brack the representative of bourgeois society.'

'H.L. [i.e. Lœvborg]'s despair arises from the fact that he wants to control the world but cannot control himself.'

'Life for Hedda is a farce which isn't worth seeing through to the end.'

As usual with Ibsen's plays, certain elements in *Hedda Gabler* can be traced to incidents in the lives of people whom he knew personally or had heard or read about. For example, when he visited Norway in 1885 he must have heard of the marriage the previous winter between a famous beauty named Sophie Magelssen and the philologist Peter Groth. Groth had married her on a research grant which he had won in competition with Hjalmar Falk, whom many thought the better scholar of the two (and who gets a consolatory mention in the play as the dead Cabinet Minister who had previously owned the Tesmans' villa). Neither Tesman nor Lœvborg, however, was modelled on either of these two. Ibsen told his son Sigurd that he had based Tesman on Julius Elias, a young German student of literature whom he had got to know in Munich. Elias's great passion was for 'putting other people's papers in order'; later he became a distinguished man of letters, and ironically enough it fell to him to put Ibsen's own papers in order when he shared with Halvdan Koht the task of editing the dramatist's literary remains.* Lœvborg was closely modelled on a Dane named Julius Hoffory who was Professor of Scandinavian Philol-

---

*In fairness to Elias, it should be stated that Tesman is a much less ridiculous character in the early draft of the play than Ibsen subsequently made him. His maddening repetition of nursery phrases such as 'Fancy that!' was added during revision.

ogy and Phonetics in Berlin. Hoffory was a gifted but unbalanced man who mixed freely with women of low repute and had once lost the manuscript of a book during a nocturnal orgy. He recognized himself delightedly when *Hedda Gabler* appeared, and thereafter adopted Lœvborg as his pseudonym.

Miss Tesman, George's aunt, was based on an old lady from Trondhejm named Elise Hokk. Ibsen had met her a number of times during the early seventies in Dresden, where she tended a sick sister for three years until the latter died. He wrote a charming poem in tribute to her in 1874. She is the only character in the play, as far as is known, who was based on a Norwegian original, and this may have influenced early critics who wrote that *Hedda Gabler* was the least Norwegian of Ibsen's plays and that the town (unnamed as usual) in which the action takes place was less suggestive of Christiania than of a Continental capital. William Archer, however, who knew Christiania well, felt sure that Ibsen had that city in mind, and added the interesting comment that Ibsen, although writing in 1890, seemed to have set the play some thirty years earlier. 'The electric cars, telephones and other conspicuous factors in the life of a modern capital', he wrote in his introduction (1907) to the English translation by himself and Edmund Gosse, 'are notably absent from the play. There is no electric light in Secretary Falk's villa. It is still the habit for ladies to return on foot from evening parties, with gallant swains escorting them. This "suburbanism" which so distressed the London critics of 1891, was characteristic of the Christiania Ibsen himself had known in the eighteen-sixties—the Christiania of *Love's Comedy*—rather than of the greatly extended and modernised city of the end of the century.'

Three further incidents which came to Ibsen's notice found their way into the play. While he was actually working on it, a young married couple came to seek his advice;

their happiness, they said, had been ruined because the husband had been hypnotized by another woman. Then there was the unfortunate case of the Norwegian composer Johan Svendsen, whose wife, Sally, in a fit of rage at discovering a letter from another woman hidden in a bouquet of flowers, had burned the score of a symphony which he had just composed. Finally, he heard of the even more unfortunate incident of the Norwegian lady whose husband had cured himself of drink and had resolved never to touch it again. To see how much power she had over him, she rolled a keg of brandy into his room as a birthday present, and before the day was over he was dead drunk. All these episodes are reflected in *Hedda Gabler*.

The original of Hedda herself is not known. She has been rather glibly assumed by some critics to be a portrait of Emilie, on the grounds that both were beautiful and aristocratic and did not know what to do with their lives, and that Ibsen's description of Hedda (aristocratic face, fine complexion, veiled expression in the eyes, etc.) corresponds to early photographs of Emilie. The same characteristics could, however, be found in the photograph of almost any well-born young lady of the period; the description would apply equally to Queen Alexandra; and few women of Ibsen's time, let alone girls of eighteen, knew what to do with their lives. In any case, the idea of creating such a character had been at the back of Ibsen's mind long before he met Emilie, for his rough notes for *Rosmersholm* (1886) contain a sketch of a girl, intended as Rosmer's elder daughter, though he finally decided not to include her in the play, who 'is in danger of succumbing to inactivity and loneliness. She has rich talents which are lying unused.' On the other hand, Emilie must certainly have been at the back of his mind when he was writing *Hedda Gabler*, and it is possible that Hedda may be a portrait, conscious or unconscious, of what Emilie might become in ten years if she did not marry the right man or find a fixed purpose in life. If so, it was a prophecy that came uncomfortably near the truth, for Emilie, though she lived to be eighty-three—she died as late as 1 November 1955—accomplished nothing and never married.

The differences between Ibsen's first draft and his final version as we know it are, as has already been remarked, numerous and revealing. Apart from changing Tesman from an ordinary bourgeois husband into a ninny spoiled (like Hjalmar Ekdal) by loving aunts, he improved him morally, for in the first draft it is Tesman who suggests hiding the manuscript to give Lœvborg a fright, and so is partly responsible for the latter's death. Miss Tesman's important account to Bertha in Act I of Hedda's life with her father was an afterthought; so were Mademoiselle Danielle, Mrs. Elvsted's abundant hair and Hedda's jealousy of it, the image of the vine-leaves, and Hedda's threat (before the play opens) to shoot Lœvborg. Act I ends much less strongly in the draft, with no mention of the pistols; and Tesman and Mrs. Elvsted both know of Hedda's former close relationship with Lœvborg. Miss Tesman's role is less complex than in the final version; she does not realize in Act I that Hedda is going to have a baby, and has a far less effective scene with Hedda in Act 4. The conversation between Hedda, Lœvborg and Tesman over the photograph album about the honeymoon contains a direct reference to Gossensass, subsequently deleted. And Brack, in a passage which one is rather sorry to lose, describes sadly to Hedda how three 'triangles' of which he was a part have been broken up during the past six months—not, as Hedda guesses, by other bachelors but by intruders far more destructive to extramarital relationships—children. Finally, one may note two remarks which Ibsen originally put into Hedda's mouth but subsequently deleted: (1) 'I can't understand how anyone could fall in love with a man who isn't married—or engaged—or at least in love with someone else.' (2) 'To take someone from someone else—I think that must be so wonderful!' He saved these thoughts for a character, already created in miniature in *The Lady from the Sea,* to whom he was to allot the principal female role in his next play two years later—Hilde Wangel in *The Master Builder.*

The repeated references to the 'vine-leaves' continue to puzzle critics, even though William Archer cleared the problem up fifty years ago. 'Surely', he wrote, 'this is a very obvious image or symbol of the beautiful, the ideal, aspect of bacchic elation and revelry. . . . Professor Dietrichson relates that among the young artists whose society Ibsen frequented during his first years in Rome it was customary, at their little festivals, for the revellers to deck themselves in this fashion. But the image is so obvious that there is no need to trace it to any personal experience. The attempt to place Hedda's vine-leaves among Ibsen's obscurities is an example of the firm resolution not to understand which animated the criticism of the nineties.' Not, alas, only of the nineties. The picture which the vine-leaves are intended to evoke is that of the young god, 'burning and unashamed', in Hedda's words; as Archer noted, it was an image which Ibsen had used previously in both *Peer Gynt* and *Emperor and Galilean.*

A point that is sometimes missed in production of *Hedda Gabler* is the importance of correct casting for Bertha, the Tesmans' maid. Ibsen never created a role, however tiny, that was not both integral to the play and rewarding to the player, and his servants are no exceptions—one thinks of the two butlers, the superior Pettersen and the inferior Jensen, in *The Wild Duck,* the housekeeper Mrs. Helseth in *Rosmersholm,* and Malene, the sour maid in *John Gabriel Borkman.* Ibsen underlined Bertha's importance in a letter which he wrote to Kristine Steen on 14 January 1891 concerning the casting of the play for Christiania. 'Mrs. Wolf', he wrote, 'wishes to be released from playing the maid Bertha in my new play, since she is of the opinion that this role could be adequately filled by any other member of the company. She is mistaken. There is no-one else at the theatre who can perform Bertha as I wish her to be performed. Only Mrs. Wolf can do it. She has evidently not taken the trouble to read the play carefully, or she could hardly fail to appreciate this. George Tesman, his old aunts and Bertha together create a picture of completeness and unity. They have common thoughts, common memories, a common attitude towards life. To Hedda they represent a force foreign and hostile to her and to everything she stands for. The harmony that exists between them must be apparent on the stage. And this can be achieved if Mrs. Wolf plays the part. But only if she does. My respect for Mrs. Wolf's soundness of judgment is too great for me seriously to believe that she regards it as artistically beneath her to create a servant. I did not regard it as artistically beneath me to create this honest, artless old creature. Here in Munich this unpretentious character is to be created by one of the Hoftheater's leading actresses, and she has embraced the task with love and interest. Besides being an actress, she is also an artist. By this I mean that she regards it as a matter of honour not merely to ''give a performance'' but to turn a created character into a thing of flesh and blood.' Ibsen's plea fell, however, on deaf ears, for Mrs. Wolf still refused to play the part.

Despite its early failures on the stages of Europe, *Hedda Gabler* has come to be accepted as one of the most popular of Ibsen's plays. London has seen no less than twenty-three separate productions, a number exceeded only, among Ibsen's other plays, by *Ghosts*. Among the actresses who have played it there are Elizabeth Robins (1891 and 1893),

Eleonora Duse (in Italian, 1903), Mrs. Patrick Campbell (1907 and 1922), Lydia Yavorska (in Russian, 1909, and in English, 1911), Jean Forbes-Robertson (1931, 1936 and 1951), Peggy Ashcroft (1954), Maggie Smith (1970) and Glenda Jackson (1975). Probably the finest English Hedda, however, was Pamela Brown, who in 1941, at the age of twenty-two, gave a performance at the Oxford Playhouse which caused James Agate seriously to compare her with the young Sarah Bernhardt. 'The moment that unquiet spirit appeared in the curtain'd doorway, drew a long breath, and paused to survey the Tesmanesque scene in marble, cold disfavour', he wrote, 'why, then we knew that Hedda was going to be present. . . . I was not playgoing in 1867, when She Who Must Not Be Named was 22, which is the age of Miss Pamela Brown. But as that great player must have been in her experimental years, so is this young actress now'. Another admired and acclaimed performance in the role was that of Catherine Lacey at the Bristol Old Vic in 1948. America first saw the play on 30 March 1898, when Elizabeth Robins presented a single performance at the Fifth Avenue Theatre in New York. *The Critic* wrote of this production that 'it was, on the whole, the most satisfactory representation of an Ibsen play ever given in this city', and described Miss Robins's performance as 'in every way a remarkable achievement'. Unfortunately, according to Norman Hapgood in *The Stage in America, 1897–1900*, 'it failed to interest the public enough to continue contemplated Ibsen experiments'. Blanche Bates played it for a single matinée in Washington in 1900; then in 1903 Minnie Fiske presented it in New York for a whole week to crowded houses, and brought it back to the Manhattan Theatre in November 1904, when it achieved the, by the standard of those days, considerable number of twenty-six performances. The cast included George Arliss as Judge Brack. In 1905 Alla Nazimova played it at the Russian Theatre, New York, in

Russian, and the following year she performed it in English, creating a tremendous impression. Subsequent Heddas in New York have included Emily Stevens, Eva le Gallienne, Tallulah Bankhead (on television), Anne Meacham and Claire Bloom.

MICHAEL MEYER

CHARACTERS

GEORGE TESMAN, research graduate in cultural history
HEDDA, his wife
MISS JULIANA TESMAN, his aunt
MRS. ELVSTED
JUDGE BRACK
EILERT LŒVBORG
BERTHA, a maid

The action takes place in Tesman's villa in the fashionable quarter of town.

This translation of *Hedda Gabler* was first performed in London on 29 June 1970 at the Cambridge Theatre, in a production by the National Theatre of Great Britain. The cast was:

GEORGE TESMAN	Jeremy Brett
HEDDA TESMAN	Maggie Smith
MISS JULIA TESMAN	Jeanne Watts
MRS. ELVSTED	Sheila Reid
JUDGE BRACK	John Moffatt
EILERT LŒVBORG	Robert Stephens
BERTHA	Julia McCarthy

Directed by Ingmar Bergman

ACT ONE

A large drawing-room, handsomely and tastefully furnished; decorated in dark colours. In the rear wall is a broad open doorway, with curtains drawn back to either side. It leads to a smaller room, decorated in the same style as the drawing-room. In the right-hand wall of the drawing-room a folding door leads out to the hall. The opposite wall, on the left, contains french windows, also with curtains drawn back on either side. Through the glass we can see part of a veranda, and trees in autumn colours. Downstage stands an oval table, covered by a cloth and surrounded by chairs. Downstage right, against the wall, is a broad stove tiled with dark porcelain; in front of it stand a high-backed armchair, a cushioned footrest and two footstools. Upstage right, in an alcove, is a corner sofa, with a small, round table. Downstage left, a little away from the wall, is another sofa. Upstage of the french windows, a piano. On either side of the open doorway in the rear wall stand what-nots holding ornaments of terra-cotta and majolica. Against the rear wall of the smaller room can be seen a sofa, a table and a couple of chairs. Above this sofa hangs the portrait of a handsome old man in general's uniform. Above the table a lamp hangs from the ceiling, with a shade of opalescent, milky glass. All round the drawing-room bunches of flowers stand in vases and glasses. More bunches lie on the tables. The floors of both rooms are covered with thick carpets.

Morning light. The sun shines in through the french windows.

> MISS JULIANA TESMAN, *wearing a hat and carrying a parasol, enters from the hall, followed by* BERTHA, *who is carrying a bunch of flowers wrapped in paper.* MISS TESMAN *is about sixty-five, of pleasant and kindly appearance. She is neatly but simply dressed in grey outdoor clothes.* BERTHA, *the maid, is rather simple and rustic-looking. She is getting on in years.*

MISS TESMAN *(stops just inside the door, listens, and says in a hushed voice)*: Well, fancy that! They're not up yet!

BERTHA *(also in hushed tones)*: What did I tell you, miss? The boat didn't get in till midnight. And when they did turn up—Jesus, miss, you should have seen all the things madam made me unpack before she'd go to bed!

MISS TESMAN: Ah, well. Let them have a good lie in. But let's have some nice fresh air waiting for them when they do come down. *(Goes to the french windows and throws them wide open.)*

BERTHA *(bewildered at the table, the bunch of flowers in her hand)*: I'm blessed if there's a square inch left to put anything. I'll have to let it lie here, miss. *(Puts it on the piano.)*

MISS TESMAN: Well, Bertha dear, so now you have a new mistress. Heaven knows it nearly broke my heart to have to part with you.

BERTHA *(snivels)*: What about me, Miss Juju? How do you suppose I felt? After all the happy years I've spent with you and Miss Rena?

MISS TESMAN: We must accept it bravely, Bertha. It was the only way. George needs you to take care of him. He could never manage without you. You've looked after him ever since he was a tiny boy.

BERTHA: Oh, but, Miss Juju, I can't help thinking about Miss Rena, lying there all helpless, poor dear. And that new girl! She'll never learn the proper way to handle an invalid.

MISS TESMAN: Oh, I'll manage to train her. I'll do most of the work myself, you know. You needn't worry about my poor sister, Bertha dear.

BERTHA: But, Miss Juju, there's another thing. I'm frightened madam may not find me suitable.

MISS TESMAN: Oh, nonsense, Bertha. There may be one or two little things to begin with—

BERTHA: She's a real lady. Wants everything just so.

MISS TESMAN: But of course she does! General Gabler's daughter! Think of what she was accustomed to when the general was alive. You remember how we used to see her out riding with her father? In that long black skirt? With the feather in her hat?

BERTHA: Oh, yes, miss. As if I could forget! But, Lord! I never dreamed I'd live to see a match between her and Master Georgie.

MISS TESMAN: Neither did I. By the way, Bertha, from now on you must stop calling him Master Georgie. You must say Dr. Tesman.

BERTHA: Yes, madam said something about that too. Last night—the moment they'd set foot inside the door. Is it true, then, miss?

MISS TESMAN: Indeed it is. Just fancy, Bertha, some foreigners have made him a doctor. It happened while they were away. I had no idea till he told me when they got off the boat.

BERTHA: Well, I suppose there's no limit to what he won't become. He's that clever. I never thought he'd go in for hospital work, though.

MISS TESMAN: No, he's not that kind of doctor. *(Nods im-*

pressively.) In any case, you may soon have to address him by an even grander title.

BERTHA: You don't say! What might that be, miss?

MISS TESMAN *(smiles):* Ah! If you only knew! *(Moved.)* Dear God, if only poor Joachim could rise out of his grave and see what his little son has grown into! *(Looks round.)* But, Bertha, why have you done this? Taken the chintz covers off all the furniture!

BERTHA: Madam said I was to. Can't stand chintz covers on chairs, she said.

MISS TESMAN: But surely they're not going to use this room as a parlour?

BERTHA: So I gathered, miss. From what madam said. He didn't say anything. The Doctor.

> GEORGE TESMAN *comes into the rear room from the right, humming, with an open, empty travelling-bag in his hand. He is about thirty-three, of medium height and youthful appearance, rather plump, with an open, round, contented face, and fair hair and beard. He wears spectacles, and is dressed in comfortable indoor clothes.*

MISS TESMAN: Good morning! Good morning, George!

TESMAN *(in open doorway):* Auntie Juju! Dear Auntie Juju! *(Comes forward and shakes her hand.)* You've come all the way out here! And so early! What?

MISS TESMAN: Well, I had to make sure you'd settled in comfortably.

TESMAN: But you can't have had a proper night's sleep.

MISS TESMAN: Oh, never mind that.

TESMAN: But you got home safely?

MISS TESMAN: Oh, yes. Judge Brack kindly saw me home.

TESMAN: We were so sorry we couldn't give you a lift. But you saw how it was—Hedda had so much luggage—and she insisted on having it all with her.

MISS TESMAN: Yes, I've never seen so much luggage.

BERTHA (*to* TESMAN): Shall I go and ask madam if there's anything I can lend her a hand with?

TESMAN: Er—thank you, Bertha, no, you needn't bother. She says if she wants you for anything she'll ring.

BERTHA (*over to right*): Oh. Very good.

TESMAN: Oh, Bertha—take this bag, will you?

BERTHA (*takes it*): I'll put it in the attic.

She goes out into the hall.

TESMAN: Just fancy, Auntie Juju, I filled that whole bag with notes for my book. You know, it's really incredible what I've managed to find rooting through those archives. By Jove! Wonderful old things no one even knew existed—

MISS TESMAN: I'm sure you didn't waste a single moment of your honeymoon, George dear.

TESMAN: No, I think I can truthfully claim that. But, Auntie Juju, do take your hat off. Here. Let me untie it for you. What?

MISS TESMAN (*as he does so*): Oh dear, oh dear! It's just as if you were still living at home with us.

TESMAN (*turns the hat in his hand and looks at it*): I say! What a splendid new hat!

MISS TESMAN: I bought it for Hedda's sake.

TESMAN: For Hedda's sake? What?

MISS TESMAN: So that Hedda needn't be ashamed of me, in case we ever go for a walk together.

TESMAN (*pats her cheek*): You still think of everything, don't you, Auntie Juju? (*Puts the hat down on a chair by the table.*) Come on, let's sit down here on the sofa. And have a little chat while we wait for Hedda.

They sit. She puts her parasol in the corner of the sofa.

MISS TESMAN (*clasps both his hands and looks at him*): Oh, George, it's so wonderful to have you back, and be able

25

to see you with my own eyes again! Poor dear Joachim's own son!

TESMAN: What about me? It's wonderful for me to see you again, Auntie Juju. You've been a mother to me. And a father, too.

MISS TESMAN: You'll always keep a soft spot in your heart for your old aunties, won't you, George dear?

TESMAN: I suppose Auntie Rena's no better? What?

MISS TESMAN: Alas, no. I'm afraid she'll never get better, poor dear. She's lying there just as she has for all these years. Please God I may be allowed to keep her for a little longer. If I lost her I don't know what I'd do. Especially now I haven't you to look after.

TESMAN *(pats her on the back):* There, there, there!

MISS TESMAN *(with a sudden change of mood):* Oh, but, George, fancy you being a married man! And to think it's you who've won Hedda Gabler! The beautiful Hedda Gabler! Fancy! She was always so surrounded by admirers.

TESMAN *(hums a little and smiles contentedly):* Yes, I suppose there are quite a few people in this town who wouldn't mind being in my shoes. What?

MISS TESMAN: And what a honeymoon! Five months! Nearly six.

TESMAN: Well, I've done a lot of work, you know. All those archives to go through. And I've had to read lots of books.

MISS TESMAN: Yes, dear, of course. *(Lowers her voice confidentially.)* But tell me, George—haven't you any—any extra little piece of news to give me?

TESMAN: You mean, arising out of the honeymoon?

MISS TESMAN: Yes.

TESMAN: No, I don't think there's anything I didn't tell you in my letters. My doctorate, of course—but I told you about that last night, didn't I?

MISS TESMAN: Yes, yes, I didn't mean that kind of thing. I was just wondering—are you—are you expecting—?

TESMAN: Expecting what?

MISS TESMAN: Oh, come on, George, I'm your old aunt!

TESMAN: Well, actually—yes, I am expecting something.

MISS TESMAN: I knew it!

TESMAN: You'll be happy to learn that before very long I expect to become a—professor.

MISS TESMAN: Professor?

TESMAN: I think I may say that the matter has been decided. But, Auntie Juju, you know about this.

MISS TESMAN *(gives a little laugh):* Yes, of course. I'd forgotten. *(Changes her tone.)* But we were talking about your honeymoon. It must have cost a dreadful amount of money, George?

TESMAN: Oh well, you know, that big research grant I got helped a good deal.

MISS TESMAN: But how on earth did you manage to make it do for two?

TESMAN: Well, to tell the truth it was a bit tricky. What?

MISS TESMAN: Especially when one's travelling with a lady. A little bird tells me that makes things very much more expensive.

TESMAN: Well, yes, of course it does make things a little more expensive. But Hedda has to do things in style, Auntie Juju. I mean, she has to. Anything less grand wouldn't have suited her.

MISS TESMAN: No, no, I suppose not. A honeymoon abroad seems to be the vogue nowadays. But tell me, have you had time to look round the house?

TESMAN: You bet. I've been up since the crack of dawn.

MISS TESMAN: Well, what do you think of it?

TESMAN: Splendid. Absolutely splendid. I'm only wondering what we're going to do with those two empty rooms between that little one and Hedda's bedroom.

MISS TESMAN (*laughs slyly*): Ah, George dear, I'm sure you'll manage to find some use for them—in time.

TESMAN: Yes, of course, Auntie Juju, how stupid of me. You're thinking of my books? What?

MISS TESMAN: Yes, yes, dear boy. I was thinking of your books.

TESMAN: You know, I'm so happy for Hedda's sake that we've managed to get this house. Before we became engaged she often used to say this was the only house in town she felt she could really bear to live in. It used to belong to Mrs. Falk—you know, the Prime Minister's widow.

MISS TESMAN: Fancy that! And what a stroke of luck it happened to come into the market. Just as you'd left on your honeymoon.

TESMAN: Yes, Auntie Juju, we've certainly had all the luck with us. What?

MISS TESMAN: But, George dear, the expense! It's going to make a dreadful hole in your pocket, all this.

TESMAN (*a little downcast*): Yes, I—I suppose it will, won't it?

MISS TESMAN: Oh, George, really!

TESMAN: How much do you think it'll cost? Roughly, I mean? What?

MISS TESMAN: I can't possibly say till I see the bills.

TESMAN: Well, luckily Judge Brack's managed to get it on very favourable terms. He wrote and told Hedda so.

MISS TESMAN: Don't you worry, George dear. Anyway, I've stood security for all the furniture and carpets.

TESMAN: Security? But dear, sweet Auntie Juju, how could you possibly stand security?

MISS TESMAN: I've arranged a mortgage on our annuity.

TESMAN (*jumps up*): What? On your annuity? And—Auntie Rena's?

MISS TESMAN: Yes. Well, I couldn't think of any other way.

TESMAN *(stands in front of her):* Auntie Juju, have you gone completely out of your mind? That annuity's all you and Auntie Rena have.

MISS TESMAN: All right, there's no need to get so excited about it. It's a pure formality, you know. Judge Brack told me so. He was so kind as to arrange it all for me. A pure formality; those were his very words.

TESMAN: I dare say. All the same—

MISS TESMAN: Anyway, you'll have a salary of your own now. And, good heavens, even if we did have to fork out a little—tighten our belts for a week or two—why, we'd be happy to do so for your sake.

TESMAN: Oh, Auntie Juju! Will you never stop sacrificing yourself for me?

MISS TESMAN *(gets up and puts her hands on his shoulders):* What else have I to live for but to smooth your road a little, my dear boy? You've never had any mother or father to turn to. And now at last we've achieved our goal. I won't deny we've had our little difficulties now and then. But now, thank the good Lord, George dear, all your worries are past.

TESMAN: Yes, it's wonderful really how everything's gone just right for me.

MISS TESMAN: Yes! And the enemies who tried to bar your way have been struck down. They have been made to bite the dust. The man who was your most dangerous rival has had the mightiest fall. And now he's lying there in the pit he dug for himself, poor misguided creature.

TESMAN: Have you heard any news of Eilert? Since I went away?

MISS TESMAN: Only that he's said to have published a new book.

TESMAN: What! Eilert Lœvborg? You mean—just recently? What?

MISS TESMAN: So they say. I don't imagine it can be of any

value, do you? When your new book comes out, that'll be another story. What's it going to be about?

TESMAN: The domestic industries of Brabant in the Middle Ages.

MISS TESMAN: Oh, George! The things you know about!

TESMAN: Mind you, it may be some time before I actually get down to writing it. I've made these very extensive notes, and I've got to file and index them first.

MISS TESMAN: Ah, yes! Making notes; filing and indexing; you've always been wonderful at that. Poor dear Joachim was just the same.

TESMAN: I'm looking forward so much to getting down to that. Especially now I've a home of my own to work in.

MISS TESMAN: And above all, now that you have the girl you set your heart on, George dear.

TESMAN *(embraces her):* Oh, yes, Auntie Juju, yes! Hedda's the loveliest thing of all! *(Looks towards the doorway.)* I think I hear her coming. What?

> HEDDA *enters the rear room from the left, and comes into the drawing-room. She is a woman of twenty-nine. Distinguished, aristocratic face and figure. Her complexion is pale and opalescent. Her eyes are steel-grey, with an expression of cold, calm serenity. Her hair is of a handsome auburn colour, but is not especially abundant. She is dressed in an elegant, somewhat loose-fitting morning gown.*

MISS TESMAN *(goes to greet her):* Good morning, Hedda dear! Good morning!

HEDDA *(holds out her hand):* Good morning, dear Miss Tesman. What an early hour to call. So kind of you.

MISS TESMAN *(seems somewhat embarrassed):* And has the young bride slept well in her new home?

HEDDA: Oh—thank you, yes. Passably well.

TESMAN *(laughs):* Passably? I say. Hedda, that's good! When I jumped out of bed, you were sleeping like a top.

HEDDA: Yes. Fortunately. One has to accustom oneself to anything new, Miss Tesman. It takes time. *(Looks left.)* Oh, that maid's left the french windows open. This room's flooded with sun.

MISS TESMAN *(goes towards the windows):* Oh—let me close them.

HEDDA: No, no, don't do that. Tesman dear, draw the curtains. This light's blinding me.

TESMAN *(at the windows):* Yes, yes, dear. There, Hedda, now you've got shade and fresh air.

HEDDA: This room needs fresh air. All these flowers—! But my dear Miss Tesman, won't you take a seat?

MISS TESMAN: No, really not, thank you. I just wanted to make sure you have everything you need. I must see about getting back home. My poor dear sister will be waiting for me.

TESMAN: Be sure to give her my love, won't you? Tell her I'll run over and see her later today.

MISS TESMAN: Oh yes, I'll tell her that. Oh, George— *(Fumbles in the pocket of her skirt.)* I almost forgot. I've brought something for you.

TESMAN: What's that, Auntie Juju? What?

MISS TESMAN *(pulls out a flat package wrapped in newspaper and gives it to him):* Open and see, dear boy.

TESMAN *(opens the package):* Good heavens! Auntie Juju, you've kept them! Hedda, this is really very touching. What?

HEDDA *(by the what-nots, on the right):* What is it, Tesman?

TESMAN: My old shoes! My slippers, Hedda!

HEDDA: Oh, them. I remember you kept talking about them on our honeymoon.

TESMAN: Yes, I missed them dreadfully. *(Goes over to her.)* Here, Hedda, take a look.

HEDDA (*goes away towards the stove*): Thanks, I won't bother.

TESMAN (*follows her*): Fancy, Hedda, Auntie Rena's embroidered them for me. Despite her being so ill. Oh, you can't imagine what memories they have for me.

HEDDA (*by the table*): Not for me.

MISS TESMAN: No, Hedda's right there, George.

TESMAN: Yes, but I thought since she's one of the family now—

HEDDA (*interrupts*): Tesman, we really can't go on keeping this maid.

MISS TESMAN: Not keep Bertha?

TESMAN: What makes you say that, dear? What?

HEDDA (*points*): Look at that! She's left her old hat lying on the chair.

TESMAN (*appalled, drops his slippers on the floor*): But, Hedda—!

HEDDA: Suppose someone came in and saw it?

TESMAN: But, Hedda—that's Auntie Juju's hat.

HEDDA: Oh?

MISS TESMAN (*picks up the hat*): Indeed it's mine. And it doesn't happen to be old, Hedda dear.

HEDDA: I didn't look at it very closely, Miss Tesman.

MISS TESMAN (*tying on the hat*): As a matter of fact, it's the first time I've worn it. As the good Lord is my witness.

TESMAN: It's very pretty, too. Really smart.

MISS TESMAN: Oh, I'm afraid it's nothing much really. (*Looks round.*) My parasol. Ah, there it is. (*Takes it.*) This is mine, too. (*Murmurs*) Not Bertha's.

TESMAN: A new hat and a new parasol! I say, Hedda, fancy that!

HEDDA: Very pretty and charming.

TESMAN: Yes, isn't it? What? But, Auntie Juju, take a good look at Hedda before you go. Isn't she pretty and charming?

MISS TESMAN: Dear boy, there's nothing new in that. Hedda's been a beauty ever since the day she was born. *(Nods and goes right.)*

TESMAN *(follows her):* Yes, but have you noticed how strong and healthy she's looking? And how she's filled out since we went away?

MISS TESMAN *(stops and turns):* Filled out?

HEDDA *(walks across the room):* Oh, can't we forget it?

TESMAN: Yes, Auntie Juju—you can't see it so clearly with that dress on. But I've good reason to know—

HEDDA *(by the french windows, impatiently):* You haven't good reason to know anything.

TESMAN: It must have been the mountain air up there in the Tyrol—

HEDDA *(curtly, interrupts him):* I'm exactly the same as when I went away.

TESMAN: You keep on saying so. But you're not. I'm right, aren't I, Auntie Juju?

MISS TESMAN *(has folded her hands and is gazing at her):* She's beautiful—beautiful. Hedda is beautiful. *(Goes over to HEDDA, takes her head between her hands, draws it down and kisses her hair.)* God bless and keep you, Hedda Tesman. For George's sake.

HEDDA *(frees herself politely):* Oh—let me go, please.

MISS TESMAN *(quietly, emotionally):* I shall come and see you both every day.

TESMAN: Yes, Auntie Juju, please do. What?

MISS TESMAN: Good-bye! Good-bye!

She goes out into the hall. TESMAN *follows her. The door remains open.* TESMAN *is heard sending his love to* AUNT RENA *and thanking* MISS TESMAN *for his slippers. Meanwhile* HEDDA *walks up and down the room, raising her arms and clenching her fists as though in desperation. Then she throws aside the curtains from the french win-*

dows and stands there, looking out. A few moments later TESMAN *returns and closes the door behind him.*

TESMAN *(picks up his slippers from the floor):* What are you looking at, Hedda?

HEDDA *(calm and controlled again):* Only the leaves. They're so golden and withered.

TESMAN *(wraps up the slippers and lays them on the table):* Well, we're in September now.

HEDDA *(restless again):* Yes. We're already into September.

TESMAN: Auntie Juju was behaving rather oddly, I thought, didn't you? Almost as though she was in church or something. I wonder what came over her. Any idea?

HEDDA: I hardly know her. Does she often act like that?

TESMAN: Not to the extent she did today.

HEDDA *(goes away from the french windows):* Do you think she was hurt by what I said about the hat?

TESMAN: Oh, I don't think so. A little at first, perhaps—

HEDDA: But what a thing to do, throw her hat down in someone's drawing-room. People don't do such things.

TESMAN: I'm sure Auntie Juju doesn't do it very often.

HEDDA: Oh well, I'll make it up with her.

TESMAN: Oh Hedda, would you?

HEDDA: When you see them this afternoon invite her to come out here this evening.

TESMAN: You bet I will! I say, there's another thing which would please her enormously.

HEDDA: Oh?

TESMAN: If you could bring yourself to call her Auntie Juju. For my sake, Hedda? What?

HEDDA: Oh no, really, Tesman, you mustn't ask me to do that. I've told you so once before. I'll try to call her Aunt Juliana. That's as far as I'll go.

TESMAN *(after a moment):* I say, Hedda, is anything wrong? What?

HEDDA: I'm just looking at my old piano. It doesn't really go with all this.

TESMAN: As soon as I start getting my salary we'll see about changing it.

HEDDA: No, no, don't let's change it. I don't want to part with it. We can move it into that little room and get another one to put in here.

TESMAN *(a little downcast)*: Yes, we—might do that.

HEDDA *(picks up the bunch of flowers from the piano)*: These flowers weren't here when we arrived last night.

TESMAN: I expect Auntie Juju brought them.

HEDDA: Here's a card. *(Takes it out and reads.)* 'Will come back later today.' Guess who it's from?

TESMAN: No idea. Who? What?

HEDDA: It says: 'Mrs. Elvsted.'

TESMAN: No, really? Mrs. Elvsted! She used to be Miss Rysing, didn't she?

HEDDA: Yes. She was the one with that irritating hair she was always showing off. I hear she used to be an old flame of yours.

TESMAN *(laughs)*: That didn't last long. Anyway, that was before I got to know you, Hedda. By Jove, fancy her being in town!

HEDDA: Strange she should call. I only knew her at school.

TESMAN: Yes, I haven't seen her for—oh, heaven knows how long. I don't know how she manages to stick it out up there in the north. What?

HEDDA *(thinks for a moment, then says suddenly)*: Tell me, Tesman, doesn't he live somewhere up in those parts? You know—Eilert Lœvborg?

TESMAN: Yes, that's right. So he does.

BERTHA *enters from the hall.*

BERTHA: She's here again, madam. The lady who came and left the flowers. *(Points.)* The ones you're holding.

35

HEDDA: Oh, is she? Well, show her in.

BERTHA opens the door for MRS. ELVSTED *and goes out.* MRS. ELVSTED *is a delicately built woman with gentle, attractive features. Her eyes are light blue, large, and somewhat prominent, with a frightened, questioning expression. Her hair is extremely fair, almost flaxen, and is exceptionally wavy and abundant. She is two or three years younger than* HEDDA. *She is wearing a dark visiting dress, in good taste but not quite in the latest fashion.*

HEDDA *(goes cordially to greet her):* Dear Mrs. Elvsted, good morning! How delightful to see you again after all this time!

MRS. ELVSTED *(nervously, trying to control herself):* Yes, it's many years since we met.

TESMAN: And since *we* met. What?

HEDDA: Thank you for your lovely flowers.

MRS. ELVSTED: I wanted to come yesterday afternoon. But they told me you were away—

TESMAN: You've only just arrived in town, then? What?

MRS. ELVSTED: I got here yesterday, around midday. Oh, I became almost desperate when I heard you weren't here.

HEDDA: Desperate? Why?

TESMAN: My dear Mrs. Rysing—Elvsted—

HEDDA: There's nothing wrong, I hope?

MRS. ELVSTED: Yes, there is. And I don't know anyone else here whom I can turn to.

HEDDA *(puts the flowers down on the table):* Come and sit with me on the sofa—

MRS. ELVSTED: Oh, I feel too restless to sit down.

HEDDA: You must. Come along, now.

She pulls MRS. ELVSTED *down on to the sofa and sits beside her.*

TESMAN: Well? Tell us, Mrs.—er—

HEDDA: Has something happened at home?

MRS. ELVSTED: Yes—that is, yes and no. Oh, I do hope you won't misunderstand me—

HEDDA: Then you'd better tell us the whole story, Mrs. Elvsted.

TESMAN: That's why you've come. What?

MRS. ELVSTED: Yes—yes, it is. Well, then—in case you don't already know—Eilert Lœvborg is in town.

HEDDA: Lœvborg here?

TESMAN: Eilert back in town? Fancy, Hedda, did you hear that?

HEDDA: Yes, of course I heard.

MRS. ELVSTED: He's been here a week. A whole week! In this city. Alone. With all those dreadful people—

HEDDA: But, my dear Mrs. Elvsted, what concern is he of yours?

MRS. ELVSTED (*gives her a frightened look and says quickly*): He's been tutoring the children.

HEDDA: Your children?

MRS. ELVSTED: My husband's. I have none.

HEDDA: Oh, you mean your stepchildren.

MRS. ELVSTED: Yes.

TESMAN (*gropingly*): But was he sufficiently—I don't know how to put it—sufficiently regular in his habits to be suited to such a post? What?

MRS. ELVSTED: For the past two to three years he has been living irreproachably.

TESMAN: You don't say! Hedda, do you hear that?

HEDDA: I hear.

MRS. ELVSTED: Quite irreproachably, I assure you. In every respect. All the same—in this big city—with money in his pockets—I'm so dreadfully frightened something may happen to him.

37

TESMAN: But why didn't he stay up there with you and your husband?

MRS. ELVSTED: Once his book had come out, he became restless.

TESMAN: Oh, yes—Auntie Juju said he's brought out a new book.

MRS. ELVSTED: Yes, a big new book about the history of civilization. A kind of general survey. It came out a fortnight ago. Everyone's been buying it and reading it—it's created a tremendous stir—

TESMAN: Has it really? It must be something he's dug up, then.

MRS. ELVSTED: You mean from the old days?

TESMAN: Yes.

MRS. ELVSTED: No, he's written it all since he came to live with us.

TESMAN: Well, that's splendid news, Hedda. Fancy that!

MRS. ELVSTED: Oh, yes! If only he can go on like this!

HEDDA: Have you met him since you came here?

MRS. ELVSTED: No, not yet. I had such dreadful difficulty finding his address. But this morning I managed to track him down at last.

HEDDA (looks searchingly at her): I must say I find it a little strange that your husband—hm—

MRS. ELVSTED (starts nervously): My husband! What do you mean?

HEDDA: That he should send you all the way here on an errand of this kind. I'm surprised he didn't come himself to keep an eye on his friend.

MRS. ELVSTED: Oh, no, no—my husband hasn't the time. Besides, I—er—wanted to do some shopping here.

HEDDA (with a slight smile): Ah. Well, that's different.

MRS. ELVSTED (gets up quickly, restlessly): Please, Mr. Tesman, I beg you—be kind to Eilert Lœvborg if he comes here. I'm sure he will. I mean, you used to be such good friends in the old days. And you're both studying the same subject, as far as I can understand. You're in the same field, aren't you?

TESMAN: Well, we used to be, anyway.

MRS. ELVSTED: Yes—so I beg you earnestly, do please, please, keep an eye on him. Oh, Mr. Tesman, do promise me you will.

TESMAN: I shall be only too happy to do so, Mrs. Rysing.

HEDDA: Elvsted.

TESMAN: I'll do everything for Eilert that lies in my power. You can rely on that.

MRS. ELVSTED: Oh, how good and kind you are! *(Presses his hands.)* Thank you, thank you, thank you. *(Frightened.)* My husband's so fond of him, you see.

HEDDA *(gets up):* You'd better send him a note, Tesman. He may not come to you of his own accord.

TESMAN: Yes, that'd probably be the best plan, Hedda. What?

HEDDA: The sooner the better. Why not do it now?

MRS. ELVSTED *(pleadingly):* Oh yes, if only you would!

TESMAN: I'll do it this very moment. Do you have his address, Mrs.—er—Elvsted?

MRS. ELVSTED: Yes. *(Takes a small piece of paper from her pocket and gives it to him.)*

TESMAN: Good, good. Right, well, I'll go inside and— *(Looks round.)* Where are my slippers? Oh yes, here. *(Picks up the package and is about to go.)*

HEDDA: Try to sound friendly. Make it a nice long letter.

TESMAN: Right, I will.

MRS. ELVSTED: Please don't say anything about my having seen you.

TESMAN: Good heavens, no, of course not. What?

He goes out through the rear room to the right.

HEDDA (*goes over to* MRS. ELVSTED, *smiles, and says softly*): Well! Now we've killed two birds with one stone.

MRS. ELVSTED: What do you mean?

HEDDA: Didn't you realize I wanted to get him out of the room?

MRS. ELVSTED: So that he could write the letter?

HEDDA: And so that I could talk to you alone.

MRS. ELVSTED (*confused*): About this?

HEDDA: Yes, about this.

MRS. ELVSTED (*in alarm*): But there's nothing more to tell, Mrs. Tesman. Really there isn't.

HEDDA: Oh, yes, there is. There's a lot more. I can see that. Come along, let's sit down and have a little chat.

She pushes MRS. ELVSTED *down into the armchair by the stove and seats herself on one of the footstools.*

MRS. ELVSTED (*looks anxiously at her watch*): Really, Mrs. Tesman, I think I ought to be going now.

HEDDA: There's no hurry. Well? How are things at home?

MRS. ELVSTED: I'd rather not speak about that.

HEDDA: But, my dear, you can tell me. Good heavens, we were at school together.

MRS. ELVSTED: Yes, but you were a year senior to me. Oh, I used to be terribly frightened of you in those days.

HEDDA: Frightened of me?

MRS. ELVSTED: Yes, terribly frightened. Whenever you met me on the staircase you used to pull my hair.

HEDDA: No, did I?

MRS. ELVSTED: Yes. And once you said you'd burn it all off.

HEDDA: Oh, that was only in fun.

MRS. ELVSTED: Yes, but I was so silly in those days. And then afterwards—I mean, we've drifted so far apart. Our backgrounds were so different.

HEDDA: Well, now we must try to drift together again. Now

listen. When we were at school we used to call each other
by our Christian names—

MRS. ELVSTED: No, I'm sure you're mistaken.

HEDDA: I'm sure I'm not. I remember it quite clearly. Let's
tell each other our secrets, as we used to in the old days.
(Moves closer on her footstool.) There, now. *(Kisses her
on the cheek.)* You must call me Hedda.

MRS. ELVSTED *(squeezes her hands and pats them)*: Oh,
you're so kind. I'm not used to people being so nice to
me.

HEDDA: Now, now, now. And I shall call you Tora, the way
I used to.

MRS. ELVSTED: My name is Thea.

HEDDA: Yes, of course. Of course. I meant Thea. *(Looks at
her sympathetically.)* So you're not used to kindness,
Thea? In your own home?

MRS. ELVSTED: Oh, if only I had a home! But I haven't. I've
never had one.

HEDDA *(looks at her for a moment)*: I thought that was it.

MRS. ELVSTED *(stares blankly and helplessly)*: Yes—yes—
yes.

HEDDA: I can't remember exactly, but didn't you first go to
Mr. Elvsted as a housekeeper?

MRS. ELVSTED: Governess, actually. But his wife—at the
time, I mean—she was an invalid, and had to spend most
of her time in bed. So I had to look after the house, too.

HEDDA: But in the end, you became mistress of the house.

MRS. ELVSTED *(sadly)*: Yes, I did.

HEDDA: Let me see. Roughly how long ago was that?

MRS. ELVSTED: When I got married, you mean?

HEDDA: Yes.

MRS. ELVSTED: About five years.

HEDDA: Yes; it must be about that.

MRS. ELVSTED: Oh, those five years! Especially the last two
or three. Oh, Mrs. Tesman, if you only knew—!

HEDDA (*slaps her hand gently*): Mrs. Tesman? Oh, Thea!

MRS. ELVSTED: I'm sorry, I'll try to remember. Yes—if you had any idea—

HEDDA (*casually*): Eilert Lœvborg's been up there, too, for about three years, hasn't he?

MRS. ELVSTED (*looks at her uncertainly*): Eilert Lœvborg? Yes, he has.

HEDDA: Did you know him before? When you were here?

MRS. ELVSTED: No, not really. That is—I knew him by name, of course.

HEDDA: But up there, he used to visit you?

MRS. ELVSTED: Yes, he used to come and see us every day. To give the children lessons. I found I couldn't do that as well as manage the house.

HEDDA: I'm sure you couldn't. And your husband—? I suppose being a magistrate he has to be away from home a good deal?

MRS. ELVSTED: Yes. You see, Mrs.—you see, Hedda, he has to cover the whole district.

HEDDA (*leans against the arm of* MRS. ELVSTED'*s chair*): Poor, pretty little Thea! Now you must tell me the whole story. From beginning to end.

MRS. ELVSTED: Well—what do you want to know?

HEDDA: What kind of a man is your husband, Thea? I mean, as a person. Is he kind to you?

MRS. ELVSTED (*evasively*): I'm sure he does his best to be.

HEDDA: I only wonder if he isn't too old for you. There's more than twenty years between you, isn't there?

MRS. ELVSTED (*irritably*): Yes, there's that, too. Oh, there are so many things. We're different in every way. We've nothing in common. Nothing whatever.

HEDDA: But he loves you, surely? In his own way?

MRS. ELVSTED: Oh, I don't know. I think he just finds me useful. And then I don't cost much to keep. I'm cheap.

HEDDA: Now you're being stupid.

MRS. ELVSTED *(shakes her head):* It can't be any different. With him. He doesn't love anyone except himself. And perhaps the children—a little.

HEDDA: He must be fond of Eilert Lœvborg, Thea.

MRS. ELVSTED *(looks at her):* Eilert Lœvborg? What makes you think that?

HEDDA: Well, if he sends you all the way down here to look for him— *(Smiles almost imperceptibly.)* Besides, you said so yourself to Tesman.

MRS. ELVSTED *(with a nervous twitch):* Did I? Oh yes, I suppose I did. *(Impulsively, but keeping her voice low.)* Well, I might as well tell you the whole story. It's bound to come out sooner or later.

HEDDA: But, my dear Thea—?

MRS. ELVSTED: My husband had no idea I was coming here.

HEDDA: What? Your husband didn't know?

MRS. ELVSTED: No, of course not. As a matter of fact, he wasn't even there. He was away at the assizes. Oh, I couldn't stand it any longer, Hedda! I just couldn't. I'd be so dreadfully lonely up there now.

HEDDA: Go on.

MRS. ELVSTED: So I packed a few things. Secretly. And went.

HEDDA: Without telling anyone?

MRS. ELVSTED: Yes. I caught the train and came straight here.

HEDDA: But, my dear Thea! How brave of you!

MRS. ELVSTED *(gets up and walks across the room):* Well, what else could I do?

HEDDA: But what do you suppose your husband will say when you get back?

MRS. ELVSTED *(by the table, looks at her):* Back there? To him?

HEDDA: Yes. Surely—?

MRS. ELVSTED: I shall never go back to him.

HEDDA (*gets up and goes closer*): You mean you've left your home for good?

MRS. ELVSTED: Yes. I didn't see what else I could do.

HEDDA: But to do it so openly!

MRS. ELVSTED: Oh, it's no use trying to keep a thing like that secret.

HEDDA: But what do you suppose people will say?

MRS. ELVSTED: They can say what they like. (*Sits sadly, wearily on the sofa.*) I had to do it.

HEDDA (*after a short silence*): What do you intend to do now? How are you going to live?

MRS. ELVSTED: I don't know. I only know that I must live wherever Eilert Lœvborg is. If I am to go on living.

HEDDA (*moves a chair from the table, sits on it near* MRS. ELVSTED *and strokes her hands*). Tell me, Thea, how did this—friendship between you and Eilert Lœvborg begin?

MRS. ELVSTED: Oh, it came about gradually. I developed a kind of—power over him.

HEDDA: Oh?

MRS. ELVSTED: He gave up his old habits. Not because I asked him to. I'd never have dared to do that. I suppose he just noticed I didn't like that kind of thing. So he gave it up.

HEDDA (*hides a smile*): So you've made a new man of him! Clever little Thea!

MRS. ELVSTED: Yes—anyway, he says I have. And he's made a—sort of—real person of me. Taught me to think— and to understand all kinds of things.

HEDDA: Did he give you lessons, too?

MRS. ELVSTED: Not exactly lessons. But he talked to me. About—oh, you've no idea—so many things! And then he let me work with him. Oh, it was wonderful. I was so happy to be allowed to help him.

HEDDA: Did he allow you to help him?

MRS. ELVSTED: Yes. Whenever he wrote anything we always—did it together.

HEDDA: Like good friends?

MRS. ELVSTED (*eagerly*): Friends! Yes—why, Hedda that's exactly the word he used! Oh, I ought to feel so happy. But I can't. I don't know if it will last.

HEDDA: You don't seem very sure of him.

MRS. ELVSTED (*sadly*): Something stands between Eilert Lœvborg and me. The shadow of another woman.

HEDDA: Who can that be?

MRS. ELVSTED: I don't know. Someone he used to be friendly with in—in the old days. Someone he's never been able to forget.

HEDDA: What has he told you about her?

MRS. ELVSTED: Oh, he only mentioned her once, casually.

HEDDA: Well! What did he say?

MRS. ELVSTED: He said when he left her she tried to shoot him with a pistol.

HEDDA (*cold, controlled*): What nonsense. People don't do such things. The kind of people we know.

MRS. ELVSTED: No. I think it must have been that red-haired singer he used to—

HEDDA: Ah yes, very probably.

MRS. ELVSTED: I remember they used to say she always carried a loaded pistol.

HEDDA: Well then, it must be her.

MRS. ELVSTED: But, Hedda, I hear she's come back, and is living here. Oh, I'm so desperate—!

HEDDA (*glances towards the rear room*): Ssh! Tesman's coming. (*Gets up and whispers*) Thea, we mustn't breathe a word about this to anyone.

MRS. ELVSTED (*jumps up*): Oh, no, no! Please don't!

GEORGE TESMAN *appears from the right in the rear*

room with a letter in his hand, and comes into the drawing-room.

TESMAN: Well, here's my little epistle all signed and sealed.

HEDDA: Good. I think Mrs. Elvsted wants to go now. Wait a moment—I'll see you as far as the garden gate.

TESMAN: Er—Hedda, do you think Bertha could deal with this?

HEDDA *(takes the letter):* I'll give her instructions.

BERTHA *enters from the hall.*

BERTHA: Judge Brack is here and asks if he may pay his respects to madam and the Doctor.

HEDDA: Yes, ask him to be so good as to come in. And—wait a moment—drop this letter in the post box.

BERTHA *(takes the letter):* Very good, madam.

She opens the door for JUDGE BRACK, *and goes out.* JUDGE BRACK *is forty-five; rather short, but well built, and elastic in his movements. He has a roundish face with an aristocratic profile. His hair, cut short, is still almost black, and is carefully barbered. Eyes lively and humorous. Thick eyebrows. His moustache is also thick, and is trimmed square at the ends. He is wearing outdoor clothes which are elegant but a little too youthful for him. He has a monocle in one eye; now and then he lets it drop.*

BRACK *(hat in hand, bows):* May one presume to call so early?

HEDDA: One may presume.

TESMAN *(shakes his hand):* You're welcome here any time. Judge Brack—Mrs. Rysing.

HEDDA *sighs.*

BRACK *(bows):* Ah—charmed—

HEDDA *(looks at him and laughs):* What fun to be able to see you by daylight for once, Judge.

BRACK: Do I look—different?

HEDDA: Yes. A little younger, I think.

BRACK: Too kind.

TESMAN: Well, what do you think of Hedda? What? Doesn't she look well? Hasn't she filled out—?

HEDDA: Oh, do stop it. You ought to be thanking Judge Brack for all the inconvenience he's put himself to—

BRACK: Nonsense, it was a pleasure—

HEDDA: You're a loyal friend. But my other friend is pining to get away, Au revoir, Judge. I won't be a minute.

Mutual salutations. MRS. ELVSTED *and* HEDDA *go out through the hall.*

BRACK: Well, is your wife satisfied with everything?

TESMAN: Yes, we can't thank you enough. That is—we may have to shift one or two things around, she tells me. And we're short of one or two little items we'll have to purchase.

BRACK: Oh? Really?

TESMAN: But you mustn't worry your head about that. Hedda says she'll get what's needed. I say, why don't we sit down? What?

BRACK: Thanks, just for a moment. *(Sits at the table.)* There's something I'd like to talk to you about, my dear Tesman.

TESMAN: Oh? Ah yes, of course. *(Sits.)* After the feast comes the reckoning. What?

BRACK: Oh, never mind about the financial side—there's no hurry about that. Though I could wish we'd arranged things a little less palatially.

TESMAN: Good heavens, that'd never have done. Think of Hedda, my dear chap. You know her. I couldn't possibly ask her to live like a petty bourgeois.

BRACK: No, no—that's just the problem.

TESMAN: Anyway, it can't be long now before my nomination comes through.

BRACK: Well, you know, these things often take time.

TESMAN: Have you heard any more news? What?

BRACK: Nothing definite. (*Changing the subject.*) Oh, by the way, I have one piece of news for you.

TESMAN: What?

BRACK: Your old friend Eilert Lœvborg is back in town.

TESMAN: I know that already.

BRACK: Oh? How did you hear that?

TESMAN: She told me. That lady who went out with Hedda.

BRACK: I see. What was her name? I didn't catch it.

TESMAN: Mrs. Elvsted.

BRACK: Oh, the magistrate's wife. Yes, Lœvborg's been living up near them, hasn't he?

TESMAN: I'm delighted to hear he's become a decent human being again.

BRACK: Yes, so they say.

TESMAN: I gather he's published a new book, too. What?

BRACK: Indeed he has.

TESMAN: I hear it's created rather a stir.

BRACK: Quite an unusual stir.

TESMAN: I say, isn't that splendid news! He's such a gifted chap—and I was afraid he'd gone to the dogs for good.

BRACK: Most people thought he had.

TESMAN: But I can't think what he'll do now. How on earth will he manage to make ends meet? What?

As he speaks his last words HEDDA *enters from the hall.*

HEDDA (*to* BRACK, *laughs slightly scornfully*): Tesman is always worrying about making ends meet.

TESMAN: We were talking about poor Eilert Lœvborg, Hedda dear.

HEDDA *(gives him a quick look)*: Oh, were you? *(Sits in the armchair by the stove and asks casually)* Is he in trouble?

TESMAN: Well, he must have run through his inheritance long ago by now. And he can't write a new book every year. What? So I'm wondering what's going to become of him.

BRACK: I may be able to enlighten you there.

TESMAN: Oh?

BRACK: You mustn't forget he has relatives who wield a good deal of influence.

TESMAN: Relatives? Oh, they've quite washed their hands of him, I'm afraid.

BRACK: They used to regard him as the hope of the family.

TESMAN: Used to, yes. But he's put an end to that.

HEDDA: Who knows? *(With a little smile.)* I hear the Elvsteds have made a new man of him.

BRACK: And then this book he's just published—

TESMAN: Well, let's hope they find something for him. I've just written him a note. Oh, by the way, Hedda, I asked him to come over and see us this evening.

BRACK: But, my dear chap, you're coming to me this evening. My bachelor party. You promised me last night when I met you at the boat.

HEDDA: Had you forgotten, Tesman?

TESMAN: Good heavens, yes, I'd quite forgotten.

BRACK: Anyway, you can be quite sure he won't turn up here.

TESMAN: Why do you think that? What?

BRACK *(a little unwillingly, gets up and rests his hands on the back of his chair)*: My dear Tesman—and you, too, Mrs. Tesman—there's something I feel you ought to know.

TESMAN: Concerning Eilert?

BRACK: Concerning him and you.

TESMAN: Well, my dear Judge, tell us, please!

BRACK: You must be prepared for your nomination not to come through quite as quickly as you hope and expect.

TESMAN *(jumps up uneasily):* Is anything wrong? What?

BRACK: There's a possibility that the appointment may be decided by competition—

TESMAN: Competition! Hedda, fancy that!

HEDDA *(leans further back in her chair):* Ah! How interesting!

TESMAN: But who else—? I say, you don't mean—?

BRACK: Exactly. By competition with Eilert Lœvborg.

TESMAN *(clasps his hands in alarm):* No, no, but this is inconceivable! It's absolutely impossible! What?

BRACK: Hm. We may find it'll happen, all the same.

TESMAN: No, but—Judge Brack, they couldn't be so inconsiderate towards me! *(Waves his arms.)* I mean, by Jove, I—I'm a married man! It was on the strength of this that Hedda and I *got* married! We've run up some pretty hefty debts. And borrowed money from Auntie Juju! I mean, good heavens, they practically promised me the appointment. What?

BRACK: Well, well, I'm sure you'll get it. But you'll have to go through a competition.

HEDDA *(motionless in her armchair):* How exciting, Tesman. It'll be a kind of duel, by Jove.

TESMAN: My dear Hedda, how can you take it so lightly?

HEDDA *(as before):* I'm not. I can't wait to see who's going to win.

BRACK: In any case, Mrs. Tesman, it's best you should know how things stand. I mean before you commit yourself to these little items I hear you're threatening to purchase.

HEDDA: I can't allow this to alter my plans.

BRACK: Indeed? Well, that's your business. Good-bye. *(To* TESMAN*)* I'll come and collect you on the way home from my afternoon walk.

TESMAN: Oh, yes, yes. I'm sorry, I'm all upside down just
now.

HEDDA *(lying in her chair, holds out her hand):* Good-bye,
Judge. See you this afternoon.

BRACK: Thank you. Good-bye, good-bye.

TESMAN *(sees him to the door):* Good-bye, my dear Judge.
You will excuse me, won't you?

JUDGE BRACK *goes out through the hall.*

TESMAN *(pacing up and down):* Oh, Hedda! One oughtn't to
go plunging off on wild adventures. What?

HEDDA *(looks at him and smiles):* Like you're doing?

TESMAN: Yes. I mean, there's no denying it, it was a pretty
big adventure to go off and get married and set up house
merely on expectation.

HEDDA: Perhaps you're right.

TESMAN: Well, anyway, we have our home, Hedda. My
word, yes! The home we dreamed of. And set our hearts
on. What?

HEDDA *(gets up slowly, wearily):* You agreed that we should
enter society. And keep open house. That was the bargain.

TESMAN: Yes. Good heavens, I was looking forward to it all
so much. To seeing you play hostess to a select circle! By
Jove! What? Ah, well, for the time being we shall have to
make do with each other's company, Hedda. Perhaps
have Auntie Juju in now and then. Oh dear, this wasn't at
all what you had in mind—

HEDDA: I won't be able to have a liveried footman. For a
start.

TESMAN: Oh no, we couldn't possibly afford a footman.

HEDDA: And the bay mare you promised me—

TESMAN *(fearfully):* Bay mare!

HEDDA: I mustn't even think of that now.

TESMAN: Heaven forbid!

HEDDA (*walks across the room*): Ah, well. I still have one thing left to amuse myself with.

TESMAN (*joyfully*): Thank goodness for that. What's that, Hedda? What?

HEDDA (*in the open doorway, looks at him with concealed scorn*): My pistols, George darling.

TESMAN (*alarmed*): Pistols!

HEDDA (*her eyes cold*): General Gabler's pistols.

She goes into the rear room and disappears.

TESMAN (*runs to the doorway and calls after her*): For heaven's sake, Hedda dear, don't touch those things. They're dangerous. Hedda—please—for my sake! What?

ACT TWO

The same as in Act One, except that the piano has been re-moved and an elegant little writing-table, with a bookcase, stands in its place. By the sofa on the left a smaller table has been placed. Most of the flowers have been removed. MRS. ELVSTED's bouquet stands on the larger table, downstage. It is afternoon.

> HEDDA, *dressed to receive callers, is alone in the room. She is standing by the open french windows, loading a revolver. The pair to it is lying in an open pistol-case on the writing-table.*

HEDDA (*looks down into the garden and calls*): Good after-noon, Judge.

BRACK (*in the distance, below*): Afternoon, Mrs. Tesman.

HEDDA (*raises the pistol and takes aim*): I'm going to shoot you, Judge Brack.

BRACK (*shouts from below*): No, no, no! Don't aim that thing at me!

HEDDA: This'll teach you to enter houses by the back door.

She fires.

BRACK (*below*): Have you gone completely out of your mind?

HEDDA: Oh dear! Did I hit you?

53

BRACK *(still outside):* Stop playing these silly tricks.

HEDDA: All right, Judge. Come along in.

> JUDGE BRACK, *dressed for a bachelor party, enters through the french windows. He has a light overcoat on his arm.*

BRACK: For God's sake, haven't you stopped fooling around with those things yet? What are you trying to hit?

HEDDA: Oh, I was just shooting at the sky.

BRACK *(takes the pistol gently from her hand):* By your leave, ma'am. *(Looks at it.)* Ah, yes—I know this old friend well. *(Looks around.)* Where's the case? Oh, yes. *(Puts the pistol in the case and closes it.)* That's enough of that little game for today.

HEDDA: Well, what on earth *am* I to do?

BRACK: You haven't had any visitors?

HEDDA *(closes the french windows):* Not one. I suppose the best people are all still in the country.

BRACK: Your husband isn't home yet?

HEDDA *(locks the pistol-case away in a drawer of the writing-table):* No. The moment he'd finished eating he ran off to his aunties. He wasn't expecting you so early.

BRACK: Ah, why didn't I think of that? How stupid of me.

HEDDA *(turns her head and looks at him):* Why stupid?

BRACK: I'd have come a little sooner.

HEDDA *(walks across the room):* There'd have been no one to receive you. I've been in my room since lunch, dressing.

BRACK: You haven't a tiny crack in the door through which we might have negotiated?

HEDDA: You forgot to arrange one.

BRACK: Another stupidity.

HEDDA: Well, we'll have to sit down here. And wait. Tesman won't be back for some time.

BRACK: Sad. Well, I'll be patient.

> HEDDA *sits on the corner of the sofa.* BRACK *puts his coat over the back of the nearest chair and seats himself, keeping his hat in his hand. Short pause. They look at each other.*

HEDDA: Well?

BRACK *(in the same tone of voice):* Well?

HEDDA: I asked first.

BRACK *(leans forward slightly):* Yes, well, now we can enjoy a nice, cosy little chat—Mrs. Hedda.

HEDDA *(leans further back in her chair):* It seems ages since we had a talk. I don't count last night or this morning.

BRACK: You mean: *à deux?*

HEDDA: Mm—yes. That's roughly what I meant.

BRACK: I've been longing so much for you to come home.

HEDDA: So have I.

BRACK: You? Really, Mrs. Hedda? And I thought you were having such a wonderful honeymoon.

HEDDA: Oh, yes. Wonderful!

BRACK: But your husband wrote such ecstatic letters.

HEDDA: He! Oh, yes! He thinks life has nothing better to offer than rooting around in libraries and copying old pieces of parchment, or whatever it is he does.

BRACK *(a little maliciously):* Well, that *is* his life. Most of it, anyway.

HEDDA: Yes, I know. Well, it's all right for him. But for me! Oh no, my dear Judge. I've been bored to death.

BRACK *(sympathetically):* Do you mean that? Seriously?

HEDDA: Yes. Can you imagine? Six whole months without ever meeting a single person who was one of us, and to whom I could talk about the kind of things we talk about.

BRACK: Yes, I can understand. I'd miss that, too.

HEDDA: That wasn't the worst, though.

BRACK: What was?

HEDDA: Having to spend every minute of one's life with—with the same person.

BRACK (nods): Yes. What a thought! Morning; noon; and—

HEDDA (coldly): As I said: every minute of one's life.

BRACK: I stand corrected. But dear Tesman is such a clever fellow, I should have thought one ought to be able—

HEDDA: Tesman is only interested in one thing, my dear Judge. His special subject.

BRACK: True.

HEDDA: And people who are only interested in one thing don't make the most amusing company. Not for long, anyway.

BRACK: Not even when they happen to be the person one loves?

HEDDA: Oh, don't use that sickly, stupid word.

BRACK (starts): But, Mrs. Hedda—!

HEDDA (half laughing, half annoyed): You just try it, Judge. Listening to the history of civilization morning, noon and—

BRACK (corrects her): Every minute of one's life.

HEDDA: All right. Oh, and those domestic industries of Brabant in the Middle Ages! That really is beyond the limit.

BRACK (looks at her searchingly): But, tell me—if you feel like this why on earth did you—? Hm—

HEDDA: Why on earth did I marry George Tesman?

BRACK: If you like to put it that way.

HEDDA: Do you think it so very strange?

BRACK: Yes—and no, Mrs. Hedda.

HEDDA: I'd danced myself tired, Judge. I felt my time was up— (Gives a slight shudder.) No, I mustn't say that. Or even think it.

BRACK: You've no rational cause to think it.

HEDDA: Oh—cause, cause— (Looks searchingly at him.)

After all, George Tesman—well, I mean, he's a very respectable man.

BRACK: Very respectable, sound as a rock. No denying that.

HEDDA: And there's nothing exactly ridiculous about him. Is there?

BRACK: Ridiculous? N-no, I wouldn't say that.

HEDDA: Mm. He's very clever at collecting material and all that, isn't he? I mean, he may go quite far in time.

BRACK *(looks at her a little uncertainly)*: I thought you believed, like everyone else, that he would become a very prominent man.

HEDDA *(looks tired)*: Yes, I did. And when he came and begged me on his bended knees to be allowed to love and to cherish me, I didn't see why I shouldn't let him.

BRACK: No, well—if one looks at it like that—

HEDDA: It was more than my other admirers were prepared to do, Judge dear.

BRACK *(laughs)*: Well, I can't answer for the others. As far as I myself am concerned, you know I've always had a considerable respect for the institution of marriage. As an institution.

HEDDA *(lightly)*: Oh, I've never entertained any hopes of you.

BRACK: All I want is to have a circle of friends whom I can trust, whom I can help with advice or—or by any other means, and into whose houses I may come and go as a—trusted friend.

HEDDA: Of the husband?

BRACK *(bows)*: Preferably, to be frank, of the wife. And of the husband too, of course. Yes, you know, this kind of triangle is a delightful arrangement for all parties concerned.

HEDDA: Yes, I often longed for a third person while I was away. Oh, those hours we spent alone in railway compartments—

BRACK: Fortunately your honeymoon is now over.

HEDDA *(shakes her head):* There's a long, long way still to go. I've only reached a stop on the line.

BRACK: Why not jump out and stretch your legs a little, Mrs. Hedda?

HEDDA: I'm not the jumping sort.

BRACK: Aren't you?

HEDDA: No. There's always someone around who—

BRACK *(laughs):* Who looks at one's legs?

HEDDA: Yes. Exactly.

BRACK: Well, but surely—

HEDDA *(with a gesture of rejection):* I don't like it. I'd rather stay where I am. Sitting in the compartment. À deux.

BRACK: But suppose a third person were to step into the compartment?

HEDDA: That would be different.

BRACK: A trusted friend—someone who understood—

HEDDA: And was lively and amusing—

BRACK: And interested in—more subjects than one—

HEDDA *(sighs audibly):* Yes, that'd be a relief.

BRACK *(hears the front door open and shut):* The triangle is completed.

HEDDA *(half under her breath):* And the train goes on.

GEORGE TESMAN, *in grey walking dress with a soft felt hat, enters from the hall. He has a number of paper-covered books under his arm and in his pockets.*

TESMAN *(goes over to the table by the corner sofa):* Phew! It's too hot to be lugging all this around. *(Puts the books down.)* I'm positively sweating, Hedda. Why, hullo, hullo! You here already, Judge? What? Bertha didn't tell me.

BRACK *(gets up):* I came in through the garden.

HEDDA: What are all those books you've got there?

TESMAN *(stands glancing through them):* Oh, some new

58

publications dealing with my special subject. I had to buy them.

HEDDA: Your special subject?

BRACK: His special subject, Mrs. Tesman.

BRACK *and* HEDDA *exchange a smile.*

HEDDA: Haven't you collected enough material on your special subject?

TESMAN: My dear Hedda, one can never have too much. One must keep abreast of what other people are writing.

HEDDA: Yes. Of course.

TESMAN (*rooting among the books*): Look—I bought a copy of Eilert Lœvborg's new book, too. (*Holds it out to her.*) Perhaps you'd like to have a look at it, Hedda? What?

HEDDA: No, thank you. Er—yes, perhaps I will, later.

TESMAN: I glanced through it on my way home.

BRACK: What's your opinion—as a specialist on the subject?

TESMAN: I'm amazed how sound and balanced it is. He never used to write like that. (*Gathers his books together.*) Well, I must get down to these at once. I can hardly wait to cut the pages. Oh, I've got to change, too. (*To* BRACK) We don't have to be off just yet, do we? What?

BRACK: Heavens, no. We've plenty of time yet.

TESMAN: Good, I needn't hurry, then. (*Goes with his books, but stops and turns in the doorway.*) Oh, by the way, Hedda, Auntie Juju won't be coming to see you this evening.

HEDDA: Won't she? Oh—the hat, I suppose.

TESMAN: Good heavens, no. How could you think such a thing of Auntie Juju? Fancy—! No, Auntie Rena's very ill.

HEDDA: She always is.

TESMAN: Yes, but today she's been taken really bad.

HEDDA: Oh, then it's quite understandable that the other one should want to stay with her. Well, I shall have to swallow my disappointment.

TESMAN: You can't imagine how happy Auntie Juju was in spite of everything. At your looking so well after the honeymoon!

HEDDA *(half beneath her breath, as she rises):* Oh, these everlasting aunts!

TESMAN: What?

HEDDA *(goes over to the french windows):* Nothing.

TESMAN: Oh. All right. *(Goes into the rear room and out of sight.)*

BRACK: What was that about the hat?

HEDDA: Oh, something that happened with Miss Tesman this morning. She'd put her hat down on a chair. *(Looks at him and smiles.)* And I pretended to think it was the servant's.

BRACK *(shakes his head):* But, my dear Mrs. Hedda, how could you do such a thing? To that poor old lady?

HEDDA *(nervously, walking across the room):* Sometimes a mood like that hits me. And I can't stop myself. *(Throws herself down in the armchair by the stove.)* Oh, I don't know how to explain it.

BRACK *(behind her chair):* You're not really happy. That's the answer.

HEDDA *(stares ahead of her):* Why on earth should I be happy? Can you give me a reason?

BRACK: Yes. For one thing you've got the home you always wanted.

HEDDA *(looks at him):* You really believe that story?

BRACK: You mean it isn't true?

HEDDA: Oh, yes, it's partly true.

BRACK: Well?

HEDDA: It's true I got Tesman to see me home from parties last summer—

BRACK: It was a pity my home lay in another direction.

HEDDA: Yes. Your interests lay in another direction, too.

BRACK *(laughs):* That's naughty of you, Mrs. Hedda. But to return to you and George—

HEDDA: Well, we walked past this house one evening. And poor Tesman was fidgeting in his boots trying to find something to talk about. I felt sorry for the great scholar—

BRACK *(smiles incredulously):* Did you? Hm.

HEDDA: Yes, honestly I did. Well, to help him out of his misery, I happened to say quite frivolously how much I'd love to live in this house.

BRACK: Was that all?

HEDDA: That evening, yes.

BRACK: But—afterwards?

HEDDA: Yes. My little frivolity had its consequences, my dear Judge.

BRACK: Our little frivolities do. Much too often, unfortunately.

HEDDA: Thank you. Well, it was our mutual admiration for the late Prime Minister's house that brought George Tesman and me together on common ground. So we got engaged, and we got married, and we went on our honeymoon, and— Ah well, Judge, I've—made my bed and I must lie in it, I was about to say.

BRACK: How utterly fantastic! And you didn't really care in the least about the house?

HEDDA: God knows I didn't.

BRACK: Yes, but now that we've furnished it so beautifully for you?

HEDDA: Ugh—all the rooms smell of lavender and dried roses. But perhaps Auntie Juju brought that in.

BRACK *(laughs):* More likely the Prime Minister's widow, rest her soul.

HEDDA: Yes, it's got the odour of death about it. It reminds me of the flowers one has worn at a ball—the morning after. *(Clasps her hands behind her neck, leans back in the*

61

chair and looks up at him.) Oh, my dear Judge, you've no idea how hideously bored I'm going to be out here.

BRACK: Couldn't you find some—occupation, Mrs. Hedda? Like your husband?

HEDDA: Occupation? That'd interest me?

BRACK: Well—preferably.

HEDDA: God knows what. I've often thought— *(Breaks off.)* No, that wouldn't work either.

BRACK: Who knows? Tell me about it.

HEDDA: I was thinking—if I could persuade Tesman to go into politics, for example.

BRACK *(laughs):* Tesman! No, honestly, I don't think he's quite cut out to be a politician.

HEDDA: Perhaps not. But if I could persuade him to have a go at it?

BRACK: What satisfaction would that give you? If he turned out to be no good? Why do you want to make him do that?

HEDDA: Because I'm bored. *(After a moment.)* You feel there's absolutely no possibility of Tesman becoming Prime Minister, then?

BRACK: Well, you know, Mrs. Hedda, for one thing he'd have to be pretty well off before he could become that.

HEDDA *(gets up impatiently):* There you are! *(Walks across the room.)* It's this wretched poverty that makes life so hateful. And ludicrous. Well, it is!

BRACK: I don't think that's the real cause.

HEDDA: What is, then?

BRACK: Nothing really exciting has ever happened to you.

HEDDA: Nothing serious, you mean?

BRACK: Call it that if you like. But now perhaps it may.

HEDDA *(tosses her head):* Oh, you're thinking of this competition for that wretched professorship? That's Tesman's affair. I'm not going to waste my time worrying about that.

BRACK: Very well, let's forget about that, then. But suppose you were to find yourself faced with what people call—to use the conventional phrase—the most solemn of human responsibilities? *(Smiles.)* A new responsibility, little Mrs. Hedda.

HEDDA *(angrily):* Be quiet! Nothing like that's going to happen.

BRACK *(warily):* We'll talk about it again in a year's time. If not earlier.

HEDDA *(curtly):* I've no leanings in that direction, Judge. I don't want any—responsibilities.

BRACK: But surely you must feel some inclination to make use of that—natural talent which every woman—

HEDDA *(over by the french windows):* Oh, be quiet, I say! I often think there's only one thing for which I have any natural talent.

BRACK *(goes closer):* And what is that, if I may be so bold as to ask?

HEDDA *(stands looking out):* For boring myself to death. Now you know. *(Turns, looks towards the rear room and laughs.)* Talking of boring, here comes the professor.

BRACK *(quietly, warningly):* Now, now, now, Mrs. Hedda!

GEORGE TESMAN, *in evening dress, with gloves and hat in his hand, enters through the rear room from the right.*

TESMAN: Hedda, hasn't any message come from Eilert? What?

HEDDA: No.

TESMAN: Ah, then we'll have him here presently. You wait and see.

BRACK: You really think he'll come?

TESMAN: Yes, I'm almost sure he will. What you were saying about him this morning is just gossip.

BRACK: Oh?

TESMAN: Yes. Auntie Juju said she didn't believe he'd ever dare to stand in my way again. Fancy that!

BRACK: Then everything in the garden's lovely.

TESMAN (*puts his hat, with his gloves in it, on a chair, right*): Yes, but you really must let me wait for him as long as possible.

BRACK: We've plenty of time. No one'll be turning up at my place before seven or half past.

TESMAN: Ah, then we can keep Hedda company a little longer. And see if he turns up. What?

HEDDA (*picks up BRACK's coat and hat and carries them over to the corner sofa*). And if the worst comes to the worst, Mr. Lœvborg can sit here and talk to me.

BRACK (*offering to take his things from her*): No, please. What do you mean by 'if the worst comes to the worst'?

HEDDA: If he doesn't want to go with you and Tesman.

TESMAN (*looks doubtfully at her*): I say, Hedda, do you think it'll be all right for him to stay here with you? What? Remember Auntie Juju isn't coming.

HEDDA: Yes, but Mrs. Elvsted is. The three of us can have a cup of tea together.

TESMAN: Ah, that'll be all right.

BRACK (*smiles*): It's probably the safest solution as far as he's concerned.

HEDDA: Why?

BRACK: My dear Mrs. Tesman, you always say of my little bachelor parties that they should only be attended by men of the strongest principles.

HEDDA: But Mr. Lœvborg is a man of principle now. You know what they say about a reformed sinner—

BERTHA *enters from the hall.*

BERTHA: Madam, there's a gentleman here who wants to see you—

HEDDA: Ask him to come in.

TESMAN *(quietly):* I'm sure it's him. By Jove. Fancy that!

> EILERT LŒVBORG *enters from the hall. He is slim and lean, of the same age as* TESMAN, *but looks older and somewhat haggard. His hair and beard are of a blackish-brown; his face is long and pale, but with a couple of reddish patches on his cheekbones. He is dressed in an elegant and fairly new black suit, and carries black gloves and a top-hat in his hand. He stops just inside the door and bows abruptly. He seems somewhat embarrassed.*

TESMAN *(goes over and shakes his hand):* My dear Eilert! How grand to see you again after all these years!

EILERT LŒVBORG *(speaks softly):* It was good of you to write, George. *(Goes near to* HEDDA.) May I shake hands with you, too, Mrs. Tesman?

HEDDA *(accepts his hand):* Delighted to see you, Mr. Lœvborg. *(With a gesture.)* I don't know if you two gentlemen—

LŒVBORG *(bows slightly):* Judge Brack, I believe.

BRACK *(also with a slight bow):* Correct. We—met some years ago—

TESMAN *(puts his hands on* LŒVBORG'S *shoulders):* Now, you're to treat this house just as though it were your own home, Eilert. Isn't that right, Hedda? I hear you've decided to settle here again. What?

LŒVBORG: Yes, I have.

TESMAN: Quite understandable. Oh, by the by—I've just bought your new book. Though to tell the truth I haven't found time to read it yet.

LŒVBORG: You needn't bother.

TESMAN: Oh? Why?

LŒVBORG: There's nothing much in it.

TESMAN: By Jove, fancy hearing that from you!

BRACK: But everyone's praising it.

LŒVBORG: That was exactly what I wanted to happen. So I only wrote what I knew everyone would agree with.

BRACK: Very sensible.

TESMAN: Yes, but my dear Eilert—

LŒVBORG: I want to try to re-establish myself. To begin again—from the beginning.

TESMAN *(a little embarrassed):* Yes, I—er—suppose you do. What?

LŒVBORG *(smiles, puts down his hat and takes a package wrapped in paper from his coat pocket):* But when this gets published—George Tesman—read it. This is my real book. The one in which I have spoken with my own voice.

TESMAN: Oh, really? What's it about?

LŒVBORG: It's the sequel.

TESMAN: Sequel? To what?

LŒVBORG: To the other book.

TESMAN: The one that's just come out?

LŒVBORG: Yes.

TESMAN: But my dear Eilert, that covers the subject right up to the present day.

LŒVBORG: It does. But this is about the future.

TESMAN: The future! But, I say, we don't know anything about that.

LŒVBORG: No. But there are one or two things that need to be said about it. *(Opens the package.)* Here, have a look.

TESMAN: Surely that's not your handwriting?

LŒVBORG: I dictated it. *(Turns the pages.)* It's in two parts. The first deals with the forces that will shape our civilization. *(Turns further on towards the end.)* And the second indicates the direction in which that civilization may develop.

TESMAN: Amazing! I'd never think of writing about anything like that.

HEDDA *(by the french windows, drumming on the pane):* No. You wouldn't.

LŒVBORG *(puts the pages back into their cover and lays the package on the table):* I brought it because I thought I might possibly read you a few pages this evening.

TESMAN: I say, what a kind idea! Oh, but this evening—?
  (Glances at BRACK.*)* I'm not quite sure whether—

LŒVBORG: Well, some other time, then. There's no hurry.

BRACK: The truth is, Mr. Lœvborg, I'm giving a little dinner
  this evening. In Tesman's honour, you know.

LŒVBORG *(looks round for his hat):* Oh—then I mustn't—

BRACK: No, wait a minute. Won't you do me the honour of
  joining us?

LŒVBORG *(curtly, with decision):* No. I can't. Thank you so
  much.

BRACK: Oh, nonsense. Do—please. There'll only be a few of
  us. And I can promise you we shall have some good sport,
  as Hed—as Mrs. Tesman puts it.

LŒVBORG: I've no doubt. Nevertheless—

BRACK: You could bring your manuscript along and read it to
  Tesman at my place. I could lend you a room.

TESMAN: Well, yes, that's an idea. What?

HEDDA *(interposes):* But, Tesman, Mr. Lœvborg doesn't want
  to go. I'm sure Mr. Lœvborg would much rather sit here and
  have supper with me.

LŒVBORG *(looks at her):* With you, Mrs. Tesman?

HEDDA: And Mrs. Elvsted.

LŒVBORG: Oh. *(Casually.)* I ran into her this afternoon.

HEDDA: Did you? Well, she's coming here this evening. So
  you really must stay, Mr. Lœvborg. Otherwise she'll have
  no one to see her home.

LŒVBORG: That's true. Well—thank you, Mrs. Tesman, I'll
  stay then.

HEDDA: I'll just tell the servant.

  She goes to the door which leads into the hall, and rings.
  BERTHA *enters.* HEDDA *talks softly to her and points to-*
  wards the rear room. BERTHA *nods and goes out.*

TESMAN *(to* LŒVBORG, *as* HEDDA *does this):* I say, Eilert. This new subject of yours—the—er—future—is that the one you're going to lecture about?

LŒVBORG: Yes.

TESMAN: They told me down at the bookshop that you're going to hold a series of lectures here during the autumn.

LŒVBORG: Yes, I am. I—hope you don't mind, Tesman.

TESMAN: Good heavens, no! But—?

LŒVBORG: I can quite understand it might queer your pitch a little.

TESMAN *(dejectedly):* Oh well, I can't expect you to put them off for my sake.

LŒVBORG: I'll wait till your appointment's been announced.

TESMAN: You'll wait! But—but—aren't you going to compete with me for the post? What?

LŒVBORG: No. I only want to defeat you in the eyes of the world.

TESMAN: Good heavens! Then Auntie Juju was right after all! Oh, I knew it, I knew it! Hear that, Hedda? Fancy! Eilert *doesn't* want to stand in our way.

HEDDA *(curtly):* Our? Leave me out of it, please.

> *She goes towards the rear room, where* BERTHA *is setting a tray with decanters and glasses on the table.* HEDDA *nods approval, and comes back into the drawing-room.* BERTHA *goes out.*

TESMAN *(while this is happening):* Judge Brack, what do you think about all this? What?

BRACK: Oh, I think honour and victory can be very splendid things—

TESMAN: Of course they can. Still—

HEDDA *(looks at* TESMAN, *with a cold smile):* You look as if you'd been hit by a thunderbolt.

TESMAN: Yes, I feel rather like it.

BRACK: There was a black cloud looming up, Mrs. Tesman. But it seems to have passed over.

HEDDA *(points towards the rear room):* Well, gentlemen, won't you go in and take a glass of cold punch?

BRACK *(glances at his watch):* One for the road? Yes, why not?

TESMAN: An admirable suggestion, Hedda. Admirable! Oh, I feel so relieved!

HEDDA: Won't you have one, too, Mr. Lœvborg?

LŒVBORG: No, thank you. I'd rather not.

BRACK: Great heavens, man, cold punch isn't poison. Take my word for it.

LŒVBORG: Not for everyone, perhaps.

HEDDA: I'll keep Mr. Lœvborg company while you drink.

TESMAN: Yes, Hedda dear, would you?

> *He and* BRACK *go into the rear room, sit down, drink punch, smoke cigarettes and talk cheerfully during the following scene.* EILERT LŒVBORG *remains standing by the stove.* HEDDA *goes to the writing-table.*

HEDDA *(raising her voice slightly):* I've some photographs I'd like to show you, if you'd care to see them. Tesman and I visited the Tyrol on our way home.

> *She comes back with an album, places it on the table by the sofa and sits in the upstage corner of the sofa.* EILERT LŒVBORG *comes towards her, stops, and looks at her. Then he takes a chair and sits down on her left, with his back towards the rear room.*

HEDDA *(opens the album):* You see these mountains, Mr. Lœvborg? That's the Ortler group. Tesman has written the name underneath. You see: 'The Ortler Group near Meran.'

LŒVBORG *(has not taken his eyes from her; says softly, slowly):* Hedda—Gabler!

HEDDA *(gives him a quick glance):* Ssh!

LŒVBORG *(repeats softly):* Hedda Gabler!

HEDDA *(looks at the album):* Yes, that used to be my name. When we first knew each other.

LŒVBORG: And from now on—for the rest of my life—I must teach myself never to say: Hedda Gabler.

HEDDA *(still turning the pages):* Yes, you must. You'd better start getting into practice. The sooner the better.

LŒVBORG *(bitterly):* Hedda Gabler married? And to George Tesman!

HEDDA: Yes. Well—that's life.

LŒVBORG: Oh, Hedda, Hedda! How could you throw yourself away like that?

HEDDA *(looks sharply at him):* Stop it.

LŒVBORG: What do you mean?

TESMAN *comes in and goes towards the sofa.*

HEDDA *(hears him coming and says casually):* And this, Mr. Lœvborg, is the view from the Ampezzo valley. Look at those mountains. *(Glances affectionately up at* TESMAN.*)* What did you say those curious mountains were called, dear?

TESMAN: Let me have a look. Oh, those are the Dolomites.

HEDDA: Of course. Those are the Dolomites, Mr. Lœvborg.

TESMAN: Hedda, I just wanted to ask you, can't we bring some punch in here? A glass for you, anyway. What?

HEDDA: Thank you, yes. And a biscuit or two, perhaps.

TESMAN: You wouldn't like a cigarette?

HEDDA: No.

TESMAN: Right.

He goes into the rear room and over to the right. BRACK *is seated there, glancing occasionally at* HEDDA *and* LŒVBORG.

LŒVBORG *(softly, as before):* Answer me, Hedda. How could you do it?

HEDDA *(apparently absorbed in the album):* If you go on calling me Hedda I won't talk to you any more.

LŒVBORG: Mayn't I even when we're alone?

70

HEDDA: No. You can think it. But you mustn't say it.

LŒVBORG: Oh, I see. Because you love George Tesman.

HEDDA *(glances at him and smiles):* Love? Don't be funny.

LŒVBORG: You don't love him?

HEDDA: I don't intend to be unfaithful to him. That's not what I want.

LŒVBORG: Hedda—just tell me one thing—

HEDDA: Ssh!

TESMAN enters from the rear room, carrying a tray.

TESMAN: Here we are! Here come the refreshments.

He puts the tray down on the table.

HEDDA: Why didn't you ask the servant to bring it in?

TESMAN *(fills the glasses):* I like waiting on you, Hedda.

HEDDA: But you've filled both glasses. Mr. Lœvborg doesn't want to drink.

TESMAN: Yes, but Mrs. Elvsted'll be here soon.

HEDDA: Oh yes, that's true. Mrs. Elvsted—

TESMAN: Had you forgotten her? What?

HEDDA: We're so absorbed with these photographs. *(Shows him one.)* You remember this little village?

TESMAN: Oh, that one down by the Brenner Pass. We spent a night there—

HEDDA: Yes, and met all those amusing people.

TESMAN: Oh yes, it was there, wasn't it? By Jove, if only we could have had you with us, Eilert! Ah, well.

He goes back into the other room and sits down with BRACK.

LŒVBORG: Tell me one thing, Hedda.

HEDDA: Yes?

LŒVBORG: Didn't you love me either? Not—just a little?

HEDDA: Well now, I wonder? No, I think we were just good friends. *(Smiles.)* You certainly poured your heart out to me.

71

LŒVBORG: You begged me to.

HEDDA: Looking back on it, there was something beautiful and fascinating—and brave—about the way we told each other everything. That secret friendship no one else knew about.

LŒVBORG: Yes, Hedda, yes! Do you remember? How I used to come up to your father's house in the afternoon—and the General sat by the window and read his newspapers—with his back towards us—

HEDDA: And we sat on the sofa in the corner—

LŒVBORG: Always reading the same illustrated magazine—

HEDDA: We hadn't any photograph album.

LŒVBORG: Yes, Hedda. I regarded you as a kind of confessor. Told you things about myself which no one else knew about—then. Those days and nights of drinking and—oh, Hedda, what power did you have to make me confess such things?

HEDDA: Power? You think I had some power over you?

LŒVBORG: Yes—I don't know how else to explain it. And all those—oblique questions you asked me—

HEDDA: You knew what they meant.

LŒVBORG: But that you could sit there and ask me such questions! So unashamedly—

HEDDA: I thought you said they were oblique.

LŒVBORG: Yes, but you asked them so unashamedly. That you could question me about—about that kind of thing!

HEDDA: You answered willingly enough.

LŒVBORG: Yes—that's what I can't understand—looking back on it. But tell me, Hedda—what you felt for me—wasn't that—love? When you asked me those questions and made me confess my sins to you, wasn't it because you wanted to wash me clean?

HEDDA: No, not exactly.

LŒVBORG: Why did you do it, then?

HEDDA: Do you find it so incredible that a young girl, given the chance in secret, should want to be allowed a glimpse into a forbidden world of whose existence she is supposed to be ignorant?

LŒVBORG: So that was it?

HEDDA: One reason. One reason—I think.

LŒVBORG: You didn't love me, then. You just wanted—knowledge. But if that was so, why did you break it off?

HEDDA: That was your fault.

LŒVBORG: It was you who put an end to it.

HEDDA: Yes, when I realized that our friendship was threatening to develop into something—something else. Shame on you, Eilert Lœvborg! How could you abuse the trust of your dearest friend?

LŒVBORG (*clenches his fist*): Oh, why didn't you do it? Why didn't you shoot me dead? As you threatened to!

HEDDA: I was afraid. Of the scandal.

LŒVBORG: Yes, Hedda. You're a coward at heart.

HEDDA: A dreadful coward. (*Changes her tone.*) Luckily for you. Well, now you've found consolation with the Elvsteds.

LŒVBORG: I know what Thea's been telling you.

HEDDA: I dare say you told her about us.

LŒVBORG: Not a word. She's too silly to understand that kind of thing.

HEDDA: Silly?

LŒVBORG: She's silly about that kind of thing.

HEDDA: And I'm a coward. (*Leans closer to him, without looking him in the eyes, and says quietly*) But let me tell you something. Something you don't know.

LŒVBORG (*tensely*): Yes?

HEDDA: My failure to shoot you wasn't my worst act of cowardice that evening.

LŒVBORG (*looks at her for a moment, realizes her meaning, and whispers passionately*): Oh, Hedda! Hedda Gabler! Now I see what was behind those questions. Yes! It wasn't knowledge you wanted! It was life!

HEDDA (*flashes a look at him and says quietly*): Take care! Don't you delude yourself!

It has begun to grow dark. BERTHA, *from outside, opens the door leading into the hall.*

HEDDA (*closes the album with a snap and cries, smiling*): Ah, at last! Come in, Thea dear!

MRS. ELVSTED *enters from the hall, in evening dress. The door is closed behind her.*

HEDDA (*on the sofa, stretches out her arms towards her*): Thea darling, I thought you were never coming!

MRS. ELVSTED *makes a slight bow to the gentlemen in the rear room as she passes the open doorway, and they to her. Then she goes to the table and holds out her hand to* HEDDA. EILERT LŒVBORG *has risen from his chair. He and* MRS. ELVSTED *nod silently to each other.*

MRS. ELVSTED: Perhaps I ought to go in and say a few words to your husband?
HEDDA: Oh, there's no need. They're happy by themselves. They'll be going soon.
MRS. ELVSTED: Going?
HEDDA: Yes, they're off on a spree this evening.
MRS. ELVSTED (*quickly, to* LŒVBORG): You're not going with them?
LŒVBORG: No.
HEDDA: Mr. Lœvborg is staying here with us.
MRS. ELVSTED (*takes a chair and is about to sit down beside him*): Oh, how nice it is to be here!
HEDDA: No, Thea darling, not there. Come over here and sit beside me. I want to be in the middle.
MRS. ELVSTED: Yes, just as you wish.

She goes round the table and sits on the sofa, on
HEDDA'*s right.* LŒVBORG *sits down again in his chair.*

LŒVBORG *(after a short pause, to* HEDDA*):* Isn't she lovely
to look at?

HEDDA *(strokes her hair gently):* Only to look at?

LŒVBORG: Yes. We're just good friends. We trust each
other implicitly. We can talk to each other quite unashamedly.

HEDDA: No need to be oblique?

MRS. ELVSTED *(nestles close to* HEDDA *and says quietly):*
Oh, Hedda, I'm so happy. Imagine—he says I've inspired him!

HEDDA *(looks at her with a smile):* Dear Thea! Does he
really?

LŒVBORG: She has the courage of her convictions, Mrs.
Tesman.

MRS. ELVSTED: I? Courage?

LŒVBORG: Absolute courage. Where friendship is concerned.

HEDDA: Yes. Courage. Yes. If only one had that—

LŒVBORG: Yes?

HEDDA: One might be able to live. In spite of everything.
(Changes her tone suddenly.) Well, Thea darling, now
you're going to drink a nice glass of cold punch.

MRS. ELVSTED: No thank you. I never drink anything like
that.

HEDDA: Oh. You, Mr. Lœvborg?

LŒVBORG: Thank you, I don't either.

MRS. ELVSTED: No, he doesn't, either.

HEDDA *(looks into his eyes):* But if I want you to.

LŒVBORG: That doesn't make any difference.

HEDDA *(laughs):* Have I no power over you at all? Poor me!

LŒVBORG: Not where this is concerned.

HEDDA: Seriously, I think you should. For your own sake.

MRS. ELVSTED: Hedda!

LŒVBORG: Why?

HEDDA: Or perhaps I should say for other people's sake.

LŒVBORG: What do you mean?

HEDDA: People might think you didn't feel absolutely and unashamedly sure of yourself. In your heart of hearts.

MRS. ELVSTED (*quietly*): Oh, Hedda, no!

LŒVBORG: People can think what they like. For the present.

MRS. ELVSTED (*happily*): Yes, that's true.

HEDDA: I saw it so clearly in Judge Brack a few minutes ago.

LŒVBORG: Oh. What did you see?

HEDDA: He smiled so scornfully when he saw you were afraid to go in there and drink with them.

LŒVBORG: Afraid! I wanted to stay here and talk to you.

MRS. ELVSTED: That was only natural, Hedda.

HEDDA: But the Judge wasn't to know that. I saw him wink at Tesman when you showed you didn't dare to join their wretched little party.

LŒVBORG: Didn't dare! Are you saying I didn't dare?

HEDDA: I'm not saying so. But that was what Judge Brack thought.

LŒVBORG: Well, let him.

HEDDA: You're not going, then?

LŒVBORG: I'm staying here with you and Thea.

MRS. ELVSTED: Yes, Hedda, of course he is.

HEDDA (*smiles, and nods approvingly to* LŒVBORG): Firm as a rock! A man of principle! That's how a man should be! (*Turns to* MRS. ELVSTED *and strokes her cheek.*) Didn't I tell you so this morning when you came here in such a panic—?

LŒVBORG (*starts*): Panic?

MRS. ELVSTED (*frightened*): Hedda! But—Hedda!

HEDDA: Well, now you can see for yourself. There's no earthly need for you to get scared to death just because—

(Stops.) Well! Let's all three cheer up and enjoy ourselves.

LŒVBORG: Mrs. Tesman, would you mind explaining to me
what this is all about?

MRS. ELVSTED: Oh, my God, my God, Hedda, what are you
saying? What are you doing?

HEDDA: Keep calm. That horrid Judge has his eye on you.

LŒVBORG: Scared to death, were you? For my sake?

MRS. ELVSTED *(quietly, trembling):* Oh, Hedda! You've
made me so unhappy!

LŒVBORG *(looks coldly at her for a moment. His face is dis-
torted):* So that was how much you trusted me.

MRS. ELVSTED: Eilert dear, please listen to me—

LŒVBORG *(takes one of the glasses of punch, raises it and
says quietly, hoarsely):* Skoal, Thea!

He empties the glass, puts it down and picks up one of
the others.

MRS. ELVSTED *(quietly):* Hedda, Hedda! Why did you want
this to happen?

HEDDA: *I*—want it? Are you mad?

LŒVBORG: Skoal to you, too, Mrs. Tesman. Thanks for telling me the truth. Here's to the truth!

He empties his glass and refills it.

HEDDA *(puts her hand on his arm):* Steady. That's enough
for now. Don't forget the party.

MRS. ELVSTED: No, no, no!

HEDDA: Ssh! They're looking at you.

LŒVBORG *(puts down his glass):* Thea, tell me the truth—

MRS. ELVSTED: Yes!

LŒVBORG: Did your husband know you were following me?

MRS. ELVSTED: Oh, Hedda!

LŒVBORG: Did you and he have an agreement that you
should come here and keep an eye on me? Perhaps he

gave you the idea? After all, he's a magistrate. I suppose he needed me back in his office. Or did he miss my companionship at the card-table?

MRS. ELVSTED (*quietly, sobbing*): Eilert, Eilert!

LŒVBORG (*seizes a glass and is about to fill it*): Let's drink to him, too.

HEDDA: No more now. Remember you're going to read your book to Tesman.

LŒVBORG (*calm again, puts down his glass*): That was silly of me, Thea. To take it like that, I mean. Don't be angry with me, my dear. You'll see—yes, and they'll see, too—that though I fell, I—I have raised myself up again. With your help, Thea.

MRS. ELVSTED (*happily*): Oh, thank God!

BRACK *has meanwhile glanced at his watch. He and* TESMAN *get up and come into the drawing-room.*

BRACK (*takes his hat and overcoat*): Well, Mrs. Tesman, it's time for us to go.

HEDDA: Yes, I suppose it must be.

LŒVBORG (*gets up*): Time for me, too, Judge.

MRS. ELVSTED (*quietly, pleadingly*): Eilert, please don't!

HEDDA (*pinches her arm*): They can hear you.

MRS. ELVSTED (*gives a little cry*): Oh!

LŒVBORG (*to* BRACK): You were kind enough to ask me to join you.

BRACK: Are you coming?

LŒVBORG: If I may.

BRACK: Delighted.

LŒVBORG (*puts the paper package in his pocket and says to* TESMAN): I'd like to show you one or two things before I send it off to the printer.

TESMAN: I say, that'll be fun. Fancy—! Oh, but, Hedda, how'll Mrs. Elvsted get home? What?

HEDDA: Oh, we'll manage somehow.

LŒVBORG (*glances over towards the ladies*): Mrs. Elvsted? I shall come back and collect her, naturally. (*Goes closer.*) About ten o'clock, Mrs. Tesman? Will that suit you?

HEDDA: Yes. That'll suit me admirably.

TESMAN: Good, that's settled. But you mustn't expect me back so early, Hedda.

HEDDA: Stay as long as you c—as long as you like, dear.

MRS. ELVSTED (*trying to hide her anxiety*): Well then, Mr. Lœvborg, I'll wait here till you come.

LŒVBORG (*his hat in his hand*): Pray do, Mrs. Elvsted.

BRACK: Well, gentlemen, now the party begins. I trust that, in the words of a certain fair lady, we shall enjoy good sport.

HEDDA: What a pity the fair lady can't be there, invisible.

BRACK: Why invisible?

HEDDA: So as to be able to hear some of your uncensored witticisms, your honour.

BRACK (*laughs*): Oh, I shouldn't advise the fair lady to do that.

TESMAN (*laughs, too*): I say, Hedda, that's good. What!

BRACK: Well, good night, ladies, good night!

LŒVBORG (*bows farewell*): About ten o'clock then.

> BRACK, LŒVBORG *and* TESMAN *go out through the hall. As they do so,* BERTHA *enters from the rear room with a lighted lamp. She puts it on the drawing-room table, then goes out the way she came.*

MRS. ELVSTED (*has got up and is walking uneasily to and fro*): Oh, Hedda, Hedda! How is all this going to end?

HEDDA: At ten o'clock, then. He'll be here. I can see him. With a crown of vine leaves in his hair. Burning and unashamed!

MRS. ELVSTED: Oh, I do hope so!

HEDDA: Can't you see? Then he'll be himself again! He'll be a free man for the rest of his days!

MRS. ELVSTED: Please God you're right.

HEDDA: That's how he'll come! *(Gets up and goes closer.)* You can doubt him as much as you like. I believe in him! Now we'll see which of us—

MRS. ELVSTED: You're after something, Hedda.

HEDDA: Yes, I am. For once in my life I want to have the power to shape a man's destiny.

MRS. ELVSTED: Haven't you that power already?

HEDDA: No, I haven't. I've never had it.

MRS. ELVSTED: What about your husband?

HEDDA: Him! Oh, if you could only understand how poor I am. And you're allowed to be so rich, so rich! *(Clasps her passionately.)* I think I'll burn your hair off after all!

MRS. ELVSTED: Let me go! Let me go! You frighten me, Hedda!

BERTHA *(in the open doorway):* I've laid tea in the dining-room, madam.

HEDDA: Good, we're coming.

MRS. ELVSTED: No, no, no! I'd rather go home alone! Now—at once!

HEDDA: Rubbish! First you're going to have some tea, you little idiot. And then—at ten o'clock—Eilert Lœvborg will come. With a crown of vine leaves in his hair!

She drags MRS. ELVSTED *almost forcibly towards the open doorway.*

ACT THREE

The same. The curtains are drawn across the open doorway, and also across the french windows. The lamp, half turned down, with a shade over it, is burning on the table. In the stove, the door of which is open, a fire has been burning, but it is now almost out. MRS. ELVSTED, *wrapped in a large shawl and with her feet resting on a footstool, is sitting near the stove, huddled in the armchair.* HEDDA *is lying asleep on the sofa, fully dressed, with a blanket over her.*

MRS. ELVSTED *(after a pause, suddenly sits up in her chair and listens tensely. Then she sinks wearily back again and sighs.)* Not back yet! Oh, God! Oh, God! Not back yet!

> BERTHA *tiptoes cautiously in from the hall. She has a letter in her hand.*

MRS. ELVSTED *(turns and whispers):* What is it? Has someone come?

BERTHA *(quietly):* Yes, a servant's just called with this letter.

MRS. ELVSTED *(quickly, holding out her hand):* A letter! Give it to me!

BERTHA: But it's for the Doctor, madam.

MRS. ELVSTED: Oh, I see.

BERTHA: Miss Tesman's maid brought it. I'll leave it here on the table.

MRS. ELVSTED: Yes, do.

BERTHA *(puts down the letter):* I'd better put the lamp out. It's starting to smoke.

MRS. ELVSTED: Yes, put it out. It'll soon be daylight.

BERTHA *(puts out the lamp):* It's daylight already, madam.

MRS. ELVSTED: Yes. Broad day. And not home yet.

BERTHA: Oh dear, I was afraid this would happen.

MRS. ELVSTED: Were you?

BERTHA: Yes. When I heard that a certain gentleman had returned to town, and saw him go off with them. I've heard all about him.

MRS. ELVSTED: Don't talk so loud. You'll wake your mistress.

BERTHA *(looks at the sofa and sighs):* Yes. Let her go on sleeping, poor dear. Shall I put some more wood on the fire?

MRS. ELVSTED: Thank you, don't bother on my account.

BERTHA: Very good.

She goes quietly out through the hall.

HEDDA *(wakes as the door closes and looks up):* What's that?

MRS. ELVSTED: It was only the maid.

HEDDA *(looks round):* What am I doing here? Oh, now I remember. *(Sits up on the sofa, stretches herself and rubs her eyes.)* What time is it, Thea?

MRS. ELVSTED: It's gone seven.

HEDDA: When did Tesman get back?

MRS. ELVSTED: He's not back yet.

HEDDA: Not home yet?

MRS. ELVSTED *(gets up):* No one's come.

HEDDA: And we sat up waiting for them till four o'clock.

MRS. ELVSTED: God! How I waited for him!

HEDDA *(yawns and says with her hand in front of her mouth):* Oh, dear. We might have saved ourselves the trouble.

MRS. ELVSTED: Did you manage to sleep?

HEDDA: Oh, yes. Quite well, I think. Didn't you get any?

MRS. ELVSTED: Not a wink. I couldn't, Hedda. I just couldn't.

HEDDA *(gets up and comes over to her)*: Now, now, now. There's nothing to worry about. I know what's happened.

MRS. ELVSTED: What? Please tell me.

HEDDA: Well, obviously the party went on very late—

MRS. ELVSTED: Oh dear, I suppose it must have. But—

HEDDA: And Tesman didn't want to come home and wake us all up in the middle of the night. *(Laughs.)* Probably wasn't too keen to show his face either, after a spree like that.

MRS. ELVSTED: But where could he have gone?

HEDDA: I should think he's probably slept at his aunts'. They keep his old room for him.

MRS. ELVSTED: No, he can't be with them. A letter came for him just now from Miss Tesman. It's over there.

HEDDA: Oh? *(Looks at the envelope.)* Yes, it's Auntie Juju's handwriting. Well, he must still be at Judge Brack's, then. And Eilert Lœvborg is sitting there, reading to him. With a crown of vine leaves in his hair.

MRS. ELVSTED: Hedda, you're only saying that. You don't believe it.

HEDDA: Thea, you really are a little fool.

MRS. ELVSTED: Perhaps I am.

HEDDA: You look tired to death.

MRS. ELVSTED: Yes. I am tired to death.

HEDDA: Go to my room and lie down for a little. Do as I say, now; don't argue.

MRS. ELVSTED: No, no. I couldn't possibly sleep.

HEDDA: Of course you can.

MRS. ELVSTED: But your husband'll be home soon. And I must know at once—

HEDDA: I'll tell you when he comes.

MRS. ELVSTED: Promise me, Hedda?

HEDDA: Yes, don't worry. Go and get some sleep.

MRS. ELVSTED: Thank you. All right, I'll try.

She goes out through the rear room. HEDDA *goes to the french windows and draws the curtains. Broad daylight floods into the room. She goes to the writing-table, takes a small hand-mirror from it and arranges her hair. Then she goes to the door leading into the hall and presses the bell. After a few moments,* BERTHA *enters.*

BERTHA: Did you want anything, madam?

HEDDA: Yes, put some more wood on the fire. I'm freezing.

BERTHA: Bless you, I'll soon have this room warmed up. *(She rakes the embers together and puts a fresh piece of wood on them. Suddenly she stops and listens.)* There's someone at the front door, madam.

HEDDA: Well, go and open it. I'll see to the fire.

BERTHA: It'll burn up in a moment.

She goes out through the hall. HEDDA *kneels on the footstool and puts more wood in the stove. After a few seconds,* GEORGE TESMAN *enters from the hall. He looks tired, and rather worried. He tiptoes towards the open doorway and is about to slip through the curtains.*

HEDDA *(at the stove, without looking up):* Good morning.

TESMAN *(turns):* Hedda! *(Comes nearer.)* Good heavens, are you up already? What?

HEDDA: Yes, I got up very early this morning.

TESMAN: I was sure you'd still be sleeping. Fancy that!

HEDDA: Don't talk so loud. Mrs. Elvsted's asleep in my room.

TESMAN: Mrs. Elvsted? Has she stayed the night here?

HEDDA: Yes. No one came to escort her home.

TESMAN: Oh. No, I suppose not.

HEDDA (*closes the door of the stove and gets up*): Well. Was it fun?

TESMAN: Have you been anxious about me? What?

HEDDA: Not in the least. I asked if you'd had fun.

TESMAN: Oh yes, rather! Well, I thought, for once in a while—! The first part was the best; when Eilert read his book to me. We arrived over an hour too early—what about that, eh? Fancy—! Brack had a lot of things to see to, so Eilert read to me.

HEDDA (*sits at the right-hand side of the table*): Well? Tell me about it.

TESMAN (*sits on a footstool by the stove*): Honestly, Hedda, you've no idea what a book that's going to be. It's really one of the most remarkable things that's ever been written. By Jove!

HEDDA: Oh, never mind about the book—

TESMAN: I'm going to make a confession to you, Hedda. When he'd finished reading a sort of beastly feeling came over me.

HEDDA: Beastly feeling?

TESMAN: I found myself envying Eilert for being able to write like that. Imagine that, Hedda!

HEDDA: Yes. I can imagine.

TESMAN: What a tragedy that with all those gifts he should be so incorrigible.

HEDDA: You mean he's less afraid of life than most men?

TESMAN: Good heavens, no. He just doesn't know the meaning of the word moderation.

HEDDA: What happened afterwards?

TESMAN: Well, looking back on it, I suppose you might almost call it an orgy, Hedda.

HEDDA: Had he vine leaves in his hair?

TESMAN: Vine leaves? No, I didn't see any of them. He made a long, rambling oration in honour of the woman who'd inspired him to write this book. Yes, those were the words he used.

HEDDA: Did he name her?

TESMAN: No. But I suppose it must be Mrs. Elvsted. You wait and see!

HEDDA: Where did you leave him?

TESMAN: On the way home. We left in a bunch—the last of us, that is—and Brack came with us to get a little fresh air. Well, then, you see, we agreed we ought to see Eilert home. He'd had a drop too much.

HEDDA: You don't say?

TESMAN: But now comes the funny part, Hedda. Or I should really say the tragic part. Oh, I'm almost ashamed to tell you. For Eilert's sake, I mean—

HEDDA: Why, what happened?

TESMAN: Well, you see, as we were walking towards town I happened to drop behind for a minute. Only for a minute—er—you understand—

HEDDA: Yes, yes—?

TESMAN: Well then, when I ran on to catch them up, what do you think I found by the roadside. What?

HEDDA: How on earth should I know?

TESMAN: You mustn't tell anyone, Hedda. What? Promise me that—for Eilert's sake. *(Takes a package wrapped in paper from his coat pocket.)* Just fancy! I found this.

HEDDA: Isn't this the one he brought here yesterday?

TESMAN: Yes! The whole of that precious, irreplaceable manuscript! And he went and lost it! Didn't even notice! What about that? Tragic.

HEDDA: But why didn't you give it back to him?

TESMAN: I didn't dare to, in the state he was in.

HEDDA: Didn't you tell any of the others?

TESMAN: Good heavens, no. I didn't want to do that. For Eilert's sake, you understand.

HEDDA: Then no one else knows you have his manuscript?

TESMAN: No. And no one must be allowed to know.

HEDDA: Didn't it come up in the conversation later?

TESMAN: I didn't get a chance to talk to him any more. As soon as we got into the outskirts of town, he and one or two of the others gave us the slip. Disappeared, by Jove!

HEDDA: Oh? I suppose they took him home.

TESMAN: Yes, I imagine that was the idea. Brack left us, too.

HEDDA: And what have you been up to since then?

TESMAN: Well, I and one or two of the others—awfully jolly chaps, they were—went back to where one of them lived and had a cup of morning coffee. Morning-after coffee—what? Ah, well. I'll just lie down for a bit and give Eilert time to sleep it off, poor chap, then I'll run over and give this back to him.

HEDDA *(holds out her hand for the package)*: No, don't do that. Not just yet. Let me read it first.

TESMAN: Oh no, really, Hedda dear, honestly, I daren't do that.

HEDDA: Daren't?

TESMAN: No—imagine how desperate he'll be when he wakes up and finds his manuscript's missing. He hasn't any copy, you see. He told me so himself.

HEDDA: Can't a thing like that be rewritten?

TESMAN: Oh no, not possibly, I shouldn't think. I mean, the inspiration, you know—

HEDDA: Oh, yes, I'd forgotten that. *(Casually.)* By the way, there's a letter for you.

TESMAN: Is there? Fancy that!

HEDDA *(holds it out to him)*: It came early this morning.

TESMAN: I say, it's from Auntie Juju! What on earth can it be? *(Puts the package on the other footstool, opens the letter, reads it and jumps up.)* Oh, Hedda! She says poor Auntie Rena's dying.

HEDDA: Well, we've been expecting that.

TESMAN: She says if I want to see her I must go quickly. I'll run over at once.

HEDDA *(hides a smile):* Run?

TESMAN: Hedda dear, I suppose you wouldn't like to come with me? What about that, eh?

HEDDA *(gets up and says wearily and with repulsion):* No, no, don't ask me to do anything like that. I can't bear illness or death. I loathe anything ugly.

TESMAN: Yes, yes. Of course. *(In a dither.)* My hat? My overcoat? Oh yes, in the hall. I do hope I won't get there too late, Hedda! What?

HEDDA: You'll be all right if you run.

BERTHA enters from the hall.

BERTHA: Judge Brack's outside and wants to know if he can come in.

TESMAN: At this hour? No, I can't possibly receive him now.

HEDDA: I can. *(To BERTHA)* Ask his honour to come in.

BERTHA goes.

HEDDA *(whispers quickly):* The manuscript, Tesman.

She snatches it from the footstool.

TESMAN: Yes, give it to me.

HEDDA: No, I'll look after it for now.

She goes over to the writing-table and puts it in the bookcase. TESMAN stands dithering, unable to get his gloves on. JUDGE BRACK enters from the hall.

HEDDA *(nods to him):* Well, you're an early bird.

BRACK: Yes, aren't I? *(To TESMAN)* Are you up and about, too?

TESMAN: Yes, I've got to go and see my aunts. Poor Auntie Rena's dying.

BRACK: Oh dear, is she? Then you mustn't let me detain you. At so tragic a—

TESMAN: Yes, I really must run. Good-bye! Good-bye!

He runs out through the hall.

HEDDA *(goes nearer):* You seem to have had excellent sport last night—Judge.

BRACK: Indeed yes, Mrs. Hedda. I haven't even had time to take my clothes off.

HEDDA: *You* haven't either?

BRACK: As you see. What's Tesman told you about last night's escapades?

HEDDA: Oh, only some boring story about having gone and drunk coffee somewhere.

BRACK: Yes, I've heard about that coffee-party. Eilert Lœvborg wasn't with them, I gather?

HEDDA: No, they took him home first.

BRACK: Did Tesman go with him?

HEDDA: No, one or two of the others, he said.

BRACK *(smiles):* George Tesman is a credulous man, Mrs. Hedda.

HEDDA: God knows. But—has something happened?

BRACK: Well, yes, I'm afraid it has.

HEDDA: I see. Sit down and tell me.

She sits on the left of the table, BRACK *at the long side of it, near her.*

HEDDA: Well?

BRACK: I had a special reason for keeping track of my guests last night. Or perhaps I should say some of my guests.

HEDDA: Including Eilert Lœvborg?

BRACK: I must confess—yes.

HEDDA: You're beginning to make me curious.

BRACK: Do you know where he and some of my other guests spent the latter half of last night, Mrs. Hedda?

HEDDA: Tell me. If it won't shock me.

BRACK: Oh, I don't think it'll shock you. They found themselves participating in an exceedingly animated *soirée.*

HEDDA: Of a sporting character?

BRACK: Of a highly sporting character.

HEDDA: Tell me more.

BRACK: Lœvborg had received an invitation in advance—as had the others. I knew all about that. But he had refused. As you know, he's become a new man.

HEDDA: Up at the Elvsteds', yes. But he went?

BRACK: Well, you see, Mrs. Hedda, last night at my house, unhappily, the spirit moved him.

HEDDA: Yes, I hear he became inspired.

BRACK: Somewhat violently inspired. And as a result, I suppose, his thoughts strayed. We men, alas, don't always stick to our principles as firmly as we should.

HEDDA: I'm sure you're an exception, Judge Brack. But go on about Lœvborg.

BRACK: Well, to cut a long story short, he ended up in the establishment of a certain Mademoiselle Danielle.

HEDDA: Mademoiselle Danielle?

BRACK: She was holding the *soirée.* For a selected circle of friends and admirers.

HEDDA: Has she got red hair?

BRACK: She has.

HEDDA: A singer of some kind?

BRACK: Yes—among other accomplishments. She's also a celebrated huntress—of men, Mrs. Hedda. I'm sure you've heard about her. Eilert Lœvborg used to be one of her most ardent patrons. In his salad days.

HEDDA: And how did all this end?

BRACK: Not entirely amicably, from all accounts. Mademoiselle Danielle began by receiving him with the utmost tenderness and ended by resorting to her fists.

HEDDA: Against Lœvborg?

BRACK: Yes. He accused her, or her friends, of having robbed him. He claimed his pocket-book had been stolen. Among other things. In short, he seems to have made a blood-thirsty scene.

HEDDA: And what did this lead to?

BRACK: It led to a general free-for-all, in which both sexes participated. Fortunately, in the end the police arrived.

HEDDA: The police, too?

BRACK: Yes. I'm afraid it may turn out to be rather an expensive joke for Master Eilert. Crazy fool!

HEDDA: Oh?

BRACK: Apparently he put up a very violent resistance. Hit one of the constables on the ear and tore his uniform. He had to accompany them to the police station.

HEDDA: Where did you learn all this?

BRACK: From the police.

HEDDA (to herself): So that's what happened. He didn't have a crown of vine leaves in his hair.

BRACK: Vine leaves, Mrs. Hedda?

HEDDA (in her normal voice again): But, tell me, Judge, why do you take such a close interest in Eilert Lœvborg?

BRACK: For one thing it'll hardly be a matter of complete indifference to me if it's revealed in court that he came there straight from my house.

HEDDA: Will it come to court?

BRACK: Of course. Well, I don't regard that as particularly serious. Still, I thought it my duty, as a friend of the family, to give you and your husband a full account of his nocturnal adventures.

HEDDA: Why?

BRACK: Because I've a shrewd suspicion that he's hoping to use you as a kind of screen.

HEDDA: What makes you think that?

BRACK: Oh, for heaven's sake, Mrs. Hedda, we're not

blind. You wait and see. This Mrs. Elvsted won't be going back to her husband just yet.

HEDDA: Well, if there were anything between those two there are plenty of other places where they could meet.

BRACK: Not in anyone's home. From now on every respectable house will once again be closed to Eilert Lœvborg.

HEDDA: And mine should be, too, you mean?

BRACK: Yes. I confess I should find it more than irksome if this gentleman were to be granted unrestricted access to this house. If he were superfluously to intrude into—

HEDDA: The triangle?

BRACK: Precisely. For me it would be like losing a home.

HEDDA (*looks at him and smiles*): I see. You want to be the cock of the walk.

BRACK (*nods slowly and lowers his voice*): Yes, that is my aim. And I shall fight for it with—every weapon at my disposal.

HEDDA (*as her smile fades*): You're a dangerous man, aren't you? When you really want something.

BRACK: You think so?

HEDDA: Yes, I'm beginning to think so. I'm deeply thankful you haven't any kind of hold over me.

BRACK (*laughs equivocally*): Well, well, Mrs. Hedda— perhaps you're right. If I had, who knows what I might not think up?

HEDDA: Come, Judge Brack. That sounds almost like a threat.

BRACK (*gets up*): Heaven forbid! In the creation of a triangle—and its continuance—the question of compulsion should never arise.

HEDDA: Exactly what I was thinking.

BRACK: Well, I've said what I came to say. I must be getting back. Good-bye, Mrs. Hedda. (*Goes towards the french windows.*)

HEDDA (*gets up*): Are you going out through the garden?

BRACK: Yes, it's shorter.

HEDDA: Yes. And it's the back door, isn't it?

BRACK: I've nothing against back doors. They can be quite intriguing—sometimes.

HEDDA: When people fire pistols out of them, for example?

BRACK (*in the doorway, laughs*): Oh, people don't shoot tame cocks.

HEDDA (*laughs, too*): I suppose not. When they've only got one.

They nod good-bye, laughing. He goes. She closes the french windows behind him, and stands for a moment, looking out pensively. Then she walks across the room and glances through the curtains in the open doorway. Goes to the writing-table, takes LŒVBORG's package from the bookcase and is about to turn through the pages when BERTHA is heard remonstrating loudly in the hall. HEDDA turns and listens. She hastily puts the package back in the drawer, locks it and puts the key on the inkstand. EILERT LŒVBORG, with his overcoat on and his hat in his hand, throws the door open. He looks somewhat confused and excited.

LŒVBORG (*shouts as he enters*): I must come in, I tell you! Let me pass!

He closes the door, turns, sees HEDDA, controls himself immediately and bows.

HEDDA (*at the writing-table*): Well, Mr. Lœvborg, this is rather a late hour to be collecting Thea.

LŒVBORG: And an early hour to call on you. Please forgive me.

HEDDA: How do you know she's still here?

LŒVBORG: They told me at her lodgings that she has been out all night.

HEDDA (*goes to the table*): Did you notice anything about their behaviour when they told you?

LŒVBORG (*looks at her, puzzled*): Notice anything?

HEDDA: Did they sound as if they thought it—strange?

LŒVBORG (*suddenly understands*): Oh, I see what you mean. I'm dragging her down with me. No, as a matter of fact I didn't notice anything. I suppose Tesman isn't up yet?

HEDDA: No, I don't think so.

LŒVBORG: When did he get home?

HEDDA: Very late.

LŒVBORG: Did he tell you anything?

HEDDA: Yes. I gather you had a merry party at Judge Brack's last night.

LŒVBORG: He didn't tell you anything else?

HEDDA: I don't think so. I was so terribly sleepy—

> MRS. ELVSTED *comes through the curtains in the open doorway.*

MRS. ELVSTED (*runs towards him*): Oh, Eilert! At last!

LŒVBORG: Yes—at last. And too late.

MRS. ELVSTED: What is too late?

LŒVBORG: Everything—now. I'm finished, Thea.

MRS. ELVSTED: Oh, no, no! Don't say that!

LŒVBORG: You'll say it yourself, when you've heard what I—

MRS. ELVSTED: I don't want to hear anything!

HEDDA: Perhaps you'd rather speak to her alone? I'd better go.

LŒVBORG: No, stay.

MRS. ELVSTED: But I don't want to hear anything, I tell you!

LŒVBORG: It's not about last night.

MRS. ELVSTED: Then what—?

LŒVBORG: I want to tell you that from now on we must stop seeing each other.

MRS. ELVSTED: Stop seeing each other!

HEDDA *(involuntarily):* I knew it!

LŒVBORG: I have no further use for you, Thea.

MRS. ELVSTED: You can stand there and say that! No further use for me! Surely I can go on helping you? We'll go on working together, won't we?

LŒVBORG: I don't intend to do any more work from now on.

MRS. ELVSTED *(desperately):* Then what use have I for my life?

LŒVBORG: You must try to live as if you had never known me.

MRS. ELVSTED: But I can't!

LŒVBORG: Try to, Thea. Go back home—

MRS. ELVSTED: Never! I want to be wherever you are! I won't let myself be driven away like this! I want to stay here—and be with you when the book comes out.

HEDDA *(whispers):* Ah, yes! The book!

LŒVBORG *(looks at her):* Our book; Thea's and mine. It belongs to both of us.

MRS. ELVSTED: Oh, yes! I feel that, too! And I've a right to be with you when it comes into the world. I want to see people respect and honour you again. And the joy! The joy! I want to share it with you!

LŒVBORG: Thea—our book will never come into the world.

HEDDA: Ah!

MRS. ELVSTED: Not—?

LŒVBORG: It cannot. Ever.

MRS. ELVSTED: Eilert—what have you done with the manuscript?

HEDDA: Yes—the manuscript?

MRS. ELVSTED: Where is it?

LŒVBORG: Oh, Thea, please don't ask me that!

MRS. ELVSTED: Yes, yes—I must know. I've a right to know. Now!

LŒVBORG: The manuscript. Yes. I've torn it up.

MRS. ELVSTED *(screams):* No, no!

HEDDA (*involuntarily*): But that's not—!

LŒVBORG (*looks at her*): Not true, you think.

HEDDA (*controls herself*): Why—yes, of course it is, if you say so. It sounded so incredible—

LŒVBORG: It's true, nevertheless.

MRS. ELVSTED: Oh, my God, my God, Hedda—he's destroyed his own book!

LŒVBORG: I have destroyed my life. Why not my life's work, too?

MRS. ELVSTED: And you—did this last night?

LŒVBORG: Yes, Thea. I tore it into a thousand pieces. And scattered them out across the fjord. It's good, clean, salt water. Let it carry them away; let them drift in the current and the wind. And in a little while, they will sink. Deeper and deeper. As I shall, Thea.

MRS. ELVSTED: Do you know, Eilert—this book—all my life I shall feel as though you'd killed a little child.

LŒVBORG: You're right. It is like killing a child.

MRS. ELVSTED: But how could you? It was my child, too!

HEDDA (*almost inaudibly*): Oh—the child—!

MRS. ELVSTED (*breathes heavily*): It's all over, then. Well— I'll go now, Hedda.

HEDDA: You're not leaving town?

MRS. ELVSTED: I don't know what I'm going to do. I can't see anything except—darkness.

She goes out through the hall.

HEDDA (*waits a moment*): Aren't you going to escort her home, Mr. Lœvborg?

LŒVBORG: I? Through the streets? Do you want me to let people see her with me?

HEDDA: Of course, I don't know what else may have happened last night. But is it so utterly beyond redress?

LŒVBORG: It isn't just last night. It'll go on happening. I know it. But the curse of it is, I don't want to live that kind of life. I don't want to start all that again. She's broken my courage. I can't spit in the eyes of the world any longer.

HEDDA *(as though to herself):* That pretty little fool's been trying to shape a man's destiny. *(Looks at him.)* But how could you be so heartless towards her?

LŒVBORG: Don't call me heartless!

HEDDA: To go and destroy the one thing that's made her life worth living? You don't call that heartless?

LŒVBORG: Do you want to know the truth, Hedda?

HEDDA: The truth?

LŒVBORG: Promise me first—give me your word—that you'll never let Thea know about this.

HEDDA: I give you my word.

LŒVBORG: Good. Well; what I told her just now was a lie.

HEDDA: About the manuscript?

LŒVBORG: Yes. I didn't tear it up. Or throw it in the fjord.

HEDDA: You didn't? But where is it, then?

LŒVBORG: I destroyed it, all the same. I destroyed it, Hedda!

HEDDA: I don't understand.

LŒVBORG: Thea said that what I had done was like killing a child.

HEDDA: Yes. That's what she said.

LŒVBORG: But to kill a child isn't the worst thing a father can do to it.

HEDDA: What could be worse than that?

LŒVBORG: Hedda—suppose a man came home one morning, after a night of debauchery, and said to the mother of his child: 'Look here. I've been wandering round all night. I've been to—such-and-such a place and such-and-such a place. And I had our child with me. I took him to—these places. And I've lost him. Just—lost him. God knows where he is or whose hands he's fallen into.'

HEDDA: I see. But when all's said and done, this was only a book—

LŒVBORG: Thea's heart and soul were in that book. It was her whole life.

HEDDA: Yes, I understand.

LŒVBORG: Well, then you must also understand that she and I cannot possibly ever see each other again.

HEDDA: Where will you go?

LŒVBORG: Nowhere. I just want to put an end to it all. As soon as possible.

HEDDA *(takes a step towards him):* Eilert Lœvborg, listen to me. Do it—beautifully!

LŒVBORG: Beautifully? *(Smiles.)* With a crown of vine leaves in my hair? The way you used to dream of me—in the old days?

HEDDA: No. I don't believe in that crown any longer. But—do it beautifully, all the same. Just this once. Good-bye. You must go now. And don't come back.

LŒVBORG: Adieu, madame. Give my love to George Tesman. *(Turns to go.)*

HEDDA: Wait. I want to give you a souvenir to take with you.

She goes over to the writing-table, opens the drawer and the pistol-case, and comes back to LŒVBORG *with one of the pistols.*

LŒVBORG *(looks at her):* This? Is this the souvenir?

HEDDA *(nods slowly):* You recognize it? You looked down its barrel once.

LŒVBORG: You should have used it then.

HEDDA: Here! Use it now!

LŒVBORG *(puts the pistol in his breast pocket):* Thank you.

HEDDA: Do it beautifully, Eilert Lœvborg. Only promise me that!

LŒVBORG: Good-bye, Hedda Gabler.

He goes out through the hall. HEDDA *stands by the door for a moment, listening. Then she goes over to the writing-table, takes out the package containing the manuscript, glances inside it, pulls some of the pages half out and looks at them. Then she takes it to the arm-chair by the stove and sits down with the package in her lap. After a moment, she opens the door of the stove; then she opens the packet.*

HEDDA *(throws one of the pages into the stove and whispers to herself):* I'm burning your child, Thea! You with your beautiful, wavy hair! *(She throws a few more pages into the stove.)* The child Eilert Lœvborg gave you. *(Throws the rest of the manuscript in.)* I'm burning it! I'm burning your child!

ACT FOUR

*The same. It is evening. The drawing-room is in darkness.
The small room is illuminated by the hanging lamp over the
table. The curtains are drawn across the french windows.*
HEDDA, *dressed in black, is walking up and down in the
darkened room. Then she goes into the small room and
crosses to the left. A few chords are heard from the piano.
She comes back into the drawing-room.*

> BERTHA *comes through the small room from the right
> with a lighted lamp, which she places on the table in
> front of the corner sofa in the drawing-room. Her eyes
> are red with crying, and she has black ribbons on her
> cap. She goes quietly out, right.* HEDDA *goes over to
> the french windows, draws the curtains slightly to one
> side and looks out into the darkness.*

> *A few moments later,* MISS TESMAN *enters from the hall.
> She is dressed in mourning, with a black hat and veil.*
> HEDDA *goes to meet her and holds out her hand.*

MISS TESMAN: Well, Hedda, here I am in the weeds of sorrow. My poor sister has ended her struggles at last.

HEDDA: I've already heard. Tesman sent me a card.

MISS TESMAN: Yes, he promised me he would. But I thought,
no, I must go and break the news of death to Hedda
myself—here, in the house of life.

HEDDA: It's very kind of you.

MISS TESMAN: Ah, Rena shouldn't have chosen a time like this to pass away. This is no moment for Hedda's house to be a place of mourning.

HEDDA *(changing the subject):* She died peacefully, Miss Tesman?

MISS TESMAN: Oh, it was quite beautiful! The end came so calmly. And she was so happy at being able to see George once again. And say good-bye to him. Hasn't he come home yet?

HEDDA: No. He wrote that I mustn't expect him too soon. But please sit down.

MISS TESMAN: No, thank you, Hedda dear—bless you. I'd like to. But I've so little time. I must dress her and lay her out as well as I can. She shall go to her grave looking really beautiful.

HEDDA: Can't I help with anything?

MISS TESMAN: Why, you mustn't think of such a thing! Hedda Tesman mustn't let her hands be soiled by contact with death. Or her thoughts. Not at this time.

HEDDA: One can't always control one's thoughts.

MISS TESMAN *(continues):* Ah, well, that's life. Now we must start to sew poor Rena's shroud. There'll be sewing to be done in this house, too, before long, I shouldn't wonder. But not for a shroud, praise God.

GEORGE TESMAN *enters from the hall.*

HEDDA: You've come at last! Thank heavens!

TESMAN: Are you here, Auntie Juju? With Hedda? Fancy that!

MISS TESMAN: I was just on the point of leaving, dear boy. Well, have you done everything you promised me?

TESMAN: No, I'm afraid I forgot half of it. I'll have to run over again tomorrow. My head's in a complete whirl today. I can't collect my thoughts.

MISS TESMAN: But, George dear, you mustn't take it like this.

TESMAN: Oh? Well—er—how should I?

MISS TESMAN: You must be happy in your grief. Happy for what's happened. As I am.

TESMAN: Oh, yes, yes. You're thinking of Aunt Rena.

HEDDA: It'll be lonely for you now, Miss Tesman.

MISS TESMAN: For the first few days, yes. But it won't last long, I hope. Poor dear Rena's little room isn't going to stay empty.

TESMAN: Oh? Whom are you going to move in there? What?

MISS TESMAN: Oh, there's always some poor invalid who needs care and attention.

HEDDA: Do you really want another cross like that to bear?

MISS TESMAN: Cross! God forgive you, child. It's been no cross for me.

HEDDA: But now—if a complete stranger comes to live with you—?

MISS TESMAN: Oh, one soon makes friends with invalids. And I need so much to have someone to live for. Like you, my dear. Well, I expect there'll soon be work in this house too for an old aunt, praise God!

HEDDA: Oh—please!

TESMAN: My word, yes! What a splendid time the three of us could have together if—

HEDDA: If?

TESMAN (uneasily): Oh, never mind. It'll all work out. Let's hope so—what?

MISS TESMAN: Yes, yes. Well, I'm sure you two would like to be alone. (Smiles.) Perhaps Hedda may have something to tell you, George. Good-bye. I must go home to Rena. (Turns to the door.) Dear God, how strange! Now Rena is with me and with poor dear Joachim.

TESMAN: Why, yes, Auntie Juju! What?

MISS TESMAN *goes out through the hall.*

HEDDA *(follows* TESMAN *coldly and searchingly with her eyes):* I really believe this death distresses you more than it does her.

TESMAN: Oh, it isn't just Auntie Rena. It's Eilert I'm so worried about.

HEDDA *(quickly):* Is there any news of him?

TESMAN: I ran over to see him this afternoon. I wanted to tell him his manuscript was in safe hands.

HEDDA: Oh? You didn't find him?

TESMAN: No. He wasn't at home. But later I met Mrs. Elvsted and she told me he'd been here early this morning.

HEDDA: Yes, just after you'd left.

TESMAN: It seems he said he'd torn the manuscript up. What?

HEDDA: Yes, he claimed to have done so.

TESMAN: You told him we had it, of course?

HEDDA: No. *(Quickly.)* Did you tell Mrs. Elvsted?

TESMAN: No, I didn't like to. But you ought to have told him. Think if he should go home and do something desperate! Give me the manuscript, Hedda. I'll run over to him with it right away. Where did you put it?

HEDDA *(cold and motionless, leaning against the armchair):* I haven't got it any longer.

TESMAN: Haven't got it? What on earth do you mean?

HEDDA: I've burned it.

TESMAN *(starts, terrified):* Burned it! Burned Eilert's manuscript!

HEDDA: Don't shout. The servant will hear you.

TESMAN: Burned it! But in heaven's name—! Oh, no, no, no! This is impossible!

HEDDA: Well, it's true.

TESMAN: But, Hedda, do you realize what you've done?

That's appropriating lost property! It's against the law! By God! You ask Judge Brack and see if I'm not right.

HEDDA: You'd be well advised not to talk about it to Judge Brack or anyone else.

TESMAN: But how could you go and do such a dreadful thing? What on earth put the idea into your head? What came over you? Answer me! What?

HEDDA *(represses an almost imperceptible smile):* I did it for your sake, George.

TESMAN: For my sake?

HEDDA: When you came home this morning and described how he'd read his book to you—

TESMAN: Yes, yes?

HEDDA: You admitted you were jealous of him.

TESMAN: But, good heavens, I didn't mean it literally!

HEDDA: No matter. I couldn't bear the thought that anyone else should push you into the background.

TESMAN *(torn between doubt and joy):* Hedda—is this true? But—but—but I never realized you loved me like that! Fancy that!

HEDDA: Well, I suppose you'd better know. I'm going to have— *(Breaks off and says violently)* No, no—you'd better ask your Auntie Juju. She'll tell you.

TESMAN: Hedda! I think I understand what you mean. *(Clasps his hands.)* Good heavens, can it really be true? What?

HEDDA: Don't shout. The servant will hear you.

TESMAN *(laughing with joy):* The servant! I say, that's good! The servant! Why, that's Bertha! I'll run out and tell her at once!

HEDDA *(clenches her hands in despair):* Oh, it's destroying me, all this—it's destroying me!

TESMAN: I say, Hedda, what's up? What?

HEDDA *(cold, controlled):* Oh, it's all so—absurd—George.

104

TESMAN: Absurd? That I'm so happy? But surely—? Ah, well—perhaps I won't say anything to Bertha.

HEDDA: No, do. She might as well know, too.

TESMAN: No, no, I won't tell her yet. But Auntie Juju—I must let her know! And you—you called me George! For the first time! Fancy that! Oh, it'll make Auntie Juju so happy, all this! So very happy!

HEDDA: Will she be happy when she hears I've burned Eilert Lœvborg's manuscript—for your sake?

TESMAN: No, I'd forgotten about that. Of course, no one must be allowed to know about the manuscript. But that you're burning with love for me, Hedda, I must certainly let Auntie Juju know that. I say, I wonder if young wives often feel like that towards their husbands? What?

HEDDA: You might ask Auntie Juju about that, too.

TESMAN: I will, as soon as I get the chance. (*Looks uneasy and thoughtful again.*) But I say, you know, that manuscript. Dreadful business. Poor Eilert!

MRS. ELVSTED, *dressed as on her first visit, with hat and overcoat, enters from the hall.*

MRS. ELVSTED (*greets them hastily and tremulously*): Oh, Hedda dear, do please forgive me for coming here again.

HEDDA: Why, Thea, what's happened?

TESMAN: Is it anything to do with Eilert Lœvborg? What?

MRS. ELVSTED: Yes—I'm so dreadfully afraid he may have met with an accident.

HEDDA (*grips her arm*): You think so?

TESMAN: But, good heavens, Mrs. Elvsted, what makes you think that?

MRS. ELVSTED: I heard them talking about him at the boarding-house, as I went in. Oh, there are the most terrible rumours being spread about him in town today.

TESMAN: Er—yes, I heard about them, too. But I can testify that he went straight home to bed. Fancy—!

HEDDA: Well—what did they say in the boarding-house?

MRS. ELVSTED: Oh, I couldn't find out anything. Either they didn't know, or else— They stopped talking when they saw me. And I didn't dare to ask.

TESMAN *(fidgets uneasily):* We must hope—we must hope you misheard them, Mrs. Elvsted.

MRS. ELVSTED: No, no, I'm sure it was him they were talking about. I heard them say something about a hospital—

TESMAN: Hospital!

HEDDA: Oh no, surely that's impossible!

MRS. ELVSTED: Oh, I became so afraid. So I went up to his rooms and asked to see him.

HEDDA: Do you think that was wise, Thea?

MRS. ELVSTED: Well, what else could I do? I couldn't bear the uncertainty any longer.

TESMAN: But *you* didn't manage to find him either? What?

MRS. ELVSTED: No. And they had no idea where he was. They said he hadn't been home since yesterday afternoon.

TESMAN: Since yesterday? Fancy that!

MRS. ELVSTED: I'm sure he must have met with an accident.

TESMAN: Hedda, I wonder if I ought to go into town and make one or two enquiries?

HEDDA: No, no, don't you get mixed up in this.

JUDGE BRACK *enters from the hall, hat in hand.* BERTHA, *who has opened the door for him, closes it. He looks serious and greets them silently.*

TESMAN: Hullo, my dear Judge. Fancy seeing you!

BRACK: I had to come and talk to you.

TESMAN: I can see Auntie Juju's told you the news.

BRACK: Yes, I've heard about that, too.

TESMAN: Tragic, isn't it?

BRACK: Well, my dear chap, that depends how you look at it.

TESMAN *(looks uncertainly at him)*: Has something else happened?

BRACK: Yes.

HEDDA: Another tragedy?

BRACK: That also depends on how you look at it, Mrs. Tesman.

MRS. ELVSTED: Oh, it's something to do with Eilert Lœvborg!

BRACK *(looks at her for a moment)*: How did you guess? Perhaps you've heard already—?

MRS. ELVSTED *(confused)*: No, no, not at all—I—

TESMAN: For heaven's sake, tell us!

BRACK *(shrugs his shoulders)*: Well, I'm afraid they've taken him to the hospital. He's dying.

MRS. ELVSTED *(screams)*: Oh God, God!

TESMAN: The hospital! Dying!

HEDDA *(involuntarily)*: So quickly!

MRS. ELVSTED *(weeping)*: Oh, Hedda! And we parted enemies!

HEDDA *(whispers)*: Thea—Thea!

MRS. ELVSTED *(ignoring her)*: I must see him! I must see him before he dies!

BRACK: It's no use, Mrs. Elvsted. No one's allowed to see him now.

MRS. ELVSTED: But what's happened to him? You must tell me!

TESMAN: He hasn't tried to do anything to himself? What?

HEDDA: Yes, he has. I'm sure of it.

TESMAN: Hedda, how can you—?

BRACK *(who has not taken his eyes from her)*: I'm afraid you've guessed correctly, Mrs. Tesman.

MRS. ELVSTED: How dreadful!

TESMAN: Attempted suicide! Fancy that!

HEDDA: Shot himself!

BRACK: Right again, Mrs. Tesman.

MRS. ELVSTED *(tries to compose herself)*: When did this happen, Judge Brack?

BRACK: This afternoon. Between three and four.

TESMAN: But, good heavens—where? What?

BRACK *(a little hesitantly)*: Where? Why, my dear chap, in his rooms, of course.

MRS. ELVSTED: No, that's impossible. I was there soon after six.

BRACK: Well, it must have been somewhere else, then. I don't know exactly. I only know that they found him. He's shot himself—through the breast.

MRS. ELVSTED: Oh, how horrible! That he should end like that!

HEDDA *(to BRACK)*: Through the breast, you said?

BRACK: That is what I said.

HEDDA: Not through the head?

BRACK: Through the breast, Mrs. Tesman.

HEDDA: The breast. Yes; yes. That's good, too.

BRACK: Why, Mrs. Tesman?

HEDDA: Oh—no, I didn't mean anything.

TESMAN: And the wound's dangerous, you say? What?

BRACK: Mortal. He's probably already dead.

MRS. ELVSTED: Yes, yes—I feel it! It's all over. All over. Oh Hedda—!

TESMAN: But, tell me, how did you manage to learn all this?

BRACK *(curtly)*: From the police. I spoke to one of them.

HEDDA *(loudly, clearly)*: Thank God! At last!

TESMAN *(appalled)*: For God's sake, Hedda, what are you saying?

HEDDA: I am saying there's beauty in what he has done.

BRACK: Hm—Mrs. Tesman—

TESMAN: Beauty! Oh, but I say!

MRS. ELVSTED: Hedda, how can you talk of beauty in connexion with a thing like this?

HEDDA: Eilert Lœvborg has settled his account with life. He's had the courage to do what—what he had to do.

MRS. ELVSTED: No, that's not why it happened. He did it because he was mad.

TESMAN: He did it because he was desperate.

HEDDA: You're wrong! I know!

MRS. ELVSTED: He must have been mad. The same as when he tore up the manuscript.

BRACK (*starts*): Manuscript? Did he tear it up?

MRS. ELVSTED: Yes. Last night.

TESMAN (*whispers*): Oh, Hedda, we shall never be able to escape from this.

BRACK: Hm. Strange.

TESMAN (*wanders round the room*): To think of Eilert dying like that. And not leaving behind him the thing that would have made his name endure.

MRS. ELVSTED: If only it could be pieced together again!

TESMAN: Yes, yes, yes! If only it could! I'd give anything—

MRS. ELVSTED: Perhaps it can, Mr. Tesman.

TESMAN: What do you mean?

MRS. ELVSTED (*searches in the pocket of her dress*): Look. I kept the notes he dictated it from.

HEDDA (*takes a step nearer*): Ah!

TESMAN: You kept them, Mrs. Elvsted! What?

MRS. ELVSTED: Yes, here they are. I brought them with me when I left home. They've been in my pocket ever since.

TESMAN: Let me have a look.

MRS. ELVSTED (*hands him a wad of small sheets of paper*): They're in a terrible muddle. All mixed up.

TESMAN: I say, just fancy if we could sort them out! Perhaps if we work on them together—?

MRS. ELVSTED: Oh, yes! Let's try, anyway!

TESMAN: We'll manage it. We must! I shall dedicate my life to this.

HEDDA: *You*, George? Your life?

TESMAN: Yes—well, all the time I can spare. My book'll have to wait. Hedda, you do understand? What? I owe it to Eilert's memory.

HEDDA: Perhaps.

TESMAN: Well, my dear Mrs. Elvsted, you and I'll have to pool our brains. No use crying over spilt milk, what? We must try to approach this matter calmly.

MRS. ELVSTED: Yes, yes, Mr. Tesman. I'll do my best.

TESMAN: Well, come over here and let's start looking at these notes right away. Where shall we sit? Here? No, the other room. You'll excuse us, won't you, Judge? Come along with me, Mrs. Elvsted.

MRS. ELVSTED: Oh, God! If only we can manage to do it!

> TESMAN *and* MRS. ELVSTED *go into the rear room. He takes off his hat and overcoat. They sit at the table beneath the hanging lamp and absorb themselves in the notes.* HEDDA *walks across to the stove and sits in the armchair. After a moment,* BRACK *goes over to her.*

HEDDA *(half aloud):* Oh, Judge! This act of Eilert Lœvborg's—doesn't it give one a sense of release!

BRACK: Release, Mrs. Hedda? Well, it's a release for him, of course—

HEDDA: Oh, I don't mean him—I mean me! The release of knowing that someone can do something really brave! Something beautiful!

BRACK *(smiles):* Hm—my dear Mrs. Hedda—

HEDDA: Oh, I know what you're going to say. You're a *bourgeois* at heart, too, just like—ah, well!

BRACK *(looks at her):* Eilert Lœvborg has meant more to you than you're willing to admit to yourself. Or am I wrong?

HEDDA: I'm not answering questions like that from you. I only know that Eilert Lœvborg has had the courage to live according to his own principles. And now, at last, he's done something big! Something beautiful! To have the courage and the will to rise from the feast of life so early!

BRACK: It distresses me deeply, Mrs. Hedda, but I'm afraid I must rob you of that charming illusion.

HEDDA: Illusion?

BRACK: You wouldn't have been allowed to keep it for long, anyway.

HEDDA: What do you mean?

BRACK: He didn't shoot himself on purpose.

HEDDA: Not on purpose?

BRACK: No. It didn't happen quite the way I told you.

HEDDA: Have you been hiding something? What is it?

BRACK: In order to spare poor Mrs. Elvsted's feelings, I permitted myself one or two small—equivocations.

HEDDA: What?

BRACK: To begin with, he is already dead.

HEDDA: He died at the hospital?

BRACK: Yes. Without regaining consciousness.

HEDDA: What else haven't you told us?

BRACK: The incident didn't take place at his lodgings.

HEDDA: Well, that's utterly unimportant.

BRACK: Not utterly. The fact is, you see, that Eilert Lœvborg was found shot in Mademoiselle Danielle's boudoir.

HEDDA (*almost jumps up, but instead sinks back in her chair*): That's impossible. He can't have been there today.

BRACK: He was there this afternoon. He went to ask for something he claimed they'd taken from him. Talked some crazy nonsense about a child which had got lost—

HEDDA: Oh! So that was the reason!

BRACK: I thought at first he might have been referring to his manuscript. But I hear he destroyed that himself. So he must have meant his pocket-book—I suppose.

HEDDA: Yes, I suppose so. So they found him there?

BRACK: Yes; there. With a discharged pistol in his breast pocket. The shot had wounded him mortally.

HEDDA: Yes. In the breast.

BRACK: No. In the—stomach. The—lower part—

HEDDA *(looks at him with an expression of repulsion):* That, too! Oh, why does everything I touch become mean and ludicrous? It's like a curse!

BRACK: There's something else, Mrs. Hedda. It's rather disagreeable, too.

HEDDA: What?

BRACK: The pistol he had on him—

HEDDA: Yes? What about it?

BRACK: He must have stolen it.

HEDDA *(jumps up):* Stolen it! That isn't true! He didn't!

BRACK: It's the only explanation. He must have stolen it. Ssh!

TESMAN and MRS. ELVSTED *have got up from the table in the rear room and come into the drawing-room.*

TESMAN *(his hands full of papers):* Hedda, I can't see properly under that lamp. Do you think—?

HEDDA: I am thinking.

TESMAN: Do you think we could possibly use your writing-table for a little? What?

HEDDA: Yes, of course. *(Quickly.)* No, wait! Let me tidy it up first.

TESMAN: Oh, don't you trouble about that. There's plenty of room.

HEDDA: No, no, let me tidy it up first, I say. I'll take these in and put them on the piano. Here.

She pulls an object, covered with sheets of music, out from under the bookcase, puts some more sheets on top and carries it all into the rear room and away to the left. TESMAN *puts his papers on the writing-table and*

moves the lamp over from the corner table. He and
MRS. ELVSTED *sit down and begin working again.*
HEDDA *comes back.*

HEDDA *(behind* MRS. ELVSTED's *chair, ruffles her hair
gently):* Well, my pretty Thea. And how is work progressing on Eilert Lœvborg's memorial?

MRS. ELVSTED *(looks up at her, dejectedly):* Oh, it's going to
be terribly difficult to get these into any order.

TESMAN: We've got to do it. We must! After all, putting
other people's papers into order is rather my speciality,
what?

HEDDA *goes over to the stove and sits on one of the
footstools.* BRACK *stands over her, leaning against the
armchair.*

HEDDA *(whispers):* What was that you were saying about the
pistol?

BRACK *(softly):* I said he must have stolen it.

HEDDA: Why do you think that?

BRACK: Because any other explanation is unthinkable, Mrs.
Hedda. Or ought to be.

HEDDA: I see.

BRACK *(looks at her for a moment):* Eilert Lœvborg was here
this morning. Wasn't he?

HEDDA: Yes.

BRACK: Were you alone with him?

HEDDA: For a few moments.

BRACK: You didn't leave the room while he was here?

HEDDA: No.

BRACK: Think again. Are you sure you didn't go out for a
moment?

HEDDA: Oh—yes, I might have gone into the hall. Just for a
few seconds.

BRACK: And where was your pistol-case during this time?

HEDDA: I'd locked it in that—

BRACK: Er—Mrs. Hedda?

HEDDA: It was lying over there on my writing-table.

BRACK: Have you looked to see if both the pistols are still there?

HEDDA: No.

BRACK: You needn't bother. I saw the pistol Lœvborg had when they found him. I recognized it at once. From yesterday. And other occasions.

HEDDA: Have you got it?

BRACK: No. The police have it.

HEDDA: What will the police do with this pistol?

BRACK: Try to trace the owner.

HEDDA: Do you think they'll succeed?

BRACK (leans down and whispers): No, Hedda Gabler. Not as long as I hold my tongue.

HEDDA (looks nervously at him): And if you don't?

BRACK (shrugs his shoulders): You could always say he'd stolen it.

HEDDA: I'd rather die!

BRACK (smiles): People say that. They never do it.

HEDDA (not replying): And suppose the pistol wasn't stolen? And they trace the owner? What then?

BRACK: There'll be a scandal, Hedda.

HEDDA: A scandal!

BRACK: Yes, a scandal. The thing you're so frightened of. You'll have to appear in court together with Mademoiselle Danielle. She'll have to explain how it all happened. Was it an accident, or was it—homicide? Was he about to take the pistol from his pocket to threaten her? And did it go off? Or did she snatch the pistol from his hand, shoot him and then put it back in his pocket? She might quite easily have done it. She's a resourceful lady, is Mademoiselle Danielle.

HEDDA: But I have nothing to do with this repulsive business.

BRACK: No. But you'll have to answer one question. Why did you give Eilert Lœvborg this pistol? And what conclusions will people draw when it is proved you did give it to him?

HEDDA *(bows her head):* That's true. I hadn't thought of that.

BRACK: Well, luckily there's no danger as long as I hold my tongue.

HEDDA *(looks up at him):* In other words, I'm in your power, Judge. From now on, you've got your hold over me.

BRACK *(whispers, more slowly):* Hedda, my dearest—believe me—I will not abuse my position.

HEDDA: Nevertheless, I'm in your power. Dependent on your will, and your demands. Not free. Still not free! *(Rises passionately.)* No. I couldn't bear that. No.

BRACK *(looks half-derisively at her):* Most people resign themselves to the inevitable, sooner or later.

HEDDA *(returns his gaze):* Possibly they do.

She goes across to the writing-table.

HEDDA *(represses an involuntary smile and says in* TESMAN's *voice):* Well, George. Think you'll be able to manage? What?

TESMAN: Heaven knows, dear. This is going to take months and months.

HEDDA *(in the same tone as before):* Fancy that, by Jove! *(Runs her hands gently through* MRS. ELVSTED's *hair.)* Doesn't it feel strange, Thea? Here you are working away with Tesman just the way you used to work with Eilert Lœvborg.

MRS. ELVSTED: Oh—if only I can inspire your husband, too!

HEDDA: Oh, it'll come. In time.

TESMAN: Yes—do you know, Hedda, I really think I'm beginning to feel a bit—well—that way. But you go back and talk to Judge Brack.

HEDDA: Can't I be of use to you two in any way?

TESMAN: No, none at all. *(Turns his head.)* You'll have to keep Hedda company from now on, Judge, and see she doesn't get bored. If you don't mind.

BRACK *(glances at HEDDA):* It'll be a pleasure.

HEDDA: Thank you. But I'm tired this evening. I think I'll lie down on the sofa in there for a little while.

TESMAN: Yes, dear—do. What?

HEDDA goes into the rear room and draws the curtains behind her. Short pause. Suddenly she begins to play a frenzied dance melody on the piano.

MRS. ELVSTED *(starts up from her chair):* Oh, what's that?

TESMAN *(runs to the doorway):* Hedda dear, please! Don't play dance music tonight! Think of Auntie Rena. And Eilert.

HEDDA *(puts her head through the curtains):* And Auntie Juju. And all the rest of them. From now on I'll be quiet.

She closes the curtains behind her.

TESMAN *(at the writing-table):* It distresses her to watch us doing this. I say, Mrs. Elvsted, I've an idea. Why don't you move in with Auntie Juju? I'll run over each evening, and we can sit and work there. What?

MRS. ELVSTED: Yes, that might be the best plan.

HEDDA *(from the rear room):* I can hear what you're saying, Tesman. But how shall I spend the evenings out here?

TESMAN *(looking through his papers):* Oh, I'm sure Judge Brack'll be kind enough to come over and keep you company. You won't mind my not being here, Judge?

BRACK *(in the armchair, calls gaily):* I'll be delighted, Mrs. Tesman. I'll be here every evening. We'll have great fun together, you and I.

HEDDA *(loud and clear)*: Yes, that'll suit you, won't it, Judge? The only cock on the dunghill—

A shot is heard from the rear room. TESMAN, MRS. ELVSTED *and* JUDGE BRACK *start from their chairs.*

TESMAN: Oh, she's playing with those pistols again.

He pulls the curtains aside and runs in. MRS. ELVSTED *follows him.* HEDDA *is lying dead on the sofa. Confusion and shouting.* BERTHA *enters in alarm from the right.*

TESMAN *(screams to* BRACK*)*: She's shot herself! Shot herself in the head! Fancy that!

BRACK *(half paralysed in the armchair)*: But, good God! People don't do such things!

Note on the Translation

The main problem in translating *Hedda Gabler* is to contrast
the snobbish and consciously upper-class speech of Hedda
and Judge Brack with the naïve and homely way of talking
shared by Miss Tesman, Bertha and George Tesman. Hedda
is a General's daughter and lets no one forget it. George
Tesman has unconsciously acquired the nanny-like mode of
speech of the old aunts who brought him up. He addresses
Aunt Juliana as *Tante Julle,* a particularly irritating and
baby-like abbreviation which drives Hedda mad every time
he uses it. The last straw is when he asks her to address the
old lady by it, too. To render this as Auntie Julie, as has usually been done, is completely to miss the point; it must be a
ridiculous nickname such as Juju. When Brack tells Hedda
where Lœvborg has shot himself, he must make it clear to
her that the bullet destroyed his sexual organs; otherwise
Hedda's reactions make no sense. To translate this as 'belly'
or 'bowels' is again to miss the point, yet Brack must not use
the phrase 'sexual organs' directly; he is far too subtle a
campaigner to speak so bluntly to a lady. What he says is:
'In the—stomach. The—lower part.' I have altered the name
of the red-haired singer from Mademoiselle Diana, which is
difficult to say in English and has an improbable ring about
it, to Mademoiselle Danielle.

In the Norwegian, Hedda addresses her husband as Tesman except on the crucial occasions at the end of Act 1 and

in Act 4, when she deliberately switches to his Christian name. Similarly, Brack calls Hedda Mrs. Tesman when anyone else is present, but Mrs. Hedda when they are alone together; only towards the very end of the play does he address her simply as Hedda. Although this usage is un-English, even for the period, it is, in fact, effective on the stage when one has the illusion of eavesdropping on a foreign nineteenth-century family, and I have let it stand. To allow Brack to call her Hedda the first time we see them alone together in Act 2 suggests an intimacy which they have not yet reached.

The Pretenders

Introduction

The Pretenders was Ibsen's first real success in the theatre; he wrote it in July and August of 1863, at the age of thirty-five.

His fortunes at this time were at their lowest ebb. Of his previous nine plays only two, *The Feast at Solhaug* and *The Vikings at Helgeland,* had received any recognition at all, and that very limited. The Norwegian Theatre in Christiania, where he had been artistic director since 1857, had gone bankrupt the previous summer, and his only employment since had been as literary adviser to the Danish-controlled Christiania Theatre; but this, too, was in such straits that the salaries of its staff were graded according to what came in, so that of his tiny stipend of one hundred crowns a month he received only a fraction. He was frequently penniless and forced to resort to money-lenders; his application in 1860 for a government grant had been rejected; and a further application early in 1863 had met a similar fate, while those of his fellow-poets, Bjœrnson and Vinje, had been granted. Worst of all, his most recent play, *Love's Comedy,* had been rejected by his own theatre, and had been poorly received when published as a New Year's Eve supplement to the magazine *Illustreret Nyhedsblad.* He had accomplished sadly little for a man half-way through his life. "I was excommunicated; everyone was against me," he wrote seven years later (28 October 1870) to Peter

123

Hansen. "And the fact that everyone was against me, that there was no uncommitted person who could be said to believe in me, could not but give rise to the strain of feeling which found utterance in *The Pretenders*."

However, that June (1863) he received an invitation from some students to attend a choral festival at Bergen, at which over a thousand singers were to gather from various parts of Norway. Ibsen accepted the invitation, and wrote a song which the three choral groups from Christiania learned for the occasion. He left with them by ship on 12 June, and reached Bergen two days later. The voyage in their company, and the festival itself, had a remarkable effect on him. Where before he had felt isolated and rejected, he now found himself surrounded by sympathy, friendship and admiration. He described his reaction in a letter which he wrote to his host at Bergen, a shipping agent named Randolph Nilsen, four days after his return to Christiania:

"It is eight days to the hour since we said goodbye, and, God be praised, I still carry within me the spirit of the festival, and I hope I shall long keep it. My hearty thanks to you and your good wife for all the indescribable warmth and friendliness you showed me. The festival up there, and the many dear and unforgettable people whom I met, are working on me like a good visit to church, and I sincerely hope that this mood will not pass. Everyone was so kind to me in Bergen. It is not so here, where there are many people who seek to hurt and wound me at every opportunity. This strong feeling of elevation, of being ennobled and purified in all one's thoughts, must I think have been common to all who attended the choral festival, and he would indeed have something hard and evil in his soul who could remain insensitive to such an atmosphere. . . ."

What particularly moved Ibsen was the generous public tribute which had been paid to him at a banquet on 16 June by his famous rival, Bjœrnsterne Bjœrnson. It is a little difficult, reading Bjœrnson's plays and novels today, to realize the immense influence that he wielded in Norway, and indeed throughout Scandinavia, for over half a century. He might have said, like Oscar Wilde, though the thought would hardly have occurred to him, that he put his genius into his life but only his talent into his writing. To Norway, a country struggling for political and cultural independence, he seemed at this time, and for the next forty years, the embodiment of noble patriotism; a kind of Parnell. Handsome, assured and a brilliant speaker, he had achieved the literary success that had eluded Ibsen, and the younger generation regarded him as their spokesman. Ibsen had directed two of Bjœrnson's plays, *King Sverre* and *Lame Hulda,* at the Christiania Norwegian Theatre, and must bitterly have noted the warmth of their reception compared with the indifference and hostility shown to his own work. "In the world of art," wrote Théophile Gautier, "there stands always below each man of genius a man of talent, preferred to him''; and at every turn Ibsen found himself contrasted with Bjœrnson, to the latter's advantage.

At the festival banquet, however, Bjœrnson spoke out most handsomely in admiration of Ibsen, and took the opportunity to denounce those people who had tried, as critics will in every age that contains writers of comparable stature, to turn them into adversaries. "Have I not experienced," he cried, "that my friend Ibsen has been held up against me for the purpose of disparaging me, and I against him, to disparage him?" This speech was followed by the song which Ibsen had written for the occasion, dealing, it so happened, with the importance of naturally dissimilar people living in harmony—a coincidence which Ibsen, no more than anyone else, can have missed. Yet the contrast between his failure and Bjœrnson's success still gnawed him, and it was the combination of this with the mood of exhilaration and confidence induced by the festival that spurred him to write *The*

Pretenders, in which a man of great gifts invalidated by self-distrust is defeated by a potentially lesser man who possesses the supreme virtue of believing in himself. Bjœrnson was very much the model for Haakon (whom incidentally he had praised in a speech at Bergen as "Norway's best king"), and Ibsen put much of himself into Skule, and also, by his own admission, into the bard Jatgeir. "I know I have the fault" he wrote to Bjœrnson on 16 September 1864 from Rome "that I can't make close contact with those people who demand that one should give oneself freely and completely. I am rather like the bard Jatgeir in *The Pretenders,* I can never bring myself to strip completely. I have the feeling that, where personal relationships are concerned, I can only give false expression to what I feel deep down inside, and that is why I prefer to shut it up within me, and why we have sometimes stood as it were observing each other from a distance."

Ibsen completed *The Pretenders* within two months of his return to Christiania. He had in fact begun to plan a play on this theme as early as five years previously, in the summer of 1858; the idea seems to have come to him through reading Volume 3 of P.A. Munch's *History of the Norwegian People,* which had appeared the previous year and which dealt with the civil wars between the accession of King Sverre in 1177 and the death of Duke Skule in 1240. But he had put the project aside, and it needed the tonic effect of the Bergen festival and the prolonged meeting with Bjœrnson to get him into the mood to write it. Unfortunately no draft manuscripts or preliminary notes relating to the play have survived, so that we do not know, as we do with so many of his plays, exactly when he began and finished each act, but from start to finish, excluding the fair-copying, it appears to have taken him from six to eight weeks.

The Pretenders was published by the Christiania bookseller Johan Dahl towards the end of October 1863 (though by an error the year 1864 appears on the title page). Seven years later, in a letter to his Danish publisher Frederik Hegel of Gyldendal (who were to publish all the original editions of Ibsen's plays from *Brand* onwards), Ibsen described how Dahl acquired the rights. "One day early in September 1863, with the fair copy of *The Pretenders* under my arm, I met Johan Dahl on the street in Christiania, told him I had written a new historical play, and offered it to him for publication. Dahl immediately expressed his willingness and agreed without demur to my request for an honorarium of 150 specie-dollars for the first edition. Dahl took the manuscript, the printing began forthwith, and on 15 September I signed the contract in Dahl's bookshop."

The book was, on the whole, favourably received by the Norwegian newspapers, though Clemens Petersen, the doyen of the Danish critics and a future enemy of Ibsen's, voiced his disapproval. Unlike *Love's Comedy*, *The Pretenders* was at once accepted for production by the Christiania Theatre, and it received its first performance there on 17 January 1864. Ibsen directed it himself—the last time that he was to direct a performance of any of his plays. Halvdan Koht has described the premiere: "It was not a really integrated performance. The young Sigvard Gundersen had not yet the strength and weight to give King Haakon the assurance of victory that is begotten of genius. The Danish actor Wolf played Duke Skule better than any role he had previously attempted . . . but in general it was the strong hero that he presented rather than the soul-sick doubter. . . . Nevertheless, the play gripped the public. Although it lasted for nearly five hours—later they managed to reduce the playing time to four—we are told that 'from start to finish it was followed with excited attention,' and that 'after the fall of the curtain there was a general cry for the author who, when he appeared, was rewarded with thunderous applause.' In less than two months, *The Pretenders* was performed eight times, a success unique for a play as long and serious as this in a town as small as the Christiania of those days. . . . Now for the first time he rested in a full and free confidence in his own ability to write, and in his calling as a poet.''

The Pretenders took some time to penetrate beyond Norway. It was not performed in Denmark until 1871, nor in Sweden until 1879. In 1876, however, it was the occasion of a notable production in Berlin by the famous Saxe-Meiningen company who had prepared it especially for their visit to the capital. Ibsen saw it, and was deeply impressed. "At the beginning of this month", he wrote to the Swedish theatre manager Ludvig Josephson on 14 June 1876, "I went to Berlin to attend the first performance of *The Pretenders* in a brilliant and spectacular presentation by the Duke of Meiningen's court ensemble. The play was received with great applause, and I was repeatedly called for. I don't think this much pleased the Berlin critics, most of whom are themselves playwrights. However, the play has run for nine successive performances, and would have continued longer if the Meiningers had not been scheduled to end their season on the 15th. After the opening performance, I was invited by the Duke to visit him at his summer palace at Liebenstein in Meiningen, where I have been staying until I came back here the day before yesterday. On my departure he decorated me with the Knight Cross of the Saxon-Ernestine Order, first class. . . ."

Largely, one imagines, because of the supposed allergy of audiences to foreign history, *The Pretenders* has been performed comparatively seldom outside Norway, where it has remained a regular item in the national repertoire. It has, however, stimulated the imagination of several famous directors. In 1904, Max Reinhardt had a big success with it at the Neues Theater in Berlin; and in 1926 the Danish actor Johannes Poulsen winkled Edward Gordon Craig out of his

Italian retirement to design and co-produce it at the Royal Theatre in Copenhagen. Craig has described the result in his book *A Production, 1926,* profusely illustrated with his designs for the sets and costumes, which are considerably more illuminating than the text. The first English production took place at the Haymarket Theatre in 1913, when it was the occasion of a brilliantly perceptive anonymous notice which has deservedly taken its place among the classics of dramatic criticism.* Earl Skule was played by Laurence Irving. In 1927, Theodore Komisarjevsky produced it at Holyhead for the National Theatre of Wales, with an all-amateur cast, for a single performance attended by ten thousand people, and the following year Terence Gray directed it at the Festival Theatre, Cambridge. The Oxford University Dramatic Society presented it in 1922, and again in 1947 (with Kenneth Tynan as Bishop Nicholas); and in 1963 there was an exciting centenary production by Val May at the Bristol Old Vic.

How accurate is *The Pretenders* historically? More than most people imagine. William Archer, who knew Norway well (he spent much of his childhood there, and was bilingual from an early age) noted: "In *The Pretenders,* Ibsen stands much nearer to history than in any other play, except perhaps *Emperor and Galilean.* All the leading characters and many of the incidents of the drama are historical; but the poet has treated chronology with a very free hand, and has made use of psychological motives which are but faintly indicated, or not at all, in the sources from which he drew." Archer went on to point out that the leading Norwegian historian of the day, J. E. Sars, writing thirteen years *after* the appearance of *The Pretenders,* assessed the characters of Haakon and Skule very similarly to Ibsen. Haakon was,

---

*In the *Daily Telegraph.* The author has now been identified as H. C. Bailey.

says Sars, "reared in the firm conviction of his right to the throne. . . . He owed his chief strength to the repose and equilibrium of mind which distinguished him, and had its root in the unwavering sense of having right and the people's will on his side." Skule, on the other hand, according to Sars, "was the centre of a hierarchic aristocratic party; but after its repeated defeats this party must have been lacking alike in numbers and confidence. . . . It was clear from the first that his attempt to reawaken the old wars of succession in Norway was undertaken in the spirit of the desperate gambler, who does not count the chances, but throws at random, in the blind hope that luck may befriend him. . . . Skule's enterprise thus had no support in opinion or in any prevailing interest, and one defeat was sufficient to crush him." Historians in general condemned Skule; Ibsen tried to portray him sympathetically (as Strindberg was to do with Göran Persson in *Erik The Fourteenth*), while admitting that it was best for his country that he should be defeated.

Of Bishop Nicholas, Sars writes (I quote again from Archer's translation) that he "represented rather the aristocracy . . . than the cloth to which he belonged. . . . During his long participation in the civil broils . . . we see in him a man to whose character any sort of religious or ecclesiastical enthusiasm must have been foreign, his leading motives being personal ambition and vengefulness rather than any care for general interests—a cold and calculating nature, shrewd but petty and without any impetus, of whom Haakon Haakonsson, in delivering his funeral speech . . . could find nothing better to say than that he had not his equal in worldly wisdom." Archer continues: "I cannot find that the Bishop played any such prominent part in the struggle between the King and the Earl as Ibsen assigns to him, and the only foundation for the great death-bed scene seems to be the following passage from *Haakon Haakonsson's Saga*,

Chap. 138: 'As Bishop Nicholas at this time lay very sick, he sent a messenger to the King praying him to come to him. The King had on this expedition seized certain letters, from which he gathered that the Bishop had not been true to him. With this he upbraided him, and the Bishop, confessing it, prayed the King to forgive him. The King replied that he did so willingly, for God's sake; and as he could discern that the Bishop lay near to death, he abode with him until God called him from the world.' A chronological conspectus of the leading events referred to in *The Pretenders* (founded on P. A. Munch's *History of the Norwegian People*) will enable the reader to estimate for himself the extent of Ibsen's adherence to, and departure from history:

1189	Skule Baardsson born.
1204	Haakon Haakonsson born.
1206	Haakon is brought by the Birchlegs to King Inge.
1217	Haakon chosen King at the Œrething (national assembly).
1218	Haakon and Skule at Bergen. Inga undergoes the ordeal.
1219	Haakon betrothed to Skule's daughter, Margrete.
1219–20	Andres Skjaldarband and Vegard Væradal, thanes of Halogaland.
1221	Vegard Væradal killed by Andres Skjaldarband's men (reason unknown).
1225	(January) Haakon's campaign in Värmland. (25 May) Haakon's marriage with Margrete. (7 November) Bishop Nicholas's death.
1227	Haakon's eldest son, Olaf, born.
1229	Andres Skjaldarband sets forth for Palestine.
1232	Haakon's second son, Haakon, born.

1235	Inga, the King's mother, dies.
1237	Skule created Duke. Dagfinn the Peasant dies.
1239	(6 November) Skule proclaims himself King at the Œrething.
1240	(6 March) Skule victorious at Laaka.
	(21 April) Haakon victorious at Oslo.
	(21 May) Skule's son Peter killed at Elgesæter.
	(24 May) Skule killed at Elgesæter, and the abbey burned.''

The Pretenders, as Ibsen wrote it, is a diffuse and un-wieldy play which, uncut, would run for between four and five hours. After I had translated it *in toto,* Mr. Val May, the director of the Bristol Old Vic, made certain cuts and trans-positions for his production of the play there in 1963, and it is this version which is given here. Apart from occasional condensations, and transpositions for the sake of clarifica-tion, the main alterations have been as follows.

Act 1, Scene 1. The two minor Pretenders to the throne, Sigurd Ribbung and Guthorm Ingesson, have been cut, to-gether with all references to them; also a good deal of histor-ical background stuff. The arguments about the respective rights of Haakon and Skule have been condensed; and Skule has been given a line not in the original: "Now *I* grasp the burning iron!"

Act 1, Scene 2. The sub-plot about the feud between Vegard Væradal and Andres Skjaldarband (Ingeborg's hus-band) has been cut; also Haakon's announcement that he is sending away his mistress, Kanga.

Act 2. All references to Sigurd Ribbung, and other digres-sions concerning the historical background, have been omitted; also the quarrel between the Earl's men and Ivar Bodde, resulting in the latter's departure from court, and the long passage about Skjaldarband's murder of Vegard Væradal.

Act 3, Scene 1. The scene in which Inga of Varteig brings Trond's letter to the Bishop has been cut. Instead, Peter hands over the letter; this involved the insertion of a short speech for him. The Bishop's deathbed monologues, which are of enormous length in the original, have been thinned down, and the short dialogue between Haakon and Skule after the Bishop's death has been cut.

Act 3, Scene 2. Skule's long monologue at the child's cradle, and the ensuing dialogue between him and Haakon, have been reduced. Inga of Varteig's melodramatic entrance at the end of the scene has been cut, and Haakon's change of heart towards Margaret condensed into a single speech.

Act 4, Scene 1. The opening of Jatgeir's song has been omitted: also part of the Skule-Jatgeir scene, in which certain transpositions were made, all references to Skule's men as the "Wolfskins", and the discussion amongst them as to what booty they will take from their enemies. Skule's monologue after their departure, and the second Skule-Jatgeir dialogue, have been condensed; also the Skule-Ingeborg dialogue.

Act 4, Scene 2. Certain lines have been added to the crowd scene to clarify the course of the battle.

Act 5, Scene 1. No significant alterations.

Act 5, Scene 2. Much of the dialogue among the citizens after Skule's flight has been cut.

Act 5, Scene 3. The scene between Skule and the Bishop's Ghost has been reduced. (A myth has been handed down from commentator to commentator, starting, I fear, with Archer, that this scene is "a blemish on the play," etc. It is in fact superbly effective if properly done, and restores the balance temporarily upset by the Bishop's death in Act 3; it also makes the part more attractive to a star actor, a consideration which Ibsen is unlikely to have overlooked.) The name of the abbey where Skule seeks refuge, and which needs to be "planted" in the audience's mind, has been altered from Elgesæter to St. Stephen's.

Act 5, Scene 4. A few slight cuts only.

These amendments are not such a heresy as may be supposed, for it so happens that Ibsen put on record his awareness that some such treatment was desirable for future productions. On 20 January 1871 he wrote to Frederik Winkel-Horn from Dresden: "You are wrong in assuming that I didn't want the play to be cut. On the contrary. During my stay in Copenhagen last summer, I explained to the director of the theatre that it neither could nor should be performed in its entirety. With his approval I therefore made an abridged version in which the Bishop's death-scene in particular was considerably reduced; moreover, I expressly urged that they should cut in rehearsal anything that they found to be superfluous."

Stylistically, as well as structurally, *The Pretenders* marks an important stage in Ibsen's development as a dramatist. Of his previous eight plays (leaving aside the short comic opera, *Norma*), three *(Catiline, The Warrior's Barrow* and *Love's Comedy)* had been written in verse and three *(St. John's Eve, Lady Inger of Œstraat* and *The Vikings at Helgeland)* in prose; while *The Feast at Solhaug* and *Olaf Liljekrans* had been composed in a mixture of the two. Although he had managed here and there to achieve a colloquial prose, he had limited it to his peasant and lower-class characters; his princes and chieftains had spoken a formal dialogue, and in his most recent prose play, *The Vikings at Helgeland*, he had deliberately imitated the antique language of the sagas. Bjœrnson had disapproved of this experiment, and Ibsen himself, in a review of Bjœrnson's historical drama *Sigurd Slembe*, had expressed his conviction that the language of a historical play should be living and colloquial, whoever might be speaking. In *The Pretenders* he attempted to create such a dialogue, retaining formal language only when the characters deliberately use a formal mode of address—as in the opening exchange between Haakon and Skule—and occasionally for special effect. He succeeded, not indeed completely, but to a considerable degree;* the play is full of terse, colloquial statements, such as Jatgeir's "Buy a dog, my lord," that we do not find in *Lady Inger* or *The Vikings*, and that shock by their unexpectedness. Parenthetically, it may be noted that Ibsen was surprised to find himself writing the play in prose at all. "I am now working on a historical drama in five acts," he wrote to Clemens Petersen on 10 August 1863, "but in prose—I *cannot* write it in verse." Within a few years, he was to renounce verse completely.

The Pretenders is full of anticipatory echoes of Ibsen's later plays; it makes a pleasant parlour game to look for them. Skule, like Brand, demands "All or Nothing." To Peter, like Solness to Hilde, he says: "You are the one I've been needing," and to Ingeborg, like Borkman to Ella: "I left you, to gain power and riches. If you had stayed. . . ." The Bishop's Ghost promises Skule, as Rubek was to promise both Maja and Irene in *When We Dead Awaken:* "I will lead you up on to a high mountain and show you all the glory of the world"; and this scene between the Ghost and Skule

---

*Not least in the delightfully easy rhymed verse given to the Bishop's Ghost in Act Five, and too glibly dismissed by some critics as "doggerel". If this is doggerel, so is much of *Peer Gynt*.

strongly anticipates the encounter in *Peer Gynt* between Peer and the Thin Person. The two priests, Aslak and Trond, whom we hear of but do not see in *The Pretenders*, were to reappear in *Peer Gynt* as a blacksmith and a troll respectively; so was the cowardly soldier of Bishop Nicholas's confession.

But it is not merely as apprentice work that *The Pretenders* demands attention. It stands solidly in its own right as a historical drama of epic sweep and intense poetic imagination, working remorselessly towards the superb climax in the abbey. It contains, in Skule, Haakon and Bishop Nicholas, three characters comparable in stature with anything that he created later; and, imaginatively produced, it works brilliantly. It should be regarded, not as an isolated rangefinder, but as the first of the great epic quartet containing *Brand, Peer Gynt* and *Emperor and Galilean*. It was no mere apprentice work that fired the imagination of Reinhardt, Craig and Komisarjevsky.

Ibsen did not at the time intend *The Pretenders* to be his last play about Norwegian history. Soon after completing it, he made plans for a drama about Magnus Heinesson, a Viking of the sixteenth century, and as late as 1870 he was meditating an opera about Sigurd Jorsalfare. But neither materialised. Nationalism began to lose its importance; other subjects, closer at hand, seemed more relevant than Norway's glorious past. The final speech of the Bishop's Ghost in Act 5 was a formidable warning of what was to come.

MICHAEL MEYER

CHARACTERS

HAAKON HAAKONSSON, chosen as King by the Birchlegs
INGA OF VARTEIG, his mother
EARL SKULE, regent of Norway during Haakon's minority
THE LADY RAGNHILD, Earl Skule's wife
SIGRID, his sister
MARGARET, his daughter
NICHOLAS ARNESSON, Bishop of Oslo
DAGFINN THE PEASANT, Haakon's marshal
IVAR BODDE, Haakon's chaplain
GREGORIUS JONSSON, a follower of Earl Skule
PAUL FLIDA, a follower of Earl Skule
INGEBORG, wife to a nobleman, Andres Skjaldarband
PETER, her son, a young priest
SIRA WILLIAM, chaplain to Bishop Nicholas
MASTER SIGARD OF BRABANT, a doctor
JATGEIR, an Icelandic bard
BAARD BRATTE, a chieftain from the Trondheim district
CITIZENS of Bergen, Oslo and Nidaros
PRIESTS, MONKS and NUNS
GUESTS, MEN-AT-ARMS, LADIES, SOLDIERS, etc.

The action takes place in Norway during the first half of the
thirteenth century.

This translation of *The Pretenders* was commissioned by the Old Vic Trust, and was first performed at the Theatre Royal, Bristol, on 12 February 1963. The cast was:

HAAKON HAAKONSSON	David Sumner
INGA OF VARTEIG	Pauline Browne
EARL SKULE	John Phillips
THE LADY RAGNHILD	Barbara Leigh-Hunt
SIGRID	Hilary Hardiman
MARGARET	Monica Evans
BISHOP NICHOLAS	John Bennett
DAGFINN THE PEASANT	Stephen Thorne
IVAR BODDE	Terrence Hardiman
GREGORIUS JONSSON	Leader Hawkins
PAUL FLIDA	Christopher Benjamin
INGEBORG	Hilary Hardiman
PETER	Leo Maguire
SIRA WILLIAM	Roger Jerome
MASTER SIGARD	Gabriel Prendergast
JATGEIR	Terrence Hardiman
BAARD BRATTE	Peter Baldwin
NUNS	Cynthia Cowdell
	Marjorie Yorke

CITIZENS, SOLDIERS,
PRIESTS, MONKS
Stanley Bates, Patrick Black, Alan Knight, Gabriel Prendergast, David Martin, Cynthia Cowdell, Marjorie Yorke, Laurence Carter, John Ainscough, William Fisher, Dirk Shoulder

Directed by Val May

138

ACT ONE

Scene One

The churchyard of Christ Church in Bergen. In the background is the church, with its main door facing the audience. Downstage left stand HAAKON HAAKONSSON, DAGFINN THE PEASANT, IVAR BODDE *and other thanes and chieftains. Facing them stand* EARL SKULE, GREGORIUS JONSSON, PAUL FLIDA, *and others of the* EARL's *followers. The approaches to the church are guarded by soldiers, and the churchyard is filled with people. Many of them are sitting up in trees or on the church wall. They all seem to be waiting tensely for something to happen. Bells can be heard from the steeples in the town, both near and in the distance.*

EARL SKULE *(impatiently, to* GREGORIUS JONSSON*)*: Why are they so slow in there?

GREGORIUS JONSSON: Ssh! They're beginning the psalm!

From within the closed church can be heard a choir of MONKS *and* NUNS *singing* Domine coeli, *to the accompaniment of trumpets. As they sing, the church door is opened from inside and* BISHOP NICHOLAS *is seen in the entrance, surrounded by* PRIESTS *and* MONKS.

139

BISHOP NICHOLAS *(moves forward into the doorway and proclaims, with upraised staff):* Now Inga of Varteig is submitting to the ordeal on behalf of her son Haakon, pretender to the crown. If the white-hot iron leaves no mark on her hands, Haakon is her son by our lamented King.

The door is closed again. The singing continues within.

GREGORIUS JONSSON *(whispers to EARL SKULE):* Pray to the blessed St. Olaf to defend your right.

EARL SKULE *(quickly, with a deprecating gesture):* Not now. Best not to put him in mind of me.

IVAR BODDE *(grips HAAKON by the arm):* Pray to the Lord your God, Haakon Haakonsson.

HAAKON: There is no need. I am sure of Him.

The singing from the church grows louder. All bare their heads. Many fall on their knees and pray.

GREGORIUS JONSSON *(to EARL SKULE):* This is a fateful hour for you, and for many.

EARL SKULE *(gazes tensely at the church):* A fateful hour for Norway.

PAUL FLIDA *(close to SKULE):* Now she is holding the burning iron.

DAGFINN *(close to HAAKON):* They are coming down the nave.

IVAR BODDE: Christ protect thine innocent hands, Inga, mother of our King!

HAAKON: All my life I shall reward her for this hour.

EARL SKULE *(who has been listening intently, suddenly exclaims):* Was that a cry? Has she let the iron fall?

PAUL FLIDA *(moves towards the church):* I don't know what it was.

GREGORIUS JONSSON: The women are weeping in the antechapel.

Act One, scene one

CHOIR IN CHURCH *(bursts forth jubilantly): Gloria in excelsis deo!*

The door is thrown open. INGA OF VARTEIG *comes out, followed by* NUNS, MONKS *and* PRIESTS.

INGA *(on the steps of the church):* God has judged! Behold these hands! In them I have held the iron!

VOICES AMONG THE CROWD: They are as fair and white as before!

OTHER VOICES: Fairer still!

WHOLE CROWD: Haakon is the King's son!

HAAKON *(embraces her):* Thank you, most blessed mother! Bravest of women, thank you!

BISHOP NICHOLAS *(wanders past* EARL SKULE*):* It was foolish to insist on the ordeal of the iron.

EARL SKULE: No, my lord. We needed the voice of God.

HAAKON *(deeply moved, clasps* INGA *by the hand):* My whole being cried out against this deed, and my heart shrank from it. But now it is done. *(Turns to the* CROWD.*)* By the ordeal of the iron I have proved my birth, and proved my right in just succession to inherit the kingdom and the crown. Six years ago they named me King, but I was a child and Earl Skule became regent. *(Pauses and looks at* SKULE.*)* Little honour has been shown me in this time! But I have been patient, borne the humiliation, and waited. Now I can wait no longer—civil war is threatening our land, and this I must prevent. I might not have risked paying so dearly to prove my right—*(looks at* INGA*)*—if I had not felt the certainty of my calling. I feel it deep within me, burning like a flame, and I am not ashamed to declare it: I *know* that I alone can guide our country to its destiny.

EARL SKULE *(after a pause):* There are others here who have belief in themselves.

HAAKON: What do you mean, my lord?

EARL SKULE: I am the late King's brother, and the law supports me when I demand to enter into my inheritance.

DAGFINN *(mutters):* More treachery!

BISHOP NICHOLAS: Blessed St. Olaf must be the judge.

HAAKON'*s men move closer together.*

HAAKON *(forces himself to be calm and takes a step towards the* EARL): I presume I have misunderstood you, my lord. Has not the ordeal just proved my right to the crown?

SEVERAL OF THE EARL'S MEN: No, no! We deny that!

EARL SKULE: It has proved only that you have a claim, and established your right to assert it against other claimants. It has not won you the crown itself.

HAAKON *(controls himself):* In short, you are saying that for six years I have falsely born the name of King, and that for six years you, my Lord, have unlawfully ruled the kingdom as my regent.

EARL SKULE: By no means. When my brother died, an heir had to be named. The Birchlegs were active in your cause, and elected you before my claim could be heard.

BISHOP NICHOLAS *(to* HAAKON): The Earl means that your election only gave you the right to use the name of King, not to wield royal power.

EARL SKULE: I believe that my right to the crown is at least as good as yours. Now let the law decide between us, and say which of us shall inherit it for himself and his descendants.

BISHOP NICHOLAS: The Earl certainly has grounds.

EARL SKULE: Moreover, if your right to the crown was already established six years ago, why did you consent to the ordeal today?

DAGFINN *(bitterly):* If my counsel had been heard, King Haakon would not have chosen hot iron but cold steel as his instrument of justice! Hear me now, men of the King! Draw your swords, and let them decide!

MANY OF HAAKON'S MEN-AT-ARMS *(storm forward):* To arms against the King's enemies!

EARL SKULE *(cries to his MEN):* Kill no one! Harm no one! Only defend yourselves!

HAAKON *(holds his men back):* Sheath your swords! Sheath them I say! *(Calmly.)* You injure my cause by such rashness. Men who are to rule a kingdom must first learn to rule themselves.

EARL SKULE: You see, Haakon, how every man stands with his sword at his neighbour's throat! It is so throughout the land. Norway is split into a hundred factions, and if you cherish peace and the lives of our countrymen, you know what you must do.

HAAKON *(pauses, then makes a decision):* Yes, now I know. My lords and justices, priests, chieftains, and men-at-arms, I hereby summon the Grand Council. The law shall judge, and the law alone. You Birchlegs, who six years ago elected me as King—I free you now from the oath you swore to me then. You, Dagfinn, are no longer my marshal. I shall not meet the Council with marshal or bodyguard, with royal men-at-arms or sworn warriors. I am a poor man; my inheritance consists only of a brooch and a gold bracelet. Take them, my mother, and God's blessing go with you for what you have done this day. Now, my fellow-claimant to the crown, we stand as equals. I want no advantage over you but the divine right I have from God. That I neither can nor will share with any man. Let the Council be summoned, and let the law decide!

He goes out left with his men. Horns and trumpets are sounded in the distance.

GREGORIUS JONSSON *(to SKULE, as the crowd disperses):* During the ordeal, I thought you seemed afraid; but now you look calm and almost joyful.

EARL SKULE *(contentedly):* Did you see? He had my

brother's eyes as he spoke. Whether it be he or I, they will have chosen well.

GREGORIUS JONSSON *(uneasily):* Do not give way to him, though. Remember how many destinies are bound to yours.

EARL SKULE: I take my stand upon justice. Now *I* grasp the burning iron! *(Goes out left with his men.)*

BISHOP NICHOLAS *(hurries after* DAGFINN*):* It will be all right, my good Dagfinn, it will be all right. But if Haakon is chosen King, keep the Earl away from him! Keep him well away!

They all go out left behind the church.

Scene Two

A hall in the palace. Downstage left is a low window. To the right, an entrance door. Upstage, a larger door which leads to the King's Hall. By the window stands a table; elsewhere there are stools and benches. THE LADY RAGNHILD, *wife to* EARL SKULE, *and her daughter* MARGARET *enter through the smaller door. A few moments later,* SIGRID *follows them.*

RAGNHILD: In here, daughter.

MARGARET: Yes, it's darkest here.

RAGNHILD *(goes to the window):* We can watch them through the window.

MARGARET *(looks cautiously through the window):* Yes. There they are, a great crowd gathered by the church. Solemn and silent. Almost as though for a burial. *(Turns, weeping.)* Oh, God! How many of us will mourn this day!

RAGNHILD: It had to come. Just to be regent could never be enough for him.

MARGARET: Yes—it had to come. To be King in name alone could never be enough for him.

RAGNHILD: Whom do you mean?

MARGARET: Haakon.

RAGNHILD: I meant the Earl.

MARGARET *(almost to herself):* The two noblest men alive—my father, and the man I love! Why couldn't it be enough for them to rule together? Now one will be master in these halls tonight, but one will be his servant.

RAGNHILD: Look at Bishop Nicholas! How slyly he sits— just like a chained wolf!

MARGARET: Yes, look at him! With his hands crossed over his staff, and his chin resting on them.

RAGNHILD: Biting his beard and smiling!

MARGARET: How horribly he smiles, mother!

RAGNHILD: Ssh! Someone is speaking. Who is it?

MARGARET: Gunnar Grœnbak.

RAGNHILD: Is he for the Earl?

MARGARET: No, for the King.

RAGNHILD *(looks at her):* For whom, did you say?

MARGARET: For Haakon.

Pause.

RAGNHILD: Who is speaking now?

MARGARET *(looks):* Tord Skolle, the thane of Ranafylke.

RAGNHILD: Is he for your father?

MARGARET: No—for Haakon.

RAGNHILD: How stilly the Earl sits and listens!

MARGARET: Haakon seems quiet and thoughtful—but how strong he looks! *(Excitedly.)* If a stranger stood here, he'd know those two among all the thousand others!

RAGNHILD: Look, Margaret. Dagfinn is bringing a gilded chair for Haakon—

MARGARET: Paul Flida is setting another behind the Earl—

RAGNHILD: Haakon's men are trying to stop him!

MARGARET: My father is clinging to the chair—!

RAGNHILD: Haakon is speaking angrily to him—oh, Jesus

Christ! Do you see how your father looks at him! His eyes—and the way he smiles! *(Turns from the window with a cry)* No, that was never the Earl!

MARGARET *(has likewise turned in fear):* Nor Haakon either! Neither the Earl nor Haakon!

SIGRID *(at the window):* Oh, pity, pity!

MARGARET: Sigrid!

RAGNHILD: You here?

SIGRID: Must they stoop so low, to climb up to the throne?

MARGARET: Oh, God, please guide them!

RAGNHILD *(pale and fearful, to SIGRID):* Did you see him? Did you see my husband? Such eyes, such a smile—I would not have known him.

SIGRID: Did he smile like the Bishop?

RAGNHILD *(quietly):* Yes. He smiled like that.

SIGRID: Then we must pray!

RAGNHILD *(with despairing strength):* They *must* choose him King. Or I fear for his soul—

SIGRID *(more strongly):* Let us pray, then!

RAGNHILD: Ssh! What is that? *(At the window.)* A great shout! They have all risen! The flags and standards are waving in the wind.

SIGRID *(grips her arm):* Pray, woman! Pray for your husband!

RAGNHILD: Yes, blessed St. Olaf, grant that he may be King!

SIGRID: Pray that he may not! Else he cannot be saved!

RAGNHILD: He must be King! All that is good in him will flower and blossom—! Listen! Margaret, look!

MARGARET *(looks):* They have raised their hands in oath. They are swearing allegiance.

RAGNHILD: God and blessed St. Olaf—to whom?

SIGRID: Pray!

MARGARET *listens and gestures to them to be silent.*

146

RAGNHILD (*after a moment*): To whom? (*Horns and trumpets sound loudly from the assembly.*) Whom have they named?

Short pause.

MARGARET (*turns her head and says*): They have chosen Haakon Haakonsson as King.

The music for the royal procession is heard, at first faintly, then gradually closer. RAGNHILD *clings weeping to* SIGRID, *who leads her quietly out right.* MARGARET *remains motionless, leaning against the window. The* KING'S SERVANTS *open the great doors, revealing the Hall, which gradually fills with the procession from the assembly.*

HAAKON (*turns in the doorway to* IVAR BODDE): Bring me a pen, and wax and silk. (*Moved and exultant, comes forward to the table and puts some parchment on it.*) Margaret, I am King!

MARGARET: I salute my lord and my King.

HAAKON (*looks at her and takes her hand*): Forgive me. I had forgotten that this must hurt you.

MARGARET (*takes away her hand*): No. You were born to be King, my lord.

HAAKON (*fervently*): Yes. Ever since I was born, it is as though God and His Saints had protected me—almost miraculously. When I was a year old, there was a plot to kill me, but I was carried to safety across the mountains in frost and storm through the midst of my enemies. In Nidaros they burned the town and I escaped unhurt while men were slain all around me. And today the ordeal—it has always been the same for me.

MARGARET: You have served a hard apprenticeship.

HAAKON (*looks earnestly at her*): Something tells me now that you might have made it less hard for me.

MARGARET: I?

HAAKON: You could have been a source of strength to me all the years we grew up together.

MARGARET: But things fell out differently.

HAAKON: Yes. Things fell out differently. We sat in the same hall, we looked at each other, each from our separate corners, but we seldom spoke. (*There is a pause.* HAAKON *looks at her, then turns impatiently away.*) Where is the pen and ink? (IVAR BODDE *enters with writing materials, followed by* BISHOP NICHOLAS.) You were slow. Give them to me.

He writes for a moment, then looks up at MARGARET.

HAAKON: Do you know what I am writing? It is a letter to my mother. I am sending her away to the east. She will live there, far from our affairs of state, quietly, but with all honour.

MARGARET: Will you not keep her with you at the palace?

HAAKON: She is too dear to me. A King must have no one by him who is near to his heart. A King must be free to act, he must stand alone, must never be swayed or influenced by affection. Then he can work with a single purpose— and there is much work to be done in Norway.

IVAR BODDE (*whispers to* BISHOP NICHOLAS): That was my counsel, to send away the King's mother.

BISHOP NICHOLAS: I recognised your touch.

IVAR BODDE: But you must keep your side of the bargain.

BISHOP NICHOLAS: Be patient. I shall not forget.

HAAKON (*hands the parchment to* IVAR BODDE): Fold this, and take it to her yourself, with my dearest greetings—

DAGFINN (*glances at the parchment*): My lord—must she sail today?

HAAKON: The wind is fair, and westerly.

MARGARET: Your Majesty—your mother did not sleep all last night. She spent it at the altar—in prayer and fasting—

DAGFINN: And the ordeal today—

HAAKON (*suddenly moved*): My blessed mother—! (*Composes himself.*) Well, if she is tired, she may wait until tomorrow.

IVAR BODDE: Your Majesty's will shall be done. (*Puts a fresh parchment before the* KING. MARGARET *rises and moves towards the door.*) And—the other matter, my lord?

BISHOP NICHOLAS (*who has meanwhile come closer*): Bind the Earl's hands now, King Haakon.

HAAKON (*softly*): You think I need to?

BISHOP NICHOLAS: You will never buy peace for Norway on cheaper terms.

HAAKON: I shall do it. Summon Earl Skule! (MARGARET *stops at the door and turns.*) Give me the pen. (*Writes.*)

The BISHOP *whispers in his ear.* EARL SKULE *enters. The* BISHOP *moves away.*

EARL SKULE (*to the* BISHOP, *as the latter passes, right*): It seems you have the King's ear, my lord.

BISHOP NICHOLAS: To your advantage.

EARL SKULE: Indeed?

BISHOP NICHOLAS: You will thank me before evening. (*Moves further off.*)

HAAKON (*holds out the parchment to* SKULE): Read this, my lord.

The BISHOP *walks across to* HAAKON, *who is watching* SKULE.

BISHOP NICHOLAS (*hovers over* HAAKON's *chair*): Your Majesty has taken a great step towards winning the Earl's friendship. Once his hands are bound, you need never fear again.

HAAKON (*tensely, to* SKULE): My lord, today I took the kingdom from you. But let your daughter share it with me.

MARGARET *catches her breath.* SKULE *slowly looks up from the parchment.*

HAAKON: Margaret—will you be my Queen? *(MARGARET is silent.* HAAKON *takes her hand.)* Answer me.

MARGARET: I will most gladly be your wife.

She looks at her father. Everyone waits for his reaction.

EARL SKULE *(finally speaks):* This is a noble action, Haakon. *(Presses his hand.)* Peace and friendship—from my heart!

HAAKON: Thank you!

IVAR BODDE *(to DAGFINN):* Heaven be praised! Now we shall have peace at last!

DAGFINN: I almost think so. I have never liked the Earl so well before.

BISHOP NICHOLAS *(behind him):* Stay on your guard, my good Dagfinn. Stay on your guard!

IVAR BODDE *(who has been waiting behind the KING with the parchments in his hand):* Here are the letters, my lord—

HAAKON: Good. Give them to the Earl.

IVAR BODDE: To the Earl? Will Your Majesty not seal them—?

HAAKON: The Earl does that. He has the seal.

IVAR BODDE *(whispers):* While he was your regent, yes. But now—

HAAKON: Now as before. The Earl has the seal. *(Moves away.)*

EARL SKULE: Give me the letters, Ivar Bodde.

He goes over to the table with them, takes out the royal seal which he has kept hidden in his belt, and seals the letters during the ensuing dialogue.

BISHOP NICHOLAS *(half to himself):* Haakon is King—and the Earl has the seal. It will pass, it will pass.

HAAKON: What are you saying, my lord Bishop?

BISHOP NICHOLAS: I was saying: "God and St. Olaf watch over our Holy Church." *(He moves away.)*

HAAKON *(goes over to* MARGARET*):* A wise Queen can do much for our land. I know you are wise, and that was what guided my choice.

MARGARET: Only that?

HAAKON: What do you mean?

MARGARET: Nothing, my lord, nothing.

HAAKON: And you will not hate me for making you renounce your fair hopes for my sake?

MARGARET: I have renounced nothing for your sake, my lord.

HAAKON: And you will stay close to me and give me good counsel?

MARGARET: I will most gladly stay close to you, my lord.

HAAKON: I shall be grateful. Every man needs a woman's counsel, and I shall have no one but you when my mother has gone.

MARGARET: No—she was too dear to you.

HAAKON: And I am King. Farewell, then, Margaret! You are young, still; but our wedding shall take place next summer—and from that hour I swear to keep you by me, in trust and honour as befits a Queen.

MARGARET *(smiles sadly):* Yes. You will not send me away.

HAAKON *(startled):* Send you away? Of course not!

MARGARET *(with tears in her eyes):* No, the King only does that to those who are too dear to him. *(Goes towards the main door.* HAAKON *watches her thoughtfully.)* Thank you for the crown, my lord. I think I am glad, even of that. *(Goes out right.)*

BISHOP NICHOLAS: A wise deed, my lord. Now Your Majesty need never fear again.

HAAKON: You have counselled me well, Bishop Nicholas.

BISHOP NICHOLAS: Now at last you are King of Norway.

HAAKON *(takes a breath):* At last!

BISHOP NICHOLAS *(shouts):* Haakon is King!

ALL OUTSIDE *(in a great shout):* Haakon is King!

> HAAKON *moves towards the door to acknowledge the cry.*

EARL SKULE *(puts the seal in his belt):* But I rule the land.

ACT TWO

The banqueting hall in the royal palace at Bergen. In the centre of the rear wall is a large bow window. Along the length of this is a dais, with seats for the women. Against the left wall, the royal throne extends several feet into the hall; in the centre of the opposite wall is a big entrance door. Banners, standards, shields, coats-of-arms and embroidered tapestries hang from the pillars and from the hewn roofbeams. Around the hall stand drinking-tables, with pitchers, horns and beakers.

> KING HAAKON *is seated on the dais, with* MARGARET, SIGRID, THE LADY RAGNHILD *and other noble women.* IVAR BODDE *stands behind the* KING. *At the drinking-tables sit the* KING'S MEN *and the* EARL'S MEN *on benches, with other* GUESTS. *At the first table, on the* KING'S *right, are, among others,* DAGFINN THE PEAS-ANT, GREGORIUS JONSSON *and* PAUL FLIDA. EARL SKULE *and* BISHOP NICHOLAS *are playing chess at a table on the left.* THE EARL'S SERVANTS *go to and fro bearing drinks. From an adjacent room, music can be heard during the ensuing dialogue.*

DAGFINN: Five days of feasting, and the ale's still flowing! (*Calls to a* SERVANT) Come on, fill these up!

DRUNKEN LORD: Don't worry, they will!

PAUL FLIDA: The Earl's never been one to stint his guests.

DAGFINN: So it seems. Norway has never known such a royal wedding feast.

PAUL FLIDA: Earl Skule has never given away a daughter before.

DAGFINN: True, true. The Earl's a mighty man, all right.

MAN-AT-ARMS: Haakon has given him a third of the kingdom. That's more than any man has ever had.

PAUL FLIDA: Except the King. The King has more.

MAN-AT-ARMS: The King has a right to more.

PAUL FLIDA *(flares up):* So has the Earl! And other rights besides—!

DAGFINN: Let's not discuss that now. We're all friends here tonight. Let things be. *(Drinks to PAUL FLIDA.)* Let the King be King and the Earl Earl.

PAUL FLIDA *(laughs):* It's easy to tell you serve the King.

DAGFINN: It's every man's duty to serve the King.

PAUL FLIDA: We serve the Earl. We have sworn an oath to him, not to the King.

DAGFINN: Not yet. But it could happen.

BISHOP NICHOLAS *(whispers to the EARL as they play):* Did you hear what Dagfinn said?

EARL SKULE *(without looking up):* I heard.

GREGORIUS JONSSON *(looks at DAGFINN):* Is that the King's intention?

DAGFINN: No, no, let's forget it. Let's have no quarrels today.

BISHOP NICHOLAS: The King is planning to make your men swear the oath of allegiance to him, my lord.

GREGORIUS JONSSON *(more loudly):* Is that the King's intention, I asked?

DAGFINN: I'm not answering. Let's drink to peace and friendship between the King and the Earl. The ale is good.

PAUL FLIDA: It's had time to mature.

GREGORIUS JONSSON: Three times the Earl made ready for the wedding, three times the King promised to come—and three times he made his excuses.

DAGFINN: Blame the Earl for that. His rebels kept us busy in the north.

BISHOP NICHOLAS (*moves a piece and says, laughing, to* SKULE): Now I'm taking your castle, my lord.

EARL SKULE (*aloud*): Take it. I can spare a castle.

DAGFINN: Yes—as your men in the north found out.

> *Subdued laughter among the* KING'S MEN. *The conversation is continued in quieter tones. After a few moments, a* MAN *enters and whispers to* GREGORIUS JONSSON.

BISHOP NICHOLAS: Now I move here; and you are mated.

EARL SKULE: So it seems.

BISHOP NICHOLAS (*leans back in his chair*): You didn't nurse your King.

EARL SKULE (*scatters the pieces and rises*): I've grown tired of nursing Kings.

GREGORIUS JONSSON (*approaches him and whispers*): My lord, Jostein Tamb says his ship is ready to sail. Have you the letter—?

EARL SKULE (*takes out a sealed parchment and says quietly*): Here it is.

GREGORIUS JONSSON (*shakes his head*): My lord, my lord! Is this wise?

EARL SKULE: What?

GREGORIUS JONSSON: It bears the King's seal.

EARL SKULE: I am acting in the King's interest.

GREGORIUS JONSSON: Then let the King write the letter himself.

EARL SKULE: He won't if it's left to him. It is for the King's good.

GREGORIUS JONSSON: Perhaps. But this is dangerous—

EARL SKULE: Leave that to me. Take the letter and tell Jostein to sail at once.

GREGORIUS JONSSON: As you command, my lord.

He goes out right, and returns after a few moments.

BISHOP NICHOLAS *(to* EARL SKULE*):* It seems you have much to do.

EARL SKULE: But little thanks for my pains.

BISHOP NICHOLAS: The King has risen.

HAAKON *descends from the dais. All the* MEN *rise from the tables.*

HAAKON *(to the* BISHOP, *ignoring* SKULE*):* My lord Bishop, we are glad to have seen you looking so well and strong during these days of rejoicing.

BISHOP NICHOLAS: I feel a flicker of life in me now and then, Your Majesty; but the next draught may snuff it out. The winter has taken its toll of my strength.

HAAKON: You have lived a full life, rich in noble deeds.

BISHOP NICHOLAS *(shakes his head):* Too much is left undone, Your Majesty. If only I could be sure there was time to finish what I have begun.

HAAKON: The living must continue the work of the dead, reverend lord. We all have the same goal: the welfare and happiness of our country.

DAGFINN *(approaches):* Shall we sound the trumpets for the jousting, Your Majesty?

HAAKON: Good! Today let us be joyful. Tomorrow our work begins.

Trumpets. All bow except EARL SKULE. HAAKON *waits.* SKULE *slowly bows.* HAAKON *goes up on to the dais, offers his hand to* MARGARET *and leads her out right. The others follow in ones and twos.*

BISHOP NICHOLAS *(to* IVAR BODDE*):* A moment. Do you know a man called Jostein Tamb?

IVAR BODDE: There is a traveller here from Orkney of that name.

BISHOP NICHOLAS: From Orkney? Indeed. And now he is sailing home?

IVAR BODDE: So I have heard.

BISHOP NICHOLAS *(lowers his voice):* With a precious cargo, Ivar Bodde!

IVAR BODDE: Corn and cloth, I believe.

BISHOP NICHOLAS: And a letter from Earl Skule.

IVAR BODDE *(suspicious):* Yes?

BISHOP NICHOLAS: Sealed with the King's seal—

IVAR BODDE *(grips his arm):* My lord—is this true?

BISHOP NICHOLAS: Tsst! Don't involve me in this! *(Moves off.)*

IVAR BODDE: I must stop him at once—! Dagfinn! Dagfinn! *(Forces his way through the crowd at the door.)*

BISHOP NICHOLAS *(sympathetically, to* GREGORIUS JONSSON*):* Every day it seems another innocent man loses his freedom. Now they are preventing some wretched traveller from leaving the country.

GREGORIUS JONSSON: Who is that?

BISHOP NICHOLAS: Jostein Tamb, I think his name was.

GREGORIUS JONSSON: Jostein—?

BISHOP NICHOLAS: Dagfinn the Peasant is after him—

GREGORIUS JONSSON: Dagfinn—?

BISHOP NICHOLAS: Yes, he's just gone to stop him sailing.

GREGORIUS JONSSON: Excuse me, my lord, I must hurry—

BISHOP NICHOLAS: Yes, do, my good lord. Dagfinn is such a hasty man—

> GREGORIUS *hurries out with the rest of the* GUESTS. *Only* EARL SKULE *and* BISHOP NICHOLAS *remain in the hall.*

EARL SKULE *(walks thoughtfully up and down. Suddenly it is as though he awakes. He looks round and says):* How quiet it is here suddenly!

BISHOP NICHOLAS: The King has gone.

EARL SKULE: And everyone followed him.

BISHOP NICHOLAS: Everyone except us.

EARL SKULE: It is a great thing to be King.

BISHOP NICHOLAS *(warily):* Would you like to try it, my lord?

EARL SKULE *(smiles seriously):* I have tried it. Every night when I sleep I am King of Norway.

BISHOP NICHOLAS: Dreams can be omens.

EARL SKULE: And tempters, too.

BISHOP NICHOLAS: Surely not to you. Not now, when you own a third of the kingdom, rule the land, and are the Queen's father—

EARL SKULE: Now most of all. Now most of all!

BISHOP NICHOLAS: Hide nothing. Confess. I see you are troubled by a great sorrow.

EARL SKULE: Now most of all, I say. That is the curse that hangs over my whole life. To stand so near to greatness—but with a gap between. Only a yard away—a single leap would do it—and there on the other side lie a crown and a purple cloak, a throne, power, everything! Every day I see them lying there—but I can never take the leap.

BISHOP NICHOLAS: True, my lord.

EARL SKULE: When they chose young Sigurd as King, I was in the full flower of manhood; and it was as though a cry sounded in my ear: "Away with this child! I am the grown, strong man!" But Sigurd was the King's son. That was the gulf that lay between me and the throne then.

BISHOP NICHOLAS: So you waited?

EARL SKULE: I waited for Sigurd to die.

BISHOP NICHOLAS: And Sigurd died, and your brother became King.

EARL SKULE: And I waited for my brother to die. He was already sick; every morning when we met at Mass, I watched to see if the sickness might not take him. Every twist of pain that crossed his face was like a breath of wind in my sail, to carry me nearer to the throne. Every moan he uttered sounded in my ears like trumpets from a distant hill, summoning me to lead my people. I stifled every brotherly thought—and my brother died—and Haakon came—and the Birchlegs chose *him* King.

BISHOP NICHOLAS: And you waited.

EARL SKULE: I sensed the divine right in me, so I thought help must surely come from above. But I was growing older. Every day that passed was a day stolen from my life's work. Each night I thought—tomorrow a sign will come that will strike him down and set me on the empty throne.

BISHOP NICHOLAS: Haakon's power was weak then. He was only a child. You only had to take a single step. But you did not take it.

EARL SKULE: It was a hard step to take. It would have divided me from my family and from my friends.

BISHOP NICHOLAS: Yes. That is the curse that has dogged your whole life, Earl Skule. You have to leave every road open behind you. You dare not burn all your bridges except one, and stand on that alone, conquering or falling there. You lay snares for your enemy—dig pits for his feet, hang swords over his head, put poison in his dishes and set a hundred traps for him—but if he enters one of them you dare not spring it—if he reaches for the poison you think he had better fall by the sword—if he is about to be caught one morning you think it would be safer if it happened in the evening. That, Earl Skule, is your tragedy.

159

EARL SKULE (*after a short pause*): Then answer me one question, reverend lord. Why does Haakon never falter on his path? He is not wiser than I, nor bolder.

BISHOP NICHOLAS: Who accomplishes most in this world?

EARL SKULE: He who is greatest.

BISHOP NICHOLAS: But who is greatest?

EARL SKULE: He who is bravest.

BISHOP NICHOLAS: That is a soldier's answer. A priest would say, he who has the greatest faith—a philosopher, he who is wisest. But neither of these is right, my lord. The greatest man is he who has the most luck. This is the man who accomplishes the greatest deeds—the hunger of his age inflames him like a passion, it generates thoughts in him which he himself does not understand, but which point for him the way which leads he knows not whither, but which he follows, and must follow, until he hears the people cry in joy, and looks about him with distended eyes, and is amazed, and realises that he has performed a mighty deed.

EARL SKULE: Yes, that is Haakon. But I could be the same if I had his luck. (*At first thoughtful, then with rising emotion.*) Was he created from another dust than I? Was he born lucky? If not, why does everything turn out right for him? Why does everything bend to his will? Even the peasant notices it—he says that the trees bear fruit twice, and the birds breed twice, every summer now that Haakon is King. Blood and ashes fertilise the land when Haakon goes to war; the Lord renews the fields that Haakon tramples; the country which he burns and harries is bright again with new-built houses, and all the fields stand heavy with crops bending richly before the wind. It is as though the powers above hastened to blot out every trace of guilt that he leaves behind him. And how easily he strode to the throne! He needed my brother's death, and my brother died; he needed an army, and men flocked to him. He needed the proof of the ordeal, and his mother underwent it for him.

BISHOP NICHOLAS *(bursts out involuntarily):* But we—we two—!

EARL SKULE: We?

BISHOP NICHOLAS: I mean you—you!

EARL SKULE: I stand in the shadow, doubting. *(Pause.)* Haakon has *right* on his side, my lord!

BISHOP NICHOLAS: Did you never see an old painting in the church at Nidaros? It shows the river of sin, swelling and rising over every mountain so that only one peak is left standing above it. Up to this peak has struggled a family, father and mother and son and the son's wife and children. The son has thrown his father down into the waters to gain a safer foothold, and he is trying to throw his mother down, and his wife and all his children, so that he may climb his way to the top—because up there is a square foot of rock on which he can survive for an hour. That, my lord, is the saga of wisdom, and the saga of every wise man.

EARL SKULE: But was he *right?*

BISHOP NICHOLAS: Of course he was right! He had the strength and the passion to live! Bow to your passion, and use your gifts. Every man has that right.

EARL SKULE: If the end is good.

BISHOP NICHOLAS: You play with words! There is no such thing as good or evil. Those are words you must forget, or you will never take that final step, never leap the gulf. *(Softly and persuasively.)* You must not hate a party or a cause because the party or the cause demands this and not that. But you must hate every man in any party who is against you, and you must hate every man who supports a cause if it does not advance your own. Everything that you can use is good. Everything that puts an obstacle in your path is evil. Don't you see that there is a stronger power than these Birchlegs behind Haakon, advancing his ambitions? He gets help from those above—from those—from those who oppose you. They were your enemies from the hour you were born! And you kneel before those enemies! Rise up, man! Straighten your back! Why else were you granted an immortal soul? Remember that the first great deed in history was performed by one who rebelled against a mighty King!

EARL SKULE: Who?

BISHOP NICHOLAS: The angel who rebelled against the light.

EARL SKULE: And was cast into a bottomless abyss—

BISHOP NICHOLAS (*passionately*): And created a kingdom there, and became a King, a mighty King—mightier than any of those ten thousand Earls who stayed above. (*Sinks down on to a bench by the drinking-table.*)

EARL SKULE (*gives him a long look and says*): Bishop Nicholas, are you a man? Or something less? Or something more?

BISHOP NICHOLAS (*smiles*): I am in a state of innocence. I do not know the difference between good and evil.

There is a pause. EARL SKULE *rises and walks agitatedly up and down.*

EARL SKULE: If only I had a son—if only I had a son who could inherit it all from me!

BISHOP NICHOLAS: If you had a son—?

EARL SKULE: I could believe in myself. But I have none.

BISHOP NICHOLAS: Haakon will have sons.

EARL SKULE (*clenches his fists*): And is a King's son.

BISHOP NICHOLAS (*rises*): My lord—what if he were not—?

EARL SKULE: He has proved it. The ordeal—

BISHOP NICHOLAS: But if he were not—despite the ordeal—?

EARL SKULE: Are you saying that God lied?

BISHOP NICHOLAS: What was it that Inga begged God to witness?

EARL SKULE: That the child she bore was the son of the King.

BISHOP NICHOLAS *(nods, looks round, and says quietly):* And if Haakon were not that child?

EARL SKULE *(starts):* Almighty—! *(Controls himself.)* That is unthinkable.

BISHOP NICHOLAS: Listen to me, my lord. I am seventy-six years old. I am beginning to wane, and I dare not take this secret with me—

EARL SKULE: Speak, speak! Is he not the King's son?

BISHOP NICHOLAS: Listen. When Inga found herself with child, it was kept secret. The King her lover had just died, and she was afraid of the new King, your brother, and of you. She bore the child secretly in the house of a priest named Trond. Nine days later she returned home. But the royal babe remained with the priest a whole year. She did not dare to visit it, and no one knew about it except Trond.

EARL SKULE: Yes, yes! And then?

BISHOP NICHOLAS: You will appreciate how dangerous it was for a humble priest to have the upbringing of a King's son. Therefore, soon after the baby was born, he revealed the truth in the confessional. His confessor counselled Trond secretly to exchange the child for another, send the true prince to a safe place, and give Inga the changeling, if she should ever claim her son.

EARL SKULE *(angrily):* Who was the dog who dared advise this?

BISHOP NICHOLAS: It was I.

EARL SKULE: You?

BISHOP NICHOLAS: I thought it would be unsafe for the prince to fall into your hands.

EARL SKULE: But the priest?

BISHOP NICHOLAS: Promised to do as I advised.

EARL SKULE *(grips his arm):* Then Haakon is the change-ling?

BISHOP NICHOLAS: If the priest kept his promise.

EARL SKULE: *If* he kept it?

BISHOP NICHOLAS: A year later, Inga revealed the existence of her child, and a baby was brought from Trond's house to the royal palace which everyone assumed was hers. But that same winter, Trond left the country on a pilgrimage to the grave of Thomas Becket, and stayed in England un-til he died.

EARL SKULE: This proves he exchanged the child! He fled the country because he feared the revenge of the Birch-legs!

BISHOP NICHOLAS: Or he did not exchange it, and feared my revenge.

EARL SKULE: Which do you believe?

BISHOP NICHOLAS: Both are equally likely.

EARL SKULE: And Inga—?

BISHOP NICHOLAS: Knows nothing, either of the priest's con-fession, or of the advice I gave him.

EARL SKULE: Her baby was only nine days old when she left him, you say?

BISHOP NICHOLAS: Yes. And the child she saw next was over a year old—

EARL SKULE: Then there is no one in the world who knows the answer! *(Walks grimly up and down several times.)* Almighty God, can it be true? Haakon an impostor! *(Goes to the window.)* See how splendidly he sits his horse! No one sits as he does. His eyes laugh and glitter like the sun, he looks at the day as though he knew himself born to go forward, always forward! The people gaze adoringly at him. In every eye shines the unshakable belief that he is their rightful King.

BISHOP NICHOLAS: That is because *he* believes it, my lord.

That is his luck. That is where his strength lies. And yet, perhaps he is not—

EARL SKULE: No. Perhaps not. *(Turns back violently to the window.)*

BISHOP NICHOLAS: Hide the fact that you don't believe in yourself. Look as though you did, speak as though you did! Swear boldly and passionately that you do, and they will all believe in *you!*

EARL SKULE *(at the window, starts and exclaims in surprise):* What's this? Dagfinn has broken through the crowd. He's whispering to the King.

BISHOP NICHOLAS *(looks out behind the EARL):* Haakon looks angry. He's clenching his fist—

EARL SKULE: He's looking up here. What can it be? *(Turns to go.)*

BISHOP NICHOLAS *(holds him back):* My lord, listen to me. There is a way to find whether Haakon is the rightful heir—

EARL SKULE: A way—?

BISHOP NICHOLAS: Before he died, Trond the priest wrote a letter revealing what he had done, and swore upon the sacrament that what he had written was the truth.

EARL SKULE: And this letter—in God's name, where is it?

BISHOP NICHOLAS: Well— *(Glances towards the door.)* Ssh, here comes the King.

EARL SKULE: The letter, my lord, the letter!

BISHOP NICHOLAS: Here is the King.

> HAAKON *enters, followed by his* MEN-AT-ARMS *and many* GUESTS. *Immediately afterwards,* MARGARET *enters. She is in great distress, and tries to run to the* KING, *but is held back by* THE LADY RAGNHILD *who, with several* WOMEN, *has accompanied her.* SIGRID *stands a little way apart, upstage. The* EARL'S MEN

165

look uneasy and gather on the right, near SKULE, *but a little way behind him.*

HAAKON *(angry but controlled):* Earl Skule, who is King in this land?

EARL SKULE: Who is King—?

HAAKON: That was my question. I bear the name of King, but who wields the royal power?

EARL SKULE: Royal power should be wielded by the lawful King.

HAAKON: It should be so. But is it?

EARL SKULE: Are you accusing me—?

HAAKON: I am. As is my royal right.

EARL SKULE: I am not afraid to answer for my actions.

HAAKON: Let us hope, for all our sakes, that you can. *(Steps up on to the dais where the throne stands and leans against the arm of the throne.)* I stand here as your King and ask you—do you know that Earl John of Orkney has rebelled against me?

EARL SKULE: Yes.

HAAKON: And is it true, my lord, that today you sent him a letter?

EARL SKULE: I did.

HAAKON: Bearing the King's seal?

EARL SKULE: Yes.

HAAKON: So you write to the King's enemies and seal your letters with the King's seal, although the King does not know what stands written there?

EARL SKULE: I have done so for many years, with your knowledge.

HAAKON: When you were my regent.

EARL SKULE: You never suffered by it, and will not suffer this time. Earl John wrote to me and asked me to mediate between him and you. He wanted peace, but on terms dishonourable to Your Majesty.

166

HAAKON: The letter should have been shown to me. What did you write?

EARL SKULE: Read my letter.

HAAKON: Give it to me.

EARL SKULE (*turns to* GREGORIUS JONSSON): Gregorius, give the King the letter.

GREGORIUS JONSSON (*approaches uneasily*): My lord—!

EARL SKULE: What is it?

GREGORIUS JONSSON: You remember, my lord, you wrote sharp words of the King—

EARL SKULE: I can answer for them. Give me the letter.

GREGORIUS JONSSON: I have not got it.

EARL SKULE: Not got it?

GREGORIUS JONSSON: Dagfinn the Peasant was on our heels. I seized the letter from Jostein, tied a stone to it—

EARL SKULE: And—?

GREGORIUS JONSSON: It is lying at the bottom of the fjord.

EARL SKULE: You have done ill—ill!

HAAKON: I am waiting for the letter, my lord.

EARL SKULE: I cannot give it to you.

HAAKON: You *can* not? (*Pause.*) Are you defying me?

EARL SKULE: If you wish—yes, I am defying you.

IVAR BODDE (*angrily*): My lord, I think no man needs further proof than this.

HAAKON (*coldly to* SKULE): Earl Skule, I order you to surrender the royal seal. Give it to Ivar Bodde.

MARGARET (*runs, her hands clasped, to the dais where the* KING *is standing*): Haakon, be a gentle and merciful husband to me!

> HAAKON *makes an imperious gesture towards her. She hides her face in her veil and goes back to her mother. Pause.*

EARL SKULE (*slowly moves towards* IVAR BODDE): Here is the seal.

Another pause. IVAR BODDE *goes towards* HAAKON *with it.*

PAUL FLIDA (*furiously to the* EARL'S MEN *around him*): Are we to endure this any longer?

GREGORIUS JONSSON (*steps forward*): We cannot and will not endure it! I say it plainly for all to hear—the Earl's men cannot serve the King with loyalty if the Earl does not keep the seal.

MANY OF THE EARL'S MEN: No, no! Give back the seal! The Earl must have the seal!

IVAR BODDE (*proffers the seal to* HAAKON): Take it into your own hands, Your Majesty. It should have rested there long ago.

HAAKON *takes the seal. The crowd is hushed.*

IVAR BODDE: God bless and prosper all your undertakings.

HAAKON (*lowers his head, kisses the seal, and looks up at* SKULE): Now, my lord—

EARL SKULE: Evil angels are coming between us two today. You must not ask more of me.

BISHOP NICHOLAS: The Earl is right, Your Majesty—

HAAKON: *You* say so, reverend lord? I say that justice must be done.

EARL SKULE: Your Majesty—more than one man's blood will be shed!

HAAKON: Perhaps. But treason must be punished. (*Draws his sword and says, calmly and firmly*) All the Earl's men shall swear an oath of allegiance.

EARL SKULE (*vehemently*): You cannot mean this! (*Almost beseechingly.*) King Haakon, do not do this!

HAAKON: No man of the Earl's shall leave this palace until he has sworn allegiance to the King.

He goes with his bodyguard towards the door. As he reaches it, SIGRID *runs forward.*

SIGRID: My lord!

> HAAKON *stops. She kneels before him.*

SIGRID: Grant me a boon, Your Majesty!

HAAKON: Rise, Sigrid. Whatever you ask shall be granted.

SIGRID: The nunnery at Rein will soon be consecrated. Write to the Archbishop and beg that I may become abbess there.

HAAKON: Why do you wish to enter a nunnery?

SIGRID *(rises):* Since the night at Nidaros, when they burned the city and murdered my husband at our wedding, the blood and fire have blinded my eyes to the outward world. But I have gained the power to see what other eyes cannot—and I see it now—a time of dreadful horror for our land!

RAGNHILD *(violently):* She is sick! Pay no heed to her!

SIGRID: A rich harvest shall ripen for him who reaps in the dark! Norway's women have but one task now—to kneel in the churches and the nunneries and pray—pray, day and night!

HAAKON *(shaken):* Take her away! The woman is mad! *(Goes out.)*

SIGRID *(to EARL SKULE):* Farewell, my brother. We shall meet once more. When you need me in your soul's extremity—when your peril is greatest—when you grasp the crown!

> *She goes out right with* MARGARET, RAGNHILD *and the* WOMEN. *The* BISHOP *and* EARL SKULE *are left alone.*

BISHOP NICHOLAS: The King has used you harshly today.

> EARL SKULE *is silent and looks speechlessly after the* KING.

BISHOP NICHOLAS *(more strongly):* And he may be the son of a peasant.

EARL SKULE (*suddenly turns passionately to the* BISHOP *and grips his arm*): The priest's confession! Where is it?

BISHOP NICHOLAS: He sent it to me from England before he died. I don't know by whom, and I have not received it.

EARL SKULE: It must be found!

BISHOP NICHOLAS: I am sure it will be.

EARL SKULE: And you will place it in my hands?

BISHOP NICHOLAS: You shall have it.

EARL SKULE: You swear it by your soul's salvation?

BISHOP NICHOLAS: I swear it by my soul's salvation.

EARL SKULE: Good. Until then I shall work against Haakon wherever I can do so, quietly and in secret. He must not be more powerful than I am when the struggle begins.

BISHOP NICHOLAS: But if the letter should prove him to be the true heir to the crown—what then?

EARL SKULE: Then I shall beseech God for a humble spirit, to serve him loyally, and with all my strength.

BISHOP NICHOLAS: And if he is not?

EARL SKULE: Then he shall yield to me! His crown and his throne, his army and his bodyguard, his treasure and his fleet, his cities and his palaces—they shall all be mine!

BISHOP NICHOLAS: He will fly to his castle—

EARL SKULE: I shall hunt him from his castle!

BISHOP NICHOLAS: He will seek refuge in sanctuary—

EARL SKULE: I shall violate the sanctuary!

BISHOP NICHOLAS: He will flee to the high altar and cling to St. Olaf's shrine—

EARL SKULE: I shall drag him down from the altar, if I have to drag the Saint's shrine with him!

BISHOP NICHOLAS: But he will still have the crown on his head, my lord.

EARL SKULE: Then I shall strike the crown off with my sword!

BISHOP NICHOLAS: But if it sits too tightly, my lord—?

EARL SKULE: Then in God's name, or in Satan's—I shall strike his head off with it! *(He goes out right.)*

BISHOP NICHOLAS *(looks after him, nods slowly, and says):* Yes—yes! This way I like the Earl!

ACT THREE

Scene One

A room in the BISHOP's *palace in Oslo. To the right, an entrance door. Upstage, a small door, standing open, leads into the chapel, which is illuminated. A door covered by a curtain in the left-hand wall leads into the* BISHOP's *bedchamber. Downstage on the same side is a padded couch. Over to the right is a desk, on which are letters, documents and a lighted lamp.*

> *At first, the room is empty. From behind the curtain on the left can be heard* MONKS *singing. After a few moments,* PAUL FLIDA *enters right in travelling clothes, stops inside the door, waits, looks around, and then strikes three times on the floor with his staff.*

SIRA WILLIAM *(enters left and exclaims, keeping his voice low):* Paul Flida! God be praised! Then the Earl is not far off?

PAUL FLIDA: His ships are past the cape. He sent me ahead. How is the Bishop?

SIRA WILLIAM: He is receiving the last sacrament. They say he cannot survive the night.

PAUL FLIDA: Then we have come too late.

SIRA WILLIAM: No, no. He is fully conscious, and has a little strength left. Every minute he asks when the Earl will be here.

PAUL FLIDA: You still call him Earl. Don't you know the King has made him a Duke?

SIRA WILLIAM: Yes, yes, of course. I'd forgotten. Ssh!

He and PAUL FLIDA *make the sign of the cross, and bow. From the* BISHOP'S *bedchamber enter two* ACO-LYTES *with candles, followed by two more with censers, and* PRIESTS *carrying chalice, paten and crucifix. Behind them follows a procession of* PRIESTS *and* MONKS. ACOLYTES *with candles and censers bring up the rear of the procession, which winds slowly into the chapel. The door of it is closed behind them.*

PAUL FLIDA: So; the old man has settled his account with this world.

SIRA WILLIAM: Can I tell him that Duke Skule will be here soon?

PAUL FLIDA: He will come straight here from the harbour. Goodbye.

He goes. Several PRIESTS, *including* PETER, *and* SER-VANTS *of the* BISHOP, *enter left with fur rugs, cushions and a large brazier.*

SIRA WILLIAM: What are these for?

PRIEST *(making the couch ready):* The Bishop wishes to lie out here.

SIRA WILLIAM: But is that wise?

PRIEST: The doctor says we must humour him. Here he is.

BISHOP NICHOLAS *enters, supported by* MASTER SIGARD *and a* PRIEST. *He is in his episcopal robes, but without his staff and mitre.*

BISHOP NICHOLAS: Light more candles! *(He is carried to the*

173

couch, placed on it in a sitting position close to the bra-
zier, and covered with furs.) William! I have received ab-
solution for my sins. They have all been taken from me. I
feel so light now!

SIRA WILLIAM: Duke Skule has sent word to you, my lord.
He will be here at any moment.

BISHOP NICHOLAS: That's good, very good! The King will
be here soon too, surely. I've been a sinful dog in my
time, William. I have sinned grievously against the King.
The priests in there said all my sins would be forgiven
me—that's all very well, it's easy for them to promise—I
haven't sinned against them. No, no—I'd best have pardon from the King's own lips. (*Shouts angrily*) Lights, I
say! It's so dark in here!

SIRA WILLIAM: The candles are lit, my lord—

SIGARD (*silences him with a gesture and goes closer to the*
BISHOP): How do you feel, my lord?

BISHOP NICHOLAS: So-so, so-so. My hands and feet are cold.

MASTER SIGARD *glances at* SIRA WILLIAM *and moves the*
brazier closer.

BISHOP NICHOLAS (*fretfully, to* SIRA WILLIAM): I've ordered
eight monks to sing and pray for me in the chapel tonight.
Keep an eye on them. They're lazy dogs, some of them.

SIRA WILLIAM *points silently towards the chapel, from*
which can be heard singing that continues throughout
the following dialogue.

BISHOP NICHOLAS: So much still undone—and to have to
leave it all! So much undone, William!

SIRA WILLIAM: Think of Heaven, my lord!

BISHOP NICHOLAS: There's no hurry. The doctor says I've
got till morning—

SIRA WILLIAM: My lord, my lord—

BISHOP NICHOLAS: Give me my mitre and my staff! You're

right—I must try to think of—! (A PRIEST *brings them.*)
No, put the mitre here, it's too heavy for me. Place my
staff in my hand. There, now I am armed. A Bishop! The
Evil One dare not touch me now! Leave me, all of you!

All go out right except PETER, *who remains in the shadows by the door.*

PETER (*quietly*): My lord.

BISHOP NICHOLAS (*starts*): Who's that? Who's there?

PETER: Peter, my lord.

BISHOP NICHOLAS: Why do you stay behind?

PETER: I have a letter for you, my lord.

BISHOP NICHOLAS: A letter?

PETER: It was given to me by a priest, newly arrived from
England. He made me promise to deliver it to you in secret. He said it was from someone named Trond.

Pause.

BISHOP NICHOLAS: Give it to me. (PETER *does so and moves
away. Pause.*): Peter.

PETER (*approaches*): My lord?

BISHOP NICHOLAS: Have you ever seen an old man die?

PETER: No.

BISHOP NICHOLAS: They're all afraid, I'll swear to that! Are
they singing in there?

PETER: Yes, my lord.

BISHOP NICHOLAS: Eight big fellows, with throats like
trumpets—that must help a little, mustn't it?

PETER: My lord, my lord, let me pray too!

BISHOP NICHOLAS: Ah, Peter. You've always been a comfort
to me. Is your mother well?

PETER: Yes, my lord.

BISHOP NICHOLAS: Did you give her my message?

PETER: Yes, my lord—but let me pray!

175

BISHOP NICHOLAS: The message! Did you give her my message?

PETER: I did, my lord.

BISHOP NICHOLAS: I've left too much unfinished, Peter. Life is too short— *(Doubles up in pain.)*

PETER: Are you in great pain?

BISHOP NICHOLAS: There is a ringing in my ears—a light flickers in my eyes—

PETER: It is the bells of Heaven ringing you home. And the light is the altar candles which God's angels have lit for you.

BISHOP NICHOLAS: Yes, yes, of course. There's nothing to fear, as long as they go on praying in there. Leave me. I am not afraid to be alone.

PETER: Farewell, my lord. We shall meet again when the bells of Heaven have sounded for me too. *(Goes out right.)*

BISHOP NICHOLAS: The bells of Heaven! Yes, it's easy to talk like that when you're young and healthy. So much left undone! *(Pause.)* Trond's confession! So it's come after all! I swore to the Duke on my soul's salvation to give it to him if I ever received it. And here it is, lying in my hand. One should never swear anything on one's soul's salvation when one's as old as I am. If I'd time left, I'd find a way out of the oath; but tonight, my last night—no, that wouldn't be wise. But how can I keep it? That would mean risking everything I've worked for all my life. If the Duke knew for sure, he would conquer or yield; and either way, one of them would become the mightiest man ever to have lived in Norway. No, no! What I can't have, no one else shall have! He must remain uncertain; then the strife will go on for ever. Towns will be burned, whole regions laid waste—neither shall profit by the other's defeat. He must never know! *(Whispers)* Oh, if only I could cheat the Evil One, just once more!

(Hides the letter under his pillow. There is distant thunder.) What's that? *(Frightened.)* Mercy, mercy! I am the one who is guilty! I started it all! I drove them on! *(More thunder. He cries)* William, William!

SIRA WILLIAM *enters right.*

BISHOP NICHOLAS: What's that horrible sighing and moaning?

SIRA WILLIAM: There's a storm blowing up.

BISHOP NICHOLAS: A storm! A storm, you say? Are they singing in there?

SIRA WILLIAM: Yes.

BISHOP NICHOLAS: Tell them to sing harder. Especially Brother Aslak. He always says such short prayers—he's a shirker, he misses bits out, the dog! *(Strikes the floor with his staff.)* Go in and tell him this is my last night. He must be diligent, or I will come and haunt him!

SIRA WILLIAM: My lord, had I not better fetch the doctor?

BISHOP NICHOLAS: Go in, I tell you!

SIRA WILLIAM *goes into the chapel. The* BISHOP *takes out the letter from beneath the pillow.*

It must be Heaven's will that I shall reconcile the King and the Duke. This is a hard thing, Nicholas—to destroy your life's work at a single blow. But this time I must obey His will. *(Opens the letter.)* I can't read a word—a mist drifts before my eyes—and I daren't let anyone else read it to me. I must, I *shall* live longer! *(Bangs with his staff. A* PRIEST *enters right.)* Bid Master Sigard come! *(The* PRIEST *goes. The* BISHOP *crumples the letter in his hand.)* Here, beneath this thin seal, rests Norway's history for the next hundred years. It lies here dreaming, like an unborn chick in its egg. *(Clasps the letter to his chest.)* Oh, if only I had time, I would hatch you into a hawk that would cast the shadow of fear over the whole land, and sink its sharp claws into every human heart! *(Starts.)* But the judgment—the punishment—! *(Cries)* No, no! You shall be a swan, a white swan! *(Throws the letter across the room, and cries)* Master Sigard, Master Sigard!

SIGARD *(enters right):* What is it, my lord?

BISHOP NICHOLAS: Master Sigard, sell me three days life!

SIGARD: I have told you—

BISHOP NICHOLAS: I'll pay well! Three days of life, Master Sigard, only three days!

SIGARD: If I had to die with you, my lord, I could not add three days to your span.

BISHOP NICHOLAS: One day, then—just one day! Let it be daylight, let the sun be shining, when I depart! Listen, Sigard! *(Beckons him over and draws him down on to the couch.)* I've given nearly all my gold and silver to the Church, to have great masses read when I am gone. I'll revoke my will—you shall have it all! What, Sigard, shall we fool those fellows in there—just the two of us? He, he, he! You'll be rich, Sigard! (MASTER SIGARD *feels his pulse. The* BISHOP *cries in anguish)* Well, why don't you answer?

SIGARD *(gets up):* I have no time, my lord. I will prepare a drink which may ease you a little at the last.

BISHOP NICHOLAS: No, wait!

SIGARD: I have no time. The drink must be ready within an hour. *(Goes out right.)*

BISHOP NICHOLAS: Within an hour! *(Knocks furiously on the floor with his staff.)* William! William!

SIRA WILLIAM *enters from the chapel.*

BISHOP NICHOLAS: Get more people to sing in there! Eight aren't enough.

SIRA WILLIAM: My lord—?

BISHOP NICHOLAS: More, I say! Brother Kolbein has been

sick in bed for five weeks—he can't have sinned much in that time—

SIRA WILLIAM: He went to confession yesterday.

BISHOP NICHOLAS: He'll do, then. Get him. (SIRA WILLIAM *goes back into the chapel.*) Within an hour! (*Wipes the sweat from his brow.*) Ugh, it's stifling in here! The dog, what's the use of all his learning if he can't give me another hour? He sits there in his room all day, fiddling with little wheels and weights and levers, trying to make something that will go on for ever, round and round and never stop. *Perpetuum mobile,* he calls it. Why doesn't he use his knowledge to make men do that? (*Stops and thinks. His eyes light up.*) Perpetuum mobile! Round and round till the end of time. What if I could set wheels and weights and levers working in the King's heart, and the Duke's— set them going so that no power on earth could stop them? If I can do that, I shall go on living, and survive through my work! Perhaps that's what's meant by immortality. O cool and comforting thoughts, to ease an old man's heart! (*Emits a deep breath, and settles himself more comfortably on the couch.*) The Devil's been after me tonight! It's all this lying idle—*otium est pulvis—pulveris*—no, damn that Latin! The Devil shan't get his claws into me again—I'll go on working to the end! (*Knocks on the floor, shouts*) Stop that din in there! I'm trying to think!

SIRA WILLIAM (*enters*): My lord, you asked for them to—?

BISHOP NICHOLAS: Tell them to keep quiet. They're distracting me.

SIRA WILLIAM (*turns to go*): Very well, my lord.

BISHOP NICHOLAS: Wait a moment. Give me that letter.

SIRA WILLIAM (*goes to the desk*): Which one, my lord?

BISHOP NICHOLAS: The one that's lying on the floor. Good. Now go and tell them to keep quiet. (SIRA WILLIAM *goes.*) To die, and yet to rule in Norway! To die, and make sure that no man will ever raise his head above the rest! How?

(Pause.) But of course! It's so easy! I shall keep the oath—the Duke shall hold the letter in his hands—and the King—hm!—the King shall know it too—he shall feel the sting of doubt in his heart. His faith in himself shall falter. Both shall believe and doubt, see-saw up and down, never feel firm ground beneath them—round and round—*perpetuum mobile! (Breathes a sigh of content.)* My spirit feels young again. I shall work on my last night! Work—till the light goes out—

DUKE SKULE *(enters right and goes over to the* BISHOP*)*: Peace and greetings, reverend lord! How goes it with you—?

BISHOP NICHOLAS: I am a corpse in bud, Your Grace. Tonight I shall flower; tomorrow you shall know my perfume.

DUKE SKULE: Tonight?

BISHOP NICHOLAS: So Master Sigard says. Within an hour.

DUKE SKULE: And the priest's letter—?

BISHOP NICHOLAS: Do you still think about that?

DUKE SKULE: It never leaves my mind.

BISHOP NICHOLAS: The King has made you a Duke. No man has ever held that rank in Norway before.

DUKE SKULE: It is not enough. If Haakon is not the rightful King, I must have everything.

BISHOP NICHOLAS: Ugh, it's cold in here. It bites through my limbs—

DUKE SKULE: The letter, my lord! In the name of God, tell me—has it come?

Pause.

BISHOP NICHOLAS: I know where it can be found.
DUKE SKULE: Then tell me, tell me!

The BISHOP *leans forward.*

SIRA WILLIAM *(enters right):* The King is coming! We can see his torches—

BISHOP NICHOLAS: He shall be made welcome. (SIRA WILLIAM *goes.*) Your Grace, in return I crave a last favour of you. When I am dead, avenge me against my enemies. *(Takes out the letter.)* I have written their names. Those at the top I should like hanged, if it could be arranged so.

DUKE SKULE: Do not think of revenge now. You have no time—

BISHOP NICHOLAS: Not revenge—punishment! Swear you will punish all my enemies when I am gone! They are as jealous of you as they were of me. When you are King, you can punish them. Swear you will do it!

DUKE SKULE: Very well. I swear it. But the letter—?

BISHOP NICHOLAS: I will tell you. *(Beckons him close.)* Not yet! Here comes the King! Hide the list of our enemies!

The DUKE hides the paper. As he does so, HAAKON enters right.

BISHOP NICHOLAS: Welcome to this funeral feast, Your Majesty.

HAAKON: Greetings, my lord Bishop. *(Turns and sees* SKULE. *Starts angrily.)* Why is the Duke here?

DUKE SKULE: My lord Bishop, will you assure King Haakon upon my faith and honour that I did not know he was coming here until I set foot on Oslo quay?

BISHOP NICHOLAS: Alas, alas! The blame is mine. I have been bedridden these last months—I thought all was now well between you noble kinsmen.

HAAKON: My friendship with the Duke prospers best when we do not see each other. Therefore, farewell, Bishop Nicholas. You have been my enemy, but Death settles all accounts, and I forgive you. God be with you, whithersoever you are bound. *(Turns to go.)*

DUKE SKULE (*whispers uneasily*): My lord, my lord, he is going!

BISHOP NICHOLAS (*suddenly and with passionate strength*): Stay, King Haakon!

HAAKON (*involuntarily lays his hand on his sword and says to the* DUKE): What trap is this? Where are your warriors?

DUKE SKULE: I did not call you back.

BISHOP NICHOLAS: Your Majesty shall not leave this room before old Bishop Nicholas has delivered his last sermon. Where there is a funeral in the house, the dead man is King. It is he who commands. My sight is dimmer, but before my inward eye, my life unfolds most clearly. Mark and learn, King! My family was the greatest in the land. Many mighty chieftains issued from it. I wanted to become the mightiest of them all. I wanted to be King. I hungered for great deeds when I was a boy—I felt I could hardly wait for manhood. Then came the day of my first battle. The sun shone, and its light flashed from a thousand polished swords. The trumpets sounded, and our ranks moved forward as though to a game. I alone felt a tightening round my heart. Our army fought bravely forward—but I could not follow. I fled across the mountain, ran and ran, and did not stop until I had reached the fjord, far from the battle. Many men washed their bloody clothes in Trondhjem fjord that night. I had to wash mine too, but not of blood. Yes, King, I was afraid! Born in love with greatness, and afraid! It smote me like a thunderbolt. I prayed secretly in the churches. I wept and kneeled before the altars, I made rich offerings and sacred vows. I tried to fight, in battle after battle, always in vain. They laughed when I stepped forth in my armour. Since then, I have hated—because I could not love. Women—ah, I could devour them even now, with glistening eyes! I am eighty years old, and still I yearn to destroy men and possess women. But it was the same in love as in battle—only the will, only the desire! Impotent from birth—tormented with the seething gift of love, and yet a cripple! So I became a priest. He who wishes to rule must either be a King or a priest! *(Laughs.)* I, a priest! A man of God! Well, Heaven had fitted me for one holy office—to sing high notes—to lead with a woman's voice at the great church festivals! A half-man—not sinning, but sinned against! Let Heaven stand in the dock! I am the accuser!

DUKE SKULE *(whispers):* My lord, the letter! You have not long left!

HAAKON: Think of your soul, and humble yourself!

BISHOP NICHOLAS: A man's life-work is his soul, and my life-work shall not die! But you, King Haakon—take care! For, just as Heaven has opposed me and suffered by it, so you oppose the man who holds the welfare of our country in his hand—

HAAKON: Enough—!

BISHOP NICHOLAS *(to HAAKON):* He will oppose you as long as his head sits on his shoulders! Share with him. I shall find no peace in my coffin, I shall walk, unless you share! Neither of you must stand on the other's shoulders—there must be no giants in Norway—for I was never one! Share, share! *(Sinks feebly back upon the couch.)*

DUKE SKULE *(throws himself on his knees beside the couch and cries to HAAKON):* Get help! For God's sake, get help! The Bishop must not die yet!

BISHOP NICHOLAS: It's getting dark! I can't see—! King, for the last time—will you share with the Duke?

HAAKON: I shall not part with one fragment of what God has given me.

BISHOP NICHOLAS: Very well! *(Whispers to himself)* Then I will split you in two myself! *(Shouts)* William!

DUKE SKULE *(whispers):* The letter, the letter!

BISHOP NICHOLAS *(not listening to him):* William! (SIRA WILLIAM *comes. The* BISHOP *draws him close, and whis-*

pers) When I received the last sacrament, all my sins were forgiven me?

SIRA WILLIAM: All your sins, from birth until unction.

BISHOP NICHOLAS: Only till then?

SIRA WILLIAM: My lord, you cannot sin tonight.

BISHOP NICHOLAS: Hm—who knows—? Take the golden chalice I had from Bishop Absalom—give it to the church—and read seven more masses!

SIRA WILLIAM: My lord, God will be merciful.

BISHOP NICHOLAS: Seven more masses, I say! For the sin I shall commit tonight! Go, go! *(SIRA WILLIAM goes. The BISHOP turns to SKULE.)* Your Grace, when you read the priest's letter, if it reveals that Haakon is the rightful King—what will you do? Search every corner of your heart. Answer as though you stood before your judge! What will you do, if you know he is the King?

DUKE SKULE: Bow my knee and serve him.

BISHOP NICHOLAS *(mutters):* Then take the consequences. *(To SKULE)* Your Grace, I am weak and weary. I feel moved by a spirit of mercy and forgiveness—

DUKE SKULE: God's death—the letter! Where is it?

BISHOP NICHOLAS: Something else first. I gave you the list of my enemies—

DUKE SKULE *(impatiently):* Yes, yes. I shall avenge you—

BISHOP NICHOLAS: No, I feel so peaceful now. I want to forgive, as the good book says we should. As you renounce power, so I renounce revenge. Burn the list.

DUKE SKULE: Yes, yes, as you wish.

BISHOP NICHOLAS: Here in the brazier, so that I can see it—

DUKE SKULE *(throws the paper in the fire):* Look, there it burns! And now, speak, speak! Thousands of lives may perish if you do not speak now!

BISHOP NICHOLAS *(his eyes sparkle):* Thousands of lives! *(Cries)* Light! Air!

HAAKON *(runs to the door and shouts):* Bring help! The Bishop is dying!

SIRA WILLIAM *and others of the* BISHOP's *men come in.*

DUKE SKULE *(shakes the* BISHOP's *arm):* Norway's glory for centuries—perhaps her greatness for all eternity—!

BISHOP NICHOLAS: For all eternity! *(Triumphantly.)* Perpetuum mobile!

DUKE SKULE: By your soul's salvation—where is the priest's letter?

BISHOP NICHOLAS *(cries):* Seven more masses, William!

DUKE SKULE *(desperately):* The letter! The letter!

BISHOP NICHOLAS *(smiles in his death agony):* You have burned it, most noble Duke! *(Falls back upon the couch and dies.)*

DUKE SKULE *(emits an involuntary cry as he starts back and covers his face with his hands):* Ah—Almighty God—!

The MONKS *flee in from the chapel.*

SOME OF THEM: Evil spirits are loose tonight!

OTHERS: One laughed from the corner! It cried: "We have him!" All the candles were quenched!

HAAKON: Bishop Nicholas is dead.

The MONKS *flee out right. Their chanting fades.*

Scene Two

A room in the palace. In the background is the entrance door. Small doors in each of the side walls. Downstage right, a window. A lamp burns in the ceiling. Close by the door on the left stands a couch, and farther back a cradle, in which the baby prince is sleeping. MARGARET *is kneeling beside the child.*

MARGARET (*sings as she rocks the cradle*):

> Above the rafters of the hall,
> Among the stars in peaceful skies,
> In answer to the angels' call
> In dreams my little Haakon flies.
>
> Out of your crib a ladder leads
> Your gentle thoughts to peace above.
> May all your mighty manhood deeds
> Be just as gentle, filled with love.
>
> God's little angels watch your rest
> To keep all evil far from you.
> God bless you, little golden child.
> Your mother watches over you.

A short pause. DUKE SKULE *enters upstage.*

MARGARET (*jumps up with a cry of joy and runs to greet him*): Father! Oh, how I've longed to see you!

DUKE SKULE: God's peace be with you, Margaret. Where is the King?

MARGARET: Ssh! Come! Come here and look—! (*Takes his hand and leads him across to the cradle.*)

DUKE SKULE: Your child!

MARGARET: Yes. This beautiful child is mine! Isn't he wonderful? His name's Haakon, like the King. Look at his eyes—no, you can't see them now—he's sleeping—but he has great blue eyes. And he knows me already—he laughs, and stretches out his hands to touch me. (*Arranges the child's clothes about him.*)

DUKE SKULE: Haakon will have sons, the Bishop prophesied.

MARGARET: I can hardly believe I'm so happy! I sleep with the cradle close by my bed every night, so that if I wake I can reach out my hand and touch it to make sure it isn't a dream.

DUKE SKULE *(listens and goes to the window):* Is that the King?

MARGARET: Yes. I'll go and fetch him. *(Takes her father's hand and leads him playfully back to the cradle.)* Duke Skule! You must stand guard over the Prince while I'm away! Yes, it's hard to get used to, but that's what he is—a Prince! If he wakes, you must bow low and salute him as you would a King! Now I'll fetch Haakon. When you see him, won't you try to settle your differences and become friends, as in the old days? Every day I pray to God that it may happen. *(Goes out right.)*

DUKE SKULE *(walks a few steps across the room, and suddenly stops by the cradle):* The King's son! What a pretty forehead—! He is dreaming. *(Settles the coverlet more comfortably over the child and looks long at it.)* A little one like you could lead a man's soul from despair. I have no son. *(Bends down over the cradle.)* He looks like Haakon. *(Suddenly shrinks back.)* "Bow low and salute him as you would a King", she said. If Haakon dies before me, this child will be set upon the throne—and I—I shall stand at his footstool, bowing before him, saluting him as King, white-haired and bent with age, seeing my life-work sleep unborn. *(Pause.)* "Burn all your bridges but one!" the Bishop said. That was three years ago, and what have I done? Left every bridge open—divided and wasted my strength. *(Sharply.)* Now I must do as he says—now or never! I have more men than Haakon— there is a storm blowing tonight, the wind is sweeping down the fjord—! What if I seized the Prince? I can count on the citizens here. What could Haakon do if his son were in my power? So be it! Let the step be taken, let the gulf be leaped! But if I did win the crown, would not doubt still consume me, gnawing and devouring me until it bored right through my brain? Yes, yes—but it is better to sit on the throne and doubt oneself than to stand below in the crowd and doubt him who sits up there! I must settle things once and for all! For once I have the advantage. I must exploit it. *(Hesitantly.)* But now—? Tonight—? *(Leans over the cradle.)* If only I could see whether you have the old King's eyes! He is asleep. I cannot tell. *(Pause.)* Sleep is a sentinel. Sleep in peace, little pretender. *(Goes over to the table.)* I shall speak to Haakon once more. He shall decide what is to be.

MARGARET *(enters with the KING right):* The Bishop dead! Oh, believe me—all our troubles will die with him.

HAAKON: Go to bed, Margaret. You must be tired after your journey.

MARGARET: Yes, yes. *(To the DUKE)* Father, be gentle and yielding. Haakon has promised to be! Goodnight, both of you! *(Waves to them in the doorway left, and goes. Two SERVANTS take the cradle after her.)*

DUKE SKULE: King Haakon, this time we must not part as enemies. Evil will follow. It will be a time of dreadful horror for our land.

HAAKON: Duke Skule, when I became King I gave you a third of the kingdom. You thirsted for more. I increased your share. Now you own half the country. You still demanded more. I made you a Duke—a title no man in Norway has ever held before—

DUKE SKULE: But you are King! There must be no King above me! I was not born to serve you.

HAAKON *(looks at him for a moment and says coldly):* Heaven protect your reason, my lord. Goodnight. *(Turns to go.)*

DUKE SKULE: Listen to me! Remember the Bishop's words. Let us share. Divide the kingdom. It has happened before. We will be friends and allies—

HAAKON: Every rock on our coasts is a stone in the house

our forefathers built! And you want me to break their work asunder? Never!

DUKE SKULE: Well, then, let us rule in turn!

HAAKON: Do you think my crown would fit your forehead?

DUKE SKULE: No crown is too broad for me!

HAAKON: A man must be called by God before he can wear a crown.

DUKE SKULE: And you are sure that God has called you?

HAAKON: I know he has.

DUKE SKULE: Very well, then. Let us fight, man against man, sword against sword, to the death!

HAAKON: Blind man! I pity you. Can't you see that it is your own pride that lures you towards the throne, not God's calling? What is it that tempts you? The golden circlet, the purple cloak, the right to sit with your chair three inches above the floor? They are nothing, nothing! If *that* were to be King, I would toss the kingdom into your hat as I throw a penny to a beggar. You have all the gifts of the mind—shrewdness, and courage. But you were born to stand next to the King, not to be King yourself.

DUKE SKULE: That is what we shall prove!

HAAKON: In all the years you ruled the country for me, name me one deed that you accomplished worthy of a King! The land was harried by rebel factions, but did you bring a single one to heel? Yet you were the mature man. I was young and inexperienced when I took power, but they all submitted to me. There are no rebels left.

DUKE SKULE: That is the last thing you should boast about, for therein lies your greatest danger. Party must vie with party, interest with interest, district with district, if the King is to stay powerful. Every region, every faction must either need the King, or fear him. If you root out all dissension, you undermine your power.

HAAKON: How can you hold a belief like that and think yourself fitted to rule? Fifty years ago, you could have been a worthy chieftain; but that time is past. Don't you see that the kingdom of Norway is like a church that has still to be consecrated? The walls stand high on strong foundations, the vaulted roof spans wide, the spire points upwards like a forest pine; but there is no life in it, no beating heart, no blood pulsing in its veins. God's spirit has not breathed into it. *I* shall consecrate our country. Norway has been a kingdom; it shall become a people! The men of Trondhjem warred with the men of the Vik, the men of Bergen with those of Oslo; henceforth all shall be one, and shall rejoice in their unity! That is the task which God has set upon my shoulders; that is the promise of our land, the mission of future Kings. And it is a task which you, my lord, would never accomplish; for, to speak plainly, you have not the gift for it.

DUKE SKULE *(bewildered):* Unite—? Unite all Norway? *(Incredulously.)* But that's impossible! Such a thing has never been known, even in legend!

HAAKON: For *you* it is impossible. You can only re-tell the old sagas. But for me it is as easy as for the hawk to cleave the clouds.

DUKE SKULE *(uneasily moved):* To unite the whole people—to make them know they are one? Where did you find such a thought? It freezes my blood, and sets my soul aflame! *(Bursts out)* You have it from the Devil, Haakon! It shall never be done, as long as I have the strength to set a helm upon my brow!

HAAKON: The idea is from God, and I shall not abandon it as long as I wear St. Olaf's crown.

DUKE SKULE: Then the crown must fall!

HAAKON: By whose hand?

DUKE SKULE: Mine, if no other. Haakon! Do not tempt God! Do not drive me to the brink of the abyss!

HAAKON *(points to the door):* Go, my lord. And let us forget that we spoke with sharp tongues tonight.

DUKE SKULE (*looks at him proudly for a moment, and says*): We shall speak with sharper tongues when next we meet. (*Goes out upstage.*)

HAAKON (*after a short pause*): He cannot mean to threaten me. He is overwrought. He must, he shall obey me. I need that strong arm and that shrewd brain. God has given him those gifts that he may serve me. To defy me is to defy Heaven.

DAGFINN (*enters upstage*): My lord, be on your guard tonight. I fear the Duke intends some mischief.

HAAKON: What?

DAGFINN: I don't know; but I saw him whispering to Paul Flida and Gregorius. I am sure something is afoot.

HAAKON: Can he be planning to attack us? Impossible, impossible.

DAGFINN (*goes to the window and looks out*): He is going on board his ship. They are hoisting sail.

HAAKON: Go and find out what is happening.

DAGFINN *goes.*

HAAKON: It's unthinkable. He would never rebel. God would not allow it. I must have peace now, peace to begin my work. I hear God's urgent voice crying within me: "Thou shalt achieve a mighty deed for Norway!"

GREGORIUS JONSSON (*enters upstage*): My lord and King!

HAAKON: Gregorius! You?

GREGORIUS JONSSON: I come to offer myself as your liegeman. Thus far I have followed the Duke. Now I dare follow him no longer.

HAAKON: What has happened?

GREGORIUS JONSSON: Something no man will believe—

HAAKON: Speak, speak!

GREGORIUS JONSSON: I dread to hear the sound of my own words. Know then—! (*Takes him by the arm and whispers.*)

HAAKON *(starts back with a cry):* What? You are mad!

GREGORIUS JONSSON: Would to God I were!

HAAKON: Impossible! It cannot be—!

GREGORIUS JONSSON: By the precious blood of Christ, it is.

HAAKON: Go, go. Bid them sound the trumpets. Call my bodyguard! Summon all my men!

GREGORIUS JONSSON *goes.*

HAAKON *(walks up and down several times, then goes quickly over to the door of* MARGARET's *bedchamber, knocks, walks up and down a couple more times, goes back to the door, knocks again and cries):* Margaret! *(He continues to pace to and fro.)*

MARGARET *(appears in the doorway to her room, dressed for bed, with her hair half down. About her shoulders she wears a red cloak, which she clasps tight across her breast):* Haakon! Is it you?

HAAKON: Yes, yes. Come in here.

MARGARET: Then you mustn't look at me. I'd just gone to bed.

HAAKON: You are wise, Margaret. I need your counsel.

MARGARET: What has happened?

HAAKON: I have just heard the worst news that ever reached my ears.

MARGARET *(alarmed):* What news?

HAAKON: There are two Kings in Norway now.

MARGARET: Two Kings—? Haakon, where is my father?

HAAKON: He has proclaimed himself King on board his ship. He is sailing to Nidaros to be crowned.

MARGARET: Oh, Almighty God—! *(Sinks down on the couch, covers her face with her hands, and weeps.)*

HAAKON: Two Kings in the land!

MARGARET: My husband one—and my father the other!

HAAKON *(paces restlessly up and down):* What shall I do, Margaret? Cross the mountains, get there before him, and prevent the coronation? No, impossible. He is stronger than I in the north. I have too few men for that. What shall I do? How can I kill him before he gets there?

MARGARET (*pleadingly, with clasped hands*): Haakon, Haakon!

HAAKON: Why does God chastise me like this? Skule is the most dangerous enemy I could have. I must kill him! Help me, Margaret. Help me to think of a way to kill him!

MARGARET (*sobs violently*): He is my father!

HAAKON (*stops suddenly*): Yes. Your father. I had forgotten.

MARGARET *weeps passionately.* HAAKON *slowly approaches her.*

HAAKON (*gently*): Don't cry, Margaret. Comfort yourself. (*Raises her and holds her.*) Why should you suffer for this madness? I ask why God punishes me—and I have my answer. I have sinned grievously against you. I have shunned your feelings, and closed my heart to you—you, who have given me so much love. Forgive me, Margaret. I need you. I need your warmth and light—

MARGARET (*throws her arms around his neck*): Oh, Haakon, my beloved husband! Am I near to you at last?

HAAKON: Yes, yes. Now you stand close to me. Not to give me wise counsel, but to light my path. If there are two Kings in Norway, there is only one in Heaven. And He will guide us.

ACT FOUR

Scene One

The great hall in Oslo Palace. KING SKULE *is feasting with his* MEN-AT-ARMS *and his* CHIEFTAINS. *Downstage left stands the high seat, on which* KING SKULE *sits, richly robed, with a purple cloak and a crown on his head. The supper table, at which the* GUESTS *are seated, stretches upstage from the high seat. Opposite* SKULE *sit* PAUL FLIDA *and* BAARD BRATTE. *Some of the humbler guests are standing on the right. It is late evening; the hall is brightly lit. The feast is drawing towards its close. The* GUESTS *are merry and partly drunk. They toast each other, laugh and converse. The bard* JATGEIR *is singing a ballad in the middle of the room.*

JATGEIR *(sings):*

> . . . And this is sure. Since the days of yore
> Was never so fierce a fight.
> The plain, like warriors' winding-sheets,
> Grew red, that had been white.
>
> And ere the battle yet was won,
> They fled, the Birchlegs bold.

But many could not turn and run,
For they lay and were icy cold.

Where Haakon hides no man can state.
King Skule holds fort and town.
Hail, King! Long, long mayst thou be great,
And wear proud Norway's crown!

SKULE'S MEN *(jump to their feet cheering, raise their cups and goblets above their heads, clash their swords and repeat):*

Hail, King! Long, long mayst thou be great,
And wear proud Norway's crown!

KING SKULE: Thank you for your song, good Jatgeir. I like a song that praises warriors.

JATGEIR: To praise your warriors is to praise you, Your Majesty.

KING SKULE: Take this bracelet as a reward. Stay with me, and be my friend. I would have many poets about me.

JATGEIR: They will be needed, my lord, if songs are to be written in praise of all your great deeds.

KING SKULE: I shall be thrice as bountiful as Haakon. Poets shall be rewarded as richly as warriors while I am King. Sit; you are now a courtier. All that you need shall be freely given you.

JATGEIR *(sits):* Your Majesty will soon run short of what I need most.

KING SKULE: What is that?

JATGEIR: Enemies, whose flight and fall I may celebrate.

MANY OF THE GUESTS *(amid laughter and applause):* Well spoken, Icelander!

JATGEIR: I promise you, my lord, I shall compose a great ode to you when you kill the Sleeper.

KING SKULE: The Sleeper?

JATGEIR: That is what they have called Haakon ever since

you beat him at Laaka. He has lain in Nidaros like a man paralysed.

BAARD BRATTE: With his eyes closed, they say. I suppose he's dreaming that he is still King!

KING SKULE: Let him dream. He will never dream himself back to the throne.

PAUL FLIDA: They say he has renounced the Church and all that is holy. He refused to attend mass on New Year's Day.

BAARD BRATTE: He had a good excuse. He spent the whole day chopping up his silver plates and cups—he had nothing else to pay his men with!

Laughter and loud comments from the GUESTS.

KING SKULE: I drink to you, Baard Bratte, and I thank you, and all my new men. You fought bravely for me at Laaka.

BAARD BRATTE: We soon found how easy it was to conquer with such a chieftain riding at our head. It was a pity we killed so many of them. I fear it will be a long time before they show their faces again.

KING SKULE: Wait till the spring comes. When they think they are strong enough, we shall hear from them.

BAARD BRATTE: They won't dare.

KING SKULE: Then we shall lure them out by guile.

MANY VOICES: Yes, yes!

BAARD BRATTE: You have a good store of cunning, King Skule. Your enemies never know where you are until you are upon them. You will enter Nidaros in triumph, Your Majesty, and this time the monks will not dare refuse to bring the shrine from the church. You will be proclaimed beside it in the market-place, and then you will be King of all Norway.

KING SKULE: But the shrine must be brought out. My coronation must be lawful. (*Turns to his* MEN.) My good men, I make you all a promise. After our next battle, each of you shall have the weapons and clothes, the gold and silver, the land and the inheritance of the men he kills; and he shall take the title that his victim held. He who kills a knight shall become a knight—he who kills a judge shall take the judge's seat upon the bench—

THE MEN *(leap to their feet in wild excitement)*: Hail, hail, King Skule! Lead us against the Birchlegs!

BAARD BRATTE: Now you are sure of victory!

KING SKULE: Go to your beds now, my good men. We have sat late at the tables tonight.

MAN-AT-ARMS *(as the others prepare to go)*: Tomorrow we'll cast lots for the Birchlegs' goods!

ANOTHER: No, let's grab what we can get.

There is a babble of excited disagreement as they go out.

BAARD BRATTE: Now the wolves are fighting for the bear's pelt.

PAUL FLIDA: Before they have killed him.

They all go out upstage except KING SKULE.

KING SKULE *(waits till his GUESTS are gone. Then his face relaxes, and he sinks down on one of the benches)*: How tired I am! Tired to death! Day in and day out to stand amidst this crowd, smiling as though I were certain of my cause, and without one friend in whom I can confide my fears. *(Rises in terror.)* Haakon sent his army against me. And the impossible happened—Haakon lost, and I won! And yet I am still afraid. When the question comes to me unawares: "Which of us is the rightful King?", my heart always answers "he", and never "I". To see myself as King I have to use art, build a throne of imagination, a crown of dreams—I have to chase away memories, and possess faith by force. *Why?* Is it because the Bishop burned the letter? No—that only made my doubt eternal—it did not increase it. *(Sits, right.)* Then what *is* it? Ha, that's strange—it dances on the tip of my tongue, like a forgotten word. *(Jumps up.)* Ah—now I remember! "Norway has been a kingdom—it shall become a people. All shall be one, and shall rejoice in their unity!" Since Haakon spoke those madman's words, I see him clearly as the rightful King. *(Stares vacantly in anguish, and whispers)* Did those words reveal God's calling? Has He chosen Haakon to be His prophet?

PAUL FLIDA *(enters upstage):* Your Majesty, I have news.

KING SKULE: News?

PAUL FLIDA: A man from down the fjord says the Birchlegs have put out to sea, and that many strangers have entered Oslo during the last few days.

KING SKULE: We will deal with them. Tomorrow, perhaps.

PAUL FLIDA: My lord, perhaps they are planning to surprise us.

KING SKULE: We shall beat them, as we did at Laaka.

PAUL FLIDA: My lord, it is not so easy to beat the Birchlegs twice in succession.

KING SKULE: Why not?

PAUL FLIDA: Because our country's saga tells us that such a thing has never happened before. Should I not send scouts to Head Isle?

KING SKULE: There is no need. It is a dark night, and misty.

PAUL FLIDA: Well, Your Majesty knows best. But remember, the citizens of Oslo hate you, and if the Birchlegs come they will make common cause with them.

KING SKULE *(on an impulse):* Paul Flida, isn't it possible that the people of Oslo might support me?

PAUL FLIDA *(looks at him amazed and shakes his head):* No, my lord, that is unthinkable.

KING SKULE: Why?

PAUL FLIDA: Because the people of Trondhjem are on your side.

KING SKULE: I want to have both!

PAUL FLIDA: No, my lord, that is impossible.

KING SKULE: Unthinkable—impossible! Why? Why shouldn't they?

PAUL FLIDA: Because the people of Trondhejm are the people of Trondhejm, and the men of Oslo are the men of Oslo, and because the sagas tell us that that is so, and because it has always been so.

KING SKULE: Yes, yes. You are right. Go.

PAUL FLIDA: Shall I not send scouts?

KING SKULE: Wait till daybreak. *(PAUL FLIDA goes.)* The sagas of Norway tell us that it is so, and it has always been so. He answers me as I answered Haakon. Has God given Haakon the power to see what I cannot see? *(Pause. He walks broodingly up and down; then stops.)* Can a man rob another of that power, as he can take arms and gold from the enemy he has slain? Can a pretender put on the divine calling like a purple cloak? Can the oak felled for ship's timber say: "I shall be the mast, I shall perform the task of the pine, point straight and shining towards the sky, fly a golden pennant at my head, arch in the sunshine with my white, bellying sails and be seen by people far, far away?" No, no, old heavy, knotted oak—your place is beneath the keel; you must lie there and do your duty, silent and unseen. Your task is to keep the ship from heeling over when the storm comes. The mast with the golden pennant and the bellying sails shall carry it forward towards the new, towards the unknown, towards the strange shore and the saga that is to come! *(Passionately.)* Since Haakon spoke of his great ideal, I can think of nothing else. Why should I not make it mine and fulfil it myself? *(Pensively.)* If it is beyond my power, why do I love it so?

JATGEIR *(enters upstage):* Forgive me, Your Majesty—

KING SKULE: You are welcome, poet.

JATGEIR: I thought it my duty to tell you—there are rumours in the town—

KING SKULE: Tell me, poet. You have travelled far and wide—have you ever seen a woman love a child that was not her own? Love it with her heart and soul?

JATGEIR: Only women with no children of their own do that.

KING SKULE: Only those?

JATGEIR: Especially women who are barren.

KING SKULE: Barren? Do they?

JATGEIR: Often.

KING SKULE: And does a barren woman ever kill someone else's child because she has none of her own?

JATGEIR: Oh, yes. But that's a foolish thing to do.

KING SKULE: Why foolish?

JATGEIR: Because then she gives the other woman something priceless. The gift of sorrow.

KING SKULE: Is that so precious?

JATGEIR: Yes, my lord.

KING SKULE (*looks earnestly at him*): There seem to dwell two men in you, Icelander. When you sit among the warriors at a feast, you draw cap and cloak over every thought. But when a man is alone with you, you seem the kind of man one would choose to have as a friend. Why is this?

JATGEIR: When you go to swim in the river, my lord, you do not undress where the people walk to church. You seek out a lonely place.

KING SKULE: Of course.

JATGEIR: My soul is shy. So I do not bare it when the hall is full.

KING SKULE: Hm. (*Short pause.*) Tell me, Jatgeir, how did you come to be a singer? From whom did you learn your art?

JATGEIR: The art of song cannot be learned, my lord.

KING SKULE: Then how did you acquire it?

JATGEIR: I received the gift of sorrow, and found myself a singer.

KING SKULE: Is that what a singer needs?

JATGEIR: I needed sorrow. Others may need faith—or joy—or doubt—

KING SKULE: Doubt too?

JATGEIR: Yes. But then he who doubts must be strong.

KING SKULE: And whom would you call a weak doubter?

JATGEIR: He who doubts his own doubt.

KING SKULE *(slowly):* That sounds to me like death.

JATGEIR: It is worse. It is twilight.

KING SKULE *(suddenly, as though casting aside his thoughts):* Where is my sword? I want to fight—not think. What did you come to tell me?

JATGEIR: The people at the inn are whispering among themselves. They ask if we are quite sure that King Haakon is still hiding in the west. They're pleased about something.

KING SKULE: The people of Oslo have always been against me.

JATGEIR: They mock you because the monks refused to bring St. Olaf's holy shrine out of the church when you were proclaimed. They say it is an evil omen.

KING SKULE: Next time I sail to Nidaros, the shrine shall be brought out. It shall stand in the square for all to see, if I have to batter the church to rubble!

JATGEIR: That will be a great deed. But I shall write a poem to match it.

KING SKULE: Have you many unsung poems in your head, Jatgeir?

JATGEIR: No. But I have many that are unborn. One by one they are freed, and so take life.

KING SKULE: If I had you killed, would all those unborn poems die within you?

JATGEIR: My lord, it is a sin to kill a beautiful thought.

KING SKULE: I am not asking if it is a sin. I am asking if it could be done.

JATGEIR: I do not know.

KING SKULE: Have you never had another poet as your friend, and has he never told you of a great and noble poem that he wished to write?

JATGEIR: Yes, my lord.

KING SKULE: Didn't you wish you could kill him, so that you might steal his thought and write the poem yourself?

JATGEIR: My lord, I am not barren. I have children of my own. I do not need to covet those of other men. *(Turns to go.)*

KING SKULE: Jatgeir! *(JATGEIR stops.)* Who gave you the gift of sorrow?

JATGEIR: The one I loved.

KING SKULE: She died?

JATGEIR: No. She played me false.

KING SKULE: And so you became a poet?

JATGEIR: Yes. I became a poet.

KING SKULE *(grips him by the arm):* What gift do *I* need to become King?

JATGEIR: Not the gift of doubt, or you would not have asked.

KING SKULE: What gift do I need?

JATGEIR: My lord, you *are* King.

KING SKULE: Are you always sure that you are a poet?

JATGEIR *(looks at him silently for a moment, then asks):* Have you never loved?

KING SKULE: Yes, once. Passionately, beautifully—sinfully.

JATGEIR: You have a wife.

KING SKULE: I took her because I wanted a son.

JATGEIR: But you have a daughter, my lord. A gentle and noble daughter.

KING SKULE: If my daughter had been a son, I would not have asked you what gift I needed. *(Passionately.)* I must have someone by me who will obey me instinctively, be-

202

lieve in me unflinchingly, stand close by me through good days and evil, live only to give light and warmth to my life—someone who, when I fall, must die! What shall I do, Jatgeir?

JATGEIR: Buy a dog, my lord.

PAUL FLIDA *(runs in):* To arms, Your Majesty! Haakon is lying off Elkness with all his fleet!

KING SKULE: Off Elkness! He has made good speed.

JATGEIR: To arms, my lord! If there is to be killing here tonight, I will gladly be the first to die for you!

KING SKULE: Can you not live for me? Be a son to me—live for my life-work, and believe in me!

JATGEIR: A man can die for another's life-work. But if he is to go on living, he must live for his own. *(Goes.)*

PAUL FLIDA *(impatiently):* What are your orders, my lord? The Birchlegs will be in Oslo within an hour!

KING SKULE: We must go to blessed Thomas Becket's grave. He has helped many souls in their hour of need.

PAUL FLIDA *(more loudly):* My lord! I tell you the Birchlegs are upon us!

KING SKULE: Let all the churches be opened. We must seek sanctuary.

PAUL FLIDA: My lord! You have the chance to destroy your enemies at a blow! This is no time to speak of churches!

KING SKULE: Yes, yes. Keep all the churches open.

PAUL FLIDA: Haakon will violate the sanctuary!

KING SKULE: No. God will guard him against such a sin. God always guards Haakon.

PAUL FLIDA *(takes him aside and whispers):* My lord, the men will hear you. They will ask: "Who is King in this land?"

KING SKULE *(smiles sadly):* Yes, Paul Flida, that is the great question. Who is King in this land?

PAUL FLIDA *(pleadingly):* You are sick tonight, my lord. Let me act for you.

KING SKULE: Yes, yes, do so.

PAUL FLIDA (*going towards the door*): First we must burn all the bridges.

KING SKULE: Madman! Stop! Burn all the bridges? Don't you know what that means? Beware of doing that!

PAUL FLIDA: Every second is precious now, Your Majesty! (*Seizes his hand.*) King Skule, let us burn all the bridges, fight like wolves and trust in Heaven!

KING SKULE (*whispers*): Heaven will not trust me. I dare not trust in Heaven.

PAUL FLIDA: Our saga has been short, King Skule. (*Goes out upstage.*)

KING SKULE: A hundred wise heads, a thousand armed men—these I command. But not one loyal and loving heart. Such is the poverty of Kings.

> SKULE *sits down pensively right. After a few moments, a* WOMAN IN BLACK *enters. She is wearing a long cloak, a hood and a thick veil which hides her face. A* PRIEST *enters after her and remains by the door.*

KING SKULE: Who are you?

WOMAN: One whom you loved.

KING SKULE (*shakes his head*): Who are you, I ask?

WOMAN: One who loves you.

KING SKULE: Then you must have come from the dead.

WOMAN (*comes closer and whispers passionately*): Skule Baardsson!

KING SKULE (*rises with a cry*): Ingeborg!

INGEBORG: You know me now, Skule?

KING SKULE: Ingeborg—Ingeborg!

INGEBORG: Oh, let me look at you! For a long, long time! (*Clasps his hands. Pause.*) How I loved you! Why were you false to me?

KING SKULE: Take off your veil. Look at me with those eyes which were once as clear and as blue as Heaven.

INGEBORG: Those eyes have been a clouded Heaven these twenty years. You would not recognise them; and you will never see them again.

KING SKULE: But your voice is still fresh, and soft, and young, as it used to be.

INGEBORG: I have only used it to whisper your name, to impress your greatness on a young heart, and to pray to the God of mercy to forgive us for our sinful love. That is why my voice is still young.

KING SKULE: A lifetime lies between us. I have put aside every memory of that fair time. Yet you have stayed in the cold loneliness of the north, keeping those memories.

INGEBORG: They have been my happiness.

KING SKULE: And I left you, to win power and riches. If you had stayed by my side, how much easier things might have been—!

INGEBORG: God prevented it. My soul needed a great sin, to turn it towards remorse and penitence.

KING SKULE: And now—?

INGEBORG: I come to you a widow.

KING SKULE: Your husband is dead?

INGEBORG: He took my guilt upon his strong and loving shoulders. He went to fight in the Holy Land, and died on the road from Jerusalem, bleeding for my sins.

KING SKULE *(quietly):* Did he know everything?

INGEBORG: From the first. Bishop Nicholas knew, too, for I confessed to him.

KING SKULE: And why do you come to me now?

INGEBORG: To make the final sacrifice.

KING SKULE: What do you mean?

INGEBORG *(points to the* PRIEST *standing by the door):* There he is. Peter, my son, come here.

KING SKULE: Your son—?

INGEBORG: And yours, King Skule.

KING SKULE: Ingeborg!

PETER *comes to them, silent and bewildered, and kneels before* KING SKULE.

INGEBORG: Take him. He has been the light and comfort of my life for twenty years. Now you are Norway's King. The King's son must enter into his inheritance. I have no right to him any longer.

KING SKULE *(raises him joyfully):* Come to my heart! Oh, I have longed for you so burningly! *(Embraces him tightly, releases him, looks at him for a moment, and embraces him again.)* My son! My son! I have a son! *(Roars with laughter.)* Who can withstand me now? *(Goes across to* INGEBORG *and clasps her hand.)* You will not take back your word, Ingeborg?

INGEBORG: Bishop Nicholas enjoined me to make this sacrifice. He sent him to me from his deathbed, imploring this penance for all my sins.

KING SKULE: Then our sin is wiped out; and now he is mine alone!

INGEBORG: Yes. But I ask one promise of you.

KING SKULE: Ask what you will!

INGEBORG: I give him into your hands, as pure as the lamb of God. But the path that leads to the throne is dangerous. Do not let his soul be stained! You hear, King Skule? Do not let my son's soul be corrupted!

KING SKULE: I promise and swear it.

INGEBORG *(clasps his arm):* Let him rather die!

KING SKULE: He shall rather die. I swear it.

INGEBORG: Then I can go north to my home in peace. Beg God to call me; and when we meet before God, he will come to his mother pure and unstained.

KING SKULE: Pure and unstained.

INGEBORG *(to herself):* To love, to sacrifice everything, and to be forgotten. That has been my saga. *(Goes silently out upstage.)*

KING SKULE *(turns to* PETER*)*: Let me look at you. Yes, you have your mother's eyes. You are the one I have been needing.

PETER: My father! My great and noble father! Let me live and fight for you! Whatever be your cause, I shall know that I am fighting for what is right.

KING SKULE: You shall renounce your vows and march beside me. The King's son must carry a sword.

PETER: We will go forward together!

KING SKULE *(clasps him to him)*: Yes, together! And when we have gained the kingdom, it shall be yours after me. Peter, my son—listen! You and I shall perform a noble deed for Norway. We shall awake the people and unite them. North and south, mountains and valleys—all shall become one mighty people, and then our country shall grow great!

PETER: Through the great thought of a great King!

KING SKULE: Do you grasp it?

PETER: Yes—yes! Clearly!

KING SKULE: And you believe in it?

PETER: Yes! Yes—because I believe in you!

KING SKULE *(passionately)*: Haakon Haakonsson shall die!

Distant trumpets are heard.

PAUL FLIDA *(enters and cries)*: Our hour has struck, King Skule! The Birchlegs are swarming in thousands down from the hills!

KING SKULE: Sound the trumpets! Call the men to arms! How shall we meet them?

PAUL FLIDA: All the churches stand open for us.

KING SKULE: The churches—? But the Birchlegs—?

PAUL FLIDA: All the bridges stand open for them.

KING SKULE: Accursed man, what have you done?

PAUL FLIDA: Obeyed my King.

KING SKULE: My son, my son! I have cast away your kingdom!

PETER: No! You will win! So great an idea cannot die!

Scene Two

A street in Oslo. On either side, low wooden houses with porches. In the background lies St. Hallvard's churchyard, enclosed by a high wall with a gate. To the left, at the end of the wall, can be seen the church, the door of which is standing open. It is still night; gradually, the day begins to dawn. The alarm bell is ringing. Far away to the right can be heard distant war-cries and confused alarums.

KING SKULE'S TRUMPETER *(enters right, sounds his trumpet and cries):* To arms! To arms, all King Skule's men! More is at stake here than life and death! To arms! *(He sounds his trumpet again and goes on. After a few moments he is heard sounding his trumpet and shouting in the next street.)*

A WOMAN *(comes out of a house on the right):* Merciful God! What's happening?

A CITIZEN *(emerges half-dressed from a house on the other side of the street):* The Birchlegs are in the town! Now God will punish Skule for all he has done!

2ND CITIZEN *(runs down a side street left with several others):* Where are they?

3RD CITIZEN *(from a house on the right):* I don't know.

4TH CITIZEN: They're storming the bridge!

OTHERS: To the bridge! To the bridge! *(They all run out.)*

WOMAN: The Saints preserve us! Is it the Birchlegs?

2ND CITIZEN: It's them all right. King Haakon's with them. His whole fleet's sailing into the harbour. He's already landed with his best men.

1ST CITIZEN: He'll avenge his losses at Laaka!

2ND CITIZEN: I'll wager he will!

1ST CITIZEN: Look! Skule's men are fleeing already!

A CROWD OF KING SKULE'S MEN *enters fleeing from the right.*

ONE OF THEM: Into the church! Into the church! The Birch-legs are fighting like devils from Hell tonight!

They run into the church and close the door from inside.

2ND CITIZEN (*looks away right*): Look! King Haakon's banner! They've taken the bridge!

5TH CITIZEN: They're charging up the hill!

1ST CITIZEN: Look, look! Skule's men are on the run!

More of KING SKULE'S MEN *enter from the right.*

KING SKULE'S MEN: Sanctuary! Sanctuary! To the church! Sanctuary! (*They rush towards the door.*) It is shut! It is shut! They've barred the door!

ONE OF THEM: Up to the mountains, then!

ANOTHER: Where is King Skule?

A THIRD: Yes, where's the King?

THE FIRST: He's abandoned us! Away! There's Haakon's banner!

They flee out left past the church. HAAKON *enters right with his* STANDARD-BEARER, GREGORIUS JONSSON, DAGFINN THE PEASANT *and several others.*

DAGFINN: Do you hear that war-cry? Skule is rallying his men!

1ST CITIZEN: They're behind the churchyard!

2ND CITIZEN: Some are fleeing up the mountain!

DAGFINN: Follow them!

OLD CITIZEN (*shouts from his loft to* HAAKON): Take care,

my dear lord! Skule's men are desperate tonight! They're fighting for their lives!

HAAKON: Is it you, old friend? You fought for my father, and his father.

OLD MAN: Would to God I could fight for you too!

HAAKON: There's no need. Go back to your fireside—you have played your part. The whole town has risen to join me.

DAGFINN (*points over the wall, right*): Here comes the Duke's banner!

GREGORIUS JONSSON: The Duke himself! He's riding on his white charger!

DAGFINN: Don't let him get through the gate!

HAAKON (*to his* TRUMPETER): Blow, blow! (*The* TRUMPETER *blows.*) Dog, you blew louder than that when you played for money on Bergen Bridge!

The TRUMPETER *blows again, louder. Many people come.*

ONE OF SKULE'S MEN (*enters right, fleeing towards the church, pursued by a* BIRCHLEG): Spare my life! Spare my life!

BIRCHLEG: Not if you were sitting on the altar! (*Cuts him down.*) That's a fine cloak you have. I can use that. (*Bends down to take it but utters a cry and flings away his sword.*) My brother! My brother! King Haakon, I have killed my own brother!

HAAKON (*to* DAGFINN): Is it true?

DAGFINN: Yes. I knew them both.

HAAKON (*shaken*): Brother against brother, father against son. Almighty God, let there be an end to this!

GREGORIUS JONSSON: Here comes the Duke!

DAGFINN: Bar the gate against him!

The combatants come into sight within the wall. KING SKULE'S MEN *fight their way towards the left, driving the* BIRCHLEGS *back step by step.* KING SKULE, *his sword drawn, is riding his white charger.* PETER *walks at his side, holding the horse's bridle, a crucifix raised in his left hand.* PAUL FLIDA *is carrying* KING SKULE'*s standard, which is blue with a golden lion rampant, but without the axe.*

KING SKULE: Cut them down! Spare no one! Norway has a new heir to the throne!

HAAKON: Skule Baardsson, let us share the kingdom!

KING SKULE: All or nothing!

HAAKON: Think of your daughter! Think of the Queen!

KING SKULE: I have a son! I have a son!

HAAKON: I have a son too. If I die, he will inherit my crown.

KING SKULE: Kill the Prince, wherever you find him! Kill him on the throne! Kill him on the altar! Kill him, kill him in the Queen's arms!

HAAKON: You have pronounced your own death!

KING SKULE *(hews about him):* Kill, kill! King Skule has a son! Kill, kill! *(The battle moves off left.)*

GREGORIUS JONSSON: They are fighting their way through!

DAGFINN: Only to flee.

GREGORIUS JONSSON: Yes, by Heaven! The other gate is open! They are escaping!

DAGFINN: Up the mountains! *(Shouts)* After them, after them! Avenge our brothers who died at Laaka!

HAAKON: You heard him. He condemned my son. My innocent child, the heir to Norway's crown.

HAAKON'S MEN: We heard him.

HAAKON: And what is the punishment for such a crime?

THE MEN: Death!

HAAKON: Then he too shall die. *(Raises his hand in an oath.)* I hereby swear it. Skule Baardsson shall die, wherever he be met on unconsecrated ground.

DAGFINN: It is every loyal man's duty to kill him.

BIRCHLEG *(from the left):* Duke Skule is fleeing!

CITIZEN: The Birchlegs have won!

HAAKON: Which way?

BIRCHLEG: Up the mountains.

HAAKON: God be thanked for His help! Where is the Queen?

GREGORIUS JONSSON *(points right):* She is here, my lord. See!

HAAKON *(to those nearest him):* My heaviest task is still before me. She loves her father. Listen. No word to her about the danger to her child! Swear to me, all of you, to protect your King's son; but no word to her.

THE MEN *(softly):* We swear.

MARGARET *(enters with* ATTENDANTS *right):* Haakon, my husband! Heaven has protected you! You have won, you are unharmed.

HAAKON: Yes, I have won. Where is our son?

MARGARET: On board your ship, in safe hands.

HAAKON: Go down there, some of you.

Several of the MEN *go.*

MARGARET: Haakon, where is—Duke Skule?

HAAKON: He has fled into the hills.

MARGARET: Then he is alive! Oh, my husband—may I thank God for preserving him?

HAAKON *(struggling with himself):* Listen to me, Margaret. You have been a loyal wife to me. You have followed me in good times and evil, you have given me your love unceasingly. Now I must cause you great grief. I would have avoided it. But I am King, and therefore I *must*—

MARGARET *(tensely):* Is it—the Duke?

HAAKON: Yes. I could suffer no greater punishment than to have to live without you—but if, after what I am going to tell you, you decide that it must be so—if you feel you can no longer stay at my side, no longer look at me without turning pale—well, then we must part, and live alone, and I shall not blame you for it.

MARGARET: Part from you? How can you think of such a thing? Give me your hand—

HAAKON: Do not touch it. I have just raised it in an oath—

MARGARET: An oath?

HAAKON: An oath that sealed a death sentence.

MARGARET *(cries):* My father! Oh, my father! *(Staggers. Two of the* WOMEN *run forward and hold her.)*

HAAKON: Yes, Margaret. As King, I have condemned your father to death. *(Pause.)* If you now decide that we must part, so be it.

MARGARET *(comes closer and says calmly):* We can never part. I am your wife, and nothing else. Only your wife.

HAAKON: Did you hear and understand? I have condemned your father.

MARGARET: I heard and understood. You have condemned my father.

HAAKON: And you do not ask to know his crime?

MARGARET: It is enough that you know.

HAAKON: But I have condemned him to death.

MARGARET *(kneels before the* KING *and kisses his hand):* My husband and most mighty lord, your judgment is just.

ACT FIVE

Scene One

A room in the palace at Nidaros. The entrance door is on the right. Downstage on the same side is a window. On the left, a smaller door. The room is in darkness. PAUL FLIDA, BAARD BRATTE, *and others of* KING SKULE's *principal* CHIEFTAINS *are standing by the window, looking upwards.*

A CHIEFTAIN: How red it glows!

ANOTHER: It covers half the sky, like a flaming sword.

BAARD BRATTE: Blessed St. Olaf, what can such a dreadful sign portend?

OLD WARRIOR: Surely the death of some great chieftain.

PAUL FLIDA: The death of Haakon, my good comrades. He is lying out in the fjord with his fleet. We can expect him tonight. This time, we shall win.

BAARD BRATTE: Don't be too sure. There is little courage in the army now.

OLD WARRIOR: Small wonder. Ever since we fled from Oslo, we have been without a leader. Why has King Skule shut himself away? *(Their eyes turn to the small door.)* Why won't he speak to his men?

1ST CHIEFTAIN: The townspeople don't know whether he is alive or dead.

214

BAARD BRATTE: I have tried to reason with him. It's no use.

PAUL FLIDA: Our lives are at stake. The King must show himself. *(Goes to the door left and knocks.)* Your Majesty, your people need you! You must rouse yourself!

KING SKULE *(from within):* I am sick, Paul Flida.

PAUL FLIDA: You have not eaten for two days.

KING SKULE: I am sick.

PAUL FLIDA: Almighty God, that cannot be helped! King Haakon is in the fjord. He may be upon us any moment!

KING SKULE: Kill him, and kill his child.

PAUL FLIDA: You must lead us, my lord.

KING SKULE: No, no. You are surer of victory without me.

PETER *(enters right, dressed for battle):* The people are restive. They are gathering in front of the palace.

BAARD BRATTE: If the King does not speak to them, they will betray him when he needs them most.

PETER: He must speak to them. *(At the door, left.)* Father! The citizens of Nidaros, your loyallest subjects, will abandon your cause unless you give them courage.

KING SKULE: I cannot give what is not mine.

PETER: Then you cannot give away the kingdom; for it is mine as well as yours!

KING SKULE *(after a pause):* I am coming!

PAUL FLIDA: God be praised!

Pause.

KING SKULE *(appears in the doorway. He is pale and haggard, and his hair is heavily streaked with grey):* Don't look at me. I am sick.

PETER *(goes over to him):* Father!

KING SKULE: Give away your kingdom, did you say? Great God, what has possessed me?

PETER: Forgive me, father—

KING SKULE: No, no! I have been asleep. But now I shall be strong—

215

A LOUD CRY *(outside):* King Skule! King Skule!

KING SKULE: What is that?

BAARD BRATTE *(at the window):* The citizens are gathering. The courtyard is filled with people. You must speak to them!

KING SKULE: Do I look like a King? Can I show myself?

PETER: You must, my noble father!

KING SKULE: So be it. *(Goes to the window and draws back the curtain but lets it go quickly and starts back in terror.)* The sword of fire! It still hangs over me!

PETER: It is an omen. A sword of victory!

KING SKULE: Would it were so! *(Goes to the window, and speaks through it.)* People of Nidaros, what do you want? Here stands your King.

CITIZEN *(outside):* Leave our town! The Birchlegs will burn it and kill us, if they find you here!

KING SKULE: We must stand together. I have been a good King to you. I have asked little from you—

MAN'S VOICE *(from the* CROWD*):* What about the blood that ran at Laaka?

A WOMAN: Give me back my husband!

A BOY: Give me my father and brother!

ANOTHER WOMAN: Give me my three sons, King Skule!

A MAN: He is not King! The monks did not bring out the shrine!

2ND MAN: He has not been proclaimed at the shrine!

3RD MAN: He is not our lawful King!

KING SKULE *(shrinks behind the curtain):* Not lawful—! Not King!

BAARD BRATTE: If the townspeople desert us, we cannot hold Nidaros.

KING SKULE: I am nothing without the shrine.

PETER: Then let it be brought forth, now!

PAUL FLIDA *(shakes his head):* Impossible.

PETER: Nothing is impossible, for his sake! Sound the trumpets, summon the assembly, and bring forth the shrine!

SEVERAL MEN (*shrink back*): Sacrilege!

PETER: It is no sacrilege. If the monks support us—

PAUL FLIDA: They fear the archbishop—

PETER: You call yourselves the King's men, and dare not help him now! My father and my King, the monks *shall* do this! I will beg them, I will entreat them on my knees! Let the trumpets sound! We shall show them who is the lawful King! (*Runs out.*)

KING SKULE (*exultantly*): Did you see him? Did you see my noble son? How his eyes shone! The people will stay with us now! We shall fight and conquer, and end this dreadful war. It is the will of Heaven. (*Points upwards.*) See how God's blazing sword hangs in the stars above our heads! The nights are troubled, women stagger in labour at their prayers, priests rave in the streets proclaiming the Day of Judgment! God is angry. He demands that it be ended. And, by all our holy Saints, it shall!

PAUL FLIDA: What are your orders, sire?

KING SKULE: Burn all the bridges!

PAUL FLIDA (*to a* MAN-AT-ARMS): Bid them burn all the bridges!

The MAN-AT-ARMS *goes out right.*

KING SKULE: Muster my army at the waterside. No man of Haakon's shall set foot in Nidaros!

PAUL FLIDA: Bravely said, my lord!

KING SKULE: Sound the trumpets when the shrine is brought forth. Summon the people.

PAUL FLIDA (*to one of the* MEN): Bid them prepare to sound.

The MAN *goes.*

KING SKULE (*speaks to the* CROWD *beneath from the window*): Hold fast to me, all ye who weep and mourn! Peace

217

and light shall return to our land, as in those first fair days when Haakon was King and the corn flowered twice in every summer! Hold fast to me! Trust and believe in me—I need your trust. I shall watch and fight for you—I shall bleed and fall for you, if God so wills it—but do not abandon me, and do not doubt—! *(A loud cry as though of terror is heard from among the* CROWD.) What is that?

DISTRAUGHT VOICE: Repent, repent!

BAARD BRATTE *(looks out):* It is a priest possessed by the Devil!

PAUL FLIDA: Rending his cassock and scourging himself.

THE VOICE: Repent, repent! The Day of Judgment is come!

MANY VOICES: Blasphemy! Sacrilege!

KING SKULE: What has happened?

BAARD BRATTE: The crowd is shrinking in terror, as though a wild beast had come amongst them.

PAUL FLIDA: They are fleeing—!

KING SKULE *(utters a cry of joy):* No matter! We are saved! Look, look! The shrine is standing in the centre of the courtyard!

PAUL FLIDA: St. Olaf's shrine!

BAARD BRATTE: Yes, by Heaven! There it is!

KING SKULE: The monks are loyal. They have shown their faith—

PAUL FLIDA: Listen! The trumpets!

KING SKULE: Now I shall be lawfully proclaimed.

PETER *(enters right):* Put on your royal robe. The shrine is standing in the courtyard.

KING SKULE: You have saved my kingdom, and yours. We shall reward the pious monks richly for yielding to our entreaties.

PETER: The monks, father? You have nothing to thank the monks for.

KING SKULE: Surely they helped you—?

PETER: They pronounced the Church's curse on any who dared to touch the holy relic.

KING SKULE: The Archbishop, then! He has yielded at last.

PETER: The Archbishop pronounced a heavier curse than the monks. Excommunication.

KING SKULE: Then I still have loyal subjects! Down there, among the common people, I have friends who dared to risk damnation for my sake.

PETER: Not one of them moved a step towards the church.

KING SKULE: Almighty God, then, has a miracle occurred? Who removed the relic?

PETER: I did, father.

KING SKULE *(cries)*: You!

THE MEN *(shrink fearfully)*: Sacrilege!

PAUL FLIDA, BAARD BRATTE *and several of the others go out.*

PETER: There was no other way. I begged, I entreated the monks, but to no avail. So I broke open the church door. No one dared follow me. I leaped on to the high altar, seized the handle of the shrine and set my knees against the wall. It seemed as though some mysterious power gave me more than mortal strength. I wrenched, and the shrine broke loose. I dragged it after me down the aisle, while their curses whispered in the rafters like a storm. I dragged it out of the church. The crowd shrank from me as I came down the steps, and fled as I crossed the courtyard. I reached the centre alone, and as I set down the shrine the handle snapped from the casket. Here it is. *(Holds it up.)*

KING SKULE *(quietly, appalled)*: Sacrilege!

PETER: For your sake! For the sake of your great ideal! You will bring light and peace—a new and shining dawn for

Norway! What does it matter if the night before is stormy? You will wipe out my guilt!

KING SKULE: When your mother brought you to me, I seemed to see a halo about your head. Now God's thunderbolt has withered it.

PETER: Father, father, don't be afraid for my soul! It's your will that I have fulfilled.

KING SKULE: I prayed for you to believe in me, and your faith has become a sin.

PETER (wildly): It was for your sake, for you! God will wash it clean!

KING SKULE: Pure and unstained, I promised Ingeborg. And he blasphemes!

PAUL FLIDA (enters): The city is in an uproar! This dreadful deed has filled your men with terror. They are fleeing into the churches!

KING SKULE: No, no! Bar the doors!

BAARD BRATTE: The people have risen against you! They are killing our soldiers in the streets!

MAN-AT-ARMS (enters): The Birchlegs are sailing up the river!

KING SKULE: Sound the trumpets! Summon my men!

PAUL FLIDA: Impossible. Fear has paralysed them.

KING SKULE (desperately): I cannot fail now! My son must not die with a mortal sin on his head!

PETER: Save yourself!

KING SKULE: Yes, we must flee. Any man who would save his life, follow me!

BAARD BRATTE: Which way?

KING SKULE: Over the bridge!

PAUL FLIDA: All the bridges have been burnt, my lord.

KING SKULE: Burnt—? All the bridges—?

PAUL FLIDA: All. You should have burnt them in Oslo. Then you could have let them stand in Nidaros.

KING SKULE: We must cross the river. Our salvation is at stake!

He and PETER *run out. The rest follow.*

Scene Two

A street. Distant and confused shouting is heard. Cheering CITIZENS *rush across the stage to greet* HAAKON.

HAAKON: Who knows where Skule Baardsson is hiding?

SEVERAL: In one of the churches, my lord.

HAAKON: Are you sure?

CITIZENS: Yes, all his men are seeking sanctuary.

HAAKON *(quietly, to* DAGFINN): He must be found. Set guards on all the churches.

DAGFINN: When we find him, is he to be killed?

HAAKON *(softly):* Killed? Dagfinn, I—!

DAGFINN: My lord, you swore a solemn oath in Oslo.

HAAKON: And every man in Norway will demand his death. *(Turns to* GREGORIUS JONSSON, *and speaks so that the others cannot hear.)* Go. You were once his friend. Find him, and tell him to flee the country.

GREGORIUS JONSSON *(joyfully):* God bless you, my lord—!

HAAKON: For my dear wife's sake.

GREGORIUS JONSSON: But if he will not flee? Or cannot—?

HAAKON: Then in God's name he must die. I cannot break my oath. Go!

GREGORIUS JONSSON: I will do my best. Heaven grant I may succeed! *(Goes out right.)*

HAAKON: Dagfinn, choose trusty men and go down to my ship. You must accompany the Queen and the Prince to St. Stephen's Abbey.

DAGFINN: My lord, will she be safe there?

HAAKON: Nowhere safer. Skule's men have locked themselves in the churches, and she has prayed so often to go there. Her mother will be with her.

DAGFINN: Very good, my lord.

HAAKON: Greet Her Majesty most dearly from me; and the Lady Ragnhild also. Tell them that as soon as our enemies have surrendered and received a royal pardon, all the bells in Nidaros shall be rung, as a sign that peace has returned to our land. *(Goes with his men.)*

CITIZENS: Let us hunt out Skule and kill him ourselves!

ALL: Yes, yes! Find him and kill him! *(Exeunt.)*

Scene Three

A pine forest in the hills above Nidaros. It is moonlight, but the night is misty, so that the background can be glimpsed only indistinctly, and sometimes hardly at all. Tree-stumps and boulders stand around. KING SKULE, PETER, PAUL FLIDA, BAARD BRATTE *and several others enter through the trees left.*

PETER: Sit down and rest, Father.

KING SKULE: Yes, let me rest, rest. *(Sinks down on a stone.)*

PETER: How is it with you?

KING SKULE: I am sick, sick! I see dead men's shadows!

PETER *(jumps up):* Help him! Bring bread for the King!

BAARD BRATTE: Every man is King here. Our lives are at stake. Stand up, Skule Baardsson, if you are King. You cannot rule the land from there!

PETER: I'll kill you if you mock my father!

BAARD BRATTE: We shall all die, unless we can think of a plan to save ourselves.

SOLDIER: Could we reach St. John's Abbey?

PAUL FLIDA: Or St. Stephen's? That is nearer.

BAARD BRATTE *(suddenly exclaims):* No. Let us go down to Haakon's ship and seize his child.

PAUL FLIDA: Are you mad?

BAARD BRATTE: No, no! We could do it. There can't be many men on board. They're all in the town, searching the houses and standing guard on the churches. The bridges are all down, so they won't reckon on any of us being this side of the river. We can take them by surprise, and if we get the Prince in our power, we can ransom him for a royal pardon. Who'll come with me?

SEVERAL: I! I will! I!

PETER: I'll join you when I've seen my father in safe hands.

BAARD BRATTE: We must be clear of the river by daybreak. Here, I know a short cut.

CHIEFTAIN: Put out the torches.

ANOTHER: We must make haste.

> *They go out right.*

PETER (*to* PAUL FLIDA): No word of this to my father. By dawn, we shall have the Prince in our hands.

PAUL FLIDA: What will you do if Haakon will not pardon us?

PETER: Kill the child.

PAUL FLIDA: Kill—!

PETER: It cannot be a sin. He stands in my father's way. Whatever happens, the child must die. Our King has a great plan to fulfil. It matters little who is sacrificed.

PAUL FLIDA: It was an evil day for you when you learned you were King Skule's son. (*Listens.*) Hush! Lie flat on the ground. Someone is coming.

> *They all throw themselves down behind the boulders and tree-stumps. A group of people, some riding and some on foot, is indistinctly glimpsed through the trees. They enter from the left and go out right.*

PETER: It is the Queen.

PAUL FLIDA: Yes, yes! Hush! Listen!

PETER *(after a moment)*: They're going to St. Stephen's Abbey. The Prince is with them!

PAUL FLIDA: And the Queen's women.

PETER: But only four men. Rise, rise, King Skule! Your kingdom is saved!

KING SKULE: My kingdom? It is dark—like the kingdom of the angel who rebelled against God.

A group of MONKS *enters right.*

A MONK: Who is there? Are you King Skule's men?

PAUL FLIDA: King Skule himself.

MONK *(to* SKULE*)*: God be praised that we have found you, my dear lord! We heard you had taken to the hills. We have brought monks' clothing for you and your men. Put them on, and you will gain entry to St. Stephen's Abbey. There you can beg Haakon for pardon.

KING SKULE: Yes, give me a cassock. I and my son must seek refuge on consecrated ground. Take us to the abbey—

PETER *(whispers to* PAUL FLIDA*)*: See that my father gets there safely—

PAUL FLIDA: Have you forgotten there are Birchlegs there?

PETER: Only four men. You can easily deal with them, and once you are inside they won't dare to touch you. I'll go and fetch Baard Bratte.

PAUL FLIDA: Think what you are doing!

PETER: It is not in the King's ship, but at St. Stephen's Abbey, that we outlaws shall save the kingdom for my father. *(Runs out right.)*

SOLDIER *(whispers to* ANOTHER*)*: Are you going to the abbey with Skule?

2ND SOLDIER: Hush! No. The Birchlegs are there.

MONK: Let us go two by two—every monk with a soldier—

ANOTHER MONK *(seated on a tree-stump behind the others)*: I will take King Skule.

KING SKULE: Do you know the way?

MONK: The broad way.

1ST MONK: Hurry! Let us take different paths, and meet outside the abbey gate.

> *They go out through the trees, right. The mist lifts, and the comet is revealed, red and shining in the hazy air.*

KING SKULE: Peter my son—! *(Starts.)* Ah—there is the burning sword again!

MONK *(sitting behind him on the tree-stump)*: And here am I.

KING SKULE: Who are you?

MONK: An old acquaintance.

KING SKULE: I never saw a man so pale.

MONK: You don't recognise me?

KING SKULE: You are the one who is to see me safe to the abbey.

MONK: I am the one who will see you safely to the throne.

KING SKULE: Can you do that?

MONK: I can, if you will it so.

KING SKULE: How?

MONK: By the means I used before. I will lead you up on to a high mountain, and show you all the glory of the world.

KING SKULE: I have seen that before. In dreams, that tempted me.

MONK: It was I who gave you those dreams.

KING SKULE: Who are you?

MONK: A messenger from the oldest pretender in the world.

KING SKULE: The oldest pretender in the world?

MONK: From the first Earl who rebelled against the greatest of Kings, and who founded a kingdom himself that shall last until doomsday.

KING SKULE *(screams)*: Bishop Nicholas!

MONK *(rises)*: You know me now? We were friends once.
In the selfsame bark for many a year
We have steered the same course together.

I was afraid when we parted. It was night-time and stormy.
A hawk had fastened its claws in my soul.
I bade them say masses and ring the bells;
I paid the monks to pray and sing.
But still I didn't get in through the gate.

KING SKULE: You've come from—?

MONK: The kingdom beneath the earth;
   That much-maligned kingdom down below.

KING SKULE: Greet your master from me, and thank him for
   the friendship he's shown me. You can tell him he's the
   only King to offer help to Skule the First of Norway.

MONK: Now listen, and I'll tell you why I've been sent.
   This Haakon Haakonsson's no man for us.
   We dislike him. He's always giving us trouble.
   So he must fall and you must reign.
   You alone must wear the crown.

KING SKULE: But how? How?

MONK: At St. Stephen's Abbey the royal Prince sleeps.
   Once you catch him in the web of death
   Your enemies will scatter like dust.
   Then you'll be King. Then you will conquer!

KING SKULE: Are you so sure?

MONK: The whole of Norway is crying for peace,
   And a King is no King without an heir;
   A son, to inherit his father's throne.
   Rise up, King Skule! The deed must be done
   Tonight! Either you or he must fall!
   Already it's growing light in the north.
   Look! Around us the mist is lifting.
   The ships are gathering noiselessly;
   The earth rings hollow with tramping feet.
   All this is yours if you say the word.
   A thousand warriors to march behind you,
   And a thousand shining sails to carry you!

KING SKULE: What must I say?

MONK: To stand on the topmost rung of the ladder
You have but to do what your heart commands.
The land and all it contains shall be yours
If your son succeeds you as King of Norway.

KING SKULE *(raises his hand as though in an oath):* My son
shall—! *(Stops suddenly and cries in terror)* A church-
robber! All power to him? Ah, now I understand you!
You want our country to be damned! Get away from me,
get away from me! *(Stretches his hands towards heaven.)*
O Thou, have mercy upon me now, when I cry unto Thee
for help in my hour of greatest need! *(Falls to the
ground.)*

MONK: Ah, well.
I'm not in a hurry. *Perpetuum mobile . . . !*
My power is assured for generations;
I shall always rule those who fear the light.
They will all be my faithful subjects here.

    Comes downstage.

When my good people pursue their ends,
Will-lessly wandering, knowing not whither,
With puckered hearts and grovelling souls,
As weak as willows before the wind,
Agreed on only one thing in the world;
That everything great must be brought low—
The mark of meanness their only banner,
And honour an outcast from their doors—
Then Bishop Nicholas rules in men's hearts!
The faithful Bishop pursuing his calling.

    He disappears through the trees into the mist.

KING SKULE *(after a few moments, half-raises himself from
the ground and looks around):* Where is he, my dark
counsellor? *(Jumps to his feet.)* Guide, guide, where are
you? Gone. No matter. Now I know my way, both to St.
Stephen's Abbey, and beyond. *(Goes out right.)*

Scene Four

St. Stephen's Abbey. On the left stands the chapel, with a door opening into the cloister. Its windows are illuminated. Along the opposite side of the cloister stretch several smaller buildings. In the background is the abbey wall, with a heavy gate which is shut. It is a clear, moonlit night. Three BIRCHLEG CHIEFTAINS *are standing at the gate.* MARGARET, THE LADY RAGNHILD *and* DAGFINN THE PEASANT *enter from the chapel.*

RAGNHILD *(half to herself)*: No, no, it cannot be! King Skule would never beg for mercy!

MARGARET: Calm yourself, dearest mother.

RAGNHILD: They cannot condemn him to death. He is the King. God will punish you for letting it come to this!

MARGARET: You don't know what you are saying. It is your grief that speaks.

RAGNHILD: Hear me, you Birchlegs! It was Haakon who begged the King for mercy! It was Haakon who pleaded for his life!

MARGARET: She is distraught—

RAGNHILD: King Skule will sit on the throne again. And when he does, beware!

MARGARET: Peace, peace!

RAGNHILD *(to* MARGARET*)*: And you can love this usurper! Are you your father's child? May God punish you for your loyalty to this man of blood!

MARGARET: Mother! *(Moves towards her.)*

RAGNHILD: Get away! Keep away from me! I must search the churches and find my husband. Open the door! I must go to Nidaros!

MARGARET: Mother, in God's blessed name—!

There is a loud banging on the abbey gate.

DAGFINN: Who's knocking?

KING SKULE *(outside):* A King.

DAGFINN: Skule Baardsson!

RAGNHILD: King Skule!

MARGARET: My father!

KING SKULE: Open, open!

DAGFINN: There is no place here for outlaws.

KING SKULE: It is a King who knocks, I say! A King without shelter.

MARGARET: Dagfinn, Dagfinn, he is my father!

DAGFINN *(goes to the gate and opens it a fraction):* How many men have you?

KING SKULE: All who stayed loyal in my hour of need.

DAGFINN: How many is that?

KING SKULE: Less than one.

MARGARET: He is alone, Dagfinn!

RAGNHILD: May the wrath of Heaven smite you, if you refuse him entry! This is consecrated ground!

DAGFINN: In God's name, then.

He opens the gate. The BIRCHLEGS *reverently bare their heads.* KING SKULE *enters the cloister.*

MARGARET *(embraces him):* Father! My blessed, unhappy father!

RAGNHILD *(passionately places herself between him and the* BIRCHLEGS*):* Do not go near him! Do not dare touch him! You pretend to honour him, but you will betray him like Judas!

DAGFINN: He is safe here, on holy ground.

MARGARET: Did no one stay with you?

KING SKULE: The monks and soldiers kept me company on the road. But they stole away from me, one by one. Paul Flida was the last to leave me. He came as far as the ab-

bey gate. There he gave me a last embrace, and thanked
me for the days when there were great chieftains in Norway.

DAGFINN *(to the* BIRCHLEGS): My lords, go in and guard the
Prince. I must ride to Nidaros, and tell the King that Skule
Baardsson is here.

MARGARET: Oh, Dagfinn, Dagfinn, can you do this?

DAGFINN: I would be a poor servant of my King and my
country if I did not. *(To the* BIRCHLEGS) Close the gate behind me, guard the child, and do not open to anyone until
the King comes. *(Softly to* SKULE) Farewell, Skule Baardsson—and God grant you a good end.

He goes out through the gate. The BIRCHLEGS *close it
behind him, and go into the chapel.*

RAGNHILD: Let Haakon come. I won't let them take you. I
shall hold you in my arms, and keep them from you.

MARGARET: Oh, how pale you look—and how aged! You're
as cold as death!

KING SKULE: I am not cold. But I am tired, tired.

MARGARET: Then come in, and rest—

KING SKULE: Yes, yes. It will soon be time for me to rest.

SIGRID *(from the chapel):* You have come at last, my
brother!

KING SKULE: Sigrid!

SIGRID: I promised you we would meet when you needed me
in your soul's extremity.

KING SKULE: Where is your child, Margaret?

MARGARET: He is sleeping in the sacristy.

KING SKULE: Then all our house is gathered here tonight.

SIGRID: Yes. We are together after the long years of
straying.

KING SKULE: Now we lack only Haakon Haakonsson.

MARGARET *(clings tightly to him):* Father!

RAGNHILD *(also clings to him):* My husband!

KING SKULE (*looks at them both, moved*): Ragnhild! Margaret! Have you loved me so much? I sought fulfilment in the world outside, and never realised I had a home where I might find it. Oh, Ragnhild, my wife, I have sinned so greatly against you, yet you come to me warm and loving in my hour of need, you tremble and fear for the life of a man who has never cast a glint of sunshine on your road.

RAGNHILD: You—sinned? Oh, Skule, do not speak so. Do you think I would ever dare blame you for that? I have never been worthy of you, my noble husband. You have done no wrong to me.

KING SKULE: Have you believed so steadfastly in me, Ragnhild?

RAGNHILD: From the first day I saw you.

KING SKULE: Oh, you gentle and loving women—it is still good to live! When Haakon comes I will beg for pardon. I will implore him for—!

SIGRID (*fearfully*): Skule, my brother! Beware, if you stray from your path tonight!

A noise without. A moment later, there is a banging on the gate.

MARGARET: Who is that?

RAGNHILD: Who is knocking at the gate?

VOICES (*without*): Citizens of Nidaros! Open up! We know Skule Baardsson is there!

KING SKULE: Yes, he is here! What do you want with him?

SHOUTS (*from without*): Come out, come out! Evil man, you must die!

MARGARET: You dare to threaten him!

A VOICE: King Haakon has condemned him to death!

ANOTHER: It is every man's duty to kill him!

MARGARET: I am the Queen! I command you to leave this place!

231

A VOICE: It is Skule's daughter who speaks, and not the Queen.

ANOTHER: You cannot save him now. The King has condemned him!

RAGNHILD: Go into the chapel, Skule! In God's blessed name, do not let these murderers come near you!

KING SKULE: Yes, into the chapel. My wife, my daughter! At last I have found peace and light. It must not be taken from me so soon! *(Turns to hasten into the chapel.)*

PETER *(outside)*: My father, my King! Victory is in our hands!

KING SKULE *(with a cry)*: Peter! *(Sinks down on the chapel steps.)*

CITIZENS *(outside)*: Look, look! The blasphemer! He is climbing over the roof!

OTHERS: Stone him! Stone him!

> PETER *appears on a roof to the right, and jumps down into the cloister.* SKULE *looks at him in horror.*

PETER *(passionately)*: Where is the Prince?

MARGARET: The Prince?

KING SKULE *(jumps to his feet)*: What do you want with him?

PETER: Baard Bratte and his men are on their way. I told them this was where they would find the Prince.

MARGARET: Oh, God!

KING SKULE: You told them!

PETER *(to MARGARET)*: Where is the Prince, woman?

MARGARET *(standing against the chapel door)*: Asleep in the sacristy.

PETER: I wouldn't care if he was asleep on the altar! I have stolen a shrine from a church, and I am not afraid to steal a prince!

RAGNHILD *(cries to SKULE)*: Is this the son you love?

KING SKULE: He was as pure as the lamb of God when his

mother brought him to me. His faith in me has damned him.

PETER *(not listening to him):* The child must be brought out! Kill him, kill him in his mother's arms! Those were King Skule's words, and a saint could obey them with a clear conscience, for the sake of his great ideal.

CITIZENS *(beating on the gate):* Open up! Come out, blasphemer, or we will burn down the abbey!

KING SKULE *(as though suddenly resolved):* My great ideal! Yes, that is what has poisoned your soul! Pure and unstained I promised to hand you back to her; your belief in me has driven you on from crime to crime, from sin to mortal sin. But I can still save you. I can save us all. *(Calls)* Wait, citizens, wait! I am coming!

MARGARET *(clasps his hand in terror):* Father, what are you going to do?

RAGNHILD *(cries, clinging to him):* Skule!

SIGRID *(tears them from him and cries, joyfully and radiantly):* Let him go, women, let him go! His soul has found wings at last.

KING SKULE *(in a strong, firm voice to PETER):* Peter, listen to me. You saw in me the chosen one of Heaven. The one who would accomplish a mighty deed for Norway. Open your eyes, blind boy, and look at me! These rags of kingship in which I have decked myself are borrowed and stolen. Now I put them off, one by one.

PETER *(in anguish):* My great and noble father, do not speak thus!

KING SKULE: The idea was Haakon's, not mine. He alone was endowed by God to fulfil it. You have believed in a lie. Turn from me now, and save your soul.

PETER *(brokenly):* The idea—Haakon's!

KING SKULE: I yearned to be the greatest man in the land. Oh, God, God! See, I humble myself before Thee, and stand in Thy sight the meanest of all.

PETER: O Lord, take me from this earth! Punish me for all my sins, but take me from this earth, for I am homeless here now. *(Sinks down on the chapel steps.)*

KING SKULE: I had a friend who died for me in Oslo. He said: "A man can die for another's life-work, but if he is to live, he must live for his own." I have no life-work of my own to live for, and I cannot live for Haakon's. But I can die for it.

MARGARET: No, no! Never!

KING SKULE *(takes her hand and looks at her gently):* Do you love your husband, Margaret?

MARGARET: More than anything in the world.

KING SKULE: You could bear to hear him sentence me to death. But could you bear it if he carried out that sentence?

MARGARET: God of Heaven, grant me strength!

KING SKULE: Could you, Margaret?

MARGARET *(quietly shuddering):* No, no. We would have to part. I could never bear to see him again.

KING SKULE: You would shut out the light from his life, and from yours. Don't be afraid, Margaret. You will not have to do it.

RAGNHILD: Flee the country, Skule! I will follow you, no matter where!

KING SKULE *(shakes his head):* With a shadow dividing us and mocking us? I have found you tonight for the first time. No shadow must come between us now, my loyal and gentle wife. We must not meet again, on this earth.

SIGRID: My royal brother! I see you do not need me. You know which way you have to go.

KING SKULE: There are men who were created to live, and men who were created to die. I always longed to go where God's finger did not point for me; and so my way has always been dark. But now I see it clearly. Margaret, look! Look upwards! See how it pales and fades, the flaming sword that has been drawn above me! Yes! God has spoken, and I have understood Him, and His wrath is stilled. My sanctuary is not here. I shall not beg for mercy from an earthly King. I shall enter the great church whose roof is the stars, and beg for mercy and forgiveness from the King of Kings.

MARGARET: Father!

SIGRID: Do not prevent him! Do not oppose the will of God! A dawn is breaking for Norway and for his restless soul! Have not we women hidden long enough in our rooms, listening to all the terror without, the blood-letting that has drained our country dry? Have we not lain pale and petrified in the churches, not daring to look out, as the disciples of Christ lay in Jerusalem on that sad Friday when He walked to Golgotha? *(To SKULE)* Use your wings, and woe to those who would bind you now!

RAGNHILD: Go hence in peace, my husband! Go where no mocking shadow will stand between us when we meet again! *(She hurries into the chapel.)*

MARGARET: Father—goodbye! Goodbye! *(She follows RAGNHILD.)*

SIGRID *(opens the chapel door and calls in):* Come forth, come forth, women! Join your voices in prayer! Let your song rise up to God and tell Him that Skule Baardsson is returning home repentant from his journey of disobedience on earth!

KING SKULE: Sigrid, my loyal sister, greet King Haakon from me. Tell him that even in my last hour I do not know whether he is royally born—but that this I know assuredly. He is the one whom God has chosen.

SIGRID: I shall give him that greeting.

KING SKULE: And there is one more greeting you must give. There sits a woman sorrowing in the north. Tell her that her son has gone ahead. He went with me, because his soul was in danger.

SIGRID: I will tell her.

KING SKULE: Tell her he did not sin with his heart. When she meets him again, she will find him pure and unstained.

SIGRID: I will tell her. *(Points to the gate.)* Listen! They are breaking the lock!

KING SKULE *(points to the chapel)*: Listen. They are singing to God of salvation and peace.

SIGRID: Listen, listen! All the bells in Nidaros are ringing—!

KING SKULE *(smiles sadly)*: They are ringing a King to his grave.

SIGRID: No. They are ringing you to your true coronation. Farewell, my brother! Let the purple cloak of blood flow over your shoulders. It will wash away all sins. Go in, go in to the great church, and receive the crown of life!

> *She hurries into the chapel. During the remainder of the scene, the singing and the sound of the bells continue.*

VOICES *(outside the gate)*: We have broken the lock! Do not force us to violate the sanctuary!

KING SKULE: I am coming!

CITIZENS: The blasphemer must come too!

KING SKULE: Yes, the blasphemer shall come too. *(Goes over to PETER.)* My son, are you ready?

PETER: Yes, father. I am ready.

KING SKULE *(looks upwards)*: O God, I am a poor man, I have only my life to give. But take it, and grant that Haakon's great ideal may be fulfilled. *(To PETER)* Come now. Give me your hand.

PETER: Here is my hand, father.

KING SKULE: And don't be afraid.

PETER: No, father. I am not afraid, when I am with you.

KING SKULE: We never trod so safe a road together. *(He opens the gate. The CITIZENS are standing outside in great numbers, their weapons raised.)* Here we are. We come freely—but do not wound him in the face.

They go out, hand in hand. The gate swings shut.

A VOICE: Aim not, spare not! Strike them where you can!

A brief clash of arms; then heavy falls are heard. For a moment, there is silence. Then the royal trumpet sounds.

A VOICE: The King!

ALL CITIZENS: Hail, King Haakon! All your enemies are dead!

GREGORIUS JONSSON *(stops for a moment by the two bodies)*: Then I have come too late. *(Goes into the cloister.)*

DAGFINN: It would have been an evil day for Norway if you had come before. *(Cries)* Enter, King Haakon!

HAAKON *(stops)*: This body lies in my way.

DAGFINN: If Haakon Haakonsson is to go forward, he must go over Skule Baardsson's body.

HAAKON *(looks down at* SKULE'S *body)*: All men judged him wrongly. He was a riddle that no man solved.

DAGFINN: A riddle?

HAAKON *(grips him by the arm and says softly)*: Skule Baardsson was God's unwanted child on earth. That was his riddle.

He steps over the body. The WOMEN'S *song rises louder from the chapel. All the bells in Nidaros are ringing.*

Note on the Translation

I have followed the text of the second (1870) edition, in the few instances wherein it differs from the original edition of 1863. In 1867 Georg Brandes, in an article in *Dansk Maanedsskrift,* while praising the play, criticised Ibsen's tendency to put generalised aphorisms into the mouths of his characters, and when *The Pretenders* came to be republished by Gyldendal of Copenhagen Ibsen amended several of these, to the obvious advantage of the dialogue.

Norwegian linguistic structure being what it is, the original text is full of combination words based on *kong* (king): *kongsbarn* (prince), *kongssæde* (throne), *kongsret* (royal right), *kongsværk* (a kingly deed). The word "king" thus echoes throughout the play in a way that cannot fully be reproduced in English. A word that recurs with particular frequency is *kongstanke* (kingly thought); I have translated this variously as "great plan," "great idea" and "great ideal"; no single English phrase quite suffices.

The Norwegian title, *Kongsemnerne,* means simply "The Claimants to the Crown" (literally "the material of which kings are made"), and lacks the secondary meaning of the English word "pretenders." But the English title loses nothing by this extra significance; indeed, this is one of the few instances where the translated title is if anything slightly better than the original.

The names of the characters should be pronounced as follows: Hawkon; Skoolë; Daagfinn; Eevar Boddë; Yoonsson; Fleeda; Ingheborg; Yatgheir; Board Brattë.

I gladly express my thanks to Mr. Val May for innumerable suggestions. As already explained in the introduction, the credit for the adaptation is almost entirely his.

Brand

Introduction

In 1863 Ibsen's fortunes were at their lowest ebb. He had written nine plays, six of them historical. Of these the first, *Catiline*, had never been performed; *The Warrior's Barrow*, *St. John's Eve*, *Lady Inger of Œstraat* and *Olaf Liljekrans* had appeared, all with disastrous results; only two, *The Feast at Solhaug* and *The Vikings at Helgeland*, had achieved any recognition at all, and that very limited. Worst of all, his most recent play, *Love's Comedy*, had been rejected, and the Norwegian Theatre of Christiania, where he had for seven years been artistic director, had gone bankrupt. Thus, at the age of thirty-five, he found himself virtually penniless, dependent on a tiny university grant and an even tinier salary which he received from the Danish Theatre of Christiania as literary adviser. With a wife and small son to support, he had to resort to moneylenders. Moreover, the Norwegian Parliament had rejected his application for a poet's stipend, while granting the applications of his fellow-poets Bjœrnson and Vinje.

Fortunately, just when he must have been very close to despair, he achieved his first real success, with *The Pretenders*. First staged on 17 January 1864, it was presented eight times in less than two months—'a success', says Professor Halvdan Koht, 'unique for a play as long and serious as this in a town as small as the Christiania of those days. . . . Now for the first time he rested in a full and free confidence in his own ability to write, and in his calling as a poet.'

At this juncture another piece of good fortune came his way, for he received the news that an order in council had allotted him 400 specie-dollars (about £100) for foreign travel. This was, in fact, much too small a sum to enable him to undertake the long journey southwards on which he had set his heart, but Bjœrnson helped him to scrape together a little more, and when the ice broke in the spring of 1864 Ibsen set off towards Rome.

The war between Denmark and Germany over Schleswig-Holstein had just broken out, and the refusal of Norway and Sweden to help her Scandinavian neighbour angered Ibsen. While he was in Copenhagen that April, on the way to Rome, news arrived of the fall of Dybbœl to German troops; and next month, when he reached Berlin, he saw the Danish cannons captured at Dybbœl being led in triumph through the streets of the capital, while Germans lining the route spat at them. 'It was for me', Ibsen wrote, 'a sign that, some day, history would spit in the eyes of Sweden and Norway for their part in this affair.' Later, looking back on this period, he wrote: 'It was now that *Brand* began to grow inside me like a foetus.'

He reached Rome in the middle of June. A few days later the Scandinavian community there held a small farewell party before breaking up to go to the country and so escape the summer heat. Ibsen attended this party, and his friend Lorentz Dietrichson has described the scene. 'It was the first evening for some while that Ibsen had spent among Scandinavians, and he began to speak of the painful and disturbing impressions of recent events in the war which he had received on his journey. Gradually and almost imperceptibly, his talk took on the character of an improvised speech; all the bitterness which had for so long been stored up within him, all the fiery indignation and passion for the Scandinavian cause which he had bottled up for so long, found an outlet. His voice began to ring, and in the evening dusk one saw only his burning eyes. When he had finished, no one cried Bravo or raised his glass, but I think we all felt that that evening the Marseillaise of the North had rung out into the Roman night air.'

Writing to his mother-in-law, Magdalene Thoresen, Ibsen angrily described how Danes in Rome were attending Sunday service in the German church, and sat silent in their pews while the German pastor prayed for victory for the Prussian arms in their righteous cause.

After a fortnight in Rome, Ibsen moved out to the small hill town of Genzano, and stayed there for two months. Lorentz Dietrichson was living there with his family, and it was during a conversation with Dietrichson that Ibsen first conceived the idea of writing a tragedy about the Emperor Julian—the play that, slowly and with many interruptions, developed over the next nine years into *Emperor and Galilean*. It was in Genzano, too, that he began to write an epic poem. Shortly after he returned to Rome in the autumn, he mentioned in a letter that 'for some time I have been working on a big poem', optimistically adding that he hoped to have both that and the play about Julian ready by the following spring or summer. This poem was called *Brand*.

Ibsen based it on a Danish poem written some twenty years previously, Frederik Paludan-Müller's *Adam Homo*. Paludan-Müller's chief character was an everyday man who shunned ideals and compromised incessantly with the world and with himself. Ibsen intended his chief character to be the exact opposite of *Adam Homo*—a man who shunned compromise.

Then, in September, a young Norwegian named Christopher Bruun arrived in Rome.

He was a theologian, but was hesitating to take Holy Orders because he felt that life and the teaching of the Norwegian State Church were incompatible. Like Ibsen, he had been angered by the German attack on Denmark but, unlike Ibsen, he had volunteered as a soldier, and had fought with the Danes at the battle of Dybbøel. Ibsen got to know Bruun at once—he had already seen a good deal of Bruun's mother and sister at Genzano. They discussed the war, and Bruun asked Ibsen why, if he felt so strongly, he had not volunteered himself. 'We poets have other tasks to perform,' Ibsen replied; but a doubt remained in his mind. He wondered whether he had been right to compromise; and with this doubt was linked another. Was he right to believe so inflexibly in his calling as a writer and thus, in all probability, condemn his wife and child to continued poverty so that he might follow this calling?

Ibsen had already decided to make the chief character of his long poem a discontented priest, and had at first based him on his own memories of a revivalist named G. A. Lammers, who had converted Ibsen's parents and brothers in Skien during the eighteen-fifties. Bruun's personality now began to intrude into the character of Brand, and his ideas into the subject-matter of the poem. Ibsen struggled painfully with it throughout the autumn, winter, spring and summer, while at the same time doing historical research for *Emperor and Galilean*. At length, in July 1865, at Ariccia, a small town south of Rome, he threw aside the poem, of which he had completed some two hundred stanzas, and decided to rewrite it as a poetic drama.

At first this, too, progressed slowly and with difficulty. Ibsen has described how the turning-point came. In a letter to Bjœrnson, dated 12 September 1865, he wrote:

'I did not know where to turn. Then, one day, I went into St. Peter's—I had gone into Rome on some business—and suddenly everything I wanted to say appeared to me in a strong and clear light. I have thrown overboard the work with which I had been torturing myself for a year without getting anywhere, and in the middle of July I started on something new which has been making such progress as no other work of mine has ever done. . . . It is a dramatic poem, of serious content; contemporary subject-matter—five acts in rhymed verse (but no *Love's Comedy*). The fourth act is almost finished, and I feel I shall be able to complete the fifth in a week. I work both morning and afternoon, which I have never been able to do before. It is blessedly peaceful out here; no one I know. I read nothing but the Bible.'

Ibsen finished the dramatic version of *Brand* in three months. The fifth act (about a third of the play) took longer than the week he had predicted, but he managed it in a little under five weeks, and by mid-October the play was ready to be posted to his Danish publisher, Hegel of Gyldendal's. Hegel could not get it out in time for Christmas, as Ibsen had hoped, and it was not until 15 March 1866 that *Brand* appeared on the bookstalls. It created an immediate and widespread sensation throughout Scandinavia, where the movement toward liberalism and individualism was just reaching its climax. *Brand* stated sharply and vividly the necessity of following one's private conscience and 'being oneself' and it ran quickly through three editions. A fourth was in the press by the end of the year. Georg Brandes has described the effect which *Brand* had on the Scandinavia of the time:

'It was a book which left no reader cold. Every receptive and unblunted mind felt, on closing the book, a penetrating, nay, an overwhelming impression of having stood face to face with a great and indignant genius, before whose piercing glance weakness felt itself compelled to cast down its eyes. What made the impression less definite, namely, the fact that this mastermind was not quite clear and transparent, rendered it, on the other hand, all the more fascinating.'

And August Strindberg, who was seventeen when *Brand* appeared, later called it 'the voice of a Savonarola'.

247

The influence of Paludan-Müller's *Adam Homo* on *Brand* has already been noted. Another important literary influence may (though some dispute it) have been the Danish philosopher Kierkegaard. Georg Brandes, writing the year after *Brand* appeared, observed: 'It actually seems as if Ibsen had aspired to the honour of being called Kierkegaard's poet'; and it has been suggested that it was Kierkegaard's *Either-Or* which gave Ibsen the idea of 'All or Nothing'. A more probable influence, in my opinion, is Kierkegaard's *Fear and Trembling*, which dwells continually on the legend of Abraham and Isaac. 'No one was as great as Abraham, and who is capable of understanding him?'; the sentence might well serve to sum up *Brand*. There are other sentences in *Fear and Trembling* which apply to *Brand*: 'There was the man who was great through his strength, and the man who was great through his wisdom, and the man who was great through his hope, and the man who was great through his love; but Abraham was greater than any of these, great through the power whose strength is weakness, great through the wisdom whose secret is foolishness, great through the hope whose expression is madness, great through the love which is hatred of oneself.' And elsewhere there is a reference to 'that vast passion which disdains the fury of the elements and the powers of creation in order to battle with God'. Moreover, *Fear and Trembling* contains a long section on the legend of Agnes and the Triton, and I think it possible that Ibsen, consciously or unconsciously, may have taken his heroine's name from this passage. He based the character of Agnes largely on Bruun's sister, Thea; and Bruun was an ardent disciple of Kierkegaard.

A journey which Ibsen had made through the Norwegian countryside in 1862 to gather folk-lore also left its mark on the play. Many of the descriptions of natural scenery in *Brand* stem from this journey—for example, the steep descent from the Sogn mountains, and the dangers of life in a fjordside village with its storms and landslips.

Although the character of Brand was based partly on that of the revivalist, G. A. Lammers, and partly on that of Christopher Bruun, Ibsen also, by his own admission, put a good deal of himself into the part: 'Brand,' he once said, 'is myself in my best moments.' He later wrote to Georg Brandes that he could, in fact, as easily have made Brand a sculptor or a politician, or even Galileo—'except that then of course he would have to have held strongly to his beliefs, and not pretended that the earth stood still'. I suspect that Ejnar, the painter, represented Ibsen's idea of himself in his worst moments; Ibsen was an accomplished painter and in his youth had seriously considered following art instead of literature as a profession.

A great deal has been written about the symbolism of *Brand*, and the different significances that might be attached to the hawk, the Ice Church, and so forth. Dr. Arne Duve, in his stimulating book *Symbolikken i Henrik Ibsens Skuespill*, suggests that the hawk represents the life of the emotions, i.e. love, and that it is Brand's fear of the powers of life and light that makes him, in the fifth act, dismiss the hawk contemptuously as 'the spirit of compromise'. The Ice Church, Dr. Duve thinks, represents the opposite of the hawk, i.e. the negation of love. Gerd, like Brand, fears and distrusts love (like him, she is the daughter of a loveless marriage), and Brand's negation of love finally leads him, too, to the terrible citadel of the Ice Church; what Ibsen, thirty years later in *John Gabriel Borkman*, was to term 'the coldness of the heart'. The Ice Church finally killed Brand, just as the coldness of the heart killed John Gabriel Borkman. On the other hand, Michael Elliott, who directed the brilliant and acclaimed 1959 production of *Brand* in London, believes that the hawk represents nothing as specific as love, but rather in a general way, 'whatever one rejects', just as Room

101 in George Orwell's *1984* contained 'the worst thing in the world', whatever that might be. I agree with this theory, and believe that the Ice Church stands for the false citadel which each of us builds in his own imagination as a refuge from his particular hawk.

Ibsen never intended *Brand* for the stage; he wrote it, as he wrote *Peer Gynt* eighteen months later, simply to be read. His years as a dramatist and a theatre director had made him bitterly aware of the technical limitations of the theatre and its audiences. Consequently he chose a form in which he need make no concessions to these limitations. He wrote scenes which demand, among other things, a storm at sea and an avalanche; and his final version was, like *Peer Gynt,* more than twice the length of an average play.

Despite *Brand*'s success with the reading public, nineteen years passed before anyone attempted to stage it. At length, on 24 March 1885, Ludvig Josephson presented it at Nya Teatern in Stockholm. August Lindberg has described the first night. 'It lasted for six and a half hours, until 12.30 a.m. Such ladies as survived to the end lay dozing on their escorts' shoulders, with their corsets and bodices unbuttoned.' In spite of its length, however, the play proved a success, and during the next two decades *Brand* was performed in almost every European country which boasted a serious theatre, except England. Lugné-Poe directed it at his Théâtre de L'Œuvre in Paris in 1895, and it was staged in several towns in Germany around the turn of the century. Strangely enough, it was not produced in Norway until 1904, but it has since been revived there on a number of occasions, and remains one of Ibsen's most admired and most quoted plays in his own country. It was especially successful in Russia in the early years of this century; it was introduced into the repertory of the Moscow Arts Theatre in 1907, and caused excitement by its outspoken criticisms of society.

The Russians introduced it to America when they visited New York in 1912; and in 1928 the Pitoëffs scored a success with it in Paris, in a production which used ultra-simple décor.

England, as usual, had to wait longer than most other countries before seeing the play, although Edmund Gosse had written about it at considerable length as early as January 1873 (in a long article in the *Fortnightly Review* entitled 'Ibsen, the Norwegian Satirist'), and at least three separate translations into English had been made before the end of the century. In June 1893 the fourth act was presented as a curtain-raiser to *The Master Builder* for two matinées and two evening performances, during a three-weeks Ibsen season at the Opera Comique in London; Bernard Gould* played Brand, Elizabeth Robins Agnes, and Frances Ivor the Gipsy Woman. On 29 November 1911 the Ibsen Club staged the fourth act (with the last act of *A Doll's House*) at the Ibsen Rehearsal Studio in London, but the play was not presented in a complete form until 10 November 1912, when the Irish actor, W. G. Fay, produced it in William Wilson's prose translation at the Royal Court Theatre for a single performance under the auspices of the Play Actors. *The Times*, after deploring the omission of the scene between Brand and his mother, and that in which Brand decides to give up his first mission and settle down in the fjordside village, went on:

'Mr. W. G. Fay, the producer, had done his work well. . . . The difficulties of arrangement he had overcome skilfully and fairly. Into his company he had instilled some at least of the speed which the passionate, soaring, plunging poem demands. In the part of Agnes . . . Miss Phyllis Relph did well, especially in that wonderful scene where Agnes, having learned from Brand to make the last sacrifice

---

*Alias Bernard Partridge, the well-known artist.

by giving away all her dead baby's clothes to the gipsy woman, soars clean above Brand's head and points him the way to his own goal. Miss Mignon Clifford gave a very lively and understanding portrait of Gerd, the wild girl. . . . As to the Brand of Mr. H. A. Saintsbury, we are in a difficulty. In appearance and bearing, he was so wholly unlike our idea of Brand that we have not yet found our way about his performance. It seemed, we must admit, very experienced, very clever, and nothing more. But we can quite believe that what we saw as a mincing, prelatical Brand, entirely lacking the burliness, the vitality, the passion of the man, had good qualities, which would emerge on further acquaintance.'

On 11 December 1936, Hilton Edwards produced *Brand* at the Gate Theatre, Dublin, with Michael Mac Liammoir as Brand and Meriel Moore as Agnes. The Cambridge A.D.C. presented it at Cambridge in December 1945, in a production by John Prudhoe, with Richard Bebb-Williams as Brand, Ann Mankowitz as Agnes, and Lyndon Brook as Ejnar. A version by James Forsyth was broadcast in the B.B.C. Third Programme on 11 December 1949, with Ralph Richardson as Brand, Sybil Thorndike as Brand's mother, Margaret Leighton as Agnes, and Louise Hutton as Gerd, and again on 30 December 1956, this time with Stephen Murray as Brand, Fay Compton as Brand's mother, Ursula Howells as Agnes and June Tobin as Gerd. Both productions were by Val Gielgud. Apart from the solitary performance in 1912, however, London had to wait until 8 April 1959 to see a full production of *Brand*. On that date it was presented at the Lyric Opera House, Hammersmith, by the 59 Theatre Company, in a production by Michael Elliott, with the cast named on page 255.

In 1906, when Ibsen was dying, Christopher Bruun, the man who had largely inspired the character of Brand nearly half a century before, came to visit him. The two had remained friends, and Bruun had baptized Ibsen's grandchild. They had always kept off the subject of religion, but now, in the presence of death, Bruun tentatively touched on the subject of Ibsen's relationship to God. Ibsen's answer was short and characteristic. 'You leave that to me!' he growled; and Bruun did.

MICHAEL MEYER

CHARACTERS

BRAND
GUIDE
GUIDE'S SON
AGNES
EJNAR, a painter
GERD
MAYOR
WOMAN FROM THE HEADLAND
VILLAGER
SECOND VILLAGER
BRAND'S MOTHER
DOCTOR
GIPSY WOMAN
SEXTON
SCHOOLMASTER
PROVOST
VILLAGERS

The action takes place in and around a village on the west coast of Norway, and in the mountains above it. Time: the middle of the last century.

This translation was commissioned by the 59 Theatre Company, and presented by them on 8 April 1959, at the Lyric Opera House, Hammersmith. The cast was:

BRAND	Patrick McGoohan
GUIDE	Robert Bernal
GUIDE'S SON	William McLaughlin
AGNES	Dilys Hamlett
EJNAR	Harold Lang
GERD	Olive McFarland
MAYOR	Patrick Wymark
WOMAN FROM	
THE HEADLAND	June Bailey
VILLAGER	Fulton MacKay
SECOND VILLAGER	Frank Windsor
BRAND'S MOTHER	Enid Lorimer
DOCTOR	Peter Sallis
GIPSY WOMAN	Anita Giorgi
SEXTON	Robert Bernal
SCHOOLMASTER	Frank Windsor
PROVOST	Peter Sallis
VILLAGERS	

June Bailey, Howard Baker, Anita Giorgi, Ronald Harwood, Harald Jensen, Patrick Kavanagh, William McLaughlin, Helen Montague, Jocelyn Page, Roy Spence, John Sterland, Frank Windsor

Designed by Richard Negri
Directed by Michael Elliott

255

ACT ONE

In the snow, high up in the wilds of the mountains. Mist hangs densely. It is raining, and nearly dark. BRAND, *dressed in black, with pack and staff, is struggling towards the west. His companions, a* GUIDE *and the* GUIDE'S YOUNG SON, *follow a short distance behind.*

GUIDE *(shouts after* BRAND*)*:
    Hi, there, stranger! Don't go so fast!
    Where are you?
BRAND: Here.
GUIDE: You'll lose your way. This mist's so thick
    I can hardly see the length of my staff.
SON: Father, there's a crack in the snow!
GUIDE: A crevasse!
BRAND: We have lost all trace of the path.
GUIDE *(shouts)*: Stop, man, for God's sake. The glacier's
    As thin as a crust here. Tread lightly.
BRAND *(listening)*: I can hear the roar of a waterfall.
GUIDE: A river has hollowed its way beneath us.
    There's an abyss here too deep to fathom.
    It will swallow us up.
BRAND: I must go on. I told you before.
GUIDE: It's beyond mortal power. Feel!
    The ground here is hollow and brittle.
    Stop! It's life or death.

BRAND: I must. I serve a great master.

GUIDE: What's his name?

BRAND: His name is God.

GUIDE: Who are you?

BRAND: A priest.

GUIDE *(goes cautiously closer)*:

Listen, priest. We've only one life.
Once that's lost, we don't get another.
There's a frozen mountain lake ahead,
And mountain lakes are treacherous.

BRAND: We will walk across it.

GUIDE: Walk on water? *(Laughs.)*

BRAND: It has been done.

GUIDE: Ah, that was long ago. There are no miracles now.
You sink without trace.

BRAND: Farewell. *(Begins to move on.)*

GUIDE: You'll die.

BRAND: If my master needs my death
Then welcome flood and cataract and storm.

GUIDE *(quietly)*: He's mad.

SON *(almost crying)*:

Father, let's turn back. There's a storm coming on.

BRAND *(stops, and goes back towards them)*: Listen, guide.
Didn't you say your daughter has sent you word
That she is dying, and cannot go in peace
Unless she sees you first?

GUIDE: It's true, God help me.

BRAND: And she cannot live beyond today?

GUIDE: Yes.

BRAND: Then, come!

GUIDE: It's impossible. Turn back.

BRAND *(gazes at him)*:

What would you give for your daughter to die in peace?

GUIDE: I'd give everything I have, my house and farm,
gladly.

257

BRAND: But not your life?

GUIDE: My life?

BRAND: Well?

GUIDE: There's a limit. I've a wife and children at home.

BRAND: Go home. Your life is the way of death.
You do not know God, and God does not know you.

GUIDE: You're hard.

SON *(tugging at his coat):* Come on, father.

GUIDE: All right. But he must come too.

BRAND: Must I? *(Turns. A hollow roar is heard in the distance.)*

SON *(screams):* An avalanche!

BRAND *(to the GUIDE, who has grabbed him by the collar):*
Let go!

GUIDE: No.

BRAND: Let go at once!

GUIDE *(wrestling with BRAND):* No, the Devil take me—!

BRAND *(tears himself loose, and throws the GUIDE in the snow):*
He will, you can be sure. In the end.

GUIDE *(sits rubbing his arm):*
Ah! Stubborn fool! But he's strong.
So that's what he calls the Lord's work.
(Shouts, as he gets up) Hi, priest!

SON: He's gone over the pass.

GUIDE: I can still see him. *(Shouts again)* Hi, there!
Where did we leave the road?

BRAND *(from the mist):*
You need no signpost. Your road is broad enough.

GUIDE: I wish to God it was.
Then I'd be warm at home by nightfall.

He and his SON *exeunt towards the east.*

BRAND *(appears higher up, and looks in the direction in which they have gone):*

258

They grope their way home. You coward!
If you'd had the will and only lacked the strength,
I would have helped you. Footsore as I am,
I could have carried you on my tired back
Gladly and easily. *(Moves on again.)*
Ha; how men love life! They'll sacrifice
Anything else, but life—no, that must be saved.

He smiles, as though remembering something.

When I was a boy, I remember,
Two thoughts kept occurring to me, and made me
    laugh.
An owl frightened by darkness, and a fish
Afraid of water. Why did I think of them?
Because I felt, dimly, the difference
Between what is and what should be; between
Having to endure, and finding one's burden
Unendurable.
                    Every man
Is such an owl and such a fish, created
To work in darkness, to live in the deep;
And yet he is afraid. He splashes
In anguish towards the shore, stares at the bright
Vault of heaven, and screams: 'Give me air
And the blaze of day.'
What was that? It sounded like singing.
Yes, there it is—laughter and song.
The sun shines. The mist is lifting.
Now I see the whole mountain plain.
A happy crowd of people stands
In the morning sunshine on the mountain top.
Now they are separating. The others
Turn to the east, but two go westwards.
They wave farewell.

The sun breaks more brightly through the mist. He stands looking down at the approaching figures.

>   Light shines about these two.
> It is as though the mist fell back before them,
> As though heather clothed every slope and ridge,
> And the sky smiled on them. They must be
> Brother and sister. Hand in hand they run
> Over the carpet of heather.

EJNAR *and* AGNES, *warm and glowing, in light travelling clothes, come dancing along the edge of the crevasse. The mist has dispersed, and a clear summer morning lies over the mountain.*

EJNAR (*sings*): Agnes, my butterfly,
>   You know I will capture you yet.
>   Though you fly, it will not save you,
>   For soon you'll be caught in my net.

AGNES (*sings, dancing backwards in front of him, evading him continuously*): If I am your butterfly,
>   With joy and delight I shall play,
>   But if you should catch me,
>   Don't crush my wings, I pray.

EJNAR: On my hand I shall lift you,
>   In my heart I shall lock you away,
>   And for ever, my butterfly,
>   Your joyful game you can play.

Without noticing it, EJNAR *and* AGNES *have come to the edge of the crevasse, and now stand on the brink.*

BRAND (*calling down to them*):
>   Stop! You're on the edge of a precipice!

EJNAR: Who's that shouting?

AGNES (*points upwards*): Look!

BRAND: That snowdrift's hollow.

It's hanging over the edge of the precipice.
Save yourselves before it's too late!

EJNAR *(throws his arms round her and laughs up at him):*
We're not afraid.

AGNES: We haven't finished
Our game; we've a whole lifetime yet.

EJNAR: We've been given a hundred years
Together in the sun.

BRAND: And then?

EJNAR: Then? Home again. *(Points to the sky.)* To Heaven.

BRAND: Ah! That's where you've come from, is it?

EJNAR: Of course. Where else? Come down here,
And I'll tell you how good God has been to us.
Then you'll understand the power of joy.
Don't stand up there like an icicle. Come on down!
Good! First, I'm a painter,
And it's a wonderful thing to give my thoughts flight,
Charming dead colours into life
As God creates a butterfly out of a chrysalis.
But the most wonderful thing God ever did
Was to give me Agnes for my bride.
I was coming from the south, after a long
Journey, with my easel on my back—

AGNES *(eagerly):* As bold as a king, fresh and gay,
Knowing a thousand songs.

EJNAR: As I was coming through the pass, I saw her.
She had come to drink the mountain air,
The sunshine, the dew, and the scent of the pines.
Some force had driven me up to the mountains.
A voice inside me said:
'Seek beauty where the pine trees grow,
By the forest river, high among the clouds.'
There I painted my masterpiece,
A blush on her cheek, two eyes bright with happiness,
A smile that sang from her heart.

I asked her to marry me, and she said yes.
They gave a feast for us which lasted three days.
Everyone was there. We tried to slip away
Last night, but they followed us, waving flags,
Leaves in their hats, singing all the way.
The mist was heavy from the north,
But it fell back before us.

BRAND: Where are you going now?

EJNAR: Over that last mountain peak, westwards down
To the mouth of the fjord, and then home to the city
For our wedding feast as fast as ship can sail.
Then south together, like swans on their first flight—

BRAND: And there?

EJNAR: A happy life
Together, like a dream, like a fairy tale.
For this Sunday morning, out there on the mountain,
Without a priest, our lives were declared free
Of sorrow, and consecrated to happiness.

BRAND: By whom?

EJNAR: By everyone.

BRAND: Farewell. *(Turns to go.)*

EJNAR *(suddenly looks closely at him in surprise):*
No, wait. Don't I know your face?

BRAND *(coldly):* I am a stranger.

EJNAR: I'm sure I remember—
Could we have known each other at school—or at
home?

BRAND: Yes, we were friends at school. But then
I was a boy. Now I am a man.

EJNAR: It can't be— *(Shouts suddenly)* Brand! Yes, it's
you!

BRAND: I knew you at once.

EJNAR: How good to see you!
Look at me! Yes, you're the same old Brand,

Who always kept to yourself and never played
With us.

BRAND: No, I was not at home
Among you southerners. I was
Of another race, born by a cold fjord,
In the shadow of a barren mountain.

EJNAR: Is your home in these parts?

BRAND: My road will take me through it.

EJNAR: Through it? You're going beyond, then?

BRAND: Yes, beyond; far beyond my home.

EJNAR: Are you a priest now?

BRAND: A mission preacher. I live
One day in one place, the next in another.

EJNAR: Where are you bound?

BRAND *(sharply):* Don't ask that.

EJNAR: Why?

BRAND *(changes his tone):*
    Well, the ship which is waiting for you will take me
        too.

EJNAR: Agnes, he's coming the same way!

BRAND: Yes; but I am going to a burial feast.

AGNES: To a burial feast?

EJNAR: Who is to be buried?

BRAND: That God you have just called yours.

AGNES: Come, Ejnar.

EJNAR: Brand!

BRAND: The God of every dull and earthbound slave
    Shall be shrouded and coffined for all to see
    And lowered into his grave. It is time, you know.
    He has been ailing for a thousand years.

EJNAR: Brand, you're ill!

BRAND: No, I am well and strong
    As mountain pine or juniper. It is
    Our time, our generation, that is sick
    And must be cured. All you want is to flirt,

And play, and laugh; to do lip-service to your faith
But not to know the truth; to leave your suffering
To someone who they say died for your sake.
He died for you, so you are free to dance.
To dance, yes; but whither?
Ah, that is another thing, my friend.

EJNAR: Oh, I see. This is the new teaching.
You're one of those pulpit-thumpers who tell us
That all joy is vanity, and hope
The fear of hell will drive us into sackcloth.

BRAND: No. I do not speak for the Church. I hardly
Know if I'm a Christian. But I know
That I am a man. And I know what it is
That has drained away our spirit.

EJNAR (smiles): We usually have the reputation of being
Too full of spirit.

BRAND: You don't understand me.
It isn't love of pleasure that is destroying us.
It would be better if it were.
Enjoy life if you will,
But be consistent, do it all the time,
Not one thing one day and another the next.
Be wholly what you are, not half and half.
Everyone now is a little of everything;
A little solemn on Sundays, a little respectful
Towards tradition; makes love to his wife after Satur-
        day
Supper, because his father did the same.
A little gay at feasts, a little lavish
In giving promises, but niggardly
In fulfilling them; a little of everything;
A little sin, a little virtue;
A little good, a little evil; the one
Destroys the other, and every man is nothing.

EJNAR: All right. I agree that we are sinful.

But what has that to do with Him
You want to bury—the God I still call mine?
BRAND: My gay friend, show me this God of yours.
You're an artist. You've painted him, I hear.
He's old, isn't he?
EJNAR: Well—yes.
BRAND: Of course.
And grey, and thin on top, as old men are?
Kindly, but severe enough to frighten
Children into bed? Did you give him slippers?
I hope you allowed him spectacles and a skull-cap.
EJNAR *(angrily):* What do you mean?
BRAND: That's just what he is,
The God of our country, the people's God.
A feeble dotard in his second childhood.
You would reduce God's kingdom,
A kingdom which should stretch from pole to pole,
To the confines of the Church. You separate
Life from faith and doctrine. You do not want
To live your faith. For that you need a God
Who'll keep one eye shut. That God is getting feeble
Like the generation that worships him.
Mine is a storm where yours is a gentle wind,
Inflexible where yours is deaf, all-loving,
Not all-doting. And He is young
And strong like Hercules. His is the voice
That spoke in thunder when He stood
Bright before Moses in the burning bush,
A giant before the dwarf of dwarfs. In the valley
Of Gideon He stayed the sun, and worked
Miracles without number—and would work
Them still, if people were not dead, like you.
EJNAR *(smiles uncertainly):* And now we are to be created
    anew?
BRAND: Yes. As surely as I know that I

265

Was born into this world to heal its sickness
And its weakness.

EJNAR: Do not blow out the match because it smokes
Before the lantern lights the road.
Do not destroy the old language
Until you have created the new.

BRAND: I do not seek
To create anything new. I uphold
What is eternal. I do not come
To bolster dogmas or the Church.
They were born and they will die.
But one thing cannot die; the Spirit, not created, but eternal,
Redeemed by Christ when it had been forfeited
In the first fresh spring of time. He threw a bridge
Of human faith from flesh back to the Spirit's source.
Now it is hawked round piecemeal, but from these stumps
Of soul, from these severed heads and hands,
A whole shall rise which God shall recognise,
Man, His greatest creation, His chosen heir,
Adam, young and strong.

EJNAR (interrupts): Goodbye. I think we had better part.

BRAND: Go westwards. I go to the north. There are two
Roads to the fjord. One is as short as the other.
Farewell.

EJNAR: Goodbye.

BRAND (turns as he is about to descend):
There is darkness and there is light. Remember,
Living is an art.

EJNAR (waving him away): Turn the world upside down.
I still have faith in my God.

BRAND: Good; but paint him
With crutches. I go to lay him in his grave.

He goes down the path. EJNAR *goes silently and looks after him.*

AGNES *(stands for a moment as though abstracted; then starts and looks round uneasily):* Has the sun gone down?

EJNAR: No, it was only
A cloud passing. Soon it will shine again.

AGNES: There's a cold wind.

EJNAR: It was a gust
Blowing through the gap. Let's go down.

AGNES: How black the mountain has become, shutting
Our road to the south.

EJNAR: You were so busy singing
And playing, you didn't notice it until
He frightened you with his shouting. Let him follow
His narrow path. We can go on with our game.

AGNES: No, not now. I am tired.

EJNAR: Yes, so am I;
And the way down isn't as easy
As the way we've come. Look, Agnes! You see
That blue streak over there with the sun on it?
That is the sea. And the dark smoke drifting along
The fjord, and that black speck which has just appeared
Off the headland? That is the steamer; yours,
And mine. Now it is moving into the fjord.
Tonight it will steam out into the open sea,
With you and me on board. Now the mist veils it,
Heavy and grey. Look, Agnes! Did you see
How the sea and sky seemed to paint each other?

AGNES *(gazes abstractedly):* Yes. But—did you see—?

EJNAR: What?

AGNES *(speaks softly, as though in church):*
How, as he spoke, he grew?

She goes down the path. EJNAR *follows.*

The scene changes to a path along the mountain wall, with a wild abyss beyond, to the right. Higher up, behind the mountain, can be glimpsed higher peaks, covered with snow. BRAND *comes along the path, descends, stops half-way on a projecting rock, and looks down into the abyss.*

BRAND: Yes. Now I know where I am. Every boathouse,
    Every cottage; the landslide hill,
    The birchtrees on the fjord, the old brown church,
    The elder bushes along the river bank.
    I remember it all
    From childhood. But it looks greyer now,
    And smaller. The snowdrift on the mountain
    Hangs further out than it used to. It cuts
    Even more from the valley's meagre strip of sky;
    It lowers, threatens, shadows, steals more sun.

He sits down and gazes into the distance.

    The fjord; was it as grim and narrow as this?
    A storm is blowing up. There's a ship
    Running for shelter. And there to the south
    Under the shadow of a crag, I can see
    A boat-house and a jetty, and behind them
    A red cottage. The widow's cottage!
    My childhood home!
            Memories swarm upon me,
    And memories of memories. There, among
    The stones on the shore, I lived my childhood alone.

    A heavy weight lies on me, the burden
    Of being tied to another human being
    Whose spirit pointed earthwards. Everything
    That I desired so passionately before

Trembles and fades. My strength and courage fail me,
My mind and soul are numbed.
Now, as I approach my home, I find
Myself a stranger; I awake bound, shorn,
And tamed, like Samson in the harlot's lap.

He looks down again into the valley.

What is all that activity?
From every cottage pour men, women and children.
Long lines of people wind up the narrow streets,
Towards the old church. *(Stands up.)*
    Oh, I know you through and through,
Dull souls and slovenly minds. Your prayers
Have not the strength nor the agony to reach
To Heaven—except to cry:
'Give us this day our daily bread!' That
Is now the watchword of this country, the remnant
Of its faith. Away from this stifling pit;
The air down here is poisoned, as in a mine.
Here no breeze can ever stir.

*He is about to go when a stone thrown from above rolls
down the path close to him.*

BRAND *(shouts up):* Hallo, there! Who is throwing stones?

  GERD, *a fifteen-year-old girl, runs along the mountain
crest with stones in her apron.*

GERD: He screeched! I hit him!
No, there he sits unhurt, rocking
On that fallen branch.

She throws a stone again, and screams.

    Here he comes again,
As savage as before. Help! Ah!
He's tearing me with his claws!

BRAND: In God's name—!

GERD: Ssh! Who are you? Stand still, stand still,
He's flying away.

BRAND: Who is flying away?

GERD: Didn't you see the hawk?

BRAND: Here? No.

GERD: The big ugly bird with the red and gold
Circled eye?

BRAND: Where are you going?

GERD: To church.

BRAND *(pointing downwards)*: But there's the church.

GERD *(smiles scornfully at him, and points downwards)*:
That?

BRAND: Yes. Come with me.

GERD: No, that's ugly.

BRAND: Ugly? Why?

GERD: Because it's small.

BRAND: Do you know a bigger one?

GERD: A bigger one? Oh, yes. Goodbye. *(Begins to climb.)*

BRAND: Is your church up there? That leads into the mountains.

GERD: Come with me, and I'll show you a church
Built of ice and snow.

BRAND: Of ice and snow?
Now I understand. I remember,
When I was a boy, up among the peaks and summits,
At the head of a valley, there was a chasm.
People called it the Ice Church.
A frozen mountain lake was its floor.
And a great piled snowdrift stretched like a roof
Over the split in the mountain wall.

GERD: Yes, it looks like rocks and ice, but really
It's a church.

BRAND: Never go there.

A gust of wind can bring the roof crashing down.
A scream, a rifle-shot, is enough.

GERD *(not listening):* Come with me, and I'll show you a herd
Of reindeer which was buried by an avalanche,
And wasn't seen again till the spring thaw.

BRAND: Don't go there. It's unsafe.

GERD *(pointing down into the valley):*
Don't go there. It's ugly!

BRAND: God's peace be with you.

GERD: No, come with me!
Up there, cataract and avalanche sing Mass.
The wind preaches along the wall of the glacier,
And the hawk can't get in; he swoops down
On to the Black Peak and sits there
On my church steeple like an ugly weathercock.

BRAND: Wild is your way, and wild your soul,
Poor, broken instrument.

GERD: Here he comes
With his clattering wings; I must get inside.
Goodbye! In the church, I'm safe.
Ah! How angry he is! *(Shrieks)*
Don't come near me! I'll throw stones at you!
I'll hit you if you try to claw me.

She runs off up the mountain side.

BRAND *(after a pause):* Another churchgoer!
On the mountain, or in the valley?
Which is best? Who gropes most blindly?
Who strays farthest from home? The light of heart
Who plays along the edge of the crevasse?
The dull of heart, plodding and slow because
His neighbours are so? Or the wild of heart,
In whose broken mind evil seems beautiful?

271

This triple enemy must be fought.
I see my calling. It shines forth like the sun.
I know my mission. If these three can be slain,
Man's sickness will be cured.
Arm, arm, my soul. Unsheath your sword.
To battle for the heirs of Heaven!

He descends into the valley.

ACT TWO

Down by the fjord. Steep mountains surround it, and the ruined church stands nearby on a small hill. A storm is building up. VILLAGERS *(men, women and children) are gathered in groups on the shore and hillside. In the midst of them, the* MAYOR *is seated on a stone. The* SEXTON *is helping him to dole out corn and other food. Some way off,* EJNAR *and* AGNES *stand surrounded by a group of people. Boats lie on the shingle.*

BRAND *appears on the hill by the church, unnoticed by the crowd.*

A MAN *(forcing his way through the crowd)*:
> Get out of the way!

A WOMAN: I was first!

MAN *(pushing her aside)*: Make way!
> *(Pushes his way to the* MAYOR.*)*
> Here, fill my sack!

MAYOR: Be patient.

MAN: I must go home. I've four children starving—
> five!

MAYOR *(sardonically)*: Don't you know how many?

MAN: One was dying when I left.

MAYOR: Well, be patient. You're on the list, I take it?

He glances through his papers.

273

No. Yes, here you are. Lucky for you. *(To* SEXTON*)*
Give number twenty-nine his. Now, now, good people,
Be patient. Nils Snemyr?

SECOND MAN: Yes?

MAYOR: You must take a quarter less than you had last time.
You've one less mouth to feed.

SECOND MAN: Yes, Ragnhild died yesterday.

MAYOR *(makes a note)*: One less. Well, a saving's a saving.

EJNAR *(to* AGNES*)*: I've given all I have—I've emptied
My pockets and my purse.

MAYOR *(catches sight of* BRAND, *and points up at him)*:
Ha, a new arrival! Welcome!
We've had drought and famine here, and now floods,
So open your purse and give what you can.
We've very little left; five small fishes
Don't feed many hungry mouths nowadays.

BRAND: Better than ten thousand issued in the name of idolatry.

MAYOR: I didn't ask you for advice.
Words are no good to hungry men.

EJNAR: Brand, you can't know how the people have suffered.
The harvest's failed, there's been famine and sickness.
People are dying—

BRAND: Yes, I can see that. These sunken eyes
Tell me what judge holds court here.

MAYOR: And yet you stand there hard as stone?

BRAND *(comes down among the crowd, and speaks earnestly)*:
If your life here was languid and easy,
I could pity your cries for bread. When day follows day
Ploddingly, like mourners at a funeral,
Then a man may well suppose that God has struck him
From His book. But to you He has been merciful,

He has made you afraid, He has scourged you
With the whip of death. The precious gift He gave you,
He has taken away—

SEVERAL VOICES *(threateningly):* He mocks us in our need!

MAYOR: He abuses us who give you bread!

BRAND *(shakes his head):*

Oh, could my heart's blood heal and refresh you,
I would pour it till my veins were dry.
But to help you now would be sin. God
Shall lift you out of your distress. A living people
Sucks strength from sorrow. The weak brace their
    backs,
Knowing that the strife will end in victory.
But where extremity breeds no courage, the flock
Is not worthy of salvation.

A WOMAN: A storm is breaking
Over the fjord. His words awake the thunder!

ANOTHER WOMAN: He tempts God!

BRAND: *Your* God will perform no miracles for you!

WOMEN: Look at the sky! The storm is rising!

CROWD: Drive him out of the village! Drive him out!
Stone him! Kill him!

The VILLAGERS *gather threateningly round* BRAND. *The*
MAYOR *tries to intervene.* A WOMAN, *crazed and di-
shevelled, runs down the hillside.*

WOMAN *(screams):*

Help me, in the name of Jesus Christ, help me!

MAYOR: What is the matter? What do you want?

WOMAN: A priest, a priest! Where can I find a priest?

MAYOR: We have no priest here.

WOMAN: Then all is lost, lost!

BRAND: Perhaps one could be found.

WOMAN *(clutches his arm):*

Where is he? Tell me! Where is he?

BRAND: Tell me why you need him, and he will come.

WOMAN: Over the fjord—my husband—
Three children, starving—we had no food.
No! Tell me he is not damned!

BRAND: Explain.

WOMAN: My breasts were dry—no one would help us—
God would not help us—my youngest child was dying.
It drove him mad. He killed the child.

CROWD *(fearfully):* Killed his own child!

WOMAN: At once, he realized what he had done.
His grief burst forth like a river, and he turned
His hand on himself. Cross the fjord and save
His soul! He cannot live, and dare not die.
He lies clasping the child's body, shrieking
The Devil's name.

BRAND *(quietly):* Your need is great.

EJNAR *(pale):* Can it be possible?

MAYOR: He doesn't belong to my district.

BRAND *(sharply, to the VILLAGERS):*
Unmoor a boat and row me over.

A MAN: In this storm? No one would dare.

BRAND: Unmoor a boat!

SECOND MAN: Impossible! Look!
The wind's blowing from the mountain! The fjord is
seething!

BRAND: The soul of a dying sinner does not wait
For wind and weather.

He goes to a boat, and unties the sail.

Will you risk your boat?

MAN: Yes, but wait—

BRAND: Good. Now, who will risk his life?

MAN: Not I.

ANOTHER MAN: Nor I.

OTHERS: It's certain death.

BRAND: Your God will help
    No one across. But mine will be on board!

WOMAN: He will die unshriven.

BRAND *(shouts from the boat):* I only need one man,
    To bale and work the sail. Come, one of you!
    You gave food just now! Won't anyone give his life?

CROWD *(retreating):* You can't ask that!

A MAN *(threateningly):*
    Get out of the boat! Don't tempt the Lord!

CROWD: The storm's rising!

BRAND *(holding himself fast with the boathook, shouts to the*
       WOMAN*):* All right, then, you come. But hurry!

WOMAN *(shrinks back):* I? When no one—!

BRAND: Let them stay.

WOMAN: No, I can't.

BRAND: Can't?

WOMAN: My children—!

BRAND *(laughs contemptuously):* You build on sand!

AGNES *(turns with flaming cheeks to* EJNAR, *and lays her*
       hand on his arm): Did you hear?

EJNAR: Yes. He is strong.

AGNES: God bless you! You know your duty. *(Cries to*
    BRAND*)*
    Here is one who is worthy to go with you.

BRAND: Come on, then.

EJNAR *(pales):* I?

AGNES: Go! I want you to. My eyes were blind; now they
    see.

EJNAR: A week ago, I would gladly have given my life
    And gone with him—

AGNES *(trembling):* But now?

EJNAR: I am young, and life is dear. I cannot go.

AGNES *(draws away from him):* What?

EJNAR: I dare not.

AGNES: This storm has driven us apart.

All God's ocean lies between us now.
    (Cries to BRAND*)* I will come.
BRAND: Good! Come on, then.
WOMEN *(in terror, as she runs on board)*:
    Help! Jesus Christ have mercy!
EJNAR *(tries desperately to seize her)*: Agnes!
CROWD *(rushing forward)*: Come back!
BRAND: Where is the house?
WOMAN: Over there, on the headland.

    The boat moves away from the shore.

EJNAR *(cries after them)*:
    Remember your family! Remember your mother!
    Save your life!
AGNES: We are three on board!

    The boat sails away. The VILLAGERS *gather on the hill-
    side and gaze after them.*

MAN: The squall's caught them!
ANOTHER MAN: The water's boiling like pitch!
EJNAR: What was that cry above the storm?
WOMAN: It came from the mountain.
ANOTHER WOMAN: There! It's the witch, Gerd, laughing
    and shouting at him!
FIRST WOMAN: Blowing a buck's horn, and throwing
    stones!
SECOND WOMAN: Hooting!
FIRST MAN: Howl and trumpet, you ugly troll! He's well
    protected.
SECOND MAN: Next time he asks, I'll sail with him in a hurri-
    cane.
FIRST MAN *(to* EJNAR*)*: What is he?
EJNAR: A priest.
SECOND MAN: Mm. Well, whatever he is, he's a man.
    Tough and strong. And brave.

FIRST MAN: That's the sort of priest we need.
VILLAGERS: Yes, that's the sort of priest we need.

They look out to sea.

On the headland, outside a hut. The day is far advanced. The fjord lies still and shining. AGNES *is seated down by the shore. After a moment,* BRAND *comes out of the door.*

BRAND: That was death. It has washed away the stains
Of fear. Now he lies, freed from his pain,
His face calm and peaceful. But those two children
Who sat huddled in the chimney corner
Staring with huge eyes,
Who only looked and looked, whose souls
Received a stain which all the toil of time
Will not wash out, even when they themselves
Are bent and grey,
Must grow up in the memory of this hour.
And what chain of sin and crime will not stretch on
From them, link upon link? Why?
The hollow answer echoes: 'They were their father's
Sons'. Silence cannot erase this,
Nor mercy. Where does responsibility
For man's inheritance from man begin?
What a hearing that will be when the great assizes sit!
Who shall bear witness where every man is guilty?
Shall the answer: 'I am my father's son'
Be admitted then?
Deep-dizzy riddle of darkness, which none can solve.
Men do not understand what a mountain of guilt
Rises from that small word: Life.

Some of the VILLAGERS *appear, and approach* BRAND.

FIRST MAN: We meet again.

BRAND: He no longer needs your help.

MAN: There are still three mouths to fill—

BRAND: Well?

MAN: We haven't much to offer, but we've brought a few
    things—

BRAND: If you give all you have, but not your life,
    You give nothing.

MAN: I would give it now, if it could save his life.

BRAND: But not to save his soul?

MAN: We are only working people.

BRAND: Then turn your eyes away from the light
    Beyond the mountains. Bend your backs to the yoke.

MAN: I thought you would tell us to throw it off.

BRAND: Yes, if you can.

MAN: You can give us the strength.

BRAND: Can I?

MAN: Many people have pointed the way, but you
    Walked in it.

BRAND *(uneasily):* What do you want with me?

MAN: Be our priest.

BRAND: I?

MAN: You are the sort of priest we need.

BRAND: Ask anything of me, but not that.
    I have a greater calling. I must speak to the world.
    Where the mountains shut one in, a voice is powerless.
    Who buries himself in a pit when the broad fields
      beckon?
    Who ploughs the desert when fertile soil awaits him?

MAN *(shakes his head):*
    I understood your deeds, but not your words.

BRAND: Ask no further; my time here is finished. *(Turns to
    go.)*

MAN: Is your calling dear to you?

BRAND: It is my life.

MAN: If you give all, but not your life,

You give nothing.

BRAND: One thing a man cannot give: his soul.

He cannot deny his calling.

He dare not block that river's course;

It forces its way towards the ocean.

MAN: Yet if it lost itself in marsh or lake,

It would reach the ocean in the end, as dew.

BRAND *(looks steadfastly at him):*

Who gave you power to speak like that?

MAN: You did. In the storm.

When you risked your life to save a sinner's soul,

Your deed rang in our ears like a bell. *(Lowers his voice.)*

Tomorrow, perhaps, we shall have forgotten it.

BRAND: Where there is no will, there is no calling. *(In a hard voice.)*

If you cannot be what you would be,

Turn your face to the earth, and till it well.

MAN *(looks at him for a moment):*

May you be cursed for quenching the flame you lit,

As we are cursed, who, for a moment, saw.

He goes. The others follow him silently.

BRAND *(gazing after him):*

Silently they go, their spirits bowed,

As Adam walked from Paradise.

No! I have dared to take upon myself

The salvation of Man. That is my work.

I must leave this narrow valley; I cannot fight

My battle here.

He turns to go, but stops as he sees AGNES *sitting on the shore.*

See how she sits and listens, as though the air

Were full of song. So she sat in the storm. *(Goes towards her.)*

What are you looking at, girl? The fjord's crooked
course?

AGNES *(without turning):*

No. Not the fjord's course, nor the earth's.

Both are hidden from me now.

But I see a greater earth, its outline

Sharp against the air.

I see oceans and the mouths of rivers.

A gleam of sunshine pierces through the mist.

I see a fiery red light playing about the mountain peaks.

I see a boundless waste of desert.

Great palm trees stand, swaying in the sharp winds.

There is no sign of life;

It is like a new world at its birth.

And I hear voices ring;

'Now shalt thou be lost or saved.

Thy task awaits thee; take up thy burden.

Thou shalt people this new earth.'

BRAND: What else?

AGNES *(lays a hand on her breast):*

I feel a force waking within me;

And I sense Him who watches over us,

Sense that He looks down

Full of sadness and of love.

A voice cries: 'Now shalt thou create and be created.

Thy task awaits thee. Take up thy burden.'

BRAND: Yes. Within, within. There is the way,

That is the path. In oneself is that earth,

Newly created, ready to receive God.

There shall the vulture that gnaws the will be slain;

There shall the new Adam be born.

A place on the earth where one can be wholly oneself;

That is Man's right; and I ask no more. *(Reflects for a
    moment.)*
To be wholly oneself! But how,
With the weight of one's inheritance of sin?
Who is that climbing the hill? Who is she—
Her body crooked and bent?
What icy gust, what cold memory from childhood
Numbs me? Merciful God!

BRAND'S MOTHER *climbs over the hilltop and stands
there, half visible, shading her eyes with her hand and
peering about her.*

MOTHER: They said he was here. *(Approaches him.)*
Curse the sun, it half blinds me.
Is that you, my son?

BRAND: Yes, mother.

MOTHER *(rubs her eyes):*
Ugh! It's enough to burn one's eyes out.

BRAND: At home I never saw the sun
From the leaves' fall to the cuckoo's song.

MOTHER *(laughs quietly):* No, it's good there—dark and
    cold.
It makes you strong, and afraid of nothing.

BRAND: Good day. My time is short.

MOTHER: Yes, you were always restless; ran away and left
    me—

BRAND: You wanted me to leave.

MOTHER: It was best. You had to be a priest. *(Looks at him
    more closely.)*
Hm! You've grown big and strong. But mark my
    words.
Take care of your life!

BRAND: Is that all?

MOTHER: All? What could be dearer than life?

Look after yours, for my sake—I gave it to you. *(Angrily.)*

I've heard about your crossing the fjord this morning.

In that storm! You are my only son,

The last of our family. You must live

To carry on my name, and all I've lived

And worked for. You'll be rich, you know, one day.

BRAND: I see. So that's why you came to look for me?

MOTHER: Keep away! *(Draws back.)* Don't come near me!

I'll hit with my stick! *(More calmly.)* Listen to me.

I'm getting older every year. Sooner or later

I've got to die, and then you'll get all I have.

It's not much, but it's enough.

You shall have it all, my son. The whole inheritance.

BRAND: On what conditions?

MOTHER: Only one. That you don't throw your life away.

Pass on our name to sons and grandsons.

That's all I ask.

BRAND: Let's be clear about one thing.

I have always defied you, even when I was a child.

I have been no son to you, and you have been

No mother to me.

MOTHER: I don't ask for sentiment.

Be what you want—be hard, be stubborn, be cold—

I shan't weep. But guard your inheritance.

Never let it leave our family.

BRAND *(takes a step towards her)*:

And if I should decide to scatter it to the winds?

MOTHER: Scatter it?

The money I've drudged all my life to save?

BRAND *(nodding slowly)*: Scatter it to the winds.

MOTHER: If you do, you scatter my soul with it.

BRAND: But if I should?

If I should come to your bedside one evening,

When a candle stands at the foot of your bed;

When, clasping a psalmbook in your hands,
You lie, sleeping your first night with death—
MOTHER (*goes towards him tensely*): Who gave you this
    idea?
BRAND: Shall I tell you?
MOTHER: Yes.
BRAND: A memory from childhood. Something
    I cannot forget. It was an autumn evening.
    Father was dead. I crept in to where he lay
    Pale in the candlelight. I stood
    And stared at him from a corner. He was holding
    A psalmbook. I wondered why he slept so deeply,
    And why his wrists were so thin; and I remember
    The smell of clammy linen. Then I heard
    A step on the stair. A woman came in.
    She didn't see me, but went straight to the bed,
    And began to grope and rummage. She moved the head
    And pulled out a bundle; then another. She counted,
    And whispered: 'More, more!' Then she pulled out
    From the pillows a packet bound with cord,
    She tore, she fumbled at it with greedy fingers,
    She bit it open with her teeth, searched on,
    Found more, counted, and whispered: 'More, more!'
    She wept, she prayed, she wailed, she swore.
    At last she had emptied every hiding-place.
    She slunk out of the room like a damned soul,
    Groaning: 'So this was all!'
MOTHER: I needed the money; and God knows
    There was precious little. I paid dearly enough for it.
BRAND: Yes, dearly. It cost you your son.
MOTHER: Maybe. But I paid a bigger price than that.
    I think I gave my life. I gave something
    Which is dead now; something foolish and beautiful.
    I gave—I hardly know what it was—
    People called it love. I remember

What a hard struggle it was. I remember
My father's advice. 'Forget the village boy',
He said, 'Take the other. Never mind that he's old
And withered. He's clever. He'll double his money.'
I took him, and it only brought me shame.
He never doubled his money. But I've worked
And slaved since then, so that now I'm not so poor.

BRAND: And do you remember, now you are near your
grave,
That you gave your soul, too?

MOTHER: I remember. But I made my son a priest.
When my time comes, you must look after my soul,
In return for your inheritance.

BRAND: And the debt?

MOTHER: Debt? What debt? I won't leave any debts.

BRAND: But if you should? I must answer every claim.
That is a son's duty when his mother
Is laid in her grave.

MOTHER: There's no such law.

BRAND: Not in the statutes; but it must be obeyed.
Blind woman, learn to see! You have debased
God's coinage, you have squandered the soul He lent
you,
You were born in His image, and you
Have dragged it in the mire. That is your debt.
Where will you go when God demands His own?

MOTHER (timidly): Where shall I go? Where?

BRAND: Have no fear. Your son
Takes all your debt on him. God's corroded image
Shall be burnt clean in me. Go to your death
In comfort. My mother shall not sleep debt-bound.

MOTHER: And my sins?

BRAND: No; only your debt; you yourself must answer
For your sins. You must repent or perish.

MOTHER (uneasily): I'd better go back home

Under the shadow of the glacier.
In this hot glare, rank thoughts sprout like weeds.
The stench is enough to make you giddy.

BRAND: Go back to your shadows. I am near.
If you feel drawn towards the light
And wish to see me, send, and I will come.

MOTHER: Yes, to judge me.

BRAND: No, as a son
To love you, and as a priest to shrive you.
I shall shield you against the chill wind
Of fear. I shall sit at the foot of your bed
And cool the burning in your blood with song.

MOTHER: Do you promise that?

BRAND: I shall come in the hour of your repentance. *(Goes
       closer to her.)*
But I, too, make one condition.
Everything that binds you to this world
You must renounce, and go naked to your grave.

MOTHER: Ask anything else! Not what I love most!

BRAND: Nothing less can mitigate His judgment.

MOTHER: My life wasted, my soul lost,
And soon my life's savings will be lost too.
I'll go home then,
And hug the little I can still call mine.
My treasure, my child of pain,
For you I tore my breast until it bled.
I will go home and weep like a mother
At the cradle of her sick child.
Why was my soul made flesh
If love of the flesh is death to the soul?
Stay near me, priest. I don't know how I shall feel
When my time is near. If I must lose everything
At least let me keep it as long as I can.

Goes.

287

BRAND *(looking after her)*:
>Your son will stay near, to answer your call.
>And if you stretch your withered, freezing hand,
>He will warm it. *(Goes down to* AGNES.*)* This evening
>Is not as the morning was. Then I was eager
>For battle. I heard distant trumpets bray,
>And longed to swing the sword of wrath
>To kill the demon of untruth,
>Filling the earth with the noise of war.

AGNES *(turns, and looks up at him with shining eyes)*:
>The morning was pale; but the evening glows.
>This morning I laughed; my laughter was a lie.
>I lived for that the loss whereof is gain.

BRAND: This morning visions flocked to me
>Like wild swans, and lifted me on their broad wings.
>I looked outwards, thinking my path lay there.
>I saw myself as the chastiser of the age,
>Striding in greatness above the tumult.
>The pomp of processions, hymns
>And incense, silken banners, golden cups,
>Songs of victory, the acclaim
>Of surging crowds, glorified my life's work.
>But it was an empty dream, a mountain mirage
>Made by the sun in the morning mist.
>Now I stand in a deep valley, where darkness
>Falls long before evening. I stand between
>The mountain and the sea, far from the tumult
>Of the world. But this is my home.
>My Sunday song is over, my winged steed
>Can be unsaddled. My duty lies here.
>There is a higher purpose than the glory of battle.
>To hallow daily toil to the praise of God.

AGNES: And that God who was to fall?

BRAND: I shall bury him.
>But secretly, in each man's soul, not openly

For all to see. I thought I knew the way
To cure man's sickness, but I was wrong.
I see it now.
It is not by spectacular achievements
That man can be transformed, but by will.
It is man's will that acquits or condemns him.

He turns towards the village, where the evening shadows are beginning to fall.

You men who wander dully in this damp
Hill-locked valley which is my home. Let us see
If we can become tablets on which God can write.

He is about to go, when EJNAR *appears, and stops him.*

EJNAR: Stop! Give me back what you took from me.

BRAND: Her? There she sits.

EJNAR (*to* AGNES): Choose between the sunny plains and this
    dark corner of sorrow.

AGNES: I have no choice.

EJNAR: Agnes, Agnes, listen to me.
    Out on the shining water, the white sails
    Cut from the shore, the high prows pearled with spray.
    They fly towards harbour in our promised land.

AGNES: Sail west or east, but think of me as one dead.
    Go, and God be with you, fair tempter.

EJNAR: Agnes, come with me as a sister.

AGNES (*shakes her head*): All God's ocean lies between us.

EJNAR: Then come home with me to your mother.

AGNES (*calmly*): He is my teacher, my brother and my
    friend.
    I shall not leave him.

BRAND (*takes a step towards them*):
    Young woman, think carefully before you decide.

Locked between mountain and mountain, shadowed by
   crag
And peak, shut in the twilight of this ravine,
My life will flow like a sad October evening.

AGNES: The darkness no longer frightens me. A star
   Pierces through the night.

BRAND: Remember, I am stern
   In my demands. I require All or Nothing.
   No half-measures. There is no forgiveness
   For failure. It may not be enough
   To offer your life. Your death may be required also.

EJNAR: Stop this mad game, leave this man of dark law.
   Live the life you know you can.

BRAND: Choose. You stand at the parting of the ways.

EJNAR: Choose between storm and calm,
   Choose between joy and sorrow, night and morning.
   Choose between death and life.

AGNES (rises): Into the night; through death.
   Beyond, the morning glows.

She goes after BRAND. EJNAR *stares after her for a moment as though lost, bows his head, and turns back towards the fjord.*

ACT THREE

Three years later. A small garden at the parsonage. High mountains tower above it; a stone wall surrounds it. The fjord is visible in the background, narrow and mountain-locked. The door of the house leads into the garden. It is afternoon.

BRAND *is standing on the step outside the house.* AGNES *is seated on the step below him.*

AGNES: My dearest husband, again your eye travels anxiously
    Along the fjord.

BRAND: I am waiting for a message.

AGNES: You are uneasy.

BRAND: I am waiting for a message from my mother.
    For three years I have waited faithfully,
    But it has never come. This morning
    I heard for certain that her hour is near.

AGNES *(quiet and loving)*:
    Brand, you ought to go to her without waiting
    For any message.

BRAND *(shakes his head)*: If she does not repent,
    I have no words to say to her, no comfort
    To offer her.

AGNES: She is your mother.

BRAND: I have no right to worship gods in my family.

AGNES: You are hard, Brand.

BRAND: Towards you?

AGNES: Oh, no!

BRAND: I told you it would be a hard life.

AGNES (*smiles*):
> It has not been so; you have not kept your word.

BRAND: Yes; this place is cold and bitter. The rose
> Has faded from your cheek; your gentle spirit freezes.
> The sun never warms this house.

AGNES: It dances so warmly and mildly on the shoulder
> Of the mountain opposite.

BRAND: For three weeks
> In the summer. But it never reaches the valley.

AGNES (*looks steadily at him, and rises to her feet*):
> Brand, there is something you are afraid of.

BRAND: I? No, you.

AGNES: No, Brand. You.

BRAND: You have a secret fear.

AGNES: So have you.

BRAND: You tremble, as though on the edge of a precipice.
> What is it? Tell me.

AGNES: Sometimes I have trembled— (*Stops.*)

BRAND: For whom?

AGNES: For our son.

BRAND: For Ulf?

AGNES: You have, too?

BRAND: Yes, sometimes. No, no!
> He cannot be taken from us. God is good.
> My son will grow well and strong. Where is he now?

AGNES: Sleeping.

BRAND (*looks in through the door*):
> Look at him; he does not dream of sickness
> Or sorrow. His little hand is round and plump.

AGNES: But pale.

BRAND: Pale, yes. But that will pass.

AGNES: How peacefully he sleeps.

BRAND: God bless you, my son. Sleep soundly. *(Closes the door.)*

You and he have given me light and peace
In my work. You have made every moment of sorrow,
Every difficult task, easy to bear.
Your courage has never failed me; his childish play
Gives me strength.
I thought my calling would be a martyrdom,
But success has followed me on my journey.

AGNES: Yes, Brand, but you deserve success.
You have fought and suffered, have toiled and drudged.
I know you have wept blood silently.

BRAND: Yes, but it all seemed easy to me. With you
Love came like a sunny spring day to warm my heart.
I had never known it before. My father and mother
Never loved me. They quenched any little flame
That faltered from the ashes. It was as though
All the gentleness I carried suppressed within me
Had been saved so that I could give it all to you
And him.

AGNES: Not only to us. To others too.

BRAND: Through you and him. You taught me
Gentleness of spirit. That was the bridge to their hearts.
No one can love all until he has first loved one.

AGNES: And yet your love is hard.
Where you would caress, you bruise.
Many have shrunk from us, at your demand
Of: All or Nothing.

BRAND: What the world calls love, I neither know nor want.
I know God's love, which is neither weak nor mild.
It is hard, even unto the terror of death;
Its caress is a scourge. What did God reply
In the olive grove when His Son lay in agony

And cried, and prayed: 'Take this cup from me'?
Did He take the cup of pain from his lips?
No child; he had to drink it to the dregs.

AGNES: Measured by that yardstick, we all stand condemned.

BRAND: No man knows whom the judgement shall touch.
But it stands written in eternal letters of fire:
'Be steadfast to the end!' It is not enough
To bathe in the sweat of anguish; you must pass
Through the fire of torture. That you *cannot*
Will be forgiven; that you *will* not, never.

AGNES: Yes, it must be so. Oh, lift me, lift me
To where you climb. Lead me towards your high heaven.
My longing is great, my courage weak.
I grow dizzy, my feet are tired
And clogged with earth.

BRAND: Listen, Agnes. There is but one law
For all men: no cowardly compromise!
If a man does his work by halves,
He stands condemned.

AGNES (*throws her arms round his neck*):
Lead, and I shall follow.

BRAND: No path is too steep for two to climb.

The DOCTOR *comes down the path and stops outside the garden wall.*

DOCTOR: Hullo, I never expected to see
Lovebirds in this cold valley.

AGNES: Dear doctor, are you here? Come in!

She runs down and opens the garden gate.

DOCTOR: No, I won't! You know quite well
I'm angry with you! Burying yourselves

In this damp cellar, where the wind from the mountain
Cuts through body and soul like a knife.

BRAND: Not through the soul.

DOCTOR: No? Well—no, it almost seems so. Well,
I must be off—I've got to visit a patient.

BRAND: My mother?

DOCTOR: Yes. Care to come with me?

BRAND: Not now.

DOCTOR: You've been to see her already, perhaps?

BRAND: No.

DOCTOR: You're a hard man. I've struggled all the way
Across the moor, through mist and sleet,
Although I know she pays like a pauper.

BRAND: May God bless your energy and skill.
Ease her suffering, if you can.

DOCTOR: I hope He may bless my sense of duty.
I came as soon as I heard she needed me.

BRAND: She sends for you; I am forgotten.
I wait, wait.

DOCTOR: Don't wait for her to send for you. Come now,
with me.

BRAND: Until she sends for me, I know no duty there.

DOCTOR *(to AGNES):* Poor child, you have a hard master.

BRAND: I am not hard.

AGNES: He would give his blood if it could wash her
soul.

BRAND: As her son, I shall pay her debts.
They are my inheritance.

DOCTOR: Pay your own!

BRAND: One man may pay for the sins of many.

DOCTOR: Not when he himself is a beggar.

BRAND: Whether I am rich or a beggar, I have the will;
That is enough.

DOCTOR *(looks sternly at him):*
Yes, in your ledger your credit account

For strength of will is full, but, priest,
Your love account is a white virgin page.

He goes.

BRAND *(watching him go)*:
Love! Has any word been so abused
And debased? It is used as a veil to cover weakness.
When the path is narrow, steep and slippery,
It can be cut short—by love.
When a man walks on the broad road of sin,
There is still hope—in love.
When he sees his goal but will not fight towards it,
He can conquer—through love.
When he goes astray, knowing what is right,
He may yet find refuge in love!

AGNES: Yes, love is a snare. And yet—
I sometimes wonder—is it?

BRAND: First there must be will.
You must will your way through fear, resolutely,
Joyfully. It is not
Martyrdom to die in agony on a cross;
But to *will* that you shall die upon a cross,
To will it in the extremity of pain,
To will it when the spirit cries in torment,
That is to find salvation.

AGNES *(clings to him)*:
Oh, Brand. When the path becomes too steep for me,
You must give me strength.

BRAND: When the will has triumphed, then comes the time
    for love.
But here, faced by a generation
Which is lax and slothful, the best love is hate. *(In
    terror.)*
Hate! Hate! But to will that simple word
Means universal war.

He rushes into the house.

AGNES: He kneels by the child; he rocks his head
As though he wept. He presses himself
Against the cot like a man desperate for comfort.
What a deep well of love exists in his soul!
He can love his child; the snake of human weakness
Has not yet bitten that small heart.

BRAND *(comes out on to the steps)*: Has no message come?

AGNES: No, no message.

BRAND *(looks back into the house)*:
His skin is dry and hot, his temple throbs,
His pulse beats fast. Don't be afraid, Agnes—

AGNES: Oh, God!

BRAND: No, don't be afraid. *(Shouts down the road.)* The
message! At last!

A MAN *(through the garden gate)*:
Father, you must come now!

BRAND *(eagerly)*: At once! What message does she send?

MAN: A strange message. She raised herself in bed,
Leaned forward, and said: 'Bring the priest,
I will give half my goods for the sacrament.'

BRAND: Half!

MAN: Half.

BRAND: Half? Half! She meant all!

MAN: Maybe; but I heard her clearly.

BRAND *(seizes him by the arm)*:
Dare you swear, on the day of judgment,
That she used that word?

MAN: Yes.

BRAND *(sternly)*: Go and say that this is my reply.
No priest will come; no sacrament.

MAN: You can't have understood. Your mother sent me.

BRAND: I know but one law for all mankind.
I cannot discriminate.

MAN: Those are hard words.

BRAND: She knows what she must offer: All or Nothing.

MAN: Priest!

BRAND: Say that the least fragment of the golden
　　Calf is as much an idol as the whole.

MAN: I will give her your answer as gently as I can.
　　She'll have one comfort: God is not as hard as you.

He goes.

BRAND: Yes; they always comfort themselves
　　With that illusion. A psalm and a few tears
　　Just before the end, and all will be forgiven.
　　Of course! They know their old God; they know
　　He is always ready to be bargained with.

The MAN *has met a* SECOND MAN *on the path. They return together.*

BRAND: Another message?

FIRST MAN: Yes.

BRAND: Tell me.

SECOND MAN: She says she will give nine-tenths of her
　　wealth.

BRAND: Not all?

SECOND MAN: No.

BRAND: She knows my answer: no priest, no sacrament.

SECOND MAN: She begged—in pain!

FIRST MAN: Priest, remember—she gave you birth!

BRAND: Go and tell her:
　　'The table for the bread and wine must be clean.'

The MEN *go.*

AGNES *(clings tightly to him):*
　　Brand, sometimes you frighten me. You flame
　　Like the sword of God.

BRAND *(with tears in his voice):* Does not the world fight me
　　With its stubborn apathy?

AGNES: Your terms are hard.

BRAND: What other terms would you dare offer?

AGNES: Could anyone meet them?

BRAND: No, you are right. So false,

So empty, so flat, so mean has man become.

AGNES: And yet, from this blind, stumbling generation,

You demand: All or Nothing?

BRAND: He who seeks victory must not weaken;

He who has sunk most low may rise most high.

*He is silent for a moment; when he speaks again, it is
with a changed voice.*

And yet, when I stand before a simple man

And make that demand, I feel as though I were floating

In a storm-wrecked sea on a shattered spar.

Go, Agnes, go in to the child.

Sing to him, and give him sweet dreams.

AGNES *(pale):*

What is it, Brand? Your thoughts always return to him.

BRAND: Oh, nothing. Take good care of him.

AGNES: Give me a text.

BRAND: Stern?

AGNES: No, gentle.

BRAND *(embracing her):* He who is without stain shall live.

AGNES *(looks up at him with shining eyes):* Yes!

There is one sacrifice which God dare not demand.

He goes into the house.

BRAND: But if He should dare? If He should test me

As He tested Abraham?

MAYOR *(over the garden gate):* Good afternoon.

BRAND: Ah, his worship the Mayor.

MAYOR: We don't see each other often.

So I thought—but perhaps this is a bad time?

BRAND *(indicates the house):* Come in.

MAYOR: Thank you.

BRAND: What do you want?

MAYOR: Your mother's sick, I hear; very sick.
  I'm sorry to hear that.

BRAND: I don't doubt it.

MAYOR: *Very* sorry.

BRAND: What do you want?

MAYOR: Well, I—er—I've a little suggestion to make.
  I hope you don't mind my broaching the subject
  At this sad time?

BRAND: Now is as good as any other time.

MAYOR: Well, I'll come straight to the point. You're going
  To be quite well off now—I may even say rich.
  You won't want to bury yourself in this little
  Backwater any longer, I presume,
  Now that you have the means to live elsewhere?

BRAND: In other words: go?

MAYOR: If you like to put it that way.
  I think it would be better for all concerned.
  Don't misunderstand me! I admire your gifts
  Greatly, but wouldn't they be better suited
  To a more sophisticated community?

BRAND: A man's native soil is to him as the root
  Is to the tree. If he is not wanted there,
  His work is doomed, his song dies.

MAYOR: If you insist on staying, of course I can't force you
      to go.
  But don't overstep the limits of your calling.

BRAND: A man must be himself.
  Only thus can he carry his cause to victory.
  And I shall carry mine to victory.
  This people whom you and your like have lulled
  To sleep shall be awakened. You have softened
  And debased the good metal of their souls.
  I declare war on you and everything
  You stand for.

MAYOR: War?

BRAND: War.

MAYOR: If you sound the call to arms, you will be
   The first to fall.

BRAND: One day it will be clear
   That the greatest victory lies in defeat.

MAYOR: Think, Brand. If you stay,
   And lose this battle, your life will have been wasted.
   You have all the good things of the world—
   Money, a child, a wife who loves you. Why
   Wage your crusade in this backwater?

BRAND: Because I must.

MAYOR: Go to rich cities where life is not so hard,
   And order them to bleed. We do not want to bleed
   But only to earn our bread in the sweat of our brows,
   Prising a living out of these rocky hillsides.

BRAND: I shall stay here. This is my home, and here
   I shall begin my war.

MAYOR: You're throwing away a great opportunity.
   And remember what you stand to lose if you should fail.

BRAND: I lose myself if I weaken.

MAYOR: Brand, no man can fight a war alone.

BRAND: My flock is strong. I have the best men on my side.

MAYOR *(smiles)*: Possibly. But I have the most.

   He goes.

BRAND *(watching him go)*:
   There goes a typical man of the people;
   Full-blooded, right-thinking, well-meaning, energetic,
   Jovial and just. And yet, no landslide, flood
   Or hurricane, no famine, frost or plague
   Does half the damage in a year that that man does.
   How much spiritual aspiration
   Has he not stifled at birth? *(Suddenly anxious.)*

Why does no message come? Ah, doctor! *(Runs to meet him.)*

Tell me—my mother—?

DOCTOR: She stands before her judge.

BRAND: Dead? But—penitent?

DOCTOR: I hardly think so. She clung fast
    To her worldly goods until God took her from them.

BRAND: What did she say?

DOCTOR: She mumbled: God is not so cruel as my son.

BRAND *(sinks down on the bench):*
    That lie that poisons every soul, even
    At the threshold of death, even in the hour of judgement.

He buries his face in his hands.

DOCTOR *(goes close to him, looks at him and shakes his head):*
    You want to resurrect an age that is dead.
    You still preach the pact Jehovah
    Made with man five thousand years ago.
    Every generation must make its own pact with God.
    Our generation is not to be scared by rods
    Of fire, or by nurses' tales about damned souls.
    Its first commandment, Brand, is: Be humane.

BRAND *(looks up at him):* Humane! That word excuses all
    our weakness.

Was God humane towards Jesus Christ?

He hides his head and sits in silent grief.

DOCTOR *(quietly):* If only you could find tears!

AGNES *(comes out on to the step; pale and frightened she whispers to the DOCTOR):*
    Come inside. Please.

DOCTOR: What is it, child?

AGNES: I am afraid.

DOCTOR: What? Why?

AGNES *(takes him by the hand):* Come!

They go into the house, unnoticed by BRAND.

BRAND *(quietly to himself):*
    She died unrepentant; unrepentant
    As she had lived. Is not this God's finger pointing?
    If I weaken now, I am damned tenfold. *(Gets up.)*
    Henceforth I shall fight unflinchingly for the victory
    Of the spirit over the weakness of the flesh.
    The Lord has armed me with the blade of His word;
    He has inflamed me with the fire of His wrath.
    Now I stand strong in my will;
    Now I dare, now I can, crush mountains.

The DOCTOR *comes hurriedly out on to the steps, followed by* AGNES.

DOCTOR: Put your affairs in order and leave this place.
BRAND: If the earth trembled, I would still remain.
DOCTOR: Then your child will die.
BRAND *(uncomprehendingly):* My child! Ulf? My child?

He rushes towards the house.

DOCTOR *(restraining him):* No, wait!
    Listen to me! There's no light or sunshine here.
    The wind cuts like a polar blast;
    The clammy mist never lifts. The child is weak;
    Another winter here will kill him.
    Go, Brand, and your son will live.
    But do it quickly. Tomorrow, if you can.
BRAND: Tonight—today—now.
    Come, Agnes, lift him gently in his sleep.
    Let us fly south. Oh Agnes, Agnes,
    Death is spinning its web about our child.
    Wrap him warmly; it will soon be evening,
    And the wind is cold.

303

AGNES *goes into the house.*

The DOCTOR *watches* BRAND *silently as he stands motionless, staring in through the door. Then he goes up to him, and places a hand on his shoulder.*

DOCTOR: So merciless towards your flock, so lenient towards yourself.
BRAND: What do you mean?
DOCTOR: You threatened your mother: 'Unless you renounce everything
And go naked to your grave, you are lost.'
Now you are the shipwrecked soul clinging
To your upturned boat, overboard now
Go all your threats of damnation. You fly south,
Away from your flock and your calling.
The priest will not preach here again.
BRAND *(clasps his head in his hands, distraught):*
Am I blind now? Or was I blind before?
DOCTOR: You act as a father should. Don't think I blame you.
I find you bigger now with your wings clipped
Than when you were the Angel of God. Goodbye.
I have given you a mirror; look at it, and ask yourself:
'Is this a man who would storm the gates of Heaven?'

He goes.

BRAND *(is silent for a moment, then cries suddenly):*
Was I wrong then, or am I now?

AGNES *comes out of the door with her cloak over her shoulders and the child in her arms.* BRAND *does not see her. She is about to speak to him, but stands as though numbed by fear as she sees the expression on his face.* A MAN *rushes in through the garden gate. The sun is setting.*

MAN: Father, father, listen to me. You've an enemy.

BRAND *(puts his hand on his heart):* Yes, here.

MAN: Be on your guard against the mayor.
He's spreading rumours. He's saying the parsonage
Will soon be empty, that you will turn your back on us
Now that your rich mother is dead.

BRAND: And if I did?

MAN: Then—you've been lying to us all!

BRAND: Have I?

MAN: How many times haven't you told us that God
Sent you here to fight for us? That it's better
For a man to die than to betray his calling?
This is your calling, here, among us.

BRAND: Here the people are deaf. Their hearts are dead.

MAN: You know better. You've shown us the light.

BRAND: For every one who has found the light, ten remain in
darkness.

MAN: I am that one; and I say to you:
'Go if you can!' I can't help myself
From the book; you have dragged me up from the
abyss.
See if you dare let me fall! You can't!
If you let me go, my soul is lost. Goodbye.
I am not afraid. My priest and my God will not fail me.

He goes.

BRAND: Every word I say echoes back at me
Like thunder from the mountain wall.

AGNES *(takes a step towards him):* I am ready.

BRAND: Ready? For what?

AGNES: To go.

GERD *runs down the path and stops outside the garden
gate.*

305

GERD (*claps her hands and shouts gleefully*): Have you
        heard? The parson's flown away!

    The trolls and demons are swarming out of the hillsides,

    Black and ugly. Big ones, small ones—oh!

    How sharply they can strike! They nearly

    Tore my eye out. They've taken half my soul.

    But I can manage with what's left.

BRAND: Child, you talk crazily. Look at me; I am still here.

GERD: You? Yes, you, but not the priest.

    My hawk swept down the mountainside

    From Black Peak. Bridled, saddled, wild and angry,

    Hissing down the evening wind. And on his back

    A man rode. The priest, it was the priest!

    The village church stands empty, locked and barred.

    Its time is up; it's ugly.

    My church's time has come now. There stands my
        priest,

    Big and strong, in his white cloak woven of ice.

    Come along with me!

BRAND: Stricken soul, who sent you to bewilder me

    With talk of idols?

GERD (*comes in through the gate*):

    Idols? There's one, do you see him?

    See those hands and feet under the blanket.

    Man, there's an idol!

BRAND: Agnes, Agnes!

    I fear a Greater One has sent her to us.

GERD: Can you see the thousand trolls

    The village priest drowned in the sea?

    That grave can't hold them; they're groping their way
        ashore,

    Cold and slimy. Look at the troll children!

    They're only skin-dead; see how they grin

    As they push up the rocks that pinned them down.

BRAND: Get out of my sight!

GERD: Listen! Can you hear that one laughing
As he sits astride the crosspoint where the road
Swings up to the moor, writing down in his book
The name of every soul that passes? He has them all.
The old church stands empty, locked and barred.
The priest flew away on the hawk's back.

She leaps over the gate and disappears among the rocks. Silence.

AGNES *(goes across to* BRAND; *says quietly):* Let us go,
Brand. It is time.

BRAND *(stares at her):* Which way? *(Points towards the gate, then towards the door of the house.)*
That way—or that?

AGNES: Brand! Your child, your child!

BRAND: Answer me;
Was I not a priest before I was a father?

AGNES: I cannot answer.

BRAND: You must. You are the mother.

AGNES: I am your wife. I shall do as you command
me.

BRAND: I cannot choose! Take this cup from me!

AGNES: Ask yourself if you have a choice.

BRAND *(seizes her hand):* You must choose, Agnes.

AGNES: Do as your God bids you.

Silence.

BRAND: Let us go. It is late.

AGNES *(tonelessly):* Which way? *(*BRAND *is silent. She points towards the gate.)*
That way?

BRAND *(points towards the door of the house):* No.
That.

AGNES *(lifts the child high in her arms):*
Oh, God! This sacrifice You dare demand

307

I dare to raise towards Your heaven.
Lead me through the fire of life.

She goes into the house.

BRAND *(stands staring silently for a moment, then bursts
    into tears and throws himself down on the step):*
Jesus! Jesus! Give me light!

ACT FOUR

In the parsonage. It is Christmas Eve. In the rear wall is the front door of the house; in one side wall is a window, in the other is another door.

> AGNES, *dressed in mourning, is standing at the window, staring out into the darkness.*

AGNES: Still no sign of him. No sign.
　　Oh, how hard it is to wait
　　Listening to the silence. The snow falls soft and thick,
　　Binding the church in a tight shroud. *(Listens.)*
　　Ssh! I hear the gate creak.
　　Footsteps. *(Runs to the door and opens it.)*
　　Is it you? Come in, come in.

> BRAND *enters, covered in snow. He begins to take off his travelling clothes.*

AGNES *(embraces him):* Oh, how long you've been away.
　　　Don't leave me,
　　Don't leave me. I cannot shake off
　　The black shadows of night alone.
BRAND: You have me back now, child.

> *He lights a single candle, which illumines the room feebly.*

309

BRAND: You are pale.

AGNES: I am tired. I have watched and yearned.

I've bound some branches together, just a few;
It was all I had saved
From the summer, to decorate the Christmas tree.
His branches, I called them, because he liked
Their leaves. He had some of them for his wreath.

She bursts into tears.

Look, it is half covered with snow,
In the—

BRAND: In the graveyard.

AGNES: That word!

BRAND: Dry your tears.

AGNES: Yes, I will. But be patient.
My soul still bleeds, the wound is fresh,
I have no strength. It will be better soon.

BRAND: Is this how you honour Our Lord's birthday?

AGNES: I know, Brand. But give me time, you must give me
time.
Think, last Christmas he was so well and strong,
And now he—

BRAND *(sharply):* Lies in the graveyard.

AGNES *(screams):* Don't say it!

BRAND: It must be said. Shouted—if you are afraid of it.

AGNES: It frightens you more than you will admit.
Your brow is wet. I know what it cost you to say it.

BRAND: It is only the spray from the fjord.

AGNES: And what is that in your eyes? Melted snow?
No, it is warm.

BRAND: Agnes, we must both be strong.
We must strengthen each other, fight our way
Step by step together. Out on the fjord
An hour ago, I was a man. The water
Seethed around us, the mast shook,

310

Our sail was slit and blew far to leeward,
Every nail in the boat screeched,
Rocks were falling on either side from the slopes.
My eight men sat at their oars like corpses,
But I exulted in it. I grew stronger.
I took command. I knew
A Great One had baptized me to my calling.

AGNES: It is easy to be strong in the storm,
Easy to live the warrior's life.
But to sit alone in silence, nursing one's grief,
Performing dull and humble tasks, is harder.
I am afraid to remember, yet I cannot forget.

BRAND: Your task is not small or humble, Agnes.
It was never as great as it is now.
Listen. I want to tell you something
That has come to me in our sorrow.
It is as though there lay a kind of joy
In being able to weep—to weep!
Agnes, then I see God closer
Than I ever saw Him before.
O, so near that it seems as though I might touch Him,
And I thirst to cast myself into His bosom,
To be sheltered by His strong, loving, fatherly arms.

AGNES: O Brand, always see Him so,
As a God you can approach,
More like a father, less like a master.

BRAND: I must see Him great and strong,
As great as Heaven. I must fight
In the heat of the day, keep watch through the cold
night.
You must give me love. Your task is not small.

AGNES: Brand, last night, when you were away,
He came into my room, rosy-cheeked,
Dressed in his little shirt; tottered
Towards my bed, and stretched out his arms,

311

Smiled, and called: 'Mother', but as though he were
   asking
To be warmed. I saw it—oh! I shivered—

BRAND: Agnes!

AGNES: Yes. The child was freezing.
   He must be cold out there, under the snow.

BRAND: His body is under the snow, but the child is in
   heaven.

AGNES: Why do you tear open the wound?
   What you call his body is still my child to me.
   I cannot separate the two.

BRAND: Your wound must remain open and bleed,
   Before it can be healed.

AGNES: Yes, but you must be patient. I can be led,
   But not driven. Stay near me, Brand.
   Give me strength. Speak to me gently.
   The God you taught me to know is a warrior God.
   How dare I go to Him with my small sorrow?

BRAND: Would you have found it easier to have turned
   To the God you worshipped before?

AGNES: No. I shall never turn to that God again.
   And yet sometimes
   I long to be where light and sunshine are.
   Your kingdom is too big for me. Everything here
   Is too big for me; you, your calling,
   This mountain that hangs over us, our grief,
   Our memories. Only the church is too small.

BRAND: The church? Why is it too small?

AGNES: I can't explain it. I feel it. The church is too small.

BRAND: Many people have said the same to me.
   Even the mad girl I met on the moor
   Said it. 'The church is ugly
   Because it is too small', she screamed.
   She couldn't explain either. Many women
   Have said it since. 'Our village church is too small.'

Agnes! You can find the right road blindfold
Where I pass by the turning.
Our Lord's church is small. Well, it must be rebuilt.
Again you guide me. You see how much I need you.
It is I who say to you, 'Do not leave me, Agnes.'

AGNES: I shall shake off my sorrow, I will dry my tears.
I will bury my memories. I will be wholly your wife.

She turns to go.

BRAND: Where are you going?

AGNES *(smiles)*: I must not forget my household duties,
Least of all tonight. Do you remember
Last Christmas you said I was wasteful, because
I had a candle burning in every window;
Green branches and pretty things,
Toys on the Christmas tree, singing and laughter?
Brand, this year I shall put lights everywhere
Again, to remind us that it is Christmas.
I shall make the house as bright as I can
For Christ's birthday. Now do you see any tears in my
eyes?

BRAND *(embraces her)*:
Light the candles, child. That is your task.

AGNES *(smiles sadly)*:
Build your big church. But have it built by the spring.

She goes.

BRAND: O God, give her strength. Take from me the cup,
The bitterest cup, of bending her to Thy law.
I have strength. I have courage.
Lay upon me a double portion of Thy load.
Only be merciful unto her.

A knock upon the door. The MAYOR *enters.*

MAYOR: Well, you've beaten me.

313

BRAND: Beaten you?

MAYOR: Yes. I reckoned I'd beat you, father.
Well, I proved a bad prophet.

BRAND: Well?

MAYOR: I'm in the right. But I shan't fight you any longer.

BRAND: Why?

MAYOR: Because you've got the people on your side.

BRAND: Have I?

MAYOR: You know that. And no man's fool enough
To fight a war alone.

BRAND: Well, what do you intend to do?

MAYOR: I'm going to build.

BRAND: Build, did you say?

MAYOR: Yes. For my own sake.
As well as for the village. Election time
Will soon be here, and I must show the people
That I have their best interests at heart.
Otherwise they may elect some worthless fellow
In my place. So I thought I'd discuss with you
What would be the best measures to improve
The welfare of our poor parishioners.

BRAND: You want to abolish poverty?

MAYOR: Certainly not. Poverty's a necessity
In every society; we've got to accept that.
But with a little skill it can be kept
Within limits, and moulded into decent forms.
I thought, for example, we might build
A poorhouse. And while we're at it, we might combine
    it
With other amenities under the same roof;
A gaol, a hall for meetings and banquets,
With a platform for speeches, and guest rooms
For distinguished visitors—

BRAND: But the money—?

MAYOR: Ah! That's the problem, as always, and that

Is what I wanted to talk to you about.
I need your help to raise it.

BRAND: I myself am going to build.

MAYOR: What? You? Steal my plan?

BRAND: Not exactly. *(Points out of the window.)* Look. Can
    you see that?

MAYOR: What? That great ugly building?
    That's your cowshed, isn't it?

BRAND: Not that. The little ugly one.

MAYOR: What? The church?

BRAND: I shall rebuild it.

MAYOR: Rebuild the church?

BRAND: Make it great.

MAYOR: The devil you don't! That'd ruin my plan.
    We'd never get the people to subscribe to both.

BRAND: That church must come down.

MAYOR: It's always been acceptable to the people,
    At least in the old days.

BRAND: Possibly, but now that time is past.
    It is too small.

MAYOR: Too small? Well, I've never seen it full.

BRAND: That is because there is not space enough in it
    For a single soul to rise.

MAYOR: Brand, take my advice. Leave the church alone.
    It's an ancient monument! You can't
    Just knock it down to satisfy a whim.
    It'd be shameful, horrible, barbaric—
    Besides, where will you get the money?

BRAND: I will build it with my own money.
    My inheritance. All I have, to the last penny,
    Shall be given to this work.

MAYOR: My dear Brand, I am dumbfounded. Such munificence
    Is without precedent, even in the rich cities.
    I am dumbfounded. Very well,

I withdraw my project. Make your plans.
I'll see what support I can work up for you.
We shall build the church together.

BRAND: Will you give up your plan?

MAYOR: Yes. I'd be a fool not to. If I went round
Asking for contributions for my plan,
While they knew that you were paying for yours
Out of your own pocket, whom do you think
They'd support? No, I'm with you,
I'm all for your plan. I'm very taken with it.
It's quite excited me. What a lucky chance
I happened to come and visit you this evening!

BRAND: But remember. The old church must come down.

MAYOR: You know, now that I see it in the moonlight,
With all this snow on it, it does look a bit
Tumbledown.

BRAND: What?

MAYOR: Brand, it is too old.
I can't think why I didn't notice it before.
We mustn't let our reverence for the past,
Or our piety, warp our judgment.

BRAND: But suppose
Our parishioners should refuse to pull it down?

MAYOR: You leave that to me.
If I don't succeed in persuading the fools to agree,
I'll pull it down with my own hands, beam by beam.
Well, I must be off. *(Takes his hat.)* I shall have to see
   about
Those ragamuffins I arrested this morning.

BRAND: Ragamuffins?

MAYOR: Gipsies. I discovered them just outside the village.
Dreadful people.
I tied them up and locked them in a stable.
Two or three gave me the slip, unfortunately.
The trouble is, they belong to the parish

In a kind of way. They're my responsibility. *(Laughs.)*
Yours, too. Did you ever hear folk talk
Of that penniless lad who wanted to marry your mother?
She sent him packing, of course. He went
Half out of his mind. In the end he married
A gipsy girl, and added another one
To their numbers before he died.

BRAND: A child?

MAYOR: Yes, the gipsy Gerd. So, in a sense,
The woman who brought you into the world
Brought her here too, for the girl was conceived
As a result of his love for your mother.
Well, I mustn't stay any longer. I'll be seeing you
Again soon. Goodbye, goodbye!
Remember me to your good wife! Happy Christmas!

He goes.

BRAND: Will atonement never cease?
How strangely, how wildly the threads of fate are
woven!
My poor, innocent son, so you were killed
For my mother's greed. A mad, stricken girl
Born of my mother's sin, made me choose to stay.
And so you died.
For I the Lord thy God am a jealous God
And visit the sins of the fathers upon the children
Even unto the third and fourth generation. *(Turns from
the window.)*
The God of Justice watches over us.
He demands retribution. *(Begins to pace up and down
the room.)* Prayer! Prayer!
How easily that word slips through our lips!
Men pray to be allowed to add their weight
To Christ's burden, they stretch their hands towards
heaven

317

While they stand knee-deep in the mire of doubt.

He stops, and reflects silently.

And yet—when I was afraid—when I saw my son
Fall into his last sleep, and his mother's kisses
Could not bring back the smile to his cheek,
Did I not pray then? Whence came that sweet delirium,
That stream of song, that melody
That sounded from afar, and floated by,
And bore me high and set me free? Did I pray?
Was I refreshed by prayer? Did I speak with God?
Did He hear me? Did He look down
On this house of grief where I wept? I do not know.
Now all is shut and barred. Darkness has fallen
On me again, and I can find no light,
No light. *(Cries.)* Light, Agnes! Bring me light!

AGNES *opens the door and enters with the Christmas
candles. Their bright light illumines the room.*

BRAND: Light!
AGNES: Look, Brand! The Christmas candles.
BRAND *(softly)*: Ah, the Christmas candles.
AGNES *(putting them on the table)*: Have I been long?
BRAND: No, no.
AGNES: How cold it is in here. You must be freezing.
BRAND: No.
AGNES *(smiles)*: How proud you are.
    You will not admit that you need light and warmth.
BRAND: Hm! Will not!
AGNES *(speaks quietly as she decorates the room)*:
    Last Christmas he groped
With his tiny fingers at their clear flames.
He stretched forward from his little chair and asked:
'Mother, is it the sun?' *(Moves the candles slightly.)*
They will stand here.

Now their light falls
On his—on the—! Now from where he sleeps,
He can see their warmth through the window pane.
Now he can peep quietly in, and see
The bright glow of our Christmas room.
But the window pane is misted. Wait a moment.
Wait a moment! It will soon be clear.

She wipes the window.

BRAND: What are you doing, Agnes?

AGNES: Ssh! Quiet!

BRAND: Close the shutters.

AGNES: Brand!

BRAND: Shut them! Shut them tightly!

AGNES: Why must you be so hard? It is not right.

BRAND: Close the shutters.

AGNES *(closes them and bursts into tears)*:
　　How much more will you demand of me?

BRAND: Unless you give all, you give nothing.

AGNES: I have given all.

BRAND *(shakes his head)*: There is more.

AGNES *(smiles)*: Ask. I have the courage of poverty.

BRAND: You have your grief, your memories,
　　Your sinful longing for what is gone.

AGNES: Take them, take them!

BRAND: Your sacrifice is worthless, if you grieve.

AGNES *(shudders)*: Your Lord's way is steep and narrow.

BRAND: It is the way of the will. There is no other.

AGNES: But the way of mercy?

BRAND: Is built of sacrificial stones.

AGNES *(trembling)*:
　　Now those words of the scripture open before me
　　Like a great abyss.

BRAND: Which words?

AGNES: He dies who sees Jehovah face to face.

319

BRAND (*throws his arms round her and holds her tightly*):
  Oh, hide, hide. Do not look at Him. Close your eyes.
AGNES: Shall I?
BRAND (*releasing her*): No.
AGNES: Brand!
BRAND: I love you.
AGNES: Your love is hard.
BRAND: Too hard?
AGNES: Do not ask. I follow where you lead.
BRAND: You are my wife, and I have the right to demand
  That you shall devote yourself wholly to our calling.

He turns to go.

AGNES: Yes. But don't leave me.
BRAND: I must. I need rest and quiet.
  Soon I shall begin to build my church. (*Embraces her.*)
  All peace be with you.

He goes towards the door.

AGNES: Brand, may I open the shutters just a little?
  Only a little? Please, Brand.
BRAND (*in the doorway*): No.

He goes into his room.

AGNES: Shut. Everything is shut.
  Even oblivion is shut to me.
  I cannot forget, and I am forbidden to weep.
  I must go out. I cannot breathe
  In this shuttered room alone. Out? But where?
  Will not those stern eyes in heaven follow me?
  Can I fly from the empty silence of my fear?

She listens for a moment at BRAND'*s door.*

He is reading aloud. He cannot hear what I say.

No help, no advice, no comfort. *(Goes cautiously to the window.)*
Shall I open the shutters, so that the clear light
May hunt the horrors of night from his black bedchamber?
No, he is not down there. Christmas
Is the children's time. He will be allowed to come here.
Perhaps he stands outside now, stretching up his hands
To tap at his mother's window, and finds it closed.
Ulf, the house is closed;
Your father closed it. I dare not open it now.
You and I have never disobeyed him.
Fly back to heaven. There is light
And happiness, there children play.
But do not let anyone see you cry. Do not say
Your father shut you out. A little child
Cannot understand what grown people must do.
Say he was grieved, say he sighed,
Tell them it was he who plucked the pretty leaves
To make your wreath. *(Listens and shakes her head.)*
    No, I am dreaming.
There is much to be done before we two
Can meet. I must work, work silently.
God's demand must be fulfilled. I must
Make myself hard. I must make my will strong.
But tonight is Christmas, a holy night.
I will bring out my relics of love
And happiness, whose worth only a mother can know.

She kneels by a chest of drawers, opens a drawer and takes out various objects. As she does this, BRAND *opens his door and is about to speak to her when he sees what she is doing and remains silent.* AGNES *does not see him.*

AGNES: Here is the veil. Here is the shawl

In which he was carried to his christening.
Here is the shirt. Dear God!

She holds it up, looks at it, and smiles.

How pretty it is. How smart he looked in it
When he sat in church. Here is his scarf,
And the coat he wore when he first went out of doors.
It was too long, but it soon became too small.
Ah, and here are the clothes I wrapped him in
To keep him warm on the long journey south.
When I put them away, I was tired to death.

BRAND: Spare me, God. I cannot destroy this last idol.
Send another, if it be Thy will.

AGNES: It is wet. Have I been crying?
How rich I am to have these treasures still!

There is a loud knock at the door. AGNES *turns with a cry, and sees* BRAND. *The door is flung open, and a* GIPSY WOMAN *in rags rushes in with a child in her arms.*

GIPSY *(sees the child's clothes on the floor, and shouts at* AGNES): Share with me, rich mother.

AGNES: You are far richer than I.

GIPSY: Oh, you're like the rest. Full of words.

BRAND *(goes towards her)*: Tell me what you want.

GIPSY: Not you, you're the priest. I'd rather go back
Into the storm than have you preach at me.
Can I help being what I am?

AGNES: Rest, and warm yourself by the fire.
If your child is hungry, it will be fed.

GIPSY: Gipsies mustn't stay where there's light and warmth.
We must wander, we must be on the road.
Houses and homes are for you others.
Just give me a rag to wrap him in. Look at him,
He's half naked and blue with cold.
The wind's made his body raw.

322

BRAND: Agnes.

AGNES: Yes?

BRAND: You see your duty.

AGNES: Brand! To her? No!

GIPSY: Give them to me. Give them all to me.
Rags or silks, nothing's too poor or too fine
As long as it's something to wrap him in
And keep him warm.

BRAND: Choose, Agnes.

GIPSY: Give them to me.

AGNES: It is sacrilege. A sin against the dead.

BRAND: If you fail now, he will have died for nothing.

AGNES: Come, woman, take them. I will share them with
you.

BRAND: Share, Agnes? Share?

AGNES: Half is enough. She needs no more.

BRAND: Would half have been enough for your child?

AGNES: Come, woman. Take them. Take the dress
He wore to his baptism. Here is his shirt, his scarf,
His coat. It will keep the night air from your child.

GIPSY: Give them to me.

BRAND: Agnes, have you given her all?

AGNES: Here is his christening robe. Take that, too.

GIPSY: Good. That seems to be all. I'll go.
I'll wrap him up outside. Then I'll be on my way.
(Goes.)

AGNES: Tell me, Brand. Haven't I given enough now?

BRAND: Did you give them willingly?

AGNES: No.

BRAND: Then your gift is nothing. The demand remains.

He turns to go.

AGNES *(is silent until he is almost at the door, then cries)*:
Brand!

BRAND: What is it?

AGNES: I lied. *(Shows him a child's cap.)*
  Look. I kept one thing.

BRAND: The cap?

AGNES: Yes.

BRAND: Stay with your idols. *(Turns.)*

AGNES: Wait!

BRAND: What do you want?

AGNES *(holds out the cap to him)*: Oh, you know.

BRAND *(turns):* Willingly?

AGNES: Willingly.

BRAND: Give it to me. The woman is still outside. *(Goes.)*

> AGNES *stands motionless for a moment. Gradually the
> expression on her face changes to one of exultation.*
> BRAND *comes back. She runs joyfully towards him, and
> throws her arms round his neck.*

AGNES: I am free, Brand! I am free!

BRAND: Agnes!

AGNES: The darkness is past. The mist has stolen away.
  The clouds have gone. Through the night, beyond
      death,
  I see the morning.

BRAND: Agnes! Yes; you have conquered.

AGNES: Yes, I have conquered now. Conquered death
  And fear. He was born to die. Ulf is in heaven.
  If I dared, if I could, I would not beg for him back
      again.
  Giving my child has saved my soul from death.
  Thank you for guiding my hand. You have fought for
      me
  Unflinchingly. Now the weight has fallen on you—
  Of All or Nothing. Now you stand
  In the valley of choice.

BRAND: Agnes, you speak in riddles. Our struggle is over.

AGNES: Have you forgotten, Brand?

He dies who sees Jehovah face to face.

BRAND: No! Agnes, no! You shall not leave me.
Let me lose everything else, everything,
But not you. Don't leave me, Agnes!

AGNES: Choose. You stand where the road divides.
Quench the light that burns in me. Give me back
My idols. The woman is still outside.
Let me go back to my blindness. Push me back
Into the mire where till now I have sinned.
You can do anything. You are free to.
I have no strength to oppose you. If you will,
And dare do it, I am your wife as before.
Choose.

BRAND: Agnes, you must not go back.
Oh, far from this place, far from our memories of sorrow,
You will find that life and light are one.

AGNES: Do you forget the thousand souls here
Whom God has called you to save? Whom your God bade you lead
Home to the fountain of redemption? Choose.

BRAND: I have no choice.

AGNES *(embraces him)*:
Thank you for this. Thank you for everything.
I am tired now. I must sleep.

BRAND: Sleep, Agnes. Your day's work is ended.

AGNES: The day is ended, and the candle is lit for the night.
The victory took all my strength.
O, but God is easy to praise! Goodnight, Brand.

BRAND: Goodnight.

AGNES: Goodnight. Thank you for everything.
Now I want to sleep. *(Goes.)*

BRAND: Soul, be steadfast to the end.
The victory of victories is to lose everything.
Only that which is lost remains eternal.

ACT FIVE

Six months later. The new church is ready, and stands decorated for the ceremony of consecration. The river runs close by. It is early morning, and misty. The SEXTON *is hanging garlands outside the church. After a few moments, the* SCHOOLMASTER *enters.*

SCHOOLMASTER: Good morning! My word!
    The village has come to life today.
    People are pouring in from miles around.
    The whole fjord's white with sails.
SEXTON: Yes. The people have woken up.
    It's not like the old days. Then we slept.
    Life used to be peaceful. Now they have
    To change everything. Well, I don't know.
SCHOOLMASTER: Life, sexton, life.
SEXTON: What has life to do with us?
SCHOOLMASTER: Ah, we are not ordinary parishioners.
    We are public officials. Our task
    Is to keep church discipline and instruct the young,
    And stand aloof from all controversy.
SEXTON: The priest's the cause of it all.
SCHOOLMASTER: He has no right to be. But he's no fool. He
    knows
    What impresses people. So he builds his church.
    As soon as people see something being done,

They go crazy. It doesn't matter what it is,
    As long as something's being done.

SEXTON: Ssh!

SCHOOLMASTER: What is it?

SEXTON: Quiet!

SCHOOLMASTER: Good gracious, someone's playing the organ.

SEXTON: It's him.

SCHOOLMASTER: Who? The priest?

SEXTON: Exactly.

SCHOOLMASTER: He's out early. He doesn't sleep well these days.

SEXTON: He's been gnawed by loneliness ever since he lost his wife.
    He tries to keep his sorrow to himself,
    But it breaks out now and then. Listen!
    Every note sounds as though he were weeping
    For his wife and child.

SCHOOLMASTER: It's as if they were talking.

SEXTON: As if one were weeping, the other consoling.
    The new church hasn't brought him much happiness.

SCHOOLMASTER: Or any of us. The day the old church fell
    It seemed to take with it everything
    In which our life had been rooted.

SEXTON: They shouted: 'Down with it, down with it!'
    But when the beams began to fall,
    They dropped their eyes guiltily, as though a sacrilege
    Had been committed against the old house of God.

SCHOOLMASTER: As long as the new church was unfinished
    They still felt they belonged to the old.
    But, as the spire climbed upwards, they grew uneasy.
    And now, yes, now the day has come.
    How quiet everything is. They are afraid,
    As though they had been summoned to elect

A new God. Where is the priest?
I feel frightened.

SEXTON: So do I, so do I!

SCHOOLMASTER: We must not forget ourselves. We are men,
Not children. Good morning. My pupils are waiting.

He goes.

SEXTON: I must get to work. Idleness is the Devil's friend.

He goes.

The organ, which has been subdued during the preceding dialogue, peals once loudly, ending in a harsh discord. A few moments later, BRAND *comes out of the church.*

BRAND: No. I can find no harmony. Only discord.
The walls and roof imprison the music,
As a coffin imprisons a corpse.
I have tried, I have tried; the organ has lost its tongue.
I lifted its voice in prayer, but it was thrown back
Broken, like the note of a cracked and rusted bell.
It was as if the Lord God stood enthroned
On high in the choir, and cast it down in His wrath,
Refusing my petition.
'I shall rebuild the Lord's house and make it greater'—
That was my boast. Is this what I envisaged?
Is this the vision I once had
Of a vault spanning the world's pain?
If Agnes had lived, it would have been different.
She would have banished my doubts.
She could see greatness where I saw only smallness.

He sees the decorations.

Garlands. Flags. They have set up my name in gold.
God, give me light, or else bury me
A thousand fathoms in the earth.

Everyone praises me, but their words burn me.
If I could hide myself. If only I could hide.

MAYOR (*enters in full uniform, and hails* BRAND *triumphantly*):

Well, the great day's arrived! Warmest congratulations,
My noble friend! You are a mighty man.
Your name will soon be famous throughout the land.
Congratulations! I feel moved, deeply moved,
But very happy. And you?

BRAND: As though a hand were pressed around my throat.

MAYOR: Well, we mustn't have that. You must preach your best
This morning. The new church has marvellous acoustics.
Everyone I've spoken to is full of admiration.

BRAND: Really?

MAYOR: Yes. The provost himself was quite amazed,
And praised them highly. What a noble building
It is! What style! What size!

BRAND: You think that?

MAYOR: Think what?

BRAND: That it seems big?

MAYOR: Seems? Why, it is big.

BRAND: Yes, so it is.
We have only exchanged an old lie for a new.
They used to say: 'How old our church is!' Now
They squeal: 'How big! How wonderfully big!'
They must be told the truth. The church, as it stands,
Is small. To hide that would be to lie.

MAYOR: God bless my soul, what strange words! What do you mean?
But I've news for you. That's why I came.
Your fame has spread, and now you have attracted
Favourable attention in the highest circles.
Royalty! You're to receive a decoration!

It will be presented to you this morning.
The Grand Cross.

BRAND: I am already crushed beneath a heavier cross.
Let who can take that from me.

MAYOR: What? You don't seem very excited by the news.

BRAND: Oh, it's useless.
You don't understand a word I say.
I'm tired. Go and chatter to someone else.

He turns and walks towards the church.

MAYOR: Well, really! He must have been drinking. *(Goes.)*

BRAND: Oh, Agnes, Agnes, why did you fail me?
I am weary of this game which no one wins
And no one loses. I am tired of fighting alone.

Enter PROVOST.

PROVOST: Dear children! Blessed lambs! I beg your
pardon—
My sermon! I've been practising it all morning.
Thank you, dear brother, thank you.
My heartfelt thanks. Others more eloquent
And wittier than I will thank you at greater length
After luncheon. There will be many speeches.
But, my dear Brand, you look so pale.

BRAND: My strength and courage failed me long ago.

PROVOST: Quite understandable.
So many things to worry about, and no one
To help you. But now the worst is over.
Your fellow-priests are deeply proud of you,
And the humble people are full of gratitude.
Heartfelt gratitude. Everyone says the same
About the church. 'What style! What size!'
And the luncheon! My goodness, what a banquet!
I was there just now, and watched them roasting the ox.
You never saw a finer animal.

They must have gone to a lot of trouble
With meat as expensive as it is these days.
But we mustn't ask about that. There was something else
I wanted to talk to you about.

BRAND: Speak.

PROVOST: Well, now, you mustn't think I'm angry with you.
You're young, you're new. You're from the city,
And don't know country people's ways.
To speak plainly, my complaint is this.
You treat each one of your parishioners
As though he were a separate spiritual problem.
Between ourselves, that's a mistake.
You must treat all alike. We can't afford to discriminate.

BRAND: Explain yourself more clearly.

PROVOST: What I mean is this.
The state sees religion as the best means
Of improving the country's moral tone.
The best insurance against unrest.
Good Christian means good citizen.
Now the state can only achieve this
Through its officials; in this case, the priests.

BRAND: Go on.

PROVOST: Your church is of benefit to the state, and therefore
You have a responsibility to the state.
With the gift goes an obligation.

BRAND: By God, I never meant that.

PROVOST: Well, now, my friend, it's too late.

BRAND: Too late? We shall see about that.

PROVOST: I don't want to argue. I'm not asking you to do
Anything wicked. I really can't see what worries you.
You can minister just as well to the souls in your care
By serving the state at the same time.

331

Your job isn't to save every Jack and Jill
From damnation, but to see that the parish as a whole
Finds grace. We want all men to be equal.
But you are creating inequality
Where it never existed before. Until now
Each man was a member of the Church.
You have taught him to look upon himself
As an individual, requiring special treatment.
This will result in the most frightful confusion.
The surest way to destroy a man
Is to turn him into an individual.
Very few men can fight the world alone.

BRAND: Do you know what you are asking me to do?
You are demanding that, at the cock-crow of the state,
I shall betray the ideal for which I have lived.

PROVOST: Betray an ideal? My dear Brand, nobody
Is asking you to do anything of the sort.
I'm just showing you your duty.
I only ask you to subdue those talents
Which are not useful to our community.
Aspire to be a saint, but be a good fellow
And keep such aspirations to yourself.
Don't encourage others to imitate you.
Why be obstinate? You'll suffer for it in the end.

BRAND: I can see the mark of Cain upon your brow.
Cowardice, greed and worldly wisdom
Have slain the pure Abel that once dwelt in you.

PROVOST: There's no call to get personal. I don't intend
To prolong this argument. I merely beg you
To consider your position if you want to get on.
Every man must curb his individuality,
Humble himself, and not always be trying
To rise above his fellows. The man who fights alone
Will never achieve anything of lasting value.
Well, goodbye. I am going to preach a sermon

On the duality of human nature,
And must take a little light refreshment first. *(Goes.)*
BRAND: No. Not yet. They have not got me yet.
This churchyard has had blood to drink.
My light, my life, lie buried here,
But they will not get my soul.
It is terrible to stand alone.
Wherever I look, I see death.
It is terrible to hunger for bread
When every hand offers me a stone.
If only one person would share my faith,
And give me strength, give me peace.

EJNAR, *pale and emaciated and dressed in black,
comes down the road. He stops on seeing* BRAND.

BRAND: Ejnar! You!
EJNAR: Yes, that is my name.
BRAND: I have been longing to meet someone whose heart
Was not of wood or stone. Come and talk to me.
EJNAR: I need no priest. I have found peace.
BRAND: You are angry with me for what happened
When we last met.
EJNAR: No, I do not blame you.
You are the blind guide Our Saviour sent me
When I was playing the world's wild game,
Wandering in the vacant paths of sin.
BRAND: What language is this?
EJNAR: The language of peace.
The language a man learns when he shakes off
The sleep of sin and wakes regenerated.
BRAND: Strange. I had heard—
EJNAR: I was seduced by pride, and belief
In my own strength. But, God be praised,
He did not abandon his foolish sheep.
When the moment was ripe, He opened my eyes.

333

BRAND: How?

EJNAR: I fell.

BRAND: Fell?

EJNAR: Yes, into drunkenness and gambling.

He gave me a taste for cards and dice—

BRAND: And you call this the Lord's doing?

EJNAR: That was my first step towards salvation.

Then He took my health from me, my talent

For painting, and my love of merriment.

I was taken to hospital, where I lay sick

A long while, lay as though in flames.

I thought I saw in all the rooms

Thousands of huge flies. At last they let me go,

And I became a child of the Lord.

BRAND: And then?

EJNAR: I became a preacher of total abstinence,

And am now a missionary.

BRAND: A missionary? Where?

EJNAR: In Africa. I am on my way there now.

I must go. My time is short.

BRAND: Won't you stay for a while? As you see,

We have a feast-day here.

EJNAR: Thank you, no.

My place is with the black souls. Goodbye.

BRAND: Don't you want to ask what happened to—?

EJNAR: To whom? Ah, that young woman

Who held me struggling in her net of lust,

Before I became cleansed by the True Faith.

Yes, what's happened to her?

BRAND: The next year, she became my wife.

EJNAR: Such matters do not concern me.

BRAND: Our life together was richly blessed

With joy, and sorrow. Our child died—

EJNAR: A triviality.

BRAND: Perhaps you are right. He was lent, not given.

And we shall meet again. But then
She left me, too. Their graves grow green
Side by side.

EJNAR: Vanity, Brand, vanity.

BRAND: That too?

EJNAR: All that is important is how she died.

BRAND: In hope of the dawn, with the heart's wealth un-
touched,
Her will steadfast even to her last night,
Grateful for all that life had given her
And had taken away, she went to her grave.

EJNAR: Vanity, vanity, man. How was her faith?

BRAND: Unshakable.

EJNAR: In whom?

BRAND: In her God.

EJNAR: Her God cannot save her. She is damned.

BRAND: What are you saying?

EJNAR: Damned, poor soul.

BRAND *(calmly):* Go your way, fool.

EJNAR: The prince of darkness will have you in his clutches.
You will burn, like her, in everlasting fire.

BRAND: You dare to pronounce judgment on her and me,
Poor, sinning fool?

EJNAR: My faith has washed me clean.

BRAND: Hold your tongue.

EJNAR: Hold yours. I smell sulphur here,
And glimpse the Devil's horns upon your brow.
I am a grain of God's immortal wheat,
But you are chaff upon the wind of Judgement.

He goes.

BRAND *(stares after him for a moment, then his eyes flame
and he cries):*
And that was the man who was to give me strength!

335

Now all my bonds are broken. I shall march
Under my own flag, even if none will follow.

MAYOR *(enters in haste)*:
Hurry, Brand! The procession is lined up
Ready to move towards the church.

BRAND: Let them come.

MAYOR: Without you? Listen, the crowd is shouting for you.
Go and calm them, or I fear they'll grow violent.

BRAND: I shall stay here.

MAYOR: Are you mad? Use your influence to control them.
Ah, it's too late.

The CROWD *streams in, forcing its way through the decorations towards the church.*

CROWD: Father! Brand! Where is the priest?
Look! There he is! Open the church, father! Open the
church!

PROVOST *(to* MAYOR*)*: Cannot you control them?

MAYOR: They won't pay any attention to me.

BRAND: At last a current has stirred this stagnant pool.
Men, you stand at the crossroads! Will yourselves to be
new!
Destroy everything in you that is rotten!
Only then can the great temple be built,
As it must and shall.

PRIESTS AND OFFICIALS: The priest is mad. He is mad.

BRAND: Yes, I was. I was mad to think
That to double the church's size would be enough.
I did not see that it was All or Nothing.
I lost myself in compromise. But today
The Lord has spoken. The trump of doom
Has sounded over this house. Now all doubt is past.
People! Compromise is the way of Satan!

CROWD *(in fury)*: Away with them, they have blinded us.

336

Away with them, they have stolen our spirit.

BRAND: No. Your enemy lurks within you, binding you;
    A worm sapping your strength.
    Why have you come to the church? Only
    To gape at the show, to gape at its steeple,
    To listen to the organ and the bells,
    Enjoy the glow of high-sounding speeches.
    This was not what I dreamed.
    I dreamed that I might build a church so great
    That it would embrace, not just faith and doctrine,
    But everything in life
    Which God has given as a part of life.
    The day's toil, the evening's rest, the night's
    Sorrows, the fresh delights of burning youth,
    The river that flows below, the waterfall
    That roars between the rocks, the cry of the storm,
    And the soft voices that call from the sea.
    These should be one with the Word of God,
    With the organ music and the people's singing.
    The thing that stands here is a lie, a monstrous lie!
    Away with it!

CROWD: Lead us! Lead us! Lead us to victory!

PROVOST: Do not listen to him. He is not a true Christian.

BRAND: No, you are right. I am not a true Christian.
    Neither are you, nor is anyone here.
    A true Christian must have a soul,
    And show me one who has kept his soul!
    You grind away God's image, live like beasts,
    Then join the grovelling queue to beg for grace.
    Has He not said that only if ye are
    As little children can ye enter the kingdom?
    Come then, both men and women;
    Show yourselves with fresh children's faces
    In the great church of life!

MAYOR: Open the door!

CROWD (*cries as though in anguish*):

No, not this church! Not this church! The church of life!

BRAND: Our church is boundless. It has no walls.

Its floor is the green earth,

The moorland, the meadow, the sea, the fjord.

Only heaven can span its roof.

There, life and faith shall melt together.

The day's toil there is a flight among the stars,

Is one with children's play round the Christmas tree,

Is one with the dance of the king before the ark.

*A storm seems to shake the CROWD. Some turn away,
but most of them press closer round BRAND.*

CROWD: You give us light! We have lived in darkness!

Show us the Church of Life! Life and faith must be one!

PROVOST: Stop him, stop him! He will take our flock from us.

MAYOR (*quietly*): Keep calm, man. Let him rave.

BRAND (*to CROWD*): Away from this place! God is not here.

His kingdom is perfect freedom.

He locks the church door, and stands with the keys in his hand.

I am priest here no longer. I withdraw my gift.

He throws the keys into the river.

If you want to enter, creep in through the cellars.

Your backs are supple.

MAYOR (*quietly, relieved*):

Well, that's the end of his decoration.

PROVOST: He'll never be a bishop now.

BRAND: Come, all you who are young and strong!

Leave this dead valley! Follow me to victory!

One day you must awaken! Arise

From your misery! Arise from your half-life!
Slay the enemy within you!

MAYOR: Stop! Stop!

CROWD: Show us the way! We will follow!

BRAND: Over the frozen ocean of the moor!
We shall wander through the land, freeing
Our souls, purifying, crushing our weakness.
Be men, be priests, renew God's faded image.
Make the earth your temple.

The CROWD, *including the* SCHOOLMASTER *and the* SEX-
TON, *swarm around him. They raise* BRAND *high on
their shoulders.*

CROWD: A vision! Follow him! Arise!
Leave the valley! Up to the moor!

*They stream up through the valley. A few remain be-
hind.*

PROVOST: Are you blind? Can't you see that the devil is in
his words?

MAYOR: Turn back, turn back!
You belong to the calm waters of this village.
Good people, stop! He will lead you to destruction.
Listen! They will not answer, the swine!

PROVOST: Think of your homes and houses.

CROWD: A greater house shall be built.

MAYOR: How will you live?

CROWD: The chosen people found manna in the wilderness.

PROVOST (*gazes after them with folded hands, and says
quietly*):
They have left me. My flock has abandoned me.

MAYOR: Do not fear, my lord. Victory will soon be ours.

PROVOST (*almost in tears*):
Victory? But our flock has left us.

339

MAYOR: We are not beaten. Not if I know my sheep.

He goes after them. The PROVOST *follows.*

By the highest farm above the village. A bleak mountain landscape towers behind. It is raining. BRAND *appears over the hillside, followed by the* CROWD *of* MEN, WOMEN *and* CHILDREN.

BRAND: Forward! Forward! Victory lies ahead.
   Forget your village. Leave it in its hollow.
   The mist has buried it. Forget that you were beasts.
   Now you are men of the Lord. Climb onward, climb!
A MAN: Wait, wait. My old father is tired.
ANOTHER: I have eaten nothing since yesterday.
SEVERAL: Yes, give us food. Quench our thirst.
BRAND: We must cross the mountain first. Follow me.
MAN: The path's too steep. We'll never get there by night-
   fall.
SEXTON: The Ice Church lies that way.
BRAND: The steep path is the shortest.
A WOMAN: My child is sick.
ANOTHER WOMAN: My feet are sore.
A THIRD: Water, water, we are thirsty.
SCHOOLMASTER: Give them strength, priest. Their courage
   is failing.
CROWD: Perform a miracle, father. A miracle.
BRAND: Your slavery has branded you vilely.
   You demand your wage before your work is done.
   Rise up, shake off your sloth.
   If you cannot, go back to your graves.
SCHOOLMASTER: He is right, victory must be won first.
   The reward will follow.
BRAND: You will be rewarded, my people,
   As surely as a God watches keen-eyed over this world.

CROWD: He prophesies! He prophesies!

OTHERS IN THE CROWD: Tell us, priest, will the battle be hard?

Will it be long? Will it be bloody?

A MAN: Will we have to be brave?

SCHOOLMASTER: There's no question of our lives being endangered?

A MAN: What will be my share of the reward?

A WOMAN: My son will not die, will he, father?

SEXTON: Will victory be ours by Tuesday?

BRAND *(stares at them bewildered):*

What are you asking? What do you want to know?

SEXTON: First, how long shall we have to fight?

Secondly, how much will it cost us?

Thirdly, what will be our reward?

BRAND: That is what you want to know?

SCHOOLMASTER: Yes; you didn't tell us.

BRAND *(angrily):* Then I shall tell you now.

CROWD: Speak! Speak!

BRAND: How long will you have to fight? Until you die!

What will it cost? Everything you hold dear.

Your reward? A new will, cleansed and strong,

A new faith, integrity of spirit;

A crown of thorns. That will be your reward.

CROWD *(screams in fury):* Betrayed! You have betrayed us!

You have tricked us!

BRAND: I have not betrayed or tricked you.

CROWD: You promised us victory. Now you ask for sacrifice.

BRAND: I have promised you victory,

And I swear it shall be won through you.

But we who march in the first rank must fall.

CROWD: He wants us to die! To save people who haven't been born!

BRAND: The only road to Canaan lies through a desert.
  That desert is self-sacrifice. Death is the only victory.
  I consecrate you soldiers of the Lord.

SCHOOLMASTER: We can't go back.

SEXTON: And we daren't go on.

WOMEN (*pointing in terror down the road*):
  Look! The provost!

SCHOOLMASTER: Now don't be frightened.

Enter PROVOST.

PROVOST: My children! My sheep! Listen to the voice
  Of your old shepherd. Do not listen
  To this man. He would trick you with false promises.

CROWD: That's true.

PROVOST: We understand weakness. We forgive those
  Who truly repent. Look into your hearts
  Before it is too late.
  Can you not see the black art he has used
  To get you into his power?

CROWD: Yes. He has bewitched us.

PROVOST: Think, my children. What can you achieve,
  Humble people born in a humble village?
  Were you created to shake the world,
  To right wrongs, liberate the oppressed?
  You have your humble tasks allotted you;
  To attempt more is presumptuous and wrong.
  Would you intervene between the hawk and the eagle?
  Would you challenge the wolf and the bear?
  You will only be preyed on by the ruthless and the
    mighty,
  My sheep, my children.

CROWD: Yes. It's true. He's right.

BRAND: Choose, men and women. Choose.

SOME OF THE CROWD: We want to go home.

OTHERS: Too late, too late. Let us go on.

342

MAYOR *(hurries in):* What luck that I managed to find you!
WOMEN: Oh, sir, please don't be angry with us.
MAYOR: No time for that. Just you come with me.
    A marvellous thing has happened for the village.
    If you behave sensibly, you will all be rich by nightfall.
CROWD: What? How?
MAYOR: A shoal of fishes has entered the fjord—
    Millions of them!
CROWD: What?
MAYOR: Do you want to spend the night on this mountain?
    Such a shoal has never entered our fjord before.
    A better time is dawning for us, my friends.
BRAND: Choose between him and God.
PROVOST: A miracle! A miracle! A sign from Heaven!
    I have often dreamed that this might happen.
    Now it has. We have been given a sign.
BRAND: If you turn back now, you are lost.
CROWD: A shoal of fishes!
MAYOR: Millions of them!
PROVOST: Food for your children! Gold for your wives!
SEXTON: Will I be allowed to keep my job?
SCHOOLMASTER: Will my school be taken from me?
PROVOST: Use your good influence with the people, and you
       will find us lenient.
MAYOR: Away, away! Don't waste time!
SEXTON: To the boats, to the boats!
SOME OF THE CROWD: What about the priest?
SCHOOLMASTER: The priest? Leave the lunatic.
CROWD: Yes—he lied to us!
PROVOST: He refused his old mother the sacrament.
MAYOR: He killed his child.
SEXTON: And his wife too.
WOMEN: Shame on him! The scoundrel!
PROVOST: A bad son, a bad father, a bad husband.
    Where could you find a worse Christian?

343

CROWD: He pulled our church down. He locked us out of the
　　new one.
BRAND: I see the mark of Cain on every brow.
　　I see where you will all end.
CROWD (*roars*): Don't listen to him!
　　Drive the hell-brand away from the village!
　　Stone him! Kill him!

They stone BRAND *and drive him up the mountain.
Gradually his pursuers return.*

PROVOST: Oh, my children! Oh, my sheep!
　　Return to your firesides. Repent of your rash folly,
　　And you will find that the simple life is good.
　　Farewell—and good luck to your fishing!
SEXTON: They are true Christians. They are gentle and mer-
　　ciful.
SCHOOLMASTER: They go their way and let us go ours.
SEXTON: They don't ask us to sacrifice our lives.
SCHOOLMASTER: They are wise.

The CROWD *goes down towards the village.*

PROVOST: God's miracle has saved us.
MAYOR: What miracle?
PROVOST: The shoal of fishes.
MAYOR: Oh, that. A lie, of course.
PROVOST: A lie? Really? Well, I—
MAYOR: I hope your reverence will think it excusable,
　　In view of the importance of the issue.
PROVOST: Of course, of course. Quite excusable.
MAYOR (*scratches his nose*):
　　I wonder, though, whether their treatment of him
　　Wasn't a little inhumane?
PROVOST: The voice of the people is the voice of God.
　　Come!

They go.

*Among the peaks. A storm is gathering, hunting the clouds
slowly across the snowfields. Black peaks are visible here
and there; then they are veiled again in mist.* BRAND *appears, blood-stained and beaten.*

BRAND *(stops and looks back):* A thousand started with me
  from the valley;
Not one has followed me to the mountain top.
All of them have the craving in their hearts,
But the sacrifice frightens them.
Their will is weak; their fear is strong.
Someone once died to save their souls,
So nothing more is required of them.

He sinks down on a stone.

It was not for us that He drained the cup of agony,
Not for us that the thorn-crown scarred His brow.
It was not for us that the lance pierced His side,
Not for us that the nails burned
Through His hands and feet. We are small and mean.
We are not worthy. We defy the call to arms.
It was not for us that He carried His cross.

*He throws himself down into the snow and covers his
face. After a while he looks up.*

Have I been dreaming? Am I awake?
Everything is hidden in mist. Was it all
Only a sick man's vision? Have we forgotten
The image in whose likeness we were made?
Is Man defeated after all? *(Listens.)*
Ah! There is a sound in the air like singing.
VOICES *(murmur in the storm):*

You can never be like Him, for you are flesh.
Do His will, or forsake Him, you are lost, lost.

BRAND: Lost. Lost? I can almost believe it.
Did He not reject my prayer in the church?
Did He not take from me all I had,
Closed every path that might have led me to light?
Made me fight until my strength was finished,
And then let me be defeated?

VOICES *(louder):* Worm, you will never be like Him.
You have drained the cup of death.
Follow or forsake Him, your work is doomed.

BRAND *(weeps quietly):* Ulf and Agnes, come back to me.
I sit alone on the mountain top.
The north wind blows through me, spectres haunt me.

He looks up. A gap opens in the mist, revealing the
FIGURE OF A WOMAN, *wrapped in a light cloak. It is*
AGNES.

FIGURE *(smiles, and opens her arms towards him):*
Brand, I have come back to you.

BRAND: Agnes? Agnes! *(Moves towards her.)*

FIGURE *(screams):* Stop! A gulf lies between us.
(Gently.) You are not dreaming. You are not asleep.
You have been sick, my dear. You have been mad.
You dreamed your wife was dead.

BRAND: You are alive? Praise be to—!

FIGURE *(quickly):* Ssh! We have not much time.
Come with me, come with me.

BRAND: But—Ulf?

FIGURE: He is alive, too.

BRAND: Alive?

FIGURE: It was all a dream. Your sorrows were a dream.
You fought no battle. Ulf is with your mother.
She is well, and he grows tall.

The old church still stands; you can pull it down, if you
    wish.
The villagers toil below, as they did before you came,
In the good old days.

BRAND: Good?

FIGURE: Yes. Then there was peace.

BRAND: Peace?

FIGURE: Quickly, Brand. Come with me.

BRAND: Ah, I am dreaming.

FIGURE: No longer. But you need tenderness and care.

BRAND: I am strong.

FIGURE: Not yet. Your dreams will lure you back again.
The mist will swallow you, and take you from me.
Your mind will grow confused again unless
You try the remedy.

BRAND: Oh, give it to me!

FIGURE: You have it.

BRAND: What is it?

FIGURE: Three words.
You must blot them out, wipe them from your memory.
Forget them.

BRAND: Say them!

FIGURE: All or Nothing.

BRAND *(shrinks)*: Ah! That?

FIGURE: As surely as I live, and as surely as you shall some-
    time die.

BRAND: Alas for us both; the drawn sword
Hangs over us as it hung before.

FIGURE: Be gentle, Brand. My breasts are warm.
Hold me in your strong arms.
Let us go and find the sun and the summer.

BRAND: The sickness will not come again.

FIGURE: It will come, Brand. Be sure.

BRAND *(shakes his head)*:
No, I have put it behind me. The horror of dreams

Is past. Now comes the horror of life.

FIGURE: Of life?

BRAND: Come with me, Agnes.

FIGURE: Stop! Brand, what will you do?

BRAND: What I must. Live what till now I dreamed;
Make the illusion real.

FIGURE: Impossible! Remember where that road led you.

BRAND: I will tread it again.

FIGURE: That road of fear in the mist of dreams?
Will you ride it freely and awake?

BRAND: Freely and awake.

FIGURE: And let your child die?

BRAND: And let my child die.

FIGURE: Brand!

BRAND: I must.

FIGURE: And kill me?

BRAND: I must.

FIGURE: Quench the candles in the night,
And shut out the sun in the day?
Never pluck life's fruit, never be soothed
By song? I remember so many songs.

BRAND: I must. Do not waste your prayer.

FIGURE: Do you forget what reward your sacrifices brought
you?
Your hopes betrayed you, everyone forsook you.
Everyone stoned you.

BRAND: I do not suffer for my own reward.
I do not strive for my own victory.

FIGURE: Remember, an Angel with a flaming rod
Drove Man from Paradise.
He set a gulf before the gate.
Over that gulf you cannot leap.

BRAND: The way of longing remains.

FIGURE (disappears; there is a clap of thunder, the mist

348

gathers where it stood, and a sharp and piercing
scream is heard as though from one in flight):

Die! The world has no use for you!

BRAND (stands for a moment as though dazed):

It disappeared in the mist,
Flying on great rough wings across the moor
Like a hawk. It was a deceitful spirit;
The spirit of compromise.

GERD (appears with a rifle):

Did you see him? Did you see the hawk?

BRAND: Yes, child. This time I saw him.

GERD: Quick, tell me—which way did he fly?

We'll go after him. This time we'll get him.

BRAND: No weapon can harm him. You think you've killed
him,
But the next moment he's after you,
As fierce as ever.

GERD: I stole the reindeer-hunter's rifle, and loaded it
With silver. I'm not as mad as they say.

BRAND: I hope you hit him. (Turns to go.)

GERD: Priest, you're limping. Your foot's hurt.

How did that happen?

BRAND: The people hunted me.

GERD (goes closer): Your forehead is red.

BRAND: The people stoned me.

GERD: Your voice used to be clear as song.

Now it creaks like leaves in autumn.

BRAND: Everything—everyone—

GERD: What?

BRAND: Betrayed me.

GERD (stares at him): Ah! Now I know who you are!

I thought you were the priest. Fie upon him and all the
others!
You're the Big Man. The Biggest of all.

BRAND: I used to think I was.

349

GERD: Let me see your hands.

BRAND: My hands?

GERD: They're scarred with nails. There's blood in your
hair.

The thorns' teeth have cut your forehead.

You've been on the cross. My father told me

It happened long ago and far away.

But now I see he was deceiving me.

I know you. You're the Saviour Man!

BRAND: Get away from me!

GERD: Shall I fall down at your feet and pray?

BRAND: Go!

GERD: You gave the blood that will save us all.

There are nail holes in your hands. You are the Chosen
One.

You are the Greatest of all.

BRAND: I am the meanest thing that crawls on earth.

GERD (*looks up; the clouds are lifting*):

Do you know where you are standing?

BRAND (*stares unseeingly*): I stand upon the lowest stair.

There is far to climb and my feet are sore.

GERD (*savagely*):

Answer me! Do you know where you are standing?

BRAND: Yes, now the mist is lifting.

GERD: Yes, it is lifting. Black Peak points its finger towards
heaven.

BRAND (*looks up*): Black Peak? The Ice Church?

GERD: Yes. You came to my church after all.

BRAND: I wish I were far away. Oh, how I long for light

And sun, and the still tenderness of peace.

I long to be where life's summer kingdoms are.
(*Weeps.*)

O Jesus, I have called upon Your name.

Why did You never receive me into Your bosom?

You passed close by me, but You never touched me.
Let me hold one poor corner of Your garment
And wet it with my tears of true repentance.

GERD *(pale)*:

What's the matter? You're crying! Hot tears.
The ice in my memory is thawing into tears.
You're melting the snow on my church roof.
The ice-priest's cloak is sliding from his shoulders.
(Trembles.) Man, why did you never weep before?

BRAND *(serene and shining, as though young again)*:

My life was a long darkness.
Now the sun is shining. It is day.
Until today I sought to be a tablet
On which God could write. Now my life
Shall flow rich and warm. The crust is breaking.
I can weep! I can kneel! I can pray! *(Sinks to his knees.)*

GERD *(looks up towards the sky and says timidly and
quietly)*:

Look, there he sits, the ugly brute. That's him
Casting the shadow. Can't you hear him beating
The sides of the peak with his great wings?
Now is the moment, now! If only the silver will bite!

*She throws the rifle to her cheek and fires. A hollow
boom, like thunder, sounds from high up on the mountain.*

BRAND *(starts up)*: What are you doing?

GERD: I hit him! Look, he's falling! Hear how he groans!
Look at his white feathers floating
Down the mountain side! Ah!
He's rolling down on top of us!

BRAND *(sinks exhausted)*:

Must each man die to atone for human sin?

GERD: Look how he tumbles and rolls!
Oh, I shan't be afraid any more.

Why, he's as white as a dove! *(Shrieks in fear)*
Oh, the horrid, horrid roar!

Throws herself down in the snow.

BRAND *(shrinks before the onrushing avalanche):*
Answer me, God, in the moment of death!
If not by Will, how can Man be redeemed?

The avalanche buries him, filling the whole valley.

A VOICE *(cries through the thunder):* He is the God of Love.

Note on the Translation

Ibsen composed *Brand* in rhymed octosyllabics, varying his rhyming scheme with extraordinary skill. If one listens to the play in Norwegian, one almost forgets that rhyme is being used, although it plays an important part in giving an epigrammatic point to key statements, and reinforcing the strength and dignity of the language.

The present translation avoids rhyme, but otherwise keeps closely to Ibsen's text, except where cuts have been made. Ibsen, writing in 1865, included long discussions on topical issues, such as the Schleswig-Holstein war, the need for land reform, and the danger of an industrial revolution. Although these sections still read vividly as satirical verse, they digress from the main thread of the play, and have been omitted. Other cuts have been made for the sake of dramatic concision, though these are fewer and shorter than might have been supposed necessary.

I gladly express my thanks to Michael Elliott for much patient advice; also to the 59 Theatre Company for commissioning this translation.

The Pillars of
Society

Introduction

Ibsen completed *The Pillars of Society* a few months after his forty-ninth birthday; he wrote it in Munich between 1875 and 1877. Enormously successful and influential at the time of its appearance, and indeed for the next quarter of a century, it has rarely been performed during the past fifty years, having rather glibly been relegated to the category of polemical dramas that have lost their topicality. It is still often thought of nowadays as an apprentice work of documentary rather than practical interest. But John Barton's successful production for the Royal Shakespeare Company at the Aldwych Theatre in 1977—the first in London since 1926—surprised the critics by showing the play to be full of theatrical life, thereby doing it the same service that Michael Elliott's 1959 production at Hammersmith did for *Brand*. *The Pillars of Society* is tightly plotted and beautifully characterized; and at this distance of time we can see that its true subject is not women's rights or the evil practices of nineteenth-century shipowners, but human emotions and relationships. The ending has been condemned as facilely happy, but the same accusation was, until recently, made against *Little Eyolf* and *The Lady from the Sea*, and has been proved false if the plays are capably handled. The chief obstacles to a professional production are the size of the cast and a tendency to verbosity on the part of Bernick and, more particularly, Dr. Rœrlund the schoolmaster. Trim them down, and *The Pillars of Society* stands as an absorbing example of Ibsen in his less familiar mood of humane comedy—the mood which pervades *Love's Comedy*, *The League of Youth* and much of *Peer Gynt* and *The Wild Duck*, and of which isolated characters in his more sombre plays, such as George Tesman in *Hedda Gabler*, Ballested in *The Lady from the Sea*, and Vilhelm Foldal in *John Gabriel Borkman*, are belated manifestations.

The Pillars of Society is often referred to as the first of Ibsen's social prose dramas. That honour in fact belongs to *The League of Youth*, a vigorous and delightful comedy completed eight years earlier which hardly deserves the oblivion which has enveloped it. To *The League of Youth*, too, belongs the credit of being Ibsen's first attempt to write dialogue that was genuinely modern and colloquial. His earlier prose plays, such as *St. John's Eve*, *Lady Inger of Œstraat*, *The Vikings at Helgeland* and *The Pretenders*, had been written in a formalised style. But *The League of Youth*, often assumed by those who have not read it to be an earnest political tract, is a loosely constructed and light-hearted frolic almost in the manner of Restoration comedy,* which happens to have a pushing young politician as its chief character—"Peer Gynt as a politician," someone has described it. *The Pillars of Society* is in a much truer sense the forerunner of the eleven great plays which followed it. Apart from the tightness of its construction, it contains, as *The League of Youth* does not, the elements we commonly associate with an Ibsen play—a marriage founded on a lie, passionate women stunted and inhibited by the conventions of their time, and an arrogant man of high intellectual and practical gifts who destroys, or nearly destroys, the happiness of those nearest to him. It also exhibits, unlike his earlier

---

*It was influenced by the eighteenth-century Norwegian dramatist Ludvig Holberg, one of the few authors Ibsen really admired.

plays, what Henry James admiringly described as "the operation of talent without glamour . . . the ugly interior on which his curtain inexorably rises and which, to be honest, I like for the queer associations it has taught us to respect: the hideous carpet and wallpaper (one may answer for them), the conspicuous stove, the lonely central table, the 'lamps with green shades' as in the sumptuous first act of *The Wild Duck,* the pervasive air of small interests and standards, the sign of limited local life." Above all, *The Pillars of Society* has, despite its overtones of comedy, that peculiarly Ibsenish quality of austerity; what Henry James, on another occasion, described as "the hard compulsion of his strangely inscrutable art."

It is indicative of the technical problems posed by this new form of tightly plotted social realism that *The Pillars of Society* took Ibsen longer to write than any of his other plays except the triple-length *Emperor and Galilean.* No less than five separate drafts of the first act have survived, and over a period of nearly eight years his letters are scattered with excuses for its lack of progress. He began to brood on it as early as December 1869, just after finishing *The League of Youth.* On the fourteenth of that month he wrote to his publisher Frederik Hegel: "I am planning a new and serious contemporary drama in three acts, and expect to start work on it in the immediate future." The following month (25 January 1870) he informed Hegel that he hoped to have it ready by the following October, but on 11 April he wrote: "My new play has not yet got beyond the draft, and since I have to get my travel notes into order it looks like being delayed for some time." These travel notes referred to the visit he had made to Egypt in November 1869 to attend, as official Norwegian representative, the opening of the Suez Canal.

October 1870 arrived, and so far from having the play ready he could only tell Hegel that it "has sufficiently developed in my mind for me to hope that any day now I may be able to start writing it.'' Two sets of notes have survived from this year which contain the first germs of the play. By now he had found a more impressive excuse than the Suez Canal: the Franco-Prussian War, which had started in July of that year. In such an atmosphere (he was living in Germany) how could he concentrate on writing a social drama set in a small Norwegian seaport? He returned instead to the broader historical canvas of *Emperor and Galilean*, on which he had been working intermittently since 1864.

It was in fact another five years before he began the actual writing of *The Pillars of Society*. Apart from completing *Emperor and Galilean*, he prepared for publication a selection of his poems covering the past twenty years; it was his deliberate farewell to poetry, the form which had been his earliest love. He explained this decision in a letter written to Edmund Gosse on 15 January 1874, shortly after the publication of *Emperor and Galilean*, and although his remarks were made with specific reference to that play, they apply even more strongly to the works which followed. I quote the passage in Gosse's own translation:

''The illusion I wanted to produce is that of reality. I wished to produce the impression on the reader that what he was reading was something that had really happened. If I had employed verse, I should have counteracted my own intention and prevented the accomplishment of the task I had set myself. The many ordinary and insignificant characters whom I have introduced into the play would have become indistinct, and indistinguishable from one another, if I had allowed all of them to speak in one and the same rhythmical measure. We are no longer living in the age of Shakespeare. Among sculptors, there is already talk of painting statues in the natural colours. Much can be said both for and against this. I have no desire to see the Venus de Milo painted, but I would rather see the head of a negro executed in black than in white marble.

"Speaking generally, the style must conform to the degree of ideality which pervades the representation. My new drama [*Emperor and Galilean*] is no tragedy in the ancient acceptation; what I desired to depict was human beings, and therefore I would not let them talk in 'the language of the gods.'"

In the summer of 1874 Ibsen returned to Norway for the first time since he had left it ten years earlier. There the strife between the conservatives and the liberals had reached its height and, as a result of *The League of Youth*, which was an attack on the hollowness of radical politicians, Ibsen found the conservatives hailing him as their champion. He had, however, no intention of attaching himself to any political party, and when he read in the right-wing newspaper *Morgenbladet* an editorial demand that a candidate for a professorship at the University should be rejected on the grounds that he was a freethinker, Ibsen seized the opportunity to advertise his independence. He withdrew his subscription to *Morgenbladet* and changed to the left-wing newspaper *Dagbladet*. The uneasiness of the conservatives on hearing this—Ibsen was famous enough by now for the students to arrange a torchlight procession in his honour before he left—would have been considerably increased if they had known what he was preparing for them.

After two and a half months in Norway, he returned briefly to Dresden and then, the following spring (1875), he moved to Munich, a city which he found much more to his liking and where he was to spend most of the next sixteen years. At last, in the autumn of that year, nearly six years after he had first begun to brood on it, he settled down to the actual writing of *The Pillars of Society*. At first things went well. On 23 October he wrote to Hegel: "My new play is progressing swiftly; in a few days I shall have completed the first act, which I always find the most difficult part. The title will be: *The Pillars of Society,* a Play in Five [*sic*] Acts. In a way it can be regarded as a counterblast to *The League of Youth,* and will touch on several of the more important questions of our time." On 25 November he writes: "Act 1 of my new play is finished and *fair-copied;* I am now working on Act 2." By 10 December he is "working at it daily and am now doubly anxious to get the manuscript to you as quickly as possible." On 26 January 1876 he expects to "have it ready by May."

But now things began to go less smoothly. After 26 February, when he writes to the director of the Bergen Theatre that it "will probably be printed during the summer," there is no further mention of the play in his letters until 15 September, when he explains rather lengthily to Hegel that he has been so distracted by productions or plans for productions of his earlier plays—*The Pretenders* in Meiningen, Schwerin and Berlin, *The Vikings at Helgeland* in Munich, Leipzig, Vienna and Dresden—that he has been "compelled to postpone completion of my new play; but on my return to Munich at the beginning of next month, I intend to get it polished off." But progress continued to be slow. 1877 arrived, and on 9 February he could only tell Hegel, who must by now have been growing a little impatient: "I shall have my new play ready in the summer, and will send you the manuscript as soon as possible." However, on 20 April he wrote that it "is now moving rapidly towards its conclusion," and at last, on 24 June 1877, he was able to report: "Today I take advantage of a free moment to tell you that on the 15th inst. I completed my new play and am now going ahead with the fair-copying." He posted the fair copy to Hegel in five instalments between 29 July and 20 August 1877.

The Pillars of Society was published by Hegel's firm, Gyldendal of Copenhagen, on 11 October 1877, and achieved immediate and widespread success. Throughout Scandinavia, the liberals and radicals hailed it with as much delight as that with which the conservatives had greeted *The League of Youth*. The first edition of 6,000 copies sold out in seven weeks, and a further 4,000 had to be printed. It was first performed on 18 November 1877 in Copenhagen, where it was received with great enthusiasm, and it was equally acclaimed in Christiania,* Stockholm and Helsinki. It also gave Ibsen his first real breakthrough in Germany. In the absence of any copyright protection, three separate German translations were published early in 1878 (one of them by a man described by Ibsen as "a frightful literary bandit"), and in February of that year it was produced at five different theatres in Berlin within a fortnight. Twenty-seven German and Austrian theatres staged it within the year. In England, William Archer, then aged twenty-two, made a "hurried translation" entitled, rather uninspiringly, *The Supports of Society;* an analysis by him of the play, with extracts from his translation, was published in the *Mirror of Literature* on 2 March 1878. Since "no publisher would look at" this version, he made another and more careful one, under the new title of *Quicksands*, and this was performed for a single matinée at the Gaiety Theatre, London, on 15 December 1880—a noteworthy occasion, for it was the first recorded performance of any Ibsen play in England. *The Pillars of Society* was not staged in America, at any rate in English—though it had been acted there in German—until 13 March 1891, when it was produced at the Lyceum Theatre, New York. In 1892 it was performed in Australia and South Africa, in 1893 in Rome; and in 1896 Lugné-Poe

---

*In Swedish at the Mœllergaten Theatre. Ibsen refused to allow the Christiania Theatre to stage it because "the new director is a quite useless man," and the play was not performed in Norwegian in the capital until the following spring.

staged it at his Théâtre de l'Œuvre in Paris. By the end of the century, according to Archer, it had been performed no less than 1,200 times in Germany and Austria, a remarkable record for those days.

The Pillars of Society dealt with two problems of extreme topicality for the eighteen-seventies, and it is a measure of the play's emotional and dramatic content that it has retained its validity despite the fact that both issues have long since been settled. One was the question of women's rights; the other, that of "floating coffins," i.e. unseaworthy ships which were deliberately sacrificed with their crews so that their owners could claim insurance. Controversy over the former problem reached its height in Norway during the seventies. The Norwegian novelist Camilla Collett had fired a warning shot as early as 1853, with her novel *The Judge's Daughters*. In 1869 John Stuart Mill published *The Subjection of Women*, which Ibsen's friend Georg Brandes translated into Danish the same year. Matilda Schjœtt's *Conversation of a Group of Ladies about the Subjection of Women* (published anonymously in 1871) and Camilla Collett's *Last Papers* (1872) set the issue squarely before the Norwegian public; in 1874 a Women's Reading Society was founded in Christiania, and in 1876 Asta Hanseen, a great champion of the cause, began a series of lectures on women's rights, but was so furiously assailed that in 1880 she emigrated to America. She was the original of Lona Hessel (Ibsen at first gave the character the surname of Hassel, but changed it, presumably so as to avoid too direct an identification with Hanseen). Camilla Collett exerted a direct influence on Ibsen, for he had seen a good deal of her in Dresden in 1871, and again in Munich in the spring of 1877 when he was writing the play, and when they had many arguments about marriage and other female problems. Another influence was Ibsen's wife Suzannah; the subject of women's rights was one about which she had long felt strongly. Ibsen had already touched tentatively on this problem in *The League of Youth,* and he was to deal with it more minutely in his next play, *A Doll's House.* His original intention in *The Pillars of Society* was to be even more outspoken than he finally was, for in one of the preliminary drafts Dina announces her decision to go off with her lover without marrying him; but he evidently doubted whether the theatres would stage a play which suggested anything quite so daring, and legalised their relationship.

The problem of the "floating coffins" was first forced upon Ibsen's attention by an English Member of Parliament. In 1868 Samuel Plimsoll had sought in the House of Commons to have the State interfere against the cold-blooded and unscrupulous sacrifice of human life by sending men to sea in rotten ships. In 1873 he succeeded in getting a law passed to enforce seaworthiness; but this proved too slack. On 22 July 1875 he created a tremendous commotion in Parliament by a boldly outspoken attack on the people responsible for such a policy; he called the owners of such ships murderers and the politicians who supported them scoundrels. This so roused the conscience of the nation that a temporary bill went through in a few days, and its principles were made permanent by the Merchant Shipping Act of the following year. Plimsoll's protest echoed throughout the world, and in a seafaring country such as Norway it rang especially loudly. A particularly scandalous case had occurred in Christiania during Ibsen's visit there in 1874. On 2 September of that year, at the annual general meeting of the shipping insurance company Norske Veritas, questions were asked about a ship which, after having been declared seaworthy, sprang a leak while at sea and was shown to be completely rotten. At the annual general meeting a year later two similar cases were mentioned, and a storm of indignation was aroused. The matter was reported in detail in the newspapers, and Ibsen can hardly have failed to read about it.

The Pillars of Society is full of memories of Grimstad, the little port where Ibsen had spent his years as a chemist's apprentice (just as *The League of Youth* is full of memories of his birthplace, Skien). The *Palm Tree* was the name of a Grimstad ship. Touring theatrical companies played in the hall of a sailmaker named Mœller; an actress belonging to one of them had returned there after being involved in a scandal, and had tried to keep herself by taking in washing and sewing like Dina Dorf's mother, but had been shooed out of town by the local gossips. Foreign ships came in for repairs, and foreign visitors turned the place upside-down, like the crew of the *Indian Girl*. In the autumn of 1849, six months before Ibsen left for Christiania, the Socialist Marcus Thrane had arrived in Grimstad and founded a Workers' Association, like the one Aune belonged to. And the Bernicks had their origin in a family named Smith Petersen. Morten Smith Petersen, the original of Karsten Bernick, returned to Grimstad from abroad in the eighteen-forties, and ran his aged mother's business for a while, but finally had to close it down. He then started his own ship-yard and an insurance company, and eventually founded the Norske Veritas company which earned the notoriety referred to above. He had died in 1872, but his sister Margrethe Petersen survived. She was an elementary schoolteacher, and was the original of Martha Bernick.

The rich quantity of notes and draft material which has been preserved enables us to plot the development of *The Pillars of Society* in some detail. His first notes, made in 1870, begin: "The main theme must be how women sit modestly in the background while the men busily pursue their petty aims with an assurance which at once infuriates and impresses." The main characters are to be an "old white-haired lady" with two sons, one a shipowner, the other a ship's officer who has been abroad for ten years on foreign service. The shipowner's wife, "a fêted beauty before she married, is full of poetry but is bitter and unsatisfied; she makes demands of life which are, or seem, excessive." In other words, Mrs. Bernick, as originally conceived, is a forerunner of the great line of Ibsen heroines—Nora Hellmer, Mrs. Alving, Rebecca West, Ellida Wangel, Hedda Gabler, Rita Allmers, the Rentheim twins in *John Gabriel Borkman,* and Maja and Irene in *When We Dead Awaken.* Martha, too, appears in these early notes, jotted down five years before the play was written: "her sister, still unsure of herself; has grown up quietly admiring the man who is absent and far away." But although several of the characters of *The Pillars of Society* as we know it are here, the plot as originally conceived bears little relation to that of the final version; the naval officer falls in love with the sister (i.e., Martha), but she is already in love with a student, and the officer's mother persuades him to give up the girl and go away. "The greatest victory," she tells him, "is to conquer oneself"—a kind of echo of Brand's "The victory of victories is to lose everything." There is also reference to "the foster-daughter of sixteen, sustained by daydreams and expectations" (i.e., Dina). The play at this stage was to be "a comedy," presumably of the same genre as *The League of Youth.*

In his next notes, made five years later, we find much more of the play as we know it. A scenic synopsis includes the schoolmaster reading to the assembled wives, the husbands discussing the railway, the foster-daughter (here called Valborg) impatient and longing to get away (to her mother, who is still alive), and Lona's arrival with the steamer; Act 1 ends with her "appearing in the doorway to the garden as the curtain falls." In Act 2, "the returned wanderers [i.e., Lona and the Captain] start turning things upside-down in the town. Rumours about the Captain's great wealth and the earlier scandal concerning Valborg's mother. The schoolmaster begins to think of getting engaged to Valborg. Conflict begins between the factory-owner and the Captain." Act 3: "News about irregularities in the repairs to the ship. The engagement is announced and celebrated. The Captain decides to leave the country. Fresh information from the yards. The factory-owner hesitates; for the moment, nothing must be said." Act 4: "Secret understanding between the Captain and Valborg. The railway project secured. Great ovations. Olaf runs away with the Captain and Valborg. Exciting final catastrophe."

The list of characters has by now grown considerably. Apart from Bennick [sic], his wife, his blind mother and his sister Margrete (Martha), Miss "Hassel," the schoolmaster "Rœrstad," Valborg (who suddenly becomes Dina), and Captain John Tennyson (later Rawlinson), we also have Madame Dorf, young Mrs. Bernick's father Mads Tœnnesen (a "shipowner and master builder nicknamed 'The Badger' "), his other son Emil (altered to Hilmar), and Evensen, "a supply teacher." As synopsis follows synopsis, the list of characters changes; Aune, Sandstad and "Knap" appear, Bennick becomes Bernick, and the whole of the older generation is removed—Bernick's mother, Madame Dorf, Evensen the supply teacher and, eventually, Mads Tœnnesen, though he was to reappear three plays later as Morten Kiil in An Enemy of the People.

The drafts which follow comprise four versions of Act 1 or part of it, a draft of the whole play, and Ibsen's final fair copy in the version familiar to us. The first draft of Act 1 is different from the final version in numerous respects, and makes interesting reading. Among other things it contains a rare example of Ibsen trying to write English. The clerk Knap announces in Norwegian that since "the Captain fell overboard in the North Sea and the mate has delirium tremens," the Indian Girl has arrived under the command of "a sailor who was on board as a passenger . . . John Rawlinson, Esqr., New Orleans." Captain Rawlinson then appears and the following lively exchange takes place in English:

BERNICK: Good morning, master Rawlinson! This way, if you please, sir! I am master Bernick!

CAPTAIN RAWLINSON (*waves his handkerchief and cries*): Very well, Karsten; but first three hurrah for the old *grævling!**

The draft makes very spirited reading, and it is only when we compare it with the final version that we realize how much Ibsen gained in the rewriting. Bernick has much superfluous talk trimmed down, Lona is given a far more effective entrance, Aune (the only sympathetic portrait of a working-class man Ibsen ever attempted) is introduced quickly instead of having to wait until Act 2, a good deal of argument as to the pros and cons of the railway is cut, and we are told far more about the characters' past, notably Lona's quarrel with Bernick and the returned brother's supposed intrigue with Madame Dorf. Hilmar (who with his hypochondria and fanciful speech anticipates Hjalmar Ekdal in *The Wild Duck*) and Lona are much more sharply characterized; and the "floating coffin" issue, absent from the first draft, is introduced. The subsequent drafts show Ibsen groping painfully towards his final conception, and together they chart his progress from the vigorous but rather artless method of *The League of Youth* towards the compactness and inevitability of *A Doll's House*.

The Pillars of Society was not the first realistic prose play. Apart from *The League of Youth*, Bjœrnson's two plays *A Bankrupt* and *The Editor*, both written in 1875, were explo-

---

*The Norwegian word for badger.

rations in this field. But these are not plays in the truest sense; they are melodramas which indict individual figures. *The Pillars of Society* was the first play to combine the three elements of colloquial dialogue, objectivity, and tightness of plot which are the requirements and characteristics of modern prose drama. The effect of the play on the younger generation of its time has been recorded by Otto Brahm, one of the founders of the Freie Bühne in Berlin, a theatre comparable in influence to Antoine's Théâtre Libre and Stanislavsky's Moscow Arts. In 1878, when Brahm was twenty-two, he saw *The Pillars of Society* at a small theatre in Berlin. Many years later he recalled that this was "the first strong theatrical impression" that he received. "It was," he said, "my first intimation of a new world of creative art."

MICHAEL MEYER

370

CHARACTERS

KARSTEN BERNICK, shipowner and consul
BETTY, his wife
OLAF, their son, aged thirteen
MARTHA, Karsten's sister
JOHAN TŒNNESEN, Betty's younger brother
LONA HESSEL, her elder half-sister
HILMAR TŒNNESEN, Betty's cousin
DR. RŒRLUND, a schoolmaster
MR. RUMMEL, a wholesale dealer
MR. VIGELAND, a merchant
MR. SANDSTAD, a merchant
DINA DORF, a young girl living with the Bernicks
KRAP, a chief clerk
AUNE, a shipyard foreman
MRS. RUMMEL
MRS. HOLT, the postmaster's wife
MRS. LYNGE, wife of the local doctor
MISS RUMMEL
MISS HOLT
TOWNSPEOPLE and OTHER RESIDENTS, FOREIGN SEAMEN,
STEAMSHIP PASSENGERS, etc.

The action takes place in Karsten Bernick's house in a small
Norwegian seaport.

ACT ONE

A spacious garden room in KARSTEN BERNICK's *house. Downstage left, a door leading to* BERNICK's *room; upstage in the same wall is a similar door. In the centre of the opposite wall is a large entrance door. The rear wall is composed almost entirely of fine, clear glass, with an open door giving on to a broad verandah over which an awning is stretched. Steps lead down from the verandah into the garden, part of which can be seen, enclosed by a fence with a small gate. Beyond the fence is a street, the far side of which is lined with small wooden houses painted in bright colours. It is summer and the sun is shining warmly. Now and then* PEOPLE *wander along the street; they stop and speak to each other, buy things from a little corner shop, etc.*

In the garden room a group of LADIES *is seated round a table. At the head of it sits* MRS. BERNICK; *on her left,* MRS. HOLT *and her* DAUGHTER; *beyond them,* MRS. RUMMEL *and* MISS RUMMEL. *On* MRS. BERNICK's *right sit* MRS. LYNGE, MARTHA BERNICK *and* DINA DORF. *All the* LADIES *are busy sewing. On the table lie large heaps of linen cut into shapes and half-finished, and other articles of clothing. Further upstage, at a little table on which stand two potted plants and a glass of lemonade,* DR. RŒRLUND, *the schoolmaster, sits reading aloud from a book with gilt edges, though only the odd word can be heard by the audience. Outside in the gar-*

den, OLAF BERNICK *is running about, shooting at a target with a bow and arrow.*

After a few moments, AUNE, *a shipyard foreman, enters quietly through the door on the right. The reading is interrupted briefly;* MRS. BERNICK *nods to* AUNE *and points to the door on the left.* AUNE *walks quietly over and knocks softly on* BERNICK's *door. Pause. He knocks again.* KRAP, *the chief clerk, comes out of the room with his hat in his hand and papers under his arm.*

KRAP: Oh, it's you?

AUNE: Mr. Bernick sent for me.

KRAP: I know: but he can't see you himself. He's deputed me to tell you—

AUNE: You? I'd much rather speak to—

KRAP: He's deputed me to tell you this. You're to stop giving these talks to the men on Saturday evenings.

AUNE: Oh? I thought my free time was my own—

KRAP: You don't get free time in order for you to stop the men working. Last Saturday you told them their interests were threatened by the new machines and these new methods we've introduced down at the yard. Why d'you do it?

AUNE: For the good of the community.

KRAP: That's odd. Mr. Bernick says this kind of thing will disintegrate the community.

AUNE: I don't mean by community what Mr. Bernick does, Mr. Krap. As foreman of the Workers' Association I—

KRAP: You're Mr. Bernick's foreman. And the only community to which you owe allegiance is the Bernick Shipbuilding Company. That's where we all get our living. Well, now you know what Mr. Bernick had to say to you.

AUNE: Mr. Bernick wouldn't have said it like that, Mr. Krap. But I know whom I've to thank for this. It's that damned American ship that's put in for repairs. Those people expect us to work like they do over there, and it isn't—

KRAP: Yes, well I haven't time to go into all that. Now you've heard Mr. Bernick's orders, so stop this nonsense. Run back to the yard, now. I'm sure they need you there. I'll be down myself shortly. Pardon me, ladies!

He bows and goes out through the garden and down the street. AUNE *exits quietly, right.* DR. RŒRLUND, *who has continued his reading during the foregoing dialogue, which has been conducted in subdued voices, finishes his book and closes it with a snap.*

RŒRLUND: And that, dear ladies, concludes our story.

MRS. RUMMEL: Oh, what an instructive book!

MRS. HOLT: And so moral!

MRS. BERNICK: Yes, a book like that certainly gives one food for thought.

RŒRLUND: Indeed, yes. It provides a salutary contrast to the horrors that confront us daily in the newspapers and magazines. This rouged and gilded exterior which Society flaunts before our eyes—what does it really hide? Hollowness and corruption—if I may use such words. No solid moral foundation. These so-called great modern communities are nothing but whited sepulchres.

MRS. HOLT: How true!

MRS. RUMMEL: We only need look at the crew of that American ship that's in port.

RŒRLUND: I would rather not sully your ears by speaking of such human refuse. But even in respectable circles, what do we see? Doubt and unrest fermenting on every side; spiritual dissension and universal uncertainty. Out there, family life is everywhere undermined. An impudent spirit of subversion challenges our most sacred principles.

DINA *(without looking up)*: But hasn't there been great progress too?

RŒRLUND: Progress? I don't understand—

MRS. HOLT *(amazed)*: Dina, really!

MRS. RUMMEL *(simultaneously)*: Dina, how can you?

RŒRLUND: I hardly think it would be healthy if this progress you speak of were to gain favour in our community. No; we in this little town should thank God that we are as we are. The occasional tare is, alas, to be found among the wheat here as elsewhere; but we strive with all the might that God has given us to root it up. We must keep our community pure, ladies. We must hold these untried theories which an impatient age would force upon us at arm's length.

MRS. HOLT: Yes, there are many too many of them about.

MRS. RUMMEL: Yes, last year we were only saved from having that horrible railway forced upon us by the skin of our teeth.

MRS. BERNICK: Karsten put a stop to that.

RŒRLUND: Providence, Mrs. Bernick, Providence. You may rest assured that in refusing to countenance the scheme your husband was but the instrument of a Higher Purpose.

MRS. BERNICK: But the way they attacked him in the newspapers! Oh, but dear Dr. Rœrlund, we've completely forgotten to thank you. It really is more than kind of you to sacrifice so much of your time for us.

RŒRLUND: Oh, nonsense. My school has its holidays.

MRS. BERNICK: Well, yes, but it's still a sacrifice, Dr. Rœrlund.

RŒRLUND *(moves his chair closer)*: Pray do not speak of it, dear lady. Are you not all making sacrifices for a noble cause? And do you not make them gladly and willingly? These depraved sinners whose moral condition we are striving to ameliorate are as wounded soldiers upon a battlefield; and you, dear ladies, are the Sisters of Mercy, the ministering angels who pick lint for these fallen creatures, wind your bandages gently round their wounds, tend and heal them—

MRS. BERNICK: How wonderful to be able to view everything in such a charitable light.

RŒRLUND: It is a gift one is born with; but much can be done to foster it. It is merely a question of having a serious vocation in life and viewing everything in the light of that vocation. What do you say, Miss Bernick? Do you not find that life has a more solid moral foundation since you decided to devote yourself to the noble task of educating the young?

MARTHA: I don't really know what to say. Sometimes as I sit there in the schoolroom I wish I were far away, on the wild sea.

RŒRLUND: Temptation, my dear Miss Bernick! You must bar the door against such unruly guests. The wild sea— well, of course you don't mean that literally; you are thinking of the turbulent ocean of modern society in which so many human souls founder. Do you really envy that life you hear murmuring, nay, thundering outside? Only look down into the street. People walk there in the sunshine sweating and wrestling with their petty problems. No, we are better off who sit coolly here behind our windows with our backs turned on the direction from which unrest and disturbance might come.

MARTHA: Yes, of course. I'm sure you're right—

RŒRLUND: And in a house such as this—a good, clean home, where family life may be seen in its fairest form— where peace and harmony reign— (To MRS. BERNICK) Are you listening for something, Mrs. Bernick?

MRS. BERNICK (has turned towards the door downstage left): How loudly they're talking in there!

RŒRLUND: Is something important being discussed?

MRS. BERNICK: I don't know. My husband seems to have someone with him.

HILMAR TŒNNESEN, *with a cigar in his mouth, enters through the door on the right, but stops when he sees the ladies.*

HILMAR: Oh, I beg your pardon— *(Turns to leave.)*

MRS. BERNICK: No, come in, Hilmar; you're not disturbing us. Did you want something?

HILMAR: No, I was just looking in. Good morning, ladies. *(To* MRS. BERNICK*)* Well, what's going to be the outcome?

MRS. BERNICK: How do you mean?

HILMAR: Your husband's called a council of war.

MRS. BERNICK: Oh? But what on earth about?

HILMAR: Oh, it's some nonsense about that confounded railway again.

MRS. RUMMEL: How disgraceful!

MRS. BERNICK: Poor Karsten! As if he hadn't enough worries already!

RŒRLUND: But how is this possible, Mr. Tœnnesen? Mr. Bernick made it perfectly clear last year that he wouldn't have anything to do with any railway.

HILMAR: Yes, that's what I thought. But I met Krap just now, and he tells me that the question's being reconsidered, and that Bernick's having a meeting with three of the other local plutocrats.

MRS. RUMMEL: Yes, I thought I heard my husband's voice.

HILMAR: Oh yes, Rummel's there all right; and Sandstad who owns that big store up the hill; and Michael Vigeland—you know, the one they call Holy Mick—

RŒRLUND *coughs.*

HILMAR: Oh, sorry, Doctor.

MRS. BERNICK: Just when everything was so nice and peaceful here.

HILMAR: Well, personally I shouldn't be sorry if they started squabbling again. Give us a bit of fun—

RŒRLUND: I think we can do without that kind of fun.

HILMAR: Depends on your temperament. Certain natures need to be harrowed by conflict occasionally. Provincial life doesn't provide many opportunities, worse luck; and not everybody has the guts to— *(Glances at* RŒRLUND'S *book.) Woman as the Servant of Society.* What's this rubbish?

MRS. BERNICK: Good heavens, Hilmar, you mustn't say that! You can't have read it.

HILMAR: No, and I don't intend to.

MRS. BERNICK: You don't seem in a very good temper today.

HILMAR: I'm not.

MRS. BERNICK: Didn't you sleep well last night?

HILMAR: No, I slept rottenly. I took a walk yesterday evening—for my health, you know—and wandered into the Club and read a book some chap had written about the North Pole. I find it very good for my nerves to read about man's struggle with the elements.

MRS. RUMMEL: It doesn't appear to have agreed with you, Mr. Tœnnesen.

HILMAR: No, it didn't really agree with me. I tossed and turned all night. Dreamed I was being chased by a horrible walrus.

OLAF *(who has come up on to the verandah):* Have you been chased by a walrus, Uncle?

HILMAR: I dreamed it, you young jackass. Are you still playing with that silly bow? Why don't you get yourself a proper rifle?

OLAF: Oh, I'd love one! But—

HILMAR: There's some sense in having a rifle. That slow pressure on the trigger, you know—good for the nerves.

OLAF: And I could shoot bears with it, Uncle! But Father won't let me.

MRS. BERNICK: You mustn't put such ideas into his head, Hilmar.

HILMAR: Hm! Fine lot his generation's going to be! All this talk about the importance of sport, and all they do is play silly games, when they ought to be toughening their characters by staring danger unflinchingly in the face. Don't stand there pointing that bow at me, you little fool, it might go off.

OLAF: But Uncle, there's no arrow in it.

HILMAR: You can never be sure. There might be. Point it somewhere else, I tell you. Why the devil don't you go over to America on one of your father's ships? You could hunt buffaloes there. Or fight redskins.

MRS. BERNICK: Hilmar, really!

OLAF: Oh yes, Uncle, I'd love to! And I might meet Uncle Johan and Aunt Lona!

HILMAR: Hm—I shouldn't bother about that.

MRS. BERNICK: You can go back into the garden now, Olaf.

OLAF: Can I go out into the street too, Mother?

MRS. BERNICK: Yes, but not too far.

OLAF *runs out through the garden gate.*

RŒRLUND: You ought not to stuff the child's head with such ideas, Mr. Tœnnesen.

HILMAR: Oh, no. Of course not. He's got to spend the rest of his life sitting safe at home, like all the others.

RŒRLUND: Why don't you go to America yourself?

HILMAR: I? In my state of health? But of course no one in this town bothers about that. Besides, one has certain responsibilities towards the community one lives in. There's got to be someone here to keep the flag of ideals flying. Ugh, now he's started shouting again.

LADIES: Who? Shouting? Who is shouting?

HILMAR: I don't know. They're raising their voices in there, and it's very bad for my nerves.

MRS. RUMMEL: Ah, that's my husband, Mr. Tœnnesen. He's so used to addressing public meetings.

RŒRLUND: The others aren't doing too badly either, by the sound of it.

HILMAR: But of course! The moment their pockets are threatened— Oh, everyone here's so petty and materialistic. Ugh!

MRS. BERNICK: Well anyway, that's better than the old days, when people thought of nothing but dissipation.

MRS. LYNGE: Were things really so dreadful here before?

MRS. RUMMEL: Indeed they were, Mrs. Lynge. You may think yourself fortunate that you didn't live here then.

MRS. HOLT: Yes, there have certainly been great changes. When I think of what things were like when I was a young girl—

MRS. RUMMEL: Oh, you only need to look back fifteen years. My word, the goings on there used to be! Why, there was a dance club, *and* a musical society—

MARTHA: And a dramatic society. I remember that well.

MRS. RUMMEL: Yes, it was they who put on that play of yours, Mr. Tœnnesen.

HILMAR (*upstage*): Really? Oh, I don't—er—

RŒRLUND: Mr. Tœnnesen wrote a play?

MRS. RUMMEL: Why, yes. Long before you came here, Dr. Rœrlund. It only ran for one night.

MRS. LYNGE: Wasn't that the play you were telling me about in which you acted one of the young lovers, Mrs. Rummel?

MRS. RUMMEL (*shoots a glance at* RŒRLUND): I? I really don't recall that, Mrs. Lynge. But I do remember all the dreadful parties that used to go on.

MRS. HOLT: Yes, I know houses where they used to hold big parties twice a week.

MRS. LYNGE: And I hear there was a company of strolling players that used to come here.

MRS. RUMMEL: Yes, they were the worst of all—

MRS. HOLT *coughs uneasily.*

MRS. RUMMEL: Er—strolling players, did you say? No, I don't remember them.

MRS. LYNGE: But I hear they got up to all kinds of wicked pranks. Tell me, is there any truth in those stories?

MRS. RUMMEL: None whatever, Mrs. Lynge, I assure you.

MRS. HOLT: Dina, my love, pass me that piece of linen, will you?

MRS. BERNICK *(simultaneously)*: Dina dear, run out and ask Katrine to bring us some coffee.

MARTHA: I'll come with you, Dina.

DINA *and* MARTHA *go out through the door upstage left.*

MRS. BERNICK: If you'll excuse me for a moment, ladies, I think we'll take coffee outside.

She goes out on to the verandah and lays a table. DR. RŒRLUND *stands in the doorway talking to her.* HILMAR TŒNNESEN *sits down outside and smokes.*

MRS. RUMMEL *(quietly)*: My goodness, Mrs. Lynge, how you frightened me!

MRS. LYNGE: I?

MRS. HOLT: Yes, but you started it really, Mrs. Rummel.

MRS. RUMMEL: I? How can you say such a thing, Mrs. Holt? I never let a single word pass my lips.

MRS. LYNGE: But what is all this?

MRS. RUMMEL: How could you bring up the subject of—! I mean, really! Didn't you see Dina was here?

MRS. LYNGE: Dina? But good heavens, is there anything the matter with—?

MRS. HOLT: And in this house? Don't you know it was Mrs. Bernick's brother who—?

MRS. LYNGE: What about him? I don't know anything—I'm a newcomer here—

MRS. RUMMEL: You mean you haven't heard about—? Hm. (*To* MISS RUMMEL) Hilda dear, run down into the garden for a few minutes.

MRS. HOLT: You too, Netta. And be sure you're nice to poor dear Dina when she comes back.

MISS RUMMEL *and* MISS HOLT *go into the garden.*

MRS. LYNGE: Well? What was this about Mrs. Bernick's brother?

MRS. RUMMEL: Don't you know it was he who was involved in that dreadful scandal?

MRS. LYNGE: Mr. Tœnnesen was involved in a dreadful scandal?

MRS. RUMMEL: Oh good heavens no, Mr. Tœnnesen is her cousin, Mrs. Lynge. I'm talking about her brother—

MRS. HOLT: The Prodigal of the family—

MRS. RUMMEL: His name was Johan. He ran away to America.

MRS. HOLT: Had to, you understand.

MRS. LYNGE: And it was he who was involved in this dreadful scandal?

MRS. RUMMEL: Yes. It was a kind of a—what shall I call it?—a kind of a—with Dina's mother. Oh, I remember it as if it had happened yesterday. Johan Tœnnesen was working in old Mrs. Bernick's office. Karsten Bernick had just come back from Paris—he hadn't got engaged yet—

MRS. LYNGE: Yes, but the dreadful scandal?

382

MRS. RUMMEL: Well, you see, that winter a theatrical troupe was here in town—

MRS. HOLT: And among them was an actor named Dorf, and his wife. All the young men were quite crazy about her.

MRS. RUMMEL: Yes, heaven knows what they could see in her. Well, Mr. Dorf came home late one night—

MRS. HOLT: Unexpectedly, you understand—

MRS. RUMMEL: And what should he find but—no, I really can't bring myself to speak of it.

MRS. HOLT: No, Mrs. Rummel, he didn't *find* anything. The door was locked. From the inside.

MRS. RUMMEL: Yes, well, that's what I'm saying—he found the door locked. And, would you believe it, he—the man who was inside—had to jump out of the window!

MRS. HOLT: Right out of one of the top windows!

MRS. LYNGE: And the man was Mrs. Bernick's brother?

MRS. RUMMEL: It was indeed.

MRS. LYNGE: And that was why he ran away to America?

MRS. HOLT: Yes. Well, of course he had to.

MRS. RUMMEL: And then afterwards they discovered something almost equally dreadful. Would you believe it, he'd stolen some of the firm's money!

MRS. HOLT: But we don't know that for sure, Mrs. Rummel. It may only have been gossip.

MRS. RUMMEL: Oh, but now, really! Didn't the whole town know about it? Didn't old Mrs. Bernick practically go bankrupt because of it? My husband told me so himself. But Heaven forbid that *I* should say anything!

MRS. HOLT: Well, anyway, Mrs. Dorf didn't get the money because she—

MRS. LYNGE: Yes, what happened between Dina's parents after that?

MRS. RUMMEL: Well, Dorf went away and left his wife and child. But Madam had the cheek to stay here a whole year more. Of course, she didn't dare show her face at the theatre. She kept herself by taking in washing and sewing—

MRS. HOLT: And tried to start a dancing academy.

MRS. RUMMEL: Of course, nothing came of it. What parents would entrust their children to the care of a person like that? Besides, as things turned out she didn't last long. She wasn't used to hard work, not that fine lady. She picked up some chest trouble, and died.

MRS. LYNGE: Well, that was a dreadful scandal indeed.

MRS. RUMMEL: Yes, it's been a terrible cross for the Bernicks to bear. It's been the one skeleton in their cupboard, as my husband once phrased it. So don't ever mention the subject in this house, Mrs. Lynge.

MRS. HOLT: Or the half-sister, for heaven's sake!

MRS. LYNGE: Mrs. Bernick has a half-sister too?

MRS. RUMMEL: Did have—fortunately. It's all over between them now. Oh, she was a queer one all right. Would you believe it, she cut her hair off, and when it rained she walked round in gumboots just like a man!

MRS. HOLT: And when the half-brother—the Prodigal—ran away, and the whole town quite naturally raised a hue and cry against him, do you know what she did? Went over and joined him!

MRS. RUMMEL: Yes, but the scandal she created before she went, Mrs. Holt!

MRS. HOLT: Hush, let's not talk of that.

MRS. LYNGE: My goodness, was she involved in a scandal too?

MRS. RUMMEL: Well, it was like this. Karsten Bernick had just got engaged to Betty Tœnnesen; and he was going in to announce the news to her aunt, with his newly-betrothed on his arm—

MRS. HOLT: The Tœnnesens had lost their parents, you see—

MRS. RUMMEL: —when Lona Hessel got up from the chair she was sitting on and gave Karsten Bernick for all his fine airs and breeding such a box on the ears she nearly split his eardrums.

MRS. LYNGE: You don't mean it!

MRS. RUMMEL: As heaven is my witness.

MRS. HOLT: And packed her bags and went to America.

MRS. LYNGE: Then she must have had her eye on him too!

MRS. RUMMEL: Of course she had! She'd been flouncing round here imagining that he'd marry her the moment he got back from Paris.

MRS. HOLT: Yes, fancy her being able to believe that! A man of the world like Karsten Bernick—so genteel and well-bred—the perfect gentleman—every woman's dream—

MRS. RUMMEL: And so virtuous with it all, Mrs. Holt. So moral.

MRS. LYNGE: But what has this Miss Hessel been doing in America?

MRS. RUMMEL: Ah. Over that hangs a veil which had best not be lifted, as my husband once phrased it.

MRS. LYNGE: What do you mean?

MRS. RUMMEL: Well, the family's no longer in contact with her, as you can imagine. But the whole town knows this much, that she's sung for money over there in—hm—places of entertainment—

MRS. HOLT: And given lectures in public—

MRS. RUMMEL: And brought out a wicked book.

MRS. LYNGE: My goodness!

MRS. RUMMEL: Yes, Lona Hessel is another skeleton in the Bernick family cupboard. Well, now you know the whole story, Mrs. Lynge. Of course I've only told you all this so that you'll be on your guard.

MRS. LYNGE: My goodness yes, you can be sure I will. But that poor Dina Dorf! I feel really sorry for her.

MRS. RUMMEL: Oh, it was a great stroke of luck as far as she was concerned. Just imagine if she'd been left in the hands of those parents of hers! We all lent her a helping hand, of course, and did what we could to try to guide her along the right paths. Then Miss Bernick arranged for her to come and live here.

MRS. HOLT: But she's always been a difficult child. Well, what can you expect, when you think of the example she's been set? A girl like that isn't like one of us. We have to take her as we find her, Mrs. Lynge.

MRS. RUMMEL: Hush, here she is. (*Loudly.*) Yes, dear Dina's a very clever girl. Oh, hullo, Dina, are you back? We're just finishing.

MRS. HOLT: Dina, my sweet, how lovely your coffee smells. There's nothing like a nice cup of morning coffee—

MRS. BERNICK (*outside on the verandah*): Everything is ready, ladies!

MISS BERNICK and DINA have meanwhile been helping the MAID to bring in the coffee things. All the LADIES go out on to the verandah and sit down. They talk to DINA with ostentatious amiability. After a few moments, she comes into the room and looks for her sewing.

MRS. BERNICK (*outside at the coffee table*): Dina, won't you join us?

DINA: No, thank you. I don't want any.

She sits down to her sewing. MRS. BERNICK and DR. RŒRLUND exchange a few words; then he comes into the room.

RŒRLUND (*pretends to need something from the table; then says softly*): Dina.

DINA: Yes.

RŒRLUND: Why don't you want to sit outside with us?

DINA: When I came in with the coffee I could see from the expression on that new lady's face that they'd been talking about me.

ROERLUND: But didn't you also notice how friendly she was to you on the verandah?

DINA: That's just what I can't bear.

ROERLUND: You have a stubborn nature, Dina.

DINA: Yes.

ROERLUND: Why?

DINA: That's the way I am.

ROERLUND: Couldn't you try to make yourself different?

DINA: No.

ROERLUND: Why not?

DINA *(looks at him):* I'm one of the depraved sinners.

ROERLUND: Dina!

DINA: Mother was a depraved sinner too.

ROERLUND: Who has told you about these things?

DINA: No one. They never tell me anything. Why don't they? They all treat me so gently, as though I might break into pieces if— Oh, how I hate all this kindness!

ROERLUND: Dina dear, I understand so well how confined you feel here, but—

DINA: Yes, if only I could go far away. I'm sure I could manage on my own if only I didn't live among people who were so—so—

ROERLUND: So what?

DINA: So virtuous and moral.

ROERLUND: Dina, you can't mean that.

DINA: Oh, you know what I mean. Every day Hilda and Netta are brought here so that I can model myself on them. I can never be as clever as them. I don't want to be. Oh, if only I were far away! Then I might be able to become someone.

ROERLUND: You are someone, Dina.

DINA: What's the use, here?

ROERLUND: Then you mean you're seriously thinking of going away?

DINA: I wouldn't stay a day longer, if you weren't here.

RŒRLUND: Tell me, Dina. Why do you like being with me?

DINA: Because you teach me so much about what's beautiful.

RŒRLUND: I teach you about what is beautiful?

DINA: Yes. Or rather—you don't teach me anything; but when I hear you talk, I understand what beauty is.

RŒRLUND: What do you mean by beauty?

DINA: I've never thought.

RŒRLUND: Well, think now. What do you mean by beauty?

DINA: Beauty—is something that is big—and far away.

RŒRLUND: Hm. Dina my dear, I'm deeply concerned about you.

DINA: Is that all?

RŒRLUND: You know how very dear you are to me.

DINA: If I were Hilda or Netta you wouldn't be afraid to let people see it.

RŒRLUND: Oh, Dina, you don't understand all the little things a man has to—! When a man is chosen to be a moral pillar for the society he lives in—well, he can't be sufficiently careful. If only I could be sure that people would not misinterpret my motives—! Well, it can't be helped. You must and shall be rescued. Dina, is it a bargain that when I come—when circumstances permit me to come to you and say: "Here is my hand"—you will take it and be my wife? Will you promise me that, Dina?

DINA: Yes.

RŒRLUND: Thank you—thank you! Because I, too—oh, Dina, you are so very dear to me. Hush, someone's coming! Dina—please—for my sake—go outside and join the others.

She goes out and joins the LADIES. *As she does so,* MR. RUMMEL, MR. SANDSTAD *and* MR. VIGELAND *enter from the room downstage left, followed by* MR. BERNICK, *with a sheaf of papers in his hand.*

388

BERNICK: Right, then, we're agreed.

VIGELAND: Yes, yes. May God's blessing rest upon our plans!

RUMMEL: Never you fear, Bernick. A Norseman's word is his bond. You know that.

BERNICK: There's to be no going back, now. No one's to drop out, whatever opposition we may encounter.

RUMMEL: We stand or fall together, Bernick.

HILMAR (*who has come to the door of the verandah*): Fall? What's going to fall? Railway shares?

BERNICK: On the contrary. The railway is to go ahead.

RUMMEL: Full steam, Mr. Tœnnesen.

HILMAR (*comes closer*): Really?

RŒRLUND: What?

MRS. BERNICK (*at the verandah door*): But Karsten dear, surely you—?

BERNICK: Betty dear, how can these things possibly interest you? (*To the* THREE GENTLEMEN) Well, we must get out a prospectus as quickly as possible. Our names will head the list, of course. The positions we occupy in the community render it our duty to support this cause to the fullest limit of our generosity.

SANDSTAD: Of course, of course.

RUMMEL: We'll see it through, Bernick. You have our word.

BERNICK: Oh yes, I'm not worried about the outcome. But we must use our authority and influence; once we can show that every section of the community is actively participating, the municipality will feel compelled to subscribe its share.

MRS. BERNICK: Karsten, you must come outside and tell us all about it.

BERNICK: My dear Betty, this is not a matter for women to concern themselves with.

HILMAR: You seriously mean you're letting this railway project go through after all?

BERNICK: Yes, of course.

RŒRLUND: But Mr. Bernick, last year you—

BERNICK: Last year the situation was different. The plan then was for a line to run along the coast—

VIGELAND: Which would have been utterly superfluous, Dr. Rœrlund. After all, we have ships—

SANDSTAD: And it'd have been prohibitively expensive—

RUMMEL: Yes, and would have damaged important interests in our town.

BERNICK: The main point is that the project as then conceived would not have benefited the community as a whole. That is why I opposed it; and as a result, they have decided to run the line inland.

HILMAR: Yes, but then it won't touch any of the towns round here.

BERNICK: It will touch our town, my dear Hilmar. We have arranged for a branch line to be built.

HILMAR: Oh? That's a new idea, isn't it?

RUMMEL: Yes—magnificent idea, isn't it? What?

RŒRLUND: Hm.

VIGELAND: There's no denying that Providence might almost have designed that little valley especially so as to accommodate a branch line.

RŒRLUND: Do you really think so, Mr. Vigeland?

BERNICK: Yes, I must confess that I, too, feel it was the hand of Providence that sent me up-country on business last spring and directed my footsteps into this valley, which I had never seen before. Suddenly it struck me like an inspiration that through this valley we could lay a branch line to our little town. I arranged for an engineer to survey the land and I have here his provisional calculations and estimates. Nothing now stands in our way.

MRS. BERNICK (*still in the doorway, with the other* LADIES): But Karsten dear, why have you kept all this hidden from us?

BERNICK: My dear Betty, you wouldn't have been able to understand what it was all about. In any case I haven't mentioned it to anyone until today. But now the decisive moment has arrived. Now we can work openly and with all our strength. Yes, I shall force this project through, even if it means staking everything I possess.

RUMMEL: Us too, Bernick. You can rely on us.

RŒRLUND: You really expect so much from this project then, gentlemen?

BERNICK: Of course we do! Think what a stimulus it will give to our whole community! Think of the great tracts of forest it will render accessible! Think of the mines it will enable us to work! Think of the river with its waterfalls one above the other, and the factories we could build to utilise their power! A whole wealth of new industries will spring into being!

RŒRLUND: But are you not afraid of the possible consequences of more frequent contact with the depraved world outside?

BERNICK: No need to fear that, my dear Doctor. Nowadays our industrious little community rests, thank God, on a sound moral foundation. We have all, if I may say so, helped to cleanse it; and we shall continue to keep it clean, each in his own way. You, Dr. Rœrlund, will maintain your splendid work at the school and in the home. We, the practical men of affairs, will strengthen the community by spreading prosperity over as broad a circle as possible. And our womenfolk—yes, ladies, come closer, you may listen to what I have to say—our womenfolk, I say, our wives and daughters—continue, ladies, I beseech you, to labour untiringly in the cause of charity, and to be a help and a shield to your dear ones, as my beloved Betty and Martha are to me and to Olaf— (*Looks round.*) Yes, where is Olaf today?

MRS. BERNICK: Oh, now the holidays have begun it's hopeless to try to keep him indoors.

BERNICK: I suppose that means he's down on the waterfront again. He'll have an accident before he's finished, you mark my word.

HILMAR: Oh, rubbish. A little skirmish with the elements—

MRS. RUMMEL: Oh, I think it's so wonderful the love you show your family, Mr. Bernick.

BERNICK: Well, the family is the basis on which society rests. A good home, loyal and trustworthy friends, a small close-knit circle with no intrusive elements to cast their shadow—

KRAP *enters right with letters and newspapers.*

KRAP: The foreign mail, Mr. Bernick. And a telegram from New York.

BERNICK *(takes it):* Ah, this'll be from the owners of the *Indian Girl.*

RUMMEL: Has the post come? Then I must ask you to excuse me—

VIGELAND: Me too.

SANDSTAD: Goodbye, Mr. Bernick.

BERNICK: Goodbye, gentlemen, goodbye. And don't forget, we meet at five o'clock this afternoon.

THE THREE GENTLEMEN: Yes, yes. Of course.

They go out right.

BERNICK *(reads the telegram):* Oh no, really, this is typically American! How absolutely disgraceful!

MRS. BERNICK: Oh, Karsten, what is it?

BERNICK: Look at this, Mr. Krap. Here, read it.

KRAP *(reads):* "Execute minimum repairs. Despatch *Indian Girl* as soon as seaworthy. Safe season. At worst, cargo will keep her afloat." Well, bless my soul!

BERNICK: "Cargo will keep her afloat"! Those fellows

know perfectly well that if anything goes wrong that cargo'll send the ship to the bottom like a stone.

RŒRLUND: Well, that only goes to show what the moral climate is like in these so-called great communities.

BERNICK: You're right. They don't even respect human life, as long as they make their profit. *(To* KRAP*)* Can we make the *Indian Girl* seaworthy in four or five days?

KRAP: Yes, if Mr. Vigeland lets us stop work on the *Palm Tree.*

BERNICK: Hm. He won't do that. Well, look through the mail. By the way, did you see Olaf down on the jetty?

KRAP: No, sir.

He goes into the room downstage left.

BERNICK *(reads the telegram again):* Eighteen human lives at stake! And those gentlemen don't turn a hair.

HILMAR: Well, it's a sailor's job to brave the elements. It must be exhilarating to have nothing but a thin plank between yourself and eternity. Good for the nerves—

BERNICK: I'd like to meet the shipowner in this town who could reconcile his conscience to giving an order like this. There isn't a man in this community, not one— *(Sees* OLAF.*)* Ah, here he is. Thank goodness for that.

OLAF, *with a fishing-line in his hand, has run up the street and in through the garden gate.*

OLAF *(still in the garden):* Uncle Hilmar, I've been down looking at the steamer!

BERNICK: Have you been on that jetty again?

OLAF: No, I only went out in a boat. Just fancy, Uncle Hilmar, a whole circus has come ashore, with horses and animals! And there were lots of tourists too!

MRS. RUMMEL: I say, are we going to see a circus?

RŒRLUND: We? I hardly think so.

MRS. RUMMEL: No, no—of course, I didn't mean *us*—I only—

DINA: I should like to see a circus.

OLAF: Yes, so would I!

HILMAR: You little fool, what's worth seeing there? *Dressage,* and all that nonsense. Now, to see a gaucho galloping across the pampas on his snorting mustang— that'd be different! Oh dear, these provincial backwaters—

OLAF (*tugs* MARTHA'S *sleeve):* Look, Aunt Martha, look! There they are!

MRS. HOLT: Oh, my goodness!

MRS. LYNGE: Dear me, what horrible people.

A crowd of TOURISTS *and* TOWNSPEOPLE *appears in the street.*

MRS. RUMMEL: My word, they're proper vagabonds. Look at that woman in the grey dress, Mrs. Holt. She's carrying a knapsack on her back!

MRS. HOLT: Yes. Fancy, she's got it tied to her parasol! I expect she's the ringmaster's—er—wife.

MRS. RUMMEL: There's the ringmaster! The one with the beard. I say, he looks just like a pirate! Don't look at him, Hilda.

MRS. HOLT: Nor you, Netta.

OLAF: Mother, he's waving to us!

BERNICK: What!

MRS. BERNICK: Olaf, what on earth do you mean?

MRS. RUMMEL: My goodness, yes! The woman's waving too!

BERNICK: This really is intolerable.

MARTHA (*gives an involuntary cry):* Oh!

MRS. BERNICK: What is it, Martha?

MARTHA: Oh, nothing. I thought for a moment it—

OLAF (*cries excitedly):* Look, look! Here come the horses

and animals! And there are the Americans, too! All the sailors from the *Indian Girl!*

"Yankee Doodle" is heard, accompanied by a clarinet and drum.

HILMAR *(puts his hands over his ears)*: Ugh, ugh, ugh!

RŒRLUND: I think we should isolate ourselves for a while, ladies. This is not for us. Let us return to our work.

MRS. BERNICK: Ought we perhaps to draw the curtains?

RŒRLUND: That is exactly what I had in mind.

The LADIES *take their places again at the table.* DR. RŒRLUND *closes the verandah door and draws the curtains across it and the windows. The room is plunged into semi-darkness.*

OLAF *(peering out)*: Mother, now the ringmaster's lady's washing her face at the pump.

MRS. BERNICK: What! In the middle of the market-place?

HILMAR: Well, if I was crossing a desert and happened on a well, I don't suppose I'd bother to look round to see if— ugh, that dreadful clarinet!

RŒRLUND: This is becoming a matter for the police.

BERNICK: Ah well, they're foreigners; one mustn't judge them too severely. These people are not born with the sense of decorum which makes us instinctively obey the laws of propriety. Let them go their way. What are they to us? This ribald behaviour, offensive to every standard of decency, fortunately has no place in our community. What the—!

The STRANGE LADY *strides in through the door, right.*

THE LADIES *(in terrified whispers)*: The circus woman! The ringmaster's—er—!

MRS. BERNICK: Good heavens! What is the meaning of this?

MARTHA *(jumps to her feet)*: Oh!

THE LADY: Morning, Betty dear. Morning, Martha. Morning, brother-in-law.

MRS. BERNICK *(with a scream)*: Lona!

BERNICK *(takes a step backwards)*: Good God!

MRS. HOLT: Oh, dear heaven!

MRS. RUMMEL: It can't be possible!

HILMAR: Well! Ugh!

MRS. BERNICK: Lona! Is it really you!

MISS HESSEL: Really me? Sure it's me. Come on, kiss me and prove it!

HILMAR: Ugh! Ugh!

MRS. BERNICK: You mean you've come here to—?

BERNICK: To perform?

MISS HESSEL: Perform? What do you mean, perform?

BERNICK: In the—er—circus.

MISS HESSEL *(roars with laughter)*: Karsten, have you gone nuts? You think I've joined the circus? No—I've learned a few tricks, and acted the clown in more ways than one—(MRS. RUMMEL *coughs*)—but I haven't started jumping through hoops yet.

BERNICK: Then you're not—!

MRS. BERNICK: Thank heaven for that!

MISS HESSEL: No, we came respectably, with the other tourists. Steerage—but we're used to that.

MRS. BERNICK: Did you say *we?*

BERNICK *(takes a step towards her)*: Whom do you mean by *we?*

MISS HESSEL: Me and the kid, of course.

THE LADIES *(shriek)*: Kid?

HILMAR: What!

RŒRLUND: Well, really!

MRS. BERNICK: But Lona, what do you mean?

MISS HESSEL: Who do you think I mean? John, of course; he's the only kid I have, to my knowledge. Johan, you used to call him.

MRS. BERNICK: Johan!

MRS. RUMMEL (sotto voce to MRS. LYNGE): The Prodigal!

BERNICK (unwillingly): Is Johan with you?

MISS HESSEL: Yes, of course. Never go anywhere without him. Say, you *are* all looking down in the mouth. Why are you sitting in the dark? What's that white stuff you're all sewing? Is someone dead?

RŒRLUND: Madam, you find yourself at a meeting of the Society for the Redemption of Fallen Women.

MISS HESSEL (lowers her voice): What! You mean all these respectable-looking ladies are—?

MRS. RUMMEL: Now, really!

MISS HESSEL: Oh, I get it, I get it. Well, if it isn't Mrs. Rummel! And Mrs. Holt! Say, we three haven't grown any shorter in the tooth since we last met! Now, listen, all of you. Let the Fallen Women wait for twenty-four hours; they won't fall any further. This is an occasion for celebration!

RŒRLUND: A homecoming is not always an occasion for celebration.

MISS HESSEL: Is that so? How do you interpret your Bible, Reverend—

RŒRLUND: I am not a Reverend.

MISS HESSEL: Never mind, you'll become one. Say, this charity stuff stinks awful. Just like a shroud. Of course, I'm used to the prairies. Air's fresher there.

BERNICK (mops his brow): Yes, it is rather close in here.

MISS HESSEL: Take it easy, Karsten. You'll surface. (Pulls aside the curtains.) Let's have some daylight in here for when the kid comes. Wait till you see him! He's scrubbed himself as clean as a—

HILMAR: Ugh!

MISS HESSEL (opens the door and windows): That's to say, he *will* have, once he gets a chance up at the hotel. On that ship he got as filthy as a pig.

HILMAR: Ugh! Ugh!

MISS HESSEL: Ugh? Well, bless me if it isn't—! (*Points at* HILMAR *and asks the others*) Does he still sit around here saying "Ugh!"?

HILMAR: I *don't* sit around. I only stay here because my health doesn't permit me to work.

RŒRLUND (*coughs*): Ladies, I hardly think—

MISS HESSEL (*catches sight of* OLAF): Is this yours, Betty? Give us your paw, kid. Are you afraid of your ugly old aunt?

RŒRLUND (*puts his book under his arm*): Ladies, I hardly think the atmosphere here is conducive to further work today. We meet again as usual tomorrow?

MISS HESSEL (*as the other* LADIES *rise to leave*): Sure, why not? You can count me in.

RŒRLUND: You? Forgive my asking, madam, but what can you possibly contribute to our Society?

MISS HESSEL: Fresh air—Reverend!

ACT TWO

The garden room in BERNICK'S *house.* MRS. BERNICK *is seated alone at the work-table with her sewing. After a few moments,* BERNICK *enters right with his hat on, carrying gloves and a stick.*

MRS. BERNICK: Home already, Karsten?

BERNICK: Yes. I have an appointment here.

MRS. BERNICK *(sighs):* Oh, dear. Johan again, I suppose.

BERNICK: No, no, it's with one of the men. *(Takes off his hat.)* Where are all the ladies today?

MRS. BERNICK: Mrs. Rummel and Hilda hadn't time.

BERNICK: Oh? They sent their excuses?

MRS. BERNICK: Yes; they had so much to do at home.

BERNICK: But of course. And the others won't be coming either, I suppose?

MRS. BERNICK: No, they're busy too.

BERNICK: I could have told you that yesterday. Where's Olaf?

MRS. BERNICK: I sent him out for a walk with Dina.

BERNICK: Hm. Dina. Flighty young hussy. Striking up like that with Johan the very first day he arrived—

MRS. BERNICK: But Karsten dear, Dina knows nothing about—

BERNICK: Well, he ought to have had the tact not to pay her so much attention. I saw the look Vigeland gave them.

MRS. BERNICK (*puts her sewing in her lap*): Karsten, why do you think they've come?

BERNICK: Well, I dare say that farm of his isn't doing too well—she said yesterday they'd had to travel steerage—

MRS. BERNICK: Yes, I'm afraid you must be right. But fancy *her* coming with him! After the dreadful way she insulted you!

BERNICK: Oh, that was a long time ago. Forget about it.

MRS. BERNICK: How can I forget about it? After all, he is my brother—but it's not so much him I'm thinking of as all the unpleasantness it's causing you. Oh, Karsten, I'm so dreadfully frightened—

BERNICK: Frightened? Of what?

MRS. BERNICK: Mightn't they arrest him for stealing that money from your mother?

BERNICK: Don't be so silly. No one can prove anything was taken.

MRS. BERNICK: Oh, but the whole town knows. And you've said yourself that—

BERNICK: I have said nothing. The town knows nothing. All they heard was just vague gossip.

MRS. BERNICK: You are so magnanimous, Karsten.

BERNICK: Try to forget these old memories, Betty. You don't know how it distresses me to be reminded about all this. (*Walks up and down; then he throws down his stick.*) Why on earth must they come home just at this moment, when I don't want any trouble in the town; or in the press? It'll get into every local paper for miles around. Whether I welcome them or whether I turn my back on them, people will talk about it and read something into it. They'll dig the whole story up again, just the way you're doing. And in a community like ours— (*Throws down his gloves on the table.*) And I haven't a single person I can talk to or look to for support.

MRS. BERNICK: Have you no one, Karsten?

BERNICK: No, who could there be? Oh, why in God's name must they come *now?* They're sure to create a scandal of some kind or another. Especially she. It really is intolerable having people like that in one's own family.

MRS. BERNICK: Well, I can't help it if—

BERNICK: You can't help what? That they're your relations? No, you can't help that.

MRS. BERNICK: I didn't ask them to come.

BERNICK: Oh, here we go again. "I didn't ask them to come. I didn't write and beg them. I didn't drag them here by the hair." I know it all by heart!

MRS. BERNICK *(begins to cry):* Oh, why must you be so unkind?

BERNICK: That's right. Start crying, and give the town something else to talk about. Stop this foolishness, Betty. Go and sit outside, someone might come. Do you want people to see you've been crying? A fine thing it'd be if people got to hear that—hush, someone's coming.

There is a knock on the door.

BERNICK: Come in!

MRS. BERNICK goes out on to the verandah with her sewing. AUNE enters, right.

AUNE: Good morning, Mr. Bernick.

BERNICK: Good morning. Well, I suppose you can guess why I've sent for you?

AUNE: Mr. Krap said something yesterday about your not being satisfied with—

BERNICK: I'm dissatisfied with the way things are going down at the yard, Aune. You're not getting on with those repairs. The *Palm Tree* ought to have been under sail days ago. Mr. Vigeland comes here to complain every day. He's a difficult man to have as a partner.

AUNE: The *Palm Tree* can sail the day after tomorrow.

BERNICK: At last! But that American ship, the *Indian Girl*, has been lying here for five weeks—

AUNE: The American? I understood we were to put all our men on to your ship till she was ready.

BERNICK: I gave no such orders. My instructions were that you should go full steam ahead with the American too. You haven't.

AUNE: But her bottom's rotten, Mr. Bernick. The more we patch her the worse she gets.

BERNICK: That's not the real reason. Mr. Krap's told me the whole story. You don't understand how to use these new machines I've bought—or rather, you won't use them.

AUNE: Mr. Bernick, I'm nearly sixty and ever since I was a boy I've been accustomed to the old methods—

BERNICK: We can't use those nowadays. Look, Aune, you mustn't think I'm doing this for money. Luckily I don't need any more of that. I've got to think of the community of which I'm a member, and of the business of which I am the head. Progress has got to come from me or it won't come at all.

AUNE: I want progress too, Mr. Bernick.

BERNICK: Yes, for your own narrow circle, the working class. Oh, I know you agitators. You make speeches and get the people worked up, but the moment anyone takes any practical steps towards improving matters, as with these machines, you refuse to co-operate, and get frightened.

AUNE: I am frightened, Mr. Bernick. I'm frightened for all the mouths from which these machines will take the bread. You keep on saying we've got to think of the community, but I reckon the community owes us a duty too. What's the use of society employing knowledge and capital to introduce all these new inventions before it's educated a generation that knows how to use them?

BERNICK: You read and think too much, Aune. And what

good do you get from it? It just makes you discontented with your position in society.

AUNE: It isn't that, Mr. Bernick. I can't bear to see one good man after another getting sacked and their families going hungry to make way for these machines.

BERNICK: When printing was invented, many scribes went hungry.

AUNE: Would you have welcomed it if you'd been a scribe?

BERNICK: I didn't send for you to argue with you. The *Indian Girl*'s got to be ready to sail the day after tomorrow.

AUNE: But, Mr. Bernick—

BERNICK: The day after tomorrow, do you hear? At the same time as our own ship; not an hour later. I've good reasons for wanting to get the job done quickly. Have you read the newspaper this morning? Then you know that the Americans have been causing trouble again. Those ruffians are turning the whole town upside down; not a night goes by without them starting a brawl in the streets or in a drinking-house. To say nothing of other things I'd rather not mention.

AUNE: Yes, they seem a bad lot.

BERNICK: And who gets the blame for all this? I do! It all comes back on to my head. These newspaper fellows grumble and try to insinuate that we've put all our labour strength on to the *Palm Tree*. And I, who am supposed to influence my fellow citizens by setting them a good example, have all this dirt thrown at me. Well, I'm not standing for it. I'm not used to having my name dragged in the mud like this.

AUNE: Oh, you don't need to bother about that kind of thing, Mr. Bernick.

BERNICK: Just now I do. I need all the respect and goodwill I can muster from my fellow citizens. I've big plans afoot, as I daresay you've heard, and if malicious-minded people succeed in shaking the community's trust in me, it could cause me very great difficulties. So I want at all costs to avoid giving these damned scribblers any food for gossip, and that's why I say the job's got to be done by the day after tomorrow.

AUNE: Mr. Bernick, you might as well tell me it's got to be done by this afternoon.

BERNICK: You mean I'm demanding the impossible?

AUNE: With our present labour strength, yes.

BERNICK: Very well. Then I'll have to start looking elsewhere.

AUNE: You don't mean you're going to dismiss still more of the older men?

BERNICK: No, that's not what I was thinking.

AUNE: It'd create bad feeling in the town if you did that. And in the newspapers.

BERNICK: Probably it might, so I won't. But if the *Indian Girl* isn't ready to sail by the day after tomorrow, there'll be a notice of dismissal served on you.

AUNE: On me! *(Laughs.)* You're joking, sir.

BERNICK: I shouldn't take that for granted if I were you.

AUNE: Dismiss me? But my father and his father worked all their lives in this yard. And so have I.

BERNICK: Who's making me do this?

AUNE: You're asking the impossible, Mr. Bernick.

BERNICK: A good worker doesn't know the meaning of the word impossible. Yes or no? Give me a straight answer, or you'll get your notice now.

AUNE *(takes a step towards him)*: Mr. Bernick, have you ever seriously thought what it means to give an old worker the sack? You think he can look round for something else? Oh, yes; he can do that; but that isn't the whole story. You ought to be present some time in a workman's house on the evening when he comes home and throws down his bag of tools behind the door.

BERNICK: Do you think I'm finding it easy to do this? Haven't I always been a good master to you?

AUNE: So much the worse for me, sir. It means no one at home will put the blame on you. They won't say anything to my face—they wouldn't dare—but they'll shoot a glance at me when they think I'm not looking and say to themselves: "Oh well, he must have deserved it." Don't you see, sir, that's the one thing I can't bear! Poor as I am, I've always been used to being regarded as lord and master in my own house. My humble home is a little community just as yours is, Mr. Bernick, and I've been able to sustain it and keep it going because my wife has believed in me and my children have believed in me. And now it's all going to fall to the ground.

BERNICK: Well, if there's no alternative the lesser must make way for the greater. The individual must be sacrificed for the common cause. That's the only answer I can give you; it's the way of the world. You're a stubborn man, Aune. You oppose me, not because you must but because you won't accept the fact that machines can work better than flesh and blood.

AUNE: And you're so dead set on this, Mr. Bernick, because you know that if you sack me at least you'll have shown the press you're anxious to do as they say you should.

BERNICK: Well, suppose I am? I've told you how much this means to me; either I have every newspaper in the district putting me in the pillory, or else I get them on my side just at the moment when I'm working to get a big project under way for the good of the community. Well then, how else can I act? My choice is either to keep your home going or to suppress the building of hundreds of new homes—hundreds of homes that will never be built, never have a fire in their hearth, unless I succeed in achieving what I'm now working for. Well, I leave the choice to you.

AUNE: I see. In that case I've no more to say.

BERNICK: Hm. My dear Aune, it really grieves me deeply that we have to part.

AUNE: We're not parting, Mr. Bernick.

BERNICK: What do you mean?

AUNE: Working men have a sense of honour too.

BERNICK: Of course they have. Then you think you can promise—?

AUNE: The *Indian Girl* will be ready to sail the day after to-morrow.

Touches his forehead and goes out right.

BERNICK: Well, I've made that obstinate old fool see sense. That's a good omen, anyway.

HILMAR TŒNNESEN *enters through the garden gate, smoking a cigar.*

HILMAR (*on the verandah*): Morning, Betty. Morning, Bernick.

MRS. BERNICK: Good morning.

HILMAR: You've been crying. You know, then?

MRS. BERNICK: Know what?

HILMAR: That the scandal's started. Ugh!

BERNICK: What do you mean?

HILMAR (*comes into the room*): Those two Americans are walking round the town in broad daylight with our little Dina Dorf.

MRS. BERNICK (*follows him*): Hilmar, you're joking!

HILMAR: I'm afraid it's the truth. Lona was actually so tactless as to shout at me. Of course I pretended not to hear her.

BERNICK: And I suppose this hasn't exactly passed unnoticed.

HILMAR: You bet your life it hasn't. People stood still and stared at them. The news spread through the town like wildfire; like a prairie blaze. In every house people stood at their windows and waited for the procession to pass; they were packed behind their curtains like sardines— ugh! You must forgive me, Betty; I can't help saying "Ugh!," this makes me so nervous. If it goes on, I shall have to think about taking a holiday. Rather a long one.

MRS. BERNICK: But you ought to have spoken to him and made it clear that—

HILMAR: What, in public? No, I'm sorry! But fancy him daring to show his face in this town at all! Well, we'll see if the newspapers can't put a spoke in his wheel. I'm sorry, Betty, but—

BERNICK: The newspapers, did you say? Have you heard anything to suggest that they may take action?

HILMAR: Oh yes, there's no doubt about that. When I left you yesterday afternoon, I took a walk up to the Club, for my health. It was quite evident from the silence that fell when I entered that they'd been talking about our American friends. Well, then that tactless editor fellow—you know, Hammer—came in and congratulated me out loud on my rich cousin's return home.

BERNICK: Rich—?

HILMAR: Yes, that's what he said. Of course I gave him a pretty piercing look and made it quite clear that I knew nothing about any riches as far as Johan Tœnnesen was concerned. "Oh, really?" he said. "That's strange. People usually do all right in America provided they have some capital, and your cousin didn't go empty-handed, did he?"

BERNICK: Hm. Look, do me the goodness to—

MRS. BERNICK (*worried*): There you are, Karsten—

HILMAR: Yes, well anyway, he's given me a sleepless night. And he has the cheek to stroll round this town looking as innocent as an angel. Why didn't that illness he had knock him off? It's really monstrous how indestructible some people are.

MRS. BERNICK: Hilmar, what are you saying?

HILMAR: Oh, I'm not saying anything. But look at him, he's survived railway accidents and attacks by grizzlies and Blackfoot Indians without a scratch to show for it all. Didn't even get scalped. Ugh, here they are!

BERNICK (glances up the street): Olaf's with them!

HILMAR: But of course! They want to remind everyone that they belong to the best family in town. Look at all those people coming out of the chemist's to stare at them and make remarks. My nerves won't stand this. How a man can be expected to keep the flag of ideals flying under circumstances like these I really don't know—

BERNICK: They're coming here. Now listen, Betty, it's my express wish that you treat them with every courtesy.

MRS. BERNICK: May I, Karsten?

BERNICK: Yes, yes; and you too, Hilmar. With luck they won't stay long, and while we're alone together I don't want there to be any insinuations. We must on no account embarrass them.

MRS. BERNICK: Oh, Karsten, how magnanimous you are!

BERNICK: Yes, well; never mind that.

MRS. BERNICK: No, you must let me thank you. And forgive me for becoming so emotional just now. Oh, you were quite justified in—

BERNICK: Never mind, I say, never *mind*.

HILMAR: Ugh!

JOHAN TŒNNESEN and DINA enter through the garden, followed by MISS HESSEL and OLAF.

MISS HESSEL: Morning, everyone.

JOHAN: We've been giving the old place the once-over, Karsten.

BERNICK: Yes, so I hear. Plenty of changes, eh?

MISS HESSEL: Everywhere there's evidence of Karsten Bernick's great and good works. We've been around the gardens you presented to the town—

BERNICK: Oh, you've been there?

MISS HESSEL: "The Gift of Karsten Bernick," it says over the entrance. Yes, you seem to be the king-pin here all right.

JOHAN: Fine ships you've got too. I ran into the captain of the *Palm Tree*—he's an old school friend of mine—

MISS HESSEL: And you've built a new school; and I hear we can thank you for the waterworks and the gas tank.

BERNICK: Well, one must do something for the community one lives in.

MISS HESSEL: The sentiment does you credit, brother-in-law. It made me proud to see what a high opinion everyone has of you. I don't reckon myself vain, but I couldn't resist reminding one or two people we spoke to that Johan and I belong to the family.

HILMAR: Ugh!

MISS HESSEL: What's "Ugh!" about that?

HILMAR: All I said was "Hm!"

MISS HESSEL: Did you? Oh, that's all right. Well, you don't seem to have any visitors today.

MRS. BERNICK: No, we're alone.

MISS HESSEL: We met a couple of your Salvationists in the market-place. They seemed to be in a great hurry. But we haven't had a real chance to talk yet, have we? Yesterday you had those three Railway Kings and the Reverend—

HILMAR: Schoolmaster.

MISS HESSEL: Well, I call him Reverend. But tell me, what do you think of what I've been doing for the past fifteen years? Hasn't he grown into a fine boy? Who'd ever think he was the same as that young good-for-nothing who ran away from home?

HILMAR: Hm.

JOHAN: Oh Lona, stop boasting.

MISS HESSEL: O.K., so I'm proud of it! Hell, it's the only thing I've ever achieved in the world; but it makes me feel I've done something to justify my existence. Yes, Johan, when I think how you and I started out there, with just our four bare paws—

HILMAR: Hands—

MISS HESSEL: I said paws. They were black.

HILMAR: Ugh!

MISS HESSEL: Yes, and empty.

HILMAR: Empty? Well, I must say—

MISS HESSEL: What must you say?

BERNICK *coughs.*

HILMAR: I must say—ugh! (*Goes out on to the verandah.*)

MISS HESSEL: What's the matter with him?

BERNICK: Oh, never mind him; he's been rather nervous these last few days. Er—wouldn't you like to have a look round the garden? You haven't seen it properly yet, and I happen to have an hour free just now.

MISS HESSEL: That's a fine idea. I'd love to.

MRS. BERNICK: There've been some big changes there too, as you'll see.

BERNICK, MRS. BERNICK *and* MISS HESSEL *descend into the garden. We see them occasionally during the following scene.*

OLAF (*in the doorway to the verandah*): Uncle Hilmar, do you know what Uncle Johan asked me? He asked if I'd like to go with him to America.

HILMAR: You, you jackass? Why, you spend your whole time clinging to your mother's petticoats.

OLAF: I don't want to do that any longer. You wait—once I'm big, I'll—!

HILMAR: Oh, stuff! You've no stomach for danger.

Act Two

They go together into the garden.

JOHAN *(to* DINA, *who has taken off her hat and is standing in the doorway on the right, shaking the dust from her dress):* I'm afraid that walk must have made you very hot.

DINA: No, I enjoyed it. I've never enjoyed a walk so much before.

JOHAN: You don't often go for walks in the morning, perhaps?

DINA: Oh, yes. But only with Olaf.

JOHAN: I see. Er—perhaps you'd rather go into the garden than stay inside here?

DINA: No, I'd rather stay here.

JOHAN: So would I. Good, that's agreed then, we'll take a walk like this every morning.

DINA: No, Mr. Tœnnesen. You mustn't.

JOHAN: Mustn't? But you promised—

DINA: Yes, but now I think about it—you ought not to be seen with me.

JOHAN: But why not?

DINA: Oh, you're a stranger here. You don't understand. I'm not—

JOHAN: Yes?

DINA: No, I'd rather not talk about it.

JOHAN: Come on. You can tell me.

DINA: Well, if you want to know—I'm not like other girls. There's something—well, something. So you mustn't.

JOHAN: Look, I don't understand this at all. You haven't done anything wrong, have you?

DINA: No—*I* haven't—but—no, I don't want to talk any more about it. You'll hear all about it from the others, I expect.

JOHAN: Hm.

DINA: But there was something else I wanted to ask you.

JOHAN: What?

411

DINA: Is it as easy as they say to become—someone—over there in America?

JOHAN: No, it isn't always easy. You often have to work your fingers to the bone at first, and live pretty rough.

DINA: I wouldn't mind that.

JOHAN: You?

DINA: I can work. I'm healthy and strong, and Aunt Martha's taught me a lot.

JOHAN: Well, for heaven's sake then, come back with us.

DINA: Oh, you're only joking. You said that to Olaf. But tell me one thing. Are people as—as moral over there as they are here?

JOHAN: Moral?

DINA: Yes. I mean—are they as good and virtuous as they are here?

JOHAN: Well, they haven't all got horns, the way people here seem to imagine. You needn't be afraid of that.

DINA: You don't understand. I want to go somewhere where people aren't good and virtuous.

JOHAN: Where they *aren't?* What do you want them to be, then?

DINA: I want them to be natural.

JOHAN: They're that all right.

DINA: Then I think it'd be good for me if I could go and live there.

JOHAN: I'm sure it would. You must come back with us.

DINA: No, I don't want to go with you. I must go alone. Oh, I'd manage. I'd make something of myself—

BERNICK (*below the verandah with the two* LADIES): No, no, stay here, Betty dear. I'll fetch it. You might easily catch cold.

He enters the room and starts looking for MRS. BERNICK's *shawl.*

MRS. BERNICK *(in the garden):* You must come with us, Johan. We're going down to the grotto.

BERNICK: No, I'm sure Johan would rather stay here. Dina, take my wife's shawl down to her, will you, and go along with them? Johan'll stay here with me, Betty dear. I want to hear about what life is like on the other side.

MRS. BERNICK: All right, but come soon. You know where we'll be.

> MRS. BERNICK, MISS HESSEL *and* DINA *go out left through the garden.*

BERNICK *(watches them go for a moment, then walks across to the door upstage left and closes it. Then he goes over to* JOHAN, *clasps both his hands, shakes and presses them):* Johan! Now we're alone—thank you! Thank you!

JOHAN: Oh, nonsense.

BERNICK: My house and home, the happiness of my family, my position in the community—I owe it all to you.

JOHAN: Well, I'm glad to hear it, my dear Karsten. Some good came out of that silly business after all, then.

BERNICK *(shakes his hands again):* Thank you, thank you! There isn't one man in ten thousand who'd have done as you did.

JOHAN: Forget it! We were both young and wild, weren't we? One of us had to take the rap.

BERNICK: But who deserved to, if not the guilty one?

JOHAN: Now wait a minute! On this occasion it was the innocent one who deserved the rap. I had no worries or responsibilities; and no parents. I was glad of a chance to get away from that drudgery at the office. You had your old mother still alive; besides, you'd just got secretly engaged to Betty, and she was deeply in love with you. What would have happened to her if she'd found out that you—?

BERNICK: I know, I know; all the same—

JOHAN: And wasn't it just for Betty's sake that you broke off that business with Mrs. Dorf? You'd only gone along that evening to put an end to it all—

BERNICK: Yes; why did that drunken ruffian have to come home just that evening? Yes, Johan, it was for Betty's sake; even so—that you could be so unselfish as to take the blame on yourself, and go away—

JOHAN: Forget it, my dear Karsten. After all, we agreed that this was the best solution; we had to get you out of it somehow, and you were my friend. Yes, how proud I was of that friendship! I was a poor country lad working in an office, you were rich and of good family, just back from Paris and London—and yet you chose me as your friend, though I was four years younger than you. Oh, I realize now it was because you were in love with Betty, but how proud I was! And who wouldn't have been? Who wouldn't gladly have sacrificed himself for you, especially when all it meant was giving the town something to gossip about for a month and having an excuse to get away from it all into the great wide world outside?

BERNICK: Hm. My dear Johan, to be frank I must tell you that the matter hasn't quite been forgotten yet.

JOHAN: Hasn't it? Well, what's that to me? Once I'm back on my ranch—

BERNICK: You're going back, then?

JOHAN: Of course.

BERNICK: But not too soon, I hope?

JOHAN: As soon as I can. I only came here to please Lona.

BERNICK: Oh? How do you mean?

JOHAN: Well, you see, Lona isn't young any longer, and these last few months she's been pining her heart out to get back here; but she wouldn't ever admit it. (Smiles.) She didn't dare leave an irresponsible young fellow like me on my own, when by the age of nineteen I'd already gone and—

BERNICK: Yes, well?

JOHAN: Karsten, I've got a confession to make to you which I'm a little ashamed about.

BERNICK: You didn't tell her?

JOHAN: Yes, I did. It was wrong of me, but I had to. You've no idea what Lona has been to me. I know you could never get along with her, but to me she's been like a mother. Those first years over there, when we were so poor—you've no idea how she worked! And when I had that long illness and couldn't earn anything, she went off and sang in cafés—I tried to stop her but I couldn't—and gave lectures which people laughed at, and wrote a book which she's since laughed over herself—yes, and cried over—all just to keep me alive. I couldn't sit there last winter and watch her pining her heart out after the way she'd slaved and toiled for me. Karsten, I couldn't! So I said to her: "Go, Lona. You needn't worry about me. I'm not as irresponsible as you think." And then—well, I told her.

BERNICK: And how did she take it?

JOHAN: Well, she quite rightly decided that since I'd proved myself innocent there was no reason why I shouldn't come back with her. But you don't need to worry. Lona won't talk, and I can keep my mouth shut. Like I did before.

BERNICK: Oh, yes, yes. I trust you.

JOHAN: Here's my hand on it. Well now, we'll say no more about that business; luckily it's the only crazy thing either of us has ever done. I intend to enjoy the few days I'm going to be here. You can't imagine what a lovely walk we had this morning. Who'd ever have imagined that that little girl who used to run around here and act cherubs at the theatre would ever—by the way, Karsten, what happened to her parents—afterwards?

BERNICK: My dear chap, I don't know any more than what I

wrote to you just after you sailed. You got my two letters all right?

JOHAN: Yes, yes, I have both of them. That drunken scoundrel left her, then?

BERNICK: Yes, and got himself killed in a brawl.

JOHAN: She died not long afterwards, didn't she? But you did all you could for her, I presume? Secretly, I mean?

BERNICK: She was proud. She revealed nothing, and refused to accept a penny.

JOHAN: You did the right thing in bringing Dina to live with you.

BERNICK: Of course, of course. Actually, it was Martha who arranged that.

JOHAN: Was it Martha? Yes, by the way, where is Martha today?

BERNICK: Where is she? Oh, when she isn't at the school she's busy with her invalids.

JOHAN: So it was Martha who took care of her?

BERNICK: Yes, Martha's always had rather a weakness for looking after children. That was why she took this job at the council school. Damn stupid idea.

JOHAN: Yes, she looked pretty worn-out yesterday. I'm afraid you're right, she isn't really strong enough for that kind of work.

BERNICK: Oh, she's strong enough for it. But it's so unpleasant for me. It makes it look as though I wasn't prepared to maintain my own sister.

JOHAN: Maintain her? I thought she had money of her own—

BERNICK: Not a penny. You remember what a difficult situation mother was in when you left? Well, she managed to keep going for a while, with my help, but I wasn't really happy with that as a long-term policy. I thought I'd go in with her, but even that wasn't enough. In the end, I had to take over the whole business, and when we finally drew up the accounts there was scarcely anything left of

mother's share. Soon afterwards she died and of course
Martha was left practically penniless.

JOHAN: Poor Martha!

BERNICK: Poor? What do you mean? You don't imagine I let
her want for anything? Oh no, I think I may say I'm a
good brother to her. She lives with us, naturally, and eats
at our table; her teacher's salary is sufficient for her clothing needs, and—well, she's a single woman, what more
does she want?

JOHAN: Hm; we don't reason like that in America.

BERNICK: No, I dare say not, in an unstable society like
theirs. But here in our little community, which immoral-
ity hasn't yet, thank God, begun to corrupt, the women
are content to occupy a modest and unassuming position.
Anyway, it's Martha's own fault; she could have been
provided for long ago, if she'd been so minded.

JOHAN: Could have married, you mean?

BERNICK: Yes, and very advantageously. She's had several
good offers; strangely enough, considering she's a
woman with no money and no longer young, and really
rather ordinary.

JOHAN: Ordinary?

BERNICK: Oh, don't think I hold it against her. Indeed, I
wouldn't have it otherwise. You know how it is, in a big
house like ours it's always useful to have a—well—
placid-natured person around whom one can ask to do
anything.

JOHAN: Yes, but what about her?

BERNICK: What do you mean, what about her? Oh, I see.
Well, she's got plenty to interest herself; she's got me and
Betty and Olaf and—me. It isn't good for people to be always thinking of themselves first, least of all women. After all, each of us has a community of one kind or another
to work for, be it great or small. I do so, anyway. *(Indicates* KRAP, *as the latter enters right.)* Here's an example

for you. This business I have to deal with now, do you suppose it's to do with my own company? Not a bit of it. *(Quickly, to* KRAP) Well?

KRAP *(shows him a sheaf of papers and whispers):* All the documents for the transaction are in order.

BERNICK: Good! Splendid! Well, brother-in-law, I'm afraid you'll have to excuse me for a while. *(Lowers his voice as he presses his hand.)* Thank you, Johan, thank you! You may rest assured that anything I can ever do for you— well, you understand. *(To* KRAP) Come with me.

They go into BERNICK'S *office.*

JOHAN *(looks after him for a moment):* Hm.

He turns to go down into the garden. As he does so, MARTHA *enters right with a small basket on her arm.*

JOHAN: Why, Martha!

MARTHA: Oh—Johan—is it you?

JOHAN: You've been out early too.

MARTHA: Yes. Wait here a minute, I'm sure the others will be along soon.

Turns to go out, left.

JOHAN: Look, Martha, are you always in such a hurry?

MARTHA: Am I—?

JOHAN: Yesterday you seemed to be avoiding me—I didn't manage to get a word with you—and today—

MARTHA: Yes, but—

JOHAN: We always used to be inseparable. Ever since we were children.

MARTHA: Oh, Johan. That's many, many years ago.

JOHAN: For heaven's sake! It's only fifteen years. You think I've changed?

MARTHA: You? Oh yes—you have too—although—

JOHAN: What do you mean?

MARTHA: Oh, nothing.

JOHAN: You don't sound very glad to see me again.

MARTHA: I've waited so long, Johan. Too long.

JOHAN: Waited? For me to come back?

MARTHA: Yes.

JOHAN: Why did you think I'd want to come back?

MARTHA: To repair the wrong you did.

JOHAN: I?

MARTHA: Have you forgotten that a woman died in destitution and disgrace because of you? Have you forgotten that because of you the best years of a young child's life were embittered?

JOHAN: You don't mean that you—? Martha, did your brother never—?

MARTHA: Do what?

JOHAN: Did he never—I mean—did he never say anything in mitigation of what I did?

MARTHA: Oh, Johan, you know how strict Karsten's principles are.

JOHAN: Hm. Yes, yes, I know how strict my old friend Karsten's principles are. But this is—! Oh, well. I spoke to him just now. I think he's changed somewhat.

MARTHA: How can you say that? Karsten has always been a fine man.

JOHAN: Yes, I didn't mean it like that; but never mind. Hm! Well, now I understand how you've been thinking about me. You've been awaiting the return of the prodigal.

MARTHA: Listen, Johan. I'll tell you how I've been thinking about you. (*Points down into the garden.*) You see that girl playing down there on the grass with Olaf? That is Dina. You remember that strange letter you wrote to me when you ran away? You wrote that I must believe in you. I have believed in you, Johan. Those wicked things people talked about afterwards—you did them in a fit of madness, you didn't know what you were doing—

419

JOHAN: What do you mean?

MARTHA: Oh, you know what I mean; don't let's talk about it any more. Anyway, you had to go away and start—a new life. Listen, Johan. You remember how we two used to play games together when we were children? Well, I have acted as your proxy here. The duties that you forgot to fulfil here, or couldn't fulfil, I have fulfilled for you. I tell you this so that you shan't have that to reproach yourself with too. I have been a mother to that wronged child; I've brought her up, as well as I could—

JOHAN: And wasted your whole life for her sake.

MARTHA: It hasn't been wasted. But you took so long in coming, Johan.

JOHAN: Martha—if only I could tell you the—! Well, anyway let me thank you for being such a loyal friend to me.

MARTHA *(smiles sadly):* Hm. Well, now we've had our talk, Johan. Hush, someone's coming. Goodbye. I can't wait now.

She goes out through the door upstage left. MISS HESSEL *enters from the garden, followed by* MRS. BERNICK.

MRS. BERNICK *(still in the garden):* For heaven's sake, Lona, what are you thinking of?

MISS HESSEL: Let me go! I tell you I must speak with him.

MRS. BERNICK: But it'd create the most dreadful scandal. Oh, Johan, are you still here?

MISS HESSEL: Get along now, son. Don't stand hanging round indoors; go down into the garden and talk to Dina.

JOHAN: Yes, I was just thinking of doing that.

MRS. BERNICK: But—

MISS HESSEL: Johan, have you bothered to take a close look at Dina?

JOHAN: Why, yes, I think so.

MISS HESSEL: So you damn well should. Now there *is* something for you.

420

MRS. BERNICK: But Lona—!

JOHAN: Something for me?

MISS HESSEL: Yes, well, something to look at, anyway. O.K., then, get going!

JOHAN: Yes, yes, I'm going. I'm going!

He goes down into the garden.

MRS. BERNICK: Lona, I'm speechless! Surely you can't be serious about this?

MISS HESSEL: Of course I'm serious! She's a healthy, honest girl, and in her right mind, isn't she? She'd make just the wife for Johan. That's the kind of girl he needs over there, not an old half-sister.

MRS. BERNICK: Dina! Dina Dorf! But Lona, think—

MISS HESSEL: All I'm thinking about is the boy's happiness. He needs me to give him a push, he's a bit timid where these things are concerned; never really had an eye for girls.

MRS. BERNICK: What, Johan? I should have thought we had sufficient evidence to the contrary—unfortunately—

MISS HESSEL: Oh, to hell with that, that's ancient history! Where's Karsten? I want to talk to him.

MRS. BERNICK: Lona, you mustn't do this, I tell you.

MISS HESSEL: I'm going to do it. If the boy likes her, and she likes him, let them have one another. Karsten's a clever guy, he'll manage to find a way—

MRS. BERNICK: Do you really imagine that these American improprieties will be permitted here?

MISS HESSEL: Betty, don't talk nonsense.

MRS. BERNICK: And that a man with such strict moral principles as Karsten—

MISS HESSEL: Oh, nonsense, they're not that strict.

MRS. BERNICK: How dare you!

MISS HESSEL: All I'm saying is that Karsten isn't any more moral than most other men.

MRS. BERNICK: You still hate him, don't you? But what do you want here, if you can't forget—? I don't understand how you dare to look him in the face after the disgraceful way you behaved towards him.

MISS HESSEL: Yes, Betty, I did overstep the mark a bit that time.

MRS. BERNICK: And he's forgiven you so generously, though he never did you any wrong. It wasn't his fault that you set your cap at him. But ever since that moment you've hated me too. (*Bursts into tears.*) You've always begrudged me my happiness. And now you come here to shame me, by showing the town what kind of a family I've made Karsten marry into! I'm the person everyone will blame; and that's what you want. Oh, it's hateful of you! (*She goes out weeping through the door upstage left.*)

MISS HESSEL (*watches her go*): Poor Betty!

BERNICK *enters from his office.*

BERNICK (*still in the doorway*): Yes, yes, Krap. Good. Excellent. Send four hundred crowns to provide food for the poor. (*Turns.*) Lona! (*Comes closer.*) Are you alone? Isn't Betty with you?

MISS HESSEL: No. Shall I go and fetch her?

BERNICK: No, no, it doesn't matter. Oh, Lona, you can't imagine how I've been longing for a chance to talk frankly with you. To ask your forgiveness.

MISS HESSEL: Look, Karsten, don't let's get sentimental. It doesn't suit us.

BERNICK: You must listen to me, Lona. I know appearances seem to be against me now that you know about Dina's mother. But I swear to you it was only a temporary infatuation. I did love you once, honestly and truly.

MISS HESSEL: Why do you think I've come back?

BERNICK: Whatever you have in mind, I beseech you not to do anything before you have given me the chance to vindicate myself. I can, Lona; at any rate I can explain to you why I acted as I did.

MISS HESSEL: Now you're afraid. You once loved me, you say. Yes, you told me so often enough in your letters— and perhaps it was true in a way, as long as you were living out there in a world which was big and free and gave you the courage to think bigly and freely yourself. You probably thought I had a bit more character and will and independence than most of the others here. Besides, it was a secret between the two of us; no one could make funny remarks about your vulgar taste.

BERNICK: Lona, how can you think that—?

MISS HESSEL: But when you came back here and heard how people were laughing at me, and making fun of what they called my peculiarities—

BERNICK: Well, you were rather headstrong in those days.

MISS HESSEL: Only because I wanted to shock the prudes this town was full of—the ones in trousers as well as the ones in petticoats. Well, then you met that charming young actress—

BERNICK: It was a momentary infatuation, nothing more. I swear to you that not a tenth part of all the rumours and slander that went round about me was true.

MISS HESSEL: Possibly. But then Betty came home, pretty and rich, and everyone's darling; and the news got around that she was to inherit all her aunt's money and I was to get nothing—

BERNICK: Yes, that was the crux of it, Lona. I shan't beat about the bush. I didn't love Betty; I didn't break with you because my affections had changed. It was only for the money. I needed it; I *had* to make sure I got it.

MISS HESSEL: And you can tell me that to my face!

BERNICK: Yes, I do. Please listen to me, Lona—

MISS HESSEL: But you wrote to me that you'd fallen passionately in love with Betty, asked me to be magnanimous, begged me for Betty's sake to say nothing about the fact that there had been anything between us—

BERNICK: I had to, I tell you.

MISS HESSEL: Then, by God, I don't regret what I did.

BERNICK: Let me explain to you calmly and objectively how things stood. My mother, you recall, was head of the family business; but she had no business sense whatever. I was urgently summoned home from Paris; things had become critical; I had to get the firm back on its feet again. What did I find? I found a business tottering on the verge of bankruptcy. We had to keep it absolutely secret, of course, but this ancient and respected house which had flourished for three generations was facing ruin. I was her son, her only son. I had to look round for some means of saving it.

MISS HESSEL: So you saved the House of Bernick at the expense of a woman.

BERNICK: You know quite well that Betty loved me.

MISS HESSEL: What about me?

BERNICK: Believe me, Lona, you would never have been happy with me.

MISS HESSEL: Was it out of consideration for my happiness that you jilted me?

BERNICK: You think I acted from selfish motives? If it had only been my interests that had been at stake, I would gladly and fearlessly have started again from nothing. But you don't understand how a man of business identifies himself with the business he inherits and with the vast responsibilities it brings with it. Do you realize that the happiness or misery of hundreds, even thousands of people depends on him? Has it ever occurred to you that the whole of our community, which both you and I call our home, would have been shattered if the House of Bernick had failed?

MISS HESSEL: Is it also for the sake of the community that for the past fifteen years your life has been based upon a lie?

BERNICK: A lie?

MISS HESSEL: How much does Betty know about the circumstances that lay behind her marriage with you?

BERNICK: Do you really believe I'd hurt her by revealing such things? What dividends would that pay?

MISS HESSEL: What dividends, did you say? Ah, well, you're a business man—I suppose you know best about dividends. Now listen to me, Karsten. I'm going to talk calmly and objectively to you. Tell me; are you really happy?

BERNICK: In my family life, you mean?

MISS HESSEL: Of course.

BERNICK: Yes, Lona, I am. The sacrifice you made for me wasn't in vain. I think I can say I've grown happier year by year. Betty's so good and acquiescent. During the years we've lived together she has learned to mould her character to mine—

MISS HESSEL: Hm.

BERNICK: She used to have a lot of over-romantic ideas about love; she couldn't accept that as the years pass it must shrink into the calm candle-flame of friendship.

MISS HESSEL: But she accepts that now?

BERNICK: Completely. As you can imagine, her daily association with me hasn't been without a maturing influence on her. People have to learn to reduce their demands on each other if they are to fulfil their functions in the community in which it has pleased God to place them. Betty has gradually learned to realize this, with the result that our house is now an example to our fellow citizens.

MISS HESSEL: But these fellow citizens know nothing about this lie?

BERNICK: Lie?

425

MISS HESSEL: Yes, the lie on which your life has been resting for the past fifteen years.

BERNICK: You call that a—?

MISS HESSEL: I call it a lie. A triple lie. You lied to me, you lied to Betty and you lied to Johan.

BERNICK: Betty has never asked to be told the truth.

MISS HESSEL: Because she doesn't know.

BERNICK: And you won't ask it. For her sake you won't.

MISS HESSEL: Oh, no. I can put up with ridicule; I've a broad back.

BERNICK: Johan won't, either. He's told me so.

MISS HESSEL: But what about you, Karsten? Isn't there something in you that cries out to be freed from this lie?

BERNICK: Do you expect me voluntarily to sacrifice the happiness of my family and my position in society?

MISS HESSEL: What right have you to that position?

BERNICK: Every day for the past fifteen years I have purchased a grain of that right—by my conduct, and my work, and my achievements.

MISS HESSEL: Yes, you've achieved plenty all right—for yourself and for others. You're the richest and most powerful man in town; no one dares oppose you, because you're supposed to be a man without fault or dishonour; your home is regarded as a pattern for other homes; your career as an example for other men to follow. But all this honour, and you too, rest on a quicksand. A moment may come, a word may be spoken, and you and all your honour will sink to the bottom, if you don't save yourself in time.

BERNICK: Why have you come, Lona?

MISS HESSEL: I want to help you to get firm ground under your feet, Karsten.

BERNICK: Revenge! You want revenge? Yes, that's it, of course. But you won't succeed! There's only one person who knows the truth, and he'll hold his tongue.

MISS HESSEL: Johan?

BERNICK: Yes, Johan. If anyone else accuses me, I shall deny everything. If anyone tries to destroy me, I shall fight for my life! You'll never succeed, I tell you! The only person who could destroy me is silent. And he's going away.

RUMMEL *and* VIGELAND *enter right.*

RUMMEL: Good morning, good morning, my dear Bernick. You must come along with us to the Chamber of Commerce. You know, to discuss the railway.

BERNICK: I can't. Not just now.

VIGELAND: But Mr. Bernick, you must—!

RUMMEL: You must, Bernick. There are people working against us. That damned newspaper editor, Hammer, and the others who wanted the coast line, are saying there are private interests behind this new proposal.

BERNICK: Well, tell them—

VIGELAND: It won't help what *we* tell them, Mr. Bernick.

RUMMEL: No, no, you must come yourself. No one will dare to suspect you of anything like that.

MISS HESSEL: Why, the very idea!

BERNICK: I can't, I tell you. I'm not well. That is—well, anyway, wait a minute and give me time to collect myself.

RŒRLUND *enters right.*

RŒRLUND: Excuse me, Mr. Bernick. I've just seen something that has deeply disturbed me.

BERNICK: Yes, yes, what is it?

RŒRLUND: I must ask you a question. Is it with your consent that the young girl who has found asylum beneath your roof is walking the public streets in the company of a person who—

MISS HESSEL: What person, Reverend?

RŒRLUND: Of the person from whom, of all people, she should be kept at the greatest possible distance.

MISS HESSEL *laughs loudly.*

RŒRLUND: Is it with your consent, Mr. Bernick?

BERNICK *(looks for his hat and gloves):* I know nothing about it. Excuse me, I'm in a hurry—I have to attend a meeting of the Chamber of Commerce.

HILMAR *(enters from the garden and goes over to the door upstage left):* Betty, Betty!

MRS. BERNICK *(in the doorway):* What is it?

HILMAR: You really must go down into the garden and put a stop to the way a certain person is flirting with Dina Dorf. It made me quite nervous to listen to them.

MISS HESSEL: Oh? What did this person say?

HILMAR: Only that he wants her to go with him to America! Ugh!

RŒRLUND: Can this be possible!

MRS. BERNICK: What are you saying!

MISS HESSEL: But it'd be a wonderful thing!

BERNICK: Impossible. You must have misheard.

HILMAR: Ask him yourself, then. Here come the happy pair. Keep me out of it, though.

BERNICK *(to RUMMEL and VIGELAND):* Go ahead, I'll join you in a moment.

RUMMEL *and* VIGELAND *go out right.* JOHAN *and* DINA *enter from the garden.*

JOHAN: Lona, Lona, she's coming with us!

MRS. BERNICK: Johan, you must be mad!

RŒRLUND: I refuse to believe my ears! This is the most disgraceful scandal! By what arts of seduction have you—?

JOHAN: Now, take it easy—!

RŒRLUND: Answer me, Dina. Do you seriously intend to do this? Have you made this decision freely and voluntarily?

DINA: I must get away from here.

RŒRLUND: But with him! With him!

DINA: Name me any other man here who would have the courage to take me away with him.

RŒRLUND: Right, then you'll have to be told who he is.

JOHAN: Be quiet!

BERNICK: Don't say another word!

RŒRLUND: If I remained silent I should be betraying the community whose moral and manners I have been chosen to protect; and I should be failing my duty towards this young girl in whose upbringing I have had no small share, and who is to me—

JOHAN: Be careful what you say!

RŒRLUND: She shall know the truth! Dina, it was this man who was responsible for your mother's misery and shame.

BERNICK: Dr. Rœrlund!

DINA: He! *(To* JOHAN*)* Is this true?

JOHAN: Karsten, you answer her.

BERNICK: Silence, all of you! The subject is closed.

DINA: It is true, then.

RŒRLUND: Of course it is true. And that's not all. This person in whom you have placed your trust did not leave home empty-handed. Old Mrs. Bernick's money—her son can testify.

MISS HESSEL: Liar!

BERNICK: Ah!

MRS. BERNICK: Oh, my God, my God!

JOHAN *(raises his arm):* You dare to—

MISS HESSEL: Don't hit him, Johan.

RŒRLUND: Yes, go on, hit me! The truth shall out—and it is the truth—Mr. Bernick has said so himself, and the whole town knows it. Well, Dina, now you know the kind of man he is.

Short silence.

JOHAN *(quietly, grips* BERNICK'S *arm):* Karsten, Karsten, what have you done?

MRS. BERNICK *(in tears, softly):* Oh, Karsten, that I should have involved you in such a scandal!

SANDSTAD *(hurries in right and shouts, with his hand still on the door-handle):* Mr. Bernick, you must come at once! The railway is hanging by a thread!

BERNICK *(abstractedly):* What? What must I do?

MISS HESSEL *(earnestly, meaningly):* You must do your duty to the community, brother-in-law.

SANDSTAD: Yes, hurry! We need all your moral authority behind us.

JOHAN *(close to* BERNICK*):* Bernick, you and I will talk about this tomorrow.

He goes out through the garden. BERNICK *helplessly and blindly walks out right with* SANDSTAD.

ACT THREE

The same. BERNICK *enters angrily through the door upstage left with a cane in his hand, leaving the door ajar behind him.*

BERNICK: There, now! He's been asking for that. I fancy he won't forget that hiding in a hurry. (*Speaks to someone through the open door.*) What? Oh, Betty, you mother the boy too much. You make excuses for him and take his side whatever he does. Irresponsible little brat! Not irresponsible? What would you call it, then? Sneaking out of the house at night, stealing one of the fishermen's boats, stays away half the day and frightens the life out of me—! As if I hadn't enough on my mind already! And then the young puppy has the nerve to threaten me that he'll run away! Well, just let him try! You? No, I'm sure you don't; you don't care what happens to him. I really believe if he went and killed himself, you'd— Oh, don't you? Possibly, but when I die I shall leave something behind me that I want carried on; I don't fancy the idea of being left childless. Don't argue, Betty, I've given my orders; he's not to leave the house. (*Listens.*) Be quiet now, I don't want anyone to notice anything.

   KRAP *enters right.*

KRAP: Can you spare me a moment, Mr. Bernick?

BERNICK *(throws down the cane):* Yes, yes, by all means. Have you come from the yard?

KRAP: Yes, I've just left there. Hm.

BERNICK: Well? Everything's going ahead all right with the *Palm Tree,* isn't it?

KRAP: Oh, the *Palm Tree* will be able to sail tomorrow, but—

BERNICK: Is it the *Indian Girl?* Don't tell me that stubborn old fool—

KRAP: The *Indian Girl* will be able to sail tomorrow too—but she won't get very far.

BERNICK: What do you mean?

KRAP: Excuse me, Mr. Bernick, but that door's open and I think there's someone in there.

BERNICK *(closes the door):* Well, what have you got to tell me that mustn't be overheard?

KRAP: It's this. Your foreman seems determined to send the *Indian Girl* to the bottom with all hands.

BERNICK: Aune? Good God, what on earth makes you think that?

KRAP: Can't think of any other explanation, Mr. Bernick.

BERNICK: Well, tell me. But be brief.

KRAP: Yes, Mr. Bernick. Well, you know how slowly the work's been going since we got those new machines and took on those untrained workmen.

BERNICK: Yes, yes.

KRAP: But when I went down there this morning I noticed they'd made the most extraordinary progress on the American ship. That big patch on her hull—you know, where she's gone rotten—

BERNICK: Yes, yes, what about it?

KRAP: Completely repaired! Apparently. They've sheathed it. Looks as good as new. Aune himself had been working on her all night with a lantern.

BERNICK: Well?

KRAP: I thought about it. Didn't like it. The men were having lunch, so I went and took a good look at her, outside and in. No one saw me. I had difficulty in getting down into the hold, because they've reloaded the cargo, but I saw enough to confirm my suspicions. There's something funny going on, Mr. Bernick.

BERNICK: You must be mistaken, Mr. Krap. I can't believe Aune would do a thing like that.

KRAP: I don't like saying it, but it's the truth. Something funny going on, I said to myself. He hadn't put in any new timbers, as far as I could see; just plugged and caulked her, and covered it up with plates and tarpaulins and so on. Real shoddy workmanship! The *Indian Girl* will never reach New York. She'll go to the bottom like a cracked kettle.

BERNICK: This is dreadful! But what motive do you suppose he can have?

KRAP: Probably wants to bring the machines into discredit. Revenge; wants to force you to take the old workmen back.

BERNICK: And for that he's willing to sacrifice all those human lives.

KRAP: He said the other day: "There aren't any human beings in the *Indian Girl*. Only beasts."

BERNICK: Possibly; but what about all the capital investment that will be lost? Hasn't he thought of that?

KRAP: Aune doesn't hold with capital investment, Mr. Bernick.

BERNICK: True enough. He's a trouble-maker, a demagogue. All the same—to be so devoid of conscience—! Look here, Krap, we must check on this. Not a word about it to anyone. It'll be bad for the yard if this leaks out.

KRAP: Of course, but—

BERNICK: You must try to get down there again during the dinner break. I must have the truth about this.

KRAP: I'll get it for you, Mr. Bernick. But may I ask—what will you do if—?

BERNICK: Report the matter, of course. We can't let ourselves be accessories to a criminal action. I can't afford to have that on my conscience. Besides, it will make a good impression on both the press and the community if they see that I am putting personal considerations aside so that justice may take its course.

KRAP: Very true, Mr. Bernick.

BERNICK: But first we must have the truth. Meanwhile, not a word to anyone.

KRAP: You can trust me, Mr. Bernick. I'll get the truth for you.

He goes out through the garden and down the street.

BERNICK *(to himself):* Terrible! But—no, it's impossible! It couldn't happen.

He turns to enter his office. HILMAR TŒNNESEN *enters right.*

HILMAR: Morning, Bernick. Well, congratulations on your triumph at the Chamber of Commerce yesterday.

BERNICK: Oh, thank you.

HILMAR: Brilliant victory, they tell me. Public-spirited visionary routs chauvinistic self-interest. Like a colonial power disciplining the savages. Remarkable achievement after that unpleasant little scene you'd—

BERNICK: Yes, yes, never mind that.

HILMAR: I gather the final *coup de grâce* hasn't been delivered yet, though.

BERNICK: You mean the railway?

HILMAR: Yes. You know what our beloved editor Mr. Hammer is cooking up, I presume?

BERNICK *(tensely):* No. What?

HILMAR: He's cottoned on to that rumour that's floating around. Says he's going to make it front-page news.

BERNICK: What rumour?

HILMAR: Why, all that buying up of property along the route of the branch line.

BERNICK: What? Is there a rumour to that effect?

HILMAR: Yes, it's all over town. I heard about it at the Club. It seems one of our lawyers has been secretly buying up all the forests and mines and waterfalls on behalf of an anonymous client.

BERNICK: Do they say who this client is?

HILMAR: The members thought he must be acting for a syndicate in some other town that had heard about your plans and thought they'd get in quickly before property values began to soar. Disgusting, isn't it, what? Ugh!

BERNICK: Disgusting?

HILMAR: Yes, absolute strangers trespassing on our property like that. And fancy one of our own lawyers lending himself to such a scheme! Now it'll be these damned outsiders who'll reap all the profit.

BERNICK: But it's only an unconfirmed rumour.

HILMAR: Yes, but everyone believes it, and tomorrow or the day after Hammer will publish it as a fact. Everyone at the Club's feeling very bitter about it already. I heard several people say that if the rumour's confirmed they'll withdraw their support.

BERNICK: But that's impossible!

HILMAR: Oh? Why do you suppose those hucksters were so keen to go in with you? Do you think they hadn't already started licking their lips at the—?

BERNICK: Impossible, I tell you! We have *some* public spirit in this little community—!

HILMAR: Here? Look, you're an optimist and you judge other people by yourself. But I know our town pretty

435

well, and I tell you there isn't one person here—apart from ourselves, of course—not one, I tell you, who attempts to keep the flag of ideals flying. *(Upstage.)* Ugh, here they are!

BERNICK: Who?

HILMAR: The two Americans. *(Looks out, right.)* Who's that with them? Oh dear, isn't that the captain of the *Indian Girl?* Ugh!

BERNICK: What on earth can they want with him?

HILMAR: Birds of a feather, I suppose. He's probably been a pirate, or a slave-trader; and heaven knows what they haven't got up to in the past fifteen years.

BERNICK: No, you've no right to think of them like that.

HILMAR: You *are* an optimist. Well, if they're descending on us again, I'll be off.

He goes towards the door, left. MISS HESSEL *enters right.*

MISS HESSEL: Hullo, Hilmar. Am I chasing you away?

HILMAR: Not at all. I just happen to be in a hurry. I've something I have to say to Betty.

Enters the room upstage left.

BERNICK *(after a short silence):* Well, Lona?

MISS HESSEL: Well?

BERNICK: How do you feel about me today?

MISS HESSEL: The same as yesterday. One lie more or less—

BERNICK: I must make you understand. Where is Johan?

MISS HESSEL: He's coming. He had something he wanted to ask someone.

BERNICK: After what you heard yesterday, surely you must understand that everything I have built up here will be destroyed if the truth gets out.

MISS HESSEL: I understand that.

BERNICK: I need hardly tell you that I was not guilty of this theft which was rumoured to have been committed.

MISS HESSEL: Oh, naturally. But who was the thief, then?

BERNICK: There was no thief. No money was stolen. Not a penny was missing.

MISS HESSEL: What?

BERNICK: I repeat; not a penny.

MISS HESSEL: Then how did that monstrous rumour get round that Johan—?

BERNICK: Lona, I can talk to you as I wouldn't to anyone else. I shan't hide anything from you. I was partly responsible for spreading that rumour.

MISS HESSEL: You? You could do a thing like that to him, when to save your skin he'd—?

BERNICK: You mustn't judge me without remembering how things stood at the time. I explained it to you yesterday. I came home and found my mother involved in a whole string of stupid enterprises. One misfortune followed after another; every disaster that could happen to us happened; our house stood on the verge of ruin. I felt desperate and reckless. Oh, Lona, I think it was mainly in the hope of trying to forget it all that I got myself involved in that—business which ended in Johan going away.

MISS HESSEL: Hm.

BERNICK: You can imagine how all sorts of rumours spread about after you and he had left. It wasn't the first thing of that kind he'd done, they said; Dorf had been well paid to go away and keep his mouth shut; others said she'd been given the money. Just then it was beginning to get whispered that our house was having difficulty in fulfilling its obligations. What more natural than that the scandalmongers should put two and two together? When she stayed on here in obvious poverty, people said he'd taken the money with him to America; the gossip increased and the sum multiplied like a snowball.

MISS HESSEL: And you, Karsten—?

BERNICK: I seized on this rumour as a drowning man clutches at a raft.

MISS HESSEL: You encouraged it?

BERNICK: I didn't contradict it. Our creditors were beginning to get restive; I had to find some way of calming them; it was essential that no one should doubt our solidarity. We'd had a temporary setback; they mustn't foreclose on us; we only needed a little time, and everyone would get their money.

MISS HESSEL: And everyone got their money?

BERNICK: Yes, Lona. This rumour saved our house, and made me the man I am now.

MISS HESSEL: In other words, a lie made you the man you are now.

BERNICK: Who suffered by it—then? Johan had sworn he'd never come back.

MISS HESSEL: You ask who suffered by it. Look at yourself, Karsten, and tell me honestly; don't you think you've suffered?

BERNICK: Look at any man you choose to name; you'll find every one of them has at least one skeleton hidden in his cupboard.

MISS HESSEL: And you call yourselves pillars of society?

BERNICK: Society has none better.

MISS HESSEL: If that's what your society is like, what does it matter whether it survives or is destroyed? What do people here set store by? Lies and pretences—that's all. You, the chief citizen of the town, sit here in honour and happiness, power and glory, simply because you once branded an innocent man as a criminal.

BERNICK: Do you think I don't know how deeply I wronged him? And do you think I'm not ready to right that wrong?

MISS HESSEL: How? By talking?

BERNICK: I can't do that, Lona.

MISS HESSEL: How else can such a wrong be righted?

BERNICK: I am rich, Lona. Johan can ask anything he wants—

MISS HESSEL: Yes, offer him money, and see what he replies.

BERNICK: Do you know what he intends to do?

MISS HESSEL: No. Since yesterday he's said nothing. It's as though all this has suddenly made him into a man.

BERNICK: I must talk to him.

MISS HESSEL: Here he is.

JOHAN *enters right.*

BERNICK *(goes towards him):* Johan—!

JOHAN *(waves him aside):* First you listen to me. Yesterday morning I gave you my word to keep my mouth shut.

BERNICK: You did.

JOHAN: I didn't know then that—

BERNICK: Johan, just let me briefly explain the circumstances—

JOHAN: There's no need; I know all about the circumstances. The firm was in difficulties; I'd left the country; you had a name and a reputation at stake. Oh, I don't blame you so much for that; we were young and reckless in those days. But now the truth will have to be revealed. I need it.

BERNICK: I can't reveal the truth just now. I need all the moral credit I can muster.

JOHAN: I don't mind about the lies you've been spreading about me. It's this business with Dina's mother. You've got to admit it was you. Dina's going to become my wife, and I want to live with her here, and build a new life with her here, in this town.

MISS HESSEL: You want to do that?

BERNICK: With Dina? As your wife? Here?

JOHAN: Yes, here. I want to stay here to silence all these

liars and scandal-mongers. But she won't marry me unless you clear my name.

BERNICK: Don't you realize that if I admit to the one I'm automatically confessing to the other? You think I only need to show the firm's books to prove nothing was stolen? But I can't do that—our books weren't kept very carefully in those days. And even if I could, what good would it do? I'd stand revealed as a man who'd saved his skin by telling a lie, and had allowed this lie with all its consequences to be believed for fifteen years without raising a finger to contradict it. You don't know this community as well as you used to, or you'd realize that to do this would ruin me completely.

JOHAN: All I can say is that I intend to make Mrs. Dorf's daughter my wife and live with her here in this town.

BERNICK (wipes the sweat from his forehead): Listen, Johan—and you too, Lona. I'm in a very particular position just now. If you do this to me you'll destroy me, and not only me but a future of great prosperity and happiness for the community which nurtured you.

JOHAN: And if I don't I shall destroy my own chances of happiness for ever.

MISS HESSEL: Go on, Karsten.

BERNICK: Now listen. It's to do with this question of the railway, and that isn't such a simple matter as you may think. I suppose you've heard there was talk last year about building a coast line? A good many influential voices were raised in support of it, both here and elsewhere in the neighbourhood, especially in the press; but I managed to stop it, because it would have damaged our steamship trade along the coast.

MISS HESSEL: Have you an interest in this steamship trade?

BERNICK: Yes. But no one dared to suspect me of acting from that motive. My name and my reputation forbade that. In any case, I could have carried the loss; but the town couldn't have. So they decided to run the line inland. Once this had been decided I secretly took steps to assure myself that it would be practicable for a branch line to be extended here.

MISS HESSEL: Why secretly, Karsten?

BERNICK: Have you heard about the big purchases that have been made of forests and mines and waterfalls—?

MISS HESSEL: Yes, by a syndicate from one of the other towns.

BERNICK: Under present conditions these properties are virtually worthless to their various owners, so they went comparatively cheaply. If one had waited till the project of the branch line had been made public, the prices of these properties would have rocketed exorbitantly.

MISS HESSEL: Yes, well; what of it?

BERNICK: Now we come to something that could bear two different interpretations—something that a member of our community could only admit to if his name and reputation were such as to set him above suspicion.

MISS HESSEL: Yes?

BERNICK: It was I who bought all those properties.

MISS HESSEL: You?

JOHAN: On your own?

BERNICK: On my own. If the branch line gets built, I am a millionaire. If it doesn't get built, I am ruined.

MISS HESSEL: That was a big risk, Karsten.

BERNICK: I have risked all the money I possess.

MISS HESSEL: I'm not thinking of your money. When it gets known that—

BERNICK: Yes, that's the point. With the reputation I have now I can accept the responsibility for this act, carry it through to its conclusion and say to my fellow citizens: "Look! I have taken this risk for the sake of the community."

MISS HESSEL: Of the community?

BERNICK: Yes. And no one will question my motive.

MISS HESSEL: But there are others here who've acted more openly than you, and with no ulterior motive.

BERNICK: Who?

MISS HESSEL: Rummel, Sandstad and Vigeland, of course.

BERNICK: In order to win their support I was compelled to take them into my confidence.

MISS HESSEL: Oh?

BERNICK: They demanded a fifth of the profits, to be shared amongst them.

MISS HESSEL: Oh, these pillars of society!

BERNICK: Doesn't society itself force us to use these back-stairs methods? What would have happened if I hadn't acted secretly? Everyone would have charged in, they'd have divided and dispersed the properties and bungled and wrecked the whole enterprise. There isn't one man in this town apart from me who understands how to organize a project of this magnitude. Up here, it's only the families who have migrated from the cities who have any talent for big business. That's why my conscience tells me I have acted correctly in this matter. Only in my hands can these properties be of any permanent value to the thousands of people whom I intend that they shall benefit.

MISS HESSEL: I think you're right there, Karsten.

JOHAN: But I don't know these thousands of people, and my life and my happiness are at stake.

BERNICK: The prosperity of your birthplace is also at stake. If anything comes to light which casts a shadow on my early career, all my enemies will unite to destroy me. A youthful indiscretion won't be forgiven in this community. People will examine my whole life under a microscope, dig up a hundred trivial incidents and reinterpret them in the light of this revelation. They will destroy me with their rumours and innuendoes. I shall have to withdraw from the railway project; and if I do that, it will fail, and I shall be ruined and ostracized.

MISS HESSEL: Johan, after what you've just heard you must go away and keep your mouth shut.

BERNICK: Yes, yes, Johan, you must!

JOHAN: All right. I'll go. And I'll keep my mouth shut. But I shall come back, and when I do I shall speak.

BERNICK: Stay over there, Johan. Keep quiet about this, and I'll gladly give you a share of—

JOHAN: Keep your money. Give me back my name and my honour.

BERNICK: And sacrifice my own?

JOHAN: You and your community must work that out between you. I want to marry Dina; I must and shall marry her. So I'm leaving tomorrow. In the *Indian Girl*—

BERNICK: The *Indian Girl*?

JOHAN: Yes. The captain's promised to take me with him. I'm going back to America, to sell my ranch and put my affairs in order. In two months I shall be here again.

BERNICK: And then you'll talk?

JOHAN: Then the guilty will have to pay for his crime.

BERNICK: Are you forgetting that I shall also have to pay for a crime of which I am not guilty?

JOHAN: Who was it who profited by the false rumour of fifteen years ago?

BERNICK: You're making me desperate. If you speak, I shall deny everything. I shall say there's a conspiracy against me; a plot for revenge. I shall say you have come here to blackmail me.

MISS HESSEL: Karsten!

BERNICK: I'm desperate, I tell you; and I'm fighting for my life. I shall deny everything, everything!

JOHAN: I have your two letters. I found them in my trunk with my other papers. I read them again this morning. They're plain enough.

BERNICK: And you intend to publish them?

JOHAN: If you force me to.

BERNICK: And in two months you say you will be back?

JOHAN: I hope so. The winds are favourable. In three weeks I shall be in New York—if the *Indian Girl* doesn't sink—

BERNICK *(starts)*: Sink? Why should the *Indian Girl* sink?

JOHAN: No, why should she?

BERNICK *(scarcely audibly)*: Sink?

JOHAN: Well, Bernick, now you know how things are. You'd better start thinking. Goodbye. You can give my love to Betty, though she's hardly received me in a very sisterly manner. But I want to see Martha. She must tell Dina—she must promise me—

He goes out through the door upstage left.

BERNICK *(to himself)*: The *Indian Girl*? *(Quickly.)* Lona, you must stop him!

MISS HESSEL: You can see for yourself, Karsten. I haven't any power over him any longer.

She follows JOHAN *into the room left.*

BERNICK *(ponders uneasily)*: Sink?

AUNE *enters right.*

AUNE: Excuse me, Mr. Bernick. Can you spare me a moment?

BERNICK *(turns angrily)*: What do you want?

AUNE: I'd like permission to ask you a question.

BERNICK: All right, but be quick. What is it?

AUNE: I wanted to ask if you're still resolved to dismiss me if the *Indian Girl* doesn't sail tomorrow?

BERNICK: Why ask me that? She'll be ready now, won't she?

AUNE: She'll be ready. But if she wasn't, it'd mean my dismissal?

BERNICK: Why are you asking me these foolish questions?

444

AUNE: I'd like to know, Mr. Bernick. Answer me; would it mean my dismissal?

BERNICK: Do I usually stand by my word?

AUNE: Then tomorrow I'd lose my position in my home, and among the people I belong to. I'd lose my influence among the workmen; lose my chance to do anything for the poor and humble of this community.

BERNICK: Aune, we've discussed all that.

AUNE: Right, then the *Indian Girl* can sail.

Short silence.

BERNICK: Look, I can't have eyes everywhere; I can't be personally responsible for everything. You give me your promise, don't you, that the repairs have been executed satisfactorily?

AUNE: You didn't give me much time, Mr. Bernick.

BERNICK: But the work has been done properly?

AUNE: The weather's good, and it's midsummer.

Another silence.

BERNICK: Have you anything else to say to me?

AUNE: I don't know of anything else, Mr. Bernick.

BERNICK: Then—the *Indian Girl* will sail—

AUNE: Tomorrow?

BERNICK: Yes.

AUNE: Very good.

Touches his forehead and goes. BERNICK *stands for a moment, torn by doubt; then he strides quickly over to the door as though to call* AUNE *back, but stops uneasily with his hand on the doorhandle. As he does so, the door is opened from the outside and* KRAP *enters.*

KRAP *(quietly):* Oh, so he's been here. Has he confessed?

BERNICK: Hm—did you discover anything?

KRAP: What's the need? Couldn't you see from his eyes that he had a bad conscience?

BERNICK: Oh, nonsense, one can't *see* things like that. I asked you if you discovered anything.

KRAP: Couldn't get to her. Too late; they'd already started hauling her out of the dock. But the very fact that they were in such a hurry proves—

BERNICK: It proves nothing. They've completed the inspection, then?

KRAP: Of course, but—

BERNICK: There, you see! And they've found nothing to complain of.

KRAP: Mr. Bernick, you know what these inspections are, especially in a yard with a reputation like ours.

BERNICK: Nevertheless, it means that no blame can be attached to us.

KRAP: But, Mr. Bernick, surely you could see from the way Aune—

BERNICK: Aune has convinced me that there is nothing to fear.

KRAP: And I tell you I'm morally convinced that—

BERNICK: Look here, Krap, what the devil are you getting at? I know you've a grudge against this man, but if you want to pick a quarrel with him you'll have to find other grounds than this. You know how vitally important it is for me—for the company—that the *Indian Girl* sails tomorrow.

KRAP: All right. Let her sail. But how far she'll get—hm!

VIGELAND *enters right.*

VIGELAND: Good morning, Mr. Bernick, good morning! Can you spare me a moment?

BERNICK: Yes, of course, Mr. Vigeland.

VIGELAND: I just wanted to ask if you agree that the *Palm Tree* shall sail tomorrow.

446

BERNICK: Why, yes. It's all settled.

VIGELAND: Only that the captain came just now to tell me there's a gale warning.

KRAP: The barometer's fallen heavily since this morning.

BERNICK: Oh? Do they expect a storm?

VIGELAND: Well, a stiff breeze. But no head wind; on the contrary—

BERNICK: Hm. Well, what do you say?

VIGELAND: I say, as I said to the captain: "The *Palm Tree* rests in the hand of Providence." Besides, she's only got the North Sea to cross on her first leg; and freight charges are pretty high in England just now, so—

BERNICK: Yes, it'd certainly be expensive to delay her.

VIGELAND: She's solidly built; and anyway, she's fully insured. She's a good risk; not like that *Indian Girl*—

BERNICK: What do you mean?

VIGELAND: She's sailing tomorrow, too.

BERNICK: Yes, we've worked overtime on her; besides—

VIGELAND: Well, if that old coffin can sail—especially with the crew she's got—it'd be a poor thing if we were afraid to—

BERNICK: Quite, quite. You have the ship's papers with you?

VIGELAND: Yes, here.

BERNICK: Good. Mr. Krap, will you see to them?

KRAP: This way, Mr. Vigeland. We'll soon get this settled.

VIGELAND: Thank you. And the outcome, Mr. Bernick, we leave in the hands of the Almighty.

> *He goes with* KRAP *into the room downstage left.* RŒRLUND *enters through the garden.*

RŒRLUND: Why, fancy seeing you here at this time of day, Mr. Bernick.

BERNICK (*abstractedly*): Mm?

447

THE PILLARS OF SOCIETY

ROERLUND: I really came to speak to your wife. I thought she might need a few words of consolation.

BERNICK: I'm sure she does. But I'd like to have a word with you too.

ROERLUND: With pleasure, Mr. Bernick. Is something the matter? You look quite pale and upset.

BERNICK: Oh? Do I? Well, what can you expect with everything piling up on me the way it has these last few days? I've got my own business to look after without this railway— Listen, Dr. Roerlund: tell me something. Let me ask you a question.

ROERLUND: By all means, Mr. Bernick.

BERNICK: It's just a thought that occurred to me. When a man stands on the threshold of a great and ambitious enterprise which has as its object the creation of prosperity for thousands of people—suppose this enterprise should claim one, just one victim—?

ROERLUND: How do you mean?

BERNICK: Well, say a man is thinking of building a great factory. He knows for certain, because all his experience has taught him, that sooner or later in this factory human life will be lost.

ROERLUND: Yes, I fear that is only too likely.

BERNICK: Or a man is planning to open a mine. He employs men with children, and young men with all their lives before them. It's certain, is it not, that some of these men will lose their lives in his service?

ROERLUND: Alas, yes.

BERNICK: Well. A man in such a position knows before he starts that the project he is launching will at some stage of its development cost human life. But this project is for the general good. For every life it takes it will, equally beyond doubt, provide the means of happiness for many hundreds of people.

448

RŒRLUND: Ah, you're thinking of the railway—all that dangerous quarrying and dynamiting and so on—

BERNICK: Yes, yes, exactly. I'm thinking of the railway. And the railway will mean mines and factories— Remembering all this, do you still feel—?

RŒRLUND: My dear Mr. Bernick, your conscience is too tender. I believe that as long as one entrusts one's work to the hands of Providence—

BERNICK: Yes; yes, of course; Providence—

RŒRLUND: —one is absolved from guilt. Build your railway, and have no fear.

BERNICK: Yes, but now I want to give you a particular example. Suppose a mountainside has to be blasted at a dangerous spot; and if this isn't done, the railway cannot be completed. I know, and the engineer knows, that it will cost the life of the man who lights the fuse; but it must be lit, and it is the engineer's duty to send a man to do it.

RŒRLUND: Hm—

BERNICK: I know what you're going to say. The engineer ought to take the match and go himself to light the fuse. But such things aren't done. He must sacrifice one of his men.

RŒRLUND: No engineer in this country would do it.

BERNICK: No engineer in a big country would think twice about doing it.

RŒRLUND: Yes, I can quite believe that. In those depraved and unscrupulous societies—

BERNICK: Oh, there's some merit in those societies—

RŒRLUND: How can you say that? Why, you yourself—

BERNICK: In big countries men at least have elbow-room to plan ambitiously for the general good. They have courage to make sacrifices for the sake of a cause; but here one's hands are tied by all kinds of petty scruples and considerations.

RŒRLUND: Is a human life a petty consideration?

BERNICK: When it's weighed against the general good, yes.

RŒRLUND: But the examples you suggest are quite unrealistic, Mr. Bernick. I really can't make you out today. These great communities you speak of—what is a human life worth there? They think of human life simply as capital. Our ethical standpoint is completely different. Look at our great shipyards! Name one shipowner in this town who would think of sacrificing a human life for mercenary motives! And then think of those scoundrels in your great communities who, to increase their profits, send out one unseaworthy ship after another—

BERNICK: I'm not talking about unseaworthy ships!

RŒRLUND: But I am talking about them, Mr. Bernick.

BERNICK: Why bring that up? That's got nothing to do with it. Oh, this wretched narrowness and timidity! If a general in this country sent his men into battle and saw them shot down, he'd have sleepless nights. It isn't so in big countries. You should hear that fellow in there talking about—

RŒRLUND: What fellow? The American?

BERNICK: Yes. You should hear him describe how people in America—

RŒRLUND: Is he in there? Why didn't you tell me? I'll soon see to him—

BERNICK: Oh, it's no use. You won't get anywhere with him.

RŒRLUND: We'll see about that. Ah, here he is.

JOHAN TŒNNESEN *enters from the room on the left.*

JOHAN *(talks back through the open door):* All right, Dina, as you wish. But I'm not giving you up. I'm coming back, and when I do everything's going to be all right.

RŒRLUND: May I ask what you mean by those words? What exactly do you want?

JOHAN: That young girl, before whom you slandered me yesterday, is going to be my wife.

RŒRLUND: *Your—?* Do you really imagine that—?

JOHAN: I want her as my wife.

RŒRLUND: Very well. I suppose you'll have to be told. *(Goes across to the door, which is still ajar.)* Mrs. Bernick, will you please come and witness this? You too, Miss Martha. And let Dina come too. *(Sees* MISS HESSEL.*)* Oh. Are you here?

MISS HESSEL *(in the doorway):* Can I come too?

RŒRLUND: By all means. The more the better.

BERNICK: What are you going to do?

MISS HESSEL, MRS. BERNICK, MARTHA, DINA *and* HILMAR *enter from the room.*

MRS. BERNICK: Oh, Dr. Rœrlund, I tried to stop him, but—

RŒRLUND: I shall stop him, Mrs. Bernick. Dina, you are a rash and thoughtless girl. But I do not reproach you. For too long you have lacked the moral support which you so grievously need. I reproach myself for not having provided you with that support earlier.

DINA: You mustn't tell them now!

MRS. BERNICK: What is all this?

RŒRLUND: I must tell them now, Dina, although your conduct yesterday and today has made it ten times more difficult for me. But you must be saved, and all other considerations must yield to that. You remember the promise I made you, and the answer you promised to give me when I should decide that the time had come. Now I dare delay no longer; therefore— *(To* JOHAN*)* This young girl after whom you lust is betrothed to me.

MRS. BERNICK: What!

BERNICK: Dina!

JOHAN: She? To you?

MARTHA: No, Dina, no!

MISS HESSEL: It's a lie!

JOHAN: Dina. Is that man speaking the truth?

451

DINA (*after a brief pause*): Yes.

RŒRLUND: Let us pray that by this the arts of the seducer will be rendered powerless. This decision, which I have resolved to take in order to secure Dina's happiness, may be revealed to the rest of our community; I raise no objection. I sincerely trust it will not be misinterpreted. Meanwhile, Mrs. Bernick, I think it would be wisest to remove her to her room and to try to restore her calm and equilibrium.

MRS. BERNICK: Yes, come with me. Oh, Dina, what a lucky girl you are!

She leads DINA *out, left.* DR. RŒRLUND *goes with them.*

MARTHA: Goodbye, Johan.

She goes.

HILMAR (*in the verandah doorway*): Hm. Well, really! I must say—!

MISS HESSEL (*who has watched* DINA *go out; to* JOHAN): Don't lose heart, son. I'll stay here to keep an eye on the Reverend.

She goes out right.

BERNICK: Well, Johan, this means you won't be sailing in the *Indian Girl.*

JOHAN: It means I shall.

BERNICK: But you won't be coming back?

JOHAN: I'll come back.

BERNICK: After this? But what can you want here now?

JOHAN: To take my revenge on you all. To break as many of you as I can.

He goes out right. VIGELAND *and* KRAP *enter from* BERNICK'*s office.*

VIGELAND: Well, all the papers are in order now, Mr. Bernick.

BERNICK: Good, good.

KRAP (*whispers*): You still want the *Indian Girl* to sail tomorrow, then?

BERNICK: Yes.

He goes into his office. VIGELAND *and* KRAP *go out right.* HILMAR *is about to follow them when* OLAF *pokes his head cautiously out of the doorway to the room left.*

OLAF: Uncle! Uncle Hilmar!

HILMAR: Ugh, is it you? Why aren't you upstairs? You're under house arrest.

OLAF (*takes a step towards him*): Ssh! Uncle Hilmar, have you heard the news?

HILMAR: Yes, I hear you've had a hiding today.

OLAF (*scowls towards his father's office*): He won't hit me again. But have you heard that Uncle Johan's sailing to America tomorrow?

HILMAR: What's that to do with you? Now you run upstairs again.

OLAF: I'll fight those redskins yet.

HILMAR: Oh, stuff! A little coward like you?

OLAF: Just you wait till tomorrow. You'll see.

HILMAR: Jackass!

He goes out through the garden. OLAF *runs back into the room and shuts the door as he sees* KRAP *enter right.*

KRAP (*goes over to* BERNICK'S *door and half-opens it*): Excuse me disturbing you again, Mr. Bernick, but there's a dreadful storm blowing up. (*Waits for a moment; there is no reply.*) Shall the *Indian Girl* sail?

Short pause.

BERNICK (*from his room*): The *Indian Girl* shall sail.

KRAP closes the door and goes out right.

ACT FOUR

The same. The work-table has been moved out. It is a stormy afternoon, already twilight; during the scene it grows gradually darker. A FOOTMAN lights the chandelier. Two MAIDS bring in pots of flowers, lamps and candles, and place them on the tables and in brackets on the walls. RUMMEL, in tails, with gloves and a white cravat, is standing in the room giving orders.

RUMMEL *(to the FOOTMAN):* Only every second candle, Jacob. We mustn't look too festive; it's meant to be a surprise. Oh, and all these flowers—? Ah, well, let them stay. People will think they're always here—

    BERNICK *enters from his office.*

BERNICK *(in the doorway):* What's the meaning of all this?
RUMMEL: Oh dear, you weren't meant to see. *(To the SERVANTS)* All right, you can go now.

    The FOOTMAN *and* MAIDS *go out through the door upstage left.*

BERNICK *(comes closer):* Rummel, what on earth does all this mean?
RUMMEL: It means that your proudest moment has come. The whole town is marching here in procession this evening to pay homage to its foremost citizen.

BERNICK: What!

RUMMEL: With banners and a brass band. We were going to have torches, but the weather was so doubtful we didn't dare risk it. Still, there's to be an illumination. That'll look well in the newspapers.

BERNICK: Look, Rummel, I'd rather we didn't have this.

RUMMEL: Well, it's too late now. They'll be here in half an hour.

BERNICK: But why didn't you tell me about it before?

RUMMEL: I was afraid you might object to the idea. I had a word with your wife, and she gave me permission to make a few arrangements. She's looking after the refreshments herself.

BERNICK *(listens):* What's that? Are they coming already? I think I hear singing.

RUMMEL *(at the verandah door):* Singing? Oh, that's only the Americans. The *Indian Girl* is being hauled out to the buoy.

BERNICK: Is she hauling out? Yes. No, I can't this evening, Rummel. I'm not feeling well.

RUMMEL: Yes, you look off-colour. But you must pull yourself together. Damn it, man, you must! I and Sandstad and Vigeland attach the utmost importance to this ceremony. So spectacular a display of public feeling will completely crush our opponents. Rumours are spreading in the town; the news of the property deals is bound to come out soon. You must let them know this evening, against a background of songs and speeches, and the merry clink of glasses—in short, in an atmosphere of holiday and carnival—how much you have staked for the welfare of the community. In such an atmosphere of holiday and carnival, as I have just phrased it, we can get the hell of a lot done. But we've got to have that atmosphere, or it'll be no good.

BERNICK: Yes, yes, yes—

RUMMEL: Especially when the issue is such a delicate and ticklish one. Thank heaven you've the name and reputation you have, Bernick. But listen, now. I must tell you about the arrangements. Hilmar Tœnnesen has written a song in your honour. It's very beautiful; it begins: "Wave high the banner of ideals!" And Dr. Rœrlund is to make the speech. You'll have to reply, of course.

BERNICK: I can't do that this evening, Rummel. Couldn't you—?

RUMMEL: Impossible! Much as I'd like to. The speech will naturally be addressed mainly to you. Possibly just a word or two about us too. I've been discussing it with Vigeland and Sandstad. We thought you might reply with a toast to the prosperity of the community. Sandstad will say something about the harmony that exists between the various strata of our society; Vigeland will want to stress how important it is that this new enterprise should not disturb the moral foundations on which our life is so firmly based; and I'm thinking of paying a brief tribute to the ladies, whose contribution to the welfare of our community, while humble and unassuming, must not be overlooked. But you're not listening.

BERNICK: Yes, yes, I am. But tell me—is the sea very rough this evening?

RUMMEL: Are you worrying about the *Palm Tree?* She's well insured.

BERNICK: Insured, yes. But—

RUMMEL: And in good trim. That's the main thing.

BERNICK: Hm. If anything should happen to a ship, it doesn't necessarily follow that human lives will be lost. The ship and her cargo, perhaps—chests and papers—

RUMMEL: Damn it, man, chests and papers aren't that important.

BERNICK: Of course not. No, no—I only meant— Quiet! They're singing again.

456

RUMMEL: That'll be the crew of the *Palm Tree*.

VIGELAND *enters right*.

VIGELAND: Well, the *Palm Tree*'s hauling out now. Good evening, Mr. Bernick.

BERNICK: You're a seaman. Do you still feel confident that—?

VIGELAND: Providence will decide, Mr. Bernick; of that I am confident. Besides, I've been on board myself and distributed a few little tracts which I trust will ensure God's blessing on her.

SANDSTAD *and* KRAP *enter right*.

SANDSTAD *(still in the doorway):* Well, if that ship survives, I'll believe in miracles. Oh—good evening, good evening!

BERNICK: Anything wrong, Mr. Krap?

KRAP: I said nothing, Mr. Bernick.

SANDSTAD: The whole crew of the *Indian Girl* is drunk. If those brutes get that ship safely across the Atlantic, I'm a Dutchman.

MISS HESSEL *enters right*.

MISS HESSEL *(to* BERNICK*):* He asked me to say goodbye to you.

BERNICK: Is he aboard already?

MISS HESSEL: He will be any moment. I left him outside the hotel.

BERNICK: And he's still determined—?

MISS HESSEL: Absolutely determined.

RUMMEL *(over by the windows):* Confound these new-fangled contraptions. I can't get these curtains down.

MISS HESSEL: You want them down? I thought they were to stay up.

RUMMEL: Down to begin with, madam. I suppose you know what's going to happen?

MISS HESSEL: Yes, I know. Let me help you. *(Takes the cords.)* Yes, I'll lower the curtain on my brother-in-law; though I'd sooner lift it.

RUMMEL: You can do that later. When the garden is filled with the surging throng, the curtains will be raised to reveal an amazed and happy family circle. A citizen's home should be as a house of glass, open to the gaze of all.

> BERNICK *seems about to speak, but turns quickly and goes into his room.*

RUMMEL: Well, let's just run through the arrangements. Come along, Mr. Krap. We need your help on a few details.

> All the GENTLEMEN *go into* BERNICK's *room.* MISS HESSEL *has drawn the curtains over the windows and is just about to do the same across the open glass door when* OLAF *jumps down on to the verandah from above. He has a plaid over his shoulder and a bundle in his hand.*

MISS HESSEL: Oh, my goodness, Olaf, how you frightened me!

OLAF *(hiding his bundle):* Ssh!

MISS HESSEL: Did you jump out of that window? Where are you going?

OLAF: Ssh! Don't tell anyone! I'm going to Uncle Johan. Only down to the jetty, of course—just to say goodbye to him. Good night, Aunt Lona!

> He runs out through the garden.

MISS HESSEL: No, wait! Olaf, Olaf!

JOHAN TŒNNESEN, *in travelling clothes, with a bag over his shoulder, enters cautiously right.*

JOHAN: Lona!

MISS HESSEL *(turns):* What! Are you here again?

JOHAN: I've still got a few minutes. I must see her just once more. We can't part like this.

MARTHA *and* DINA, *both wearing overcoats, and the latter with a small travelling-bag in her hand, enter through the door upstage left.*

DINA: I must see him, I must see him!

MARTHA: Yes, Dina. You'll see him.

DINA: There he is!

JOHAN: Dina!

DINA: Take me with you.

JOHAN: What?

MISS HESSEL: You want to go with him?

DINA: Yes! Take me with you! That man says he's going to make a public announcement this evening in front of the whole town about—

JOHAN: Dina! You don't love him?

DINA: I have never loved him. I'd die rather than be engaged to him. Oh, how he humiliated me yesterday with his fine phrases! He made me feel he was raising something contemptible up to his own level. I'm not going to be humiliated like that any more. I'm going away. Can I come with you?

JOHAN: Yes! Yes!

DINA: I shan't trouble you for long. Just help me to get over there; help me to find my feet—

JOHAN: Yippee! Don't you worry about that, Dina!

MISS HESSEL *(points towards* BERNICK's *door):* Ssh! Quiet, quiet!

JOHAN: I'll take care of you, Dina!

DINA: No. I won't let you do that. I'm going to look after myself. I'll manage to do that over there. If only I can get away from here! Oh, these women—you've no idea! They've written to me today begging me to realize how lucky I am, and reminding me how noble and magnanimous he's been. Tomorrow and the next day and every day they'll be squinting at me to see whether I'm proving myself worthy of him. Oh, all this respectability frightens me so much!

JOHAN: Tell me, Dina. Is that the only reason you're leaving? Am I nothing to you?

DINA: Oh, no, Johan. You mean more to me than anyone else in the world.

JOHAN: Oh, Dina!

DINA: Everyone here tells me I ought to hate you and detest you. They say it's my duty. But I don't understand all this about duty. I never shall.

MISS HESSEL: That's right, child! Don't you!

MARTHA: Yes, Dina. Go with him. As his wife.

JOHAN: Yes! Yes!

MISS HESSEL: What? I'll have to kiss you for that, Martha. I hadn't expected that from you.

MARTHA: No, I suppose not. I hadn't expected it myself. But I've got to speak out some time. Oh, how we suffer here under this tyranny of duty and convention! Rebel against it, Dina! Marry him. Do something to defy all their stupid ideals!

JOHAN: What do you say, Dina?

DINA: Yes. I will be your wife.

JOHAN: Dina!

DINA: But first I want to work and become someone. The way you have. I don't just want to be something someone takes.

MISS HESSEL: Sensible girl! That's the way!

JOHAN: Right! I'll wait, and hope—

MISS HESSEL: You'll win her, son. But now it's time for you both to go aboard.

JOHAN: Yes—aboard! Oh, Lona, my dear sister! Here, I want a word with you—

He leads her upstage and whispers quickly to her.

MARTHA: Dina, my dear, let me look at you. Let me kiss you once again. For the last time.

DINA: Not for the last time. No, dear, dear Aunt Martha! We'll meet again!

MARTHA: No; we never shall. Promise me, Dina—don't ever come back. *(Clasps both* DINA'*s hands and looks at her.)* Go, my dear child—go to your happiness across the sea. Oh, down in that schoolroom I've so often longed to be over there! It must be beautiful there. The sky is larger and the clouds fly higher than they do here. The air that blows on the faces of the people is freer—

DINA: Oh, Aunt Martha, you must come and join us. Some day.

MARTHA: I? Never; never. My little task lies here. Now I think I can resign myself to being what I must be.

DINA: I can't imagine being without you.

MARTHA: Oh, one can learn to manage without almost anything, Dina. *(Kisses her.)* But you'll never have to test the truth of that, my dear. Promise me you'll make him happy.

DINA: I won't promise anything. I hate promises. What will be will be.

MARTHA: Yes, yes, my dear. Always be as you are now. Be true to yourself. And believe in yourself.

DINA: I will, Aunt Martha.

MISS HESSEL *(puts some papers which* JOHAN *has given her into her pocket):* Good boy, Johan. All right, I'll do that. But now be off with you!

JOHAN: Yes, we've no time to waste. Goodbye, Lona—

thanks for everything you've done for me. Goodbye, Martha. Thank you too. You've been a wonderful friend.

MARTHA: Goodbye, Johan! Goodbye, Dina! God bless you and make you happy—always!

> MARTHA *and* MISS HESSEL *hurry them to the verandah door.* JOHAN *and* DINA *run out through the garden.* MISS HESSEL *closes the door and draws the curtain over it.*

MISS HESSEL: Now we're alone, Martha. You've lost her, and I've lost him.

MARTHA: *You*'ve lost him?

MISS HESSEL: Oh, I'd half-lost him already over there. The boy wanted to stand on his own feet, so I pretended I was pining to come back here.

MARTHA: Was that why? Now I see why you came. But he wants you to go back and join them.

MISS HESSEL: An old half-sister? What good can she be to him now? Men destroy a lot of things to find happiness.

MARTHA: It happens sometimes.

MISS HESSEL: But we'll stick together, Martha.

MARTHA: Can I be of any use to you?

MISS HESSEL: Who better? We two foster-mothers—haven't we both lost our children? Now we're alone.

MARTHA: Yes; alone. You might as well know now. I loved him more than anything else in the world.

MISS HESSEL: Martha! *(Grips her arm.)* Is this true?

MARTHA: That's been my life. I loved him, and waited for him. Every summer I waited for him to come through that door. At last he came; but he didn't see me.

MISS HESSEL: You loved him! But it was you yourself who put happiness into his hands.

MARTHA: What else should I have done, if I loved him? Yes, I loved him. I've only lived for him, ever since he went away. What ground did I have for hope, you're wondering? Oh, I thought I had a little. But then, when he came back, it was just as though everything had been wiped clean from his memory. He didn't see me.

MISS HESSEL: Because of Dina, Martha. You stood in her shadow.

MARTHA: I'm glad. When he left, we were the same age; but when I saw him again—oh, that dreadful moment!—I suddenly realized that now I was ten years older than him. He'd been walking over there in the bright, quivering sunlight, drawing in youth and strength with every breath, while I'd been sitting in here, spinning and spinning—

MISS HESSEL: The thread of his happiness, Martha.

MARTHA: Yes, it was gold I was spinning. I mustn't be bitter. It's true, isn't it, Lona—we two have been good sisters to him?

MISS HESSEL (*throws her arms round her*): Martha!

BERNICK *enters from his room.*

BERNICK (*to the* GENTLEMEN *inside his room*): Yes, yes, yes, make what arrangements you please. I'll manage when the time comes— (*Closes the door.*) Oh, are you here? Look, Martha, you'd better go and dress up a bit. And tell Betty to do the same. Nothing grand, of course. Just something neat and simple. You must be quick, though.

MISS HESSEL: And you must look happy and excited, Martha. This is a joyful occasion for us all.

BERNICK: Olaf must come down too. I want to have him by my side.

MISS HESSEL: Hm. Olaf—

MARTHA: I'll go and tell Betty.

She goes out through the door upstage left.

MISS HESSEL: Well. Now the great moment's arrived.

BERNICK (*paces uneasily up and down*): Yes, so it has.

MISS HESSEL: I imagine a man must feel very proud and happy at such a moment.

BERNICK (*looks at her*): Hm.

MISS HESSEL: The whole town's to be illuminated, I hear.

BERNICK: Yes, they've planned something of the kind.

MISS HESSEL: All the guilds are to march here with their banners. Your name is to shine in letters of fire. Tonight the news will be telegraphed to every corner of the land: "Surrounded by his happy family, Karsten Bernick was acclaimed by his fellow citizens as a pillar of society."

BERNICK: Yes, that's right. And they're going to give three cheers for me outside there, and the crowd will demand that I show myself in the doorway here, and I shall be forced to bow and make a speech of thanks.

MISS HESSEL: Forced?

BERNICK: Do you think I feel happy at this moment?

MISS HESSEL: No, I don't imagine you can feel all that happy.

BERNICK: You despise me, don't you, Lona?

MISS HESSEL: Not yet.

BERNICK: You've no right to do that. To despise me. Oh, Lona, you can't imagine how dreadfully alone I am in this narrow, stunted society—how, year by year, I've had to renounce my hopes of really fulfilling myself and becoming what I might and could have become. What have I accomplished? It seems a lot, but really it's nothing—a patchwork of trivialities. But they wouldn't tolerate anything else here, or anything bigger. If I tried to move a step outside their conception of right and wrong, my power would vanish. Do you know what we are, we whom they call the pillars of society? We are the instruments of society. Nothing more.

MISS HESSEL: Why have you only begun to realize this now?

BERNICK: Because I've been thinking a great deal lately—since you came back. Especially this evening. Oh, Lona, why didn't I appreciate you then for what you were?

MISS HESSEL: And if you had?

BERNICK: I'd never have let you go. And if I'd had you beside me, I wouldn't stand where I do today.

MISS HESSEL: What about Betty? Haven't you ever thought what she might have been to you?

BERNICK: I only know she hasn't been the wife I needed.

MISS HESSEL: Because you've never let her share your work with you, or tried to establish a free and truthful relationship with her. Because you've allowed her to spend her life reproaching herself for the disgrace to her family for which you yourself are responsible.

BERNICK: Yes, yes, yes. Lying and cheating—that's the cause of it all.

MISS HESSEL: Then why don't you start telling the truth?

BERNICK: Now? It's too late now, Lona.

MISS HESSEL: Tell me, Karsten. What satisfaction does all this lying and cheating bring you?

BERNICK: None. I shall be destroyed, like the whole of this rotten society. But a generation will grow up after us. It's my son I'm working for; it's for him that I'm doing all this. A time will come when society will be founded on honesty and truth, and then he will be able to live a happier life than his father has.

MISS HESSEL: With a lie as the cornerstone of his existence? Think what an inheritance you're leaving your son.

BERNICK (*in subdued despair*): I am leaving him an inheritance a thousand times worse than you know. But some time the curse must end. And yet—in spite of everything— (*Violently.*) How could you do all this to me? Well, now it's happened. Now I must go on. I won't let you destroy me!

HILMAR TŒNNESEN, *an open letter in his hand, hastens in right, confused.*

HILMAR: But this is utterly—! Betty, Betty!

BERNICK: What is it now? Have they come already?

HILMAR: No, no. I must speak to someone—

He goes out through the door upstage left.

MISS HESSEL: Karsten, you say we came here to destroy you. Then let me tell you the metal he's made of, this prodigal whom your virtuous community treated like a leper. He can manage without you now. He's gone.

BERNICK: But he's coming back.

MISS HESSEL: Johan will never come back. He's gone for ever, and Dina has gone with him.

BERNICK: Never come back? And Dina—gone with him?

MISS HESSEL: Yes, to become his wife. There's a slap in the face for your virtuous community! Reminds me of the day I gave you a—ah well!

BERNICK: Gone? She too? In the *Indian Girl?*

MISS HESSEL: No. He didn't dare to risk so precious a cargo with that gang of ruffians. Johan and Dina have sailed in the *Palm Tree.*

BERNICK: Ah! Then it was all for nothing—! *(Goes quickly to the door of his room, flings it open and shouts)* Krap, stop the *Indian Girl!* She mustn't sail tonight!

KRAP *(from the other room):* The *Indian Girl* is already standing out to sea, Mr. Bernick.

BERNICK *(closes the door and says dully):* Too late! And for nothing—!

MISS HESSEL: What do you mean?

BERNICK: Nothing, nothing. Get away from me—!

MISS HESSEL: Hm. Look here, Karsten. Johan told me to tell you that he's entrusted to me the keeping of his good name, which he once entrusted to you and which you robbed him of while he was away. Johan will keep his mouth shut. And I can do as I choose. Look. I have your two letters here in my hand.

BERNICK: You have them! And now—now you're going to—this evening—when the procession arrives—?

MISS HESSEL: I didn't come here to unmask you. I came to shake you from your sleep, so that you'd stand up and tell the truth. I have failed. Very well, then. Go on living your lie. Look. I'm tearing your two letters up. Take the pieces. Now you have them. There's no evidence against you now, Karsten. You've nothing left to fear. Be happy—if you can.

BERNICK (*a shiver runs through his whole body*): Lona, why didn't you do this before? Now it's too late. Now my whole life is ruined. After today, I can't go on living.

MISS HESSEL: What has happened?

BERNICK: Don't ask me. And yet—I must live! I shall live! For Olaf's sake! He'll make everything right—he'll atone for everything—!

MISS HESSEL: Karsten!

HILMAR TŒNNESEN *hurries back.*

HILMAR: I can't find him. He's gone. Betty too.

BERNICK: What's the matter with you?

HILMAR: I daren't tell you.

BERNICK: What is it? You must tell me!

HILMAR: Very well. Olaf has run away. He's gone—in the *Indian Girl.*

BERNICK: (*recoils*): Olaf! In the *Indian Girl!* No! No!

MISS HESSEL: Yes, it's true. Now I understand. I saw him jump out of the window.

BERNICK (*in the doorway to his room, cries desperately*): Krap, stop the *Indian Girl!* Stop her at all costs!

KRAP (*comes out*): Impossible, Mr. Bernick. How can we?

BERNICK: We must stop her. Olaf is on board.

KRAP: What!

RUMMEL *(enters from* BERNICK'*s room):* Olaf run away? Impossible!

SANDSTAD *(enters):* They'll send him back with the pilot, Mr. Bernick.

HILMAR: No, no. He's left me a letter. *(Shows it.)* He says he'll hide among the cargo until they've reached the open sea.

BERNICK: I shall never see him again.

RUMMEL: Oh, rubbish. She's a good, strong ship, newly repaired—

VIGELAND *(who has also come out):* In your own yard, Mr. Bernick.

BERNICK: I shall never see him again, I tell you. I've lost him, Lona. No—I realize it now. He never belonged to me. *(Listens.)* What's that?

RUMMEL: Music. The procession's arriving.

BERNICK: I can't receive anyone. I won't!

RUMMEL: What on earth do you mean? You must!

SANDSTAD: You must, Mr. Bernick. Remember what you have at stake.

BERNICK: What does that matter now? Whom have I to work for now?

RUMMEL: What a question to ask! You have us. And the community.

VIGELAND: Of course!

SANDSTAD: And you surely haven't forgotten that we too—

MARTHA *enters through the door upstage left. The music can be faintly heard from far down the street.*

MARTHA: The procession's arriving. I can't find Betty anywhere. I can't think where she—

BERNICK: Can't find her! You see, Lona! In sorrow as in joy, I stand alone.

RUMMEL: Up with those curtains! Come and help me, Mr.

Krap. You too, Mr. Sandstad. Most regrettable that the whole family isn't here. That's not at all according to programme.

The curtains are raised from the windows and the door. The whole street is illuminated. On the house opposite is a big transparency, bearing the inscription: 'Long live Karsten Bernick, The Pillar of our Society!'

BERNICK *(recoils):* Take that away! I don't want to see it! Put it out, put it out!

RUMMEL: My dear fellow, have you taken leave of your senses?

MARTHA: What's the matter with him, Lona?

MISS HESSEL: Ssh!

Whispers to her.

BERNICK: Take away this nonsense, I tell you! Can't you see that all these lights are a mockery!

RUMMEL: Well, really!

BERNICK: Oh, how could you understand? But I—I—! These are torches to light the dead to their graves!

KRAP: Hm!

RUMMEL: Now look! You're making too much of this.

SANDSTAD: The boy'll just take a trip across the Atlantic, and then you'll have him back home again.

VIGELAND: Put your trust in the hand of the Almighty, Mr. Bernick.

RUMMEL: That ship's not ready to sink yet.

KRAP: Hm.

RUMMEL: It's not as though she was one of these floating coffins they send out in foreign countries—

MRS. BERNICK, *a big shawl over her head, enters from the verandah.*

MRS. BERNICK: Karsten, Karsten, have you heard?

469

BERNICK: Yes, I've heard. But you—you see nothing! You're his mother, why didn't you look after him?

MRS. BERNICK: Karsten, listen—

BERNICK: Why didn't you keep a watch on him? I've lost him! Give him back to me, if you can.

MRS. BERNICK: Yes, I can. I have him safe.

BERNICK: You have him?

THE OTHERS: Ah!

HILMAR: Yes, I thought as much.

MARTHA: You've got him back, Karsten!

MISS HESSEL: Yes. Now you must win him too.

BERNICK: You have him safe! Do you really mean it? Where is he?

MRS. BERNICK: I shan't tell you until you've forgiven him.

BERNICK: Forgiven—! But how did you find out—?

MRS. BERNICK: Do you think a mother hasn't eyes? I was terrified you might find out. Those few words he let fall yesterday—then I found his room was empty and his clothes and rucksack missing—

BERNICK: Yes, yes.

MRS. BERNICK: So I ran down and got hold of Aune. We went out in his boat. The American ship was just getting ready to sail. Thank heaven, we got there in time—went aboard—had the ship searched—found him. Oh, Karsten, you mustn't punish him!

BERNICK: Betty!

MRS. BERNICK: Or Aune either!

BERNICK: Aune? What do you know about him? Is the *Indian Girl* under sail again?

MRS. BERNICK: No, that's just it—

BERNICK: Speak, speak!

MRS. BERNICK: Aune was as frightened as I was. It took a long time to search the ship—darkness was falling, the pilot began to complain—so Aune took his courage in his hands and told them in your name—

BERNICK: Yes?

MRS. BERNICK: To hold the ship until morning.

KRAP: Hm.

BERNICK: Oh, what luck! What incredible luck!

MRS. BERNICK: You aren't angry?

BERNICK: Oh, Betty, thank God, thank God!

RUMMEL: Come, man, you're being over-sensitive.

HILMAR: Yes, as soon as anyone's bold enough to risk a little skirmish with the elements—ugh!

KRAP *(by the windows):* The procession's just coming through the garden gate!

BERNICK: Let them come.

RUMMEL: The whole garden's filling with people.

SANDSTAD: The street's crammed too.

RUMMEL: The entire town's here, Bernick. This is really an inspiring moment.

VIGELAND: Let us accept it in a humble spirit, Mr. Bernick.

RUMMEL: All the flags are out. What a procession! There's the festival committee, with Dr. Rœrlund at its head.

BERNICK: Let them come, I say!

RUMMEL: Look; you're in a rather disturbed state of mind just now—

BERNICK: So?

RUMMEL: Well, if you don't feel up to it, I wouldn't mind saying a few words on your behalf.

BERNICK: No, thank you. This evening I shall speak for myself.

RUMMEL: But do you know what you have to say?

BERNICK: Yes, Rummel. Don't worry. I know what I have to say.

The music has ceased. The verandah door is thrown open. DR. RŒRLUND *enters at the head of the festival committee, accompanied by two* FOOTMEN *carrying a covered basket. After them come* CITIZENS *of all classes, as many as the room will hold. A huge crowd, with banners and flags, can be glimpsed outside in the garden and the street.*

RŒRLUND: Most honoured sir! I see by the amazement on your face that our intrusion into this happy family circle, where you sit gathered at your peaceful fireside surrounded by active and honourable fellow citizens, takes you completely by surprise. But our hearts commanded that we should come and pay you homage. It is not the first time we have done this, but it is the first time we have done so on such a comprehensive scale. We have often expressed to you our thanks for the solid moral foundation on which you have, as one might say, grounded our community. But tonight we hail you as the far-sighted, indefatigable and selfless—nay, self-sacrificing—fellow-citizen who has seized the initiative in launching an enterprise which, so expert opinion assures us, will give a powerful impetus to the material welfare and prosperity of our community.

VOICES FROM THE CROWD: Bravo, bravo!

RŒRLUND: Mr. Bernick, you have for many years been a shining example to our town. I am speaking now not of your model family life, nor of your untarnished moral record. These are matters for private admiration rather than public acclaim. I speak rather of your work as a citizen, which is apparent for all to see. Stately ships sail forth from your shipyards and show our country's flag upon the furthest corners of the globe. A numerous and contented family of workers reveres you as a father. By calling into existence new branches of industry you have given prosperity to hundreds of homes. You are, in a word, the cornerstone of our community.

VOICES: Hear, hear! Bravo!

RŒRLUND: But what we especially bless in you is the shining altruism which irradiates your every action—a rare quality indeed in this modern age. You are now in the process of procuring for the community a—I do not flinch from the plain, prosaic word—a railway.

MANY VOICES: Bravo, bravo!

RŒRLUND: But this enterprise is threatened by obstacles deliberately placed in its path by narrow and selfish interests.

VOICES: Hear, hear!

RŒRLUND: It is not unknown that certain individuals who do not belong to our community have stolen a march on our own industrious citizens, and have secured certain advantages which rightly belonged to this town.

VOICES: Yes, yes. Hear, hear!

RŒRLUND: This regrettable information has, sir, doubtless come to your knowledge. None the less you are pursuing your project inflexibly, knowing that a true patriot's vision cannot be confined by the needs of his own parish.

VARIOUS VOICES: Hm. No, no! Yes, yes!

RŒRLUND: It is therefore to the patriot and, in the largest sense, the model citizen, that we are gathered here tonight to pay homage. May God grant that your enterprise may result in true and lasting prosperity for this community! The railway is a road which may expose us to corrupting influences from without, but it will also be a road by which we shall swiftly be able to rid ourselves of them. We can, alas, no longer hope to isolate ourselves completely from the evil of the outside world. But the fact that on this evening of rejoicing we have, so it is rumoured, been rid with unexpected speed of one such influence—

VOICES: Ssh! Ssh!

RŒRLUND: —I take as a happy omen for this enterprise. I only mention this as evidence that we stand here in a house in which ethical considerations carry greater weight than the ties of blood.

VOICES: Hear, hear! Bravo!

BERNICK *(simultaneously):* Allow me to—

RŒRLUND: One word more, sir. What you have done for this parish you have, of course, done with no ulterior motive or thought of material advantage. But we trust you will not refuse to accept a small token of appreciation from your fellow citizens, least of all at this significant moment when, so men of practical experience assure us, we stand on the threshold of a new era.

MANY VOICES: Bravo! Hear, hear!

He nods to the FOOTMEN, *who bring the basket closer. During the following,* MEMBERS OF THE COMMITTEE *take out and present the objects described.*

RŒRLUND: We therefore have the honour, Mr. Bernick, to present you with this silver coffee-service. May it adorn your table when, in the days to come, as so often in days gone by, we shall enjoy the pleasure of gathering at your hospitable board. And you too, gentlemen, who have so steadfastly supported our foremost citizen, we beg to accept these small tokens of our affection. To you, Mr. Rummel, this silver cup. You have often, in well-winged words, amid the clinking of cups, championed the civic interests of this community. May you often find worthy opportunities for raising and emptying this cup. To you, Mr. Sandstad, I present this album containing photographs of your fellow citizens. Your famed and acknowledged generosity places you in the agreeable position of numbering friends in every stratum of the community, regardless of political differences. And to you, Mr. Vigeland, to adorn your bedside, I offer this book of sermons, printed on vellum, and luxuriously bound. Under the ripening influence of the years you have arrived at a mature wisdom; your interest in temporal matters has been purified and sublimated by reflection upon loftier

and less worldly things. *(Turns to the* CROWD.*)* And now,
my friends, three cheers for Mr. Bernick and his fellows
in the fight! Three cheers for the pillars of our society!

WHOLE CROWD: Long live Mr. Bernick! Long live the pillars of our society! Hurrah! Hurrah! Hurrah!

MISS HESSEL: Good luck, brother-in-law.

An expectant silence.

BERNICK *(begins slowly and earnestly):* Fellow-citizens!
Your Chairman has said that we stand this evening on the
threshold of a new era; and I hope this will prove to be the
case. But for this to happen, we must face the truth, which
until this evening has been an outcast from this community. *(General amazement.)* I must therefore begin by re-
jecting the words of praise with which you, Dr. Rœrlund,
as is the custom on such occasions, addressed me. I am
unworthy of them, for until today I have not acted
selflessly. If I have not always acted from pecuniary motives, I none the less now realize that a desire for power,
for influence and for reputation, has been the driving
force behind most of my actions.

RUMMEL *(aside):* What's this?

BERNICK: However, I do not therefore reproach myself before my fellow citizens. For I still believe that I can be
reckoned among the most useful of us who stand here tonight.

MANY VOICES: Hear, hear! Yes, yes!

BERNICK: I condemn myself most for having so often been
weak enough to use backstairs methods, because I knew
and feared our community's fondness for scenting impure
motives behind everything a man does here. And that
brings me to a case in point.

RUMMEL *(uneasily):* Hm-hm!

BERNICK: Rumours have been spreading about the big purchases of land that have been made in the neighbourhood.

475

All these purchases have been made by me, and by me alone.

VOICES *(whisper):* What did he say? Him? Mr. Bernick?

BERNICK: All that land belongs, at this moment, to me. I have of course confided this information to my partners in this enterprise, Messrs Rummel, Vigeland and Sandstad, and we have agreed that—

RUMMEL: It isn't true! Where's the proof? Show us the proof!

VIGELAND: We agreed nothing!

SANDSTAD: Well, I must say!

BERNICK: That is quite correct; we have not yet agreed on what I was about to propose. But I am confident that these three gentlemen will agree with me now when I say that I have this evening convinced myself that these properties should be turned into a public company, so that any citizen who wishes may buy a share in them.

MANY VOICES: Hurrah! Long live Mr. Bernick!

RUMMEL *(quietly to* BERNICK*):* You damned traitor!

SANDSTAD *(also quietly):* You've cheated us!

VIGELAND: May the devil—oh, good heavens, what am I saying?

CROWD *(outside):* Hurrah, hurrah, hurrah!

BERNICK: Quiet, gentlemen! I am unworthy of this applause, for the decision I have now reached is not what I originally intended. I intended to keep all the land for myself, and I still believe that these properties can be best exploited if they come under the control of a single hand. But that is for you to decide. If it is the general wish, I am willing to administer them to the best of my ability.

VOICES: Yes! Yes! Yes!

BERNICK: But first my fellow citizens must know me as I really am. Let each man look into his own heart, and let us resolve that from tonight we shall in fact enter upon a new era. Let the old life, with its painted façade, its hypocrisy and its hollowness, its sham propriety and its miserable prejudices, survive only as a museum. And to this museum we shall give—shall we not, gentlemen?—our coffee-service, our silver cup, our photograph album and our book of sermons printed on vellum and luxuriously bound.

RUMMEL: Yes, of course.

VIGELAND (*mutters*): You've taken all the rest from us, so why not this?

SANDSTAD: Yes, yes.

BERNICK: And now to the chief issue that remains between me and my community. You have heard it asserted that evil influences have left us this evening. To that piece of news I can add another. The man in question did not leave alone. A girl went with him, to become his wife—

MISS HESSEL (*loudly*): Dina Dorf!

RŒRLUND: What?

MRS. BERNICK: Lona!

Great excitement.

RŒRLUND: Fled? Run away—with him? Impossible!

BERNICK: To become his wife, Dr. Rœrlund. And I will tell you something else. (*Quietly.*) Prepare yourself, Betty, for what I am about to say. (*Loudly.*) I say: "Hats off to that man, for he had the courage to shoulder the blame for another man's crime." Oh, fellow citizens, I am weary of lies. They have poisoned every fibre of my being. You shall know everything. It was I who was guilty fifteen years ago.

MRS. BERNICK (*quietly, emotionally*): Karsten!

MARTHA (*similarly*): Oh—Johan—!

MISS HESSEL: At last!

Dumb astonishment among the ONLOOKERS.

BERNICK: Yes, fellow-citizens! I was the guilty one, and he

477

was the one who fled. The false and evil rumours which were afterwards spread about him it is now too late to refute. But who am I to complain of this? Fifteen years ago I raised myself on these rumours. Whether they are now to bring me down is a question that each one of you must argue with his own conscience.

RŒRLUND: What a thunderbolt! The town's foremost citizen! *(Softly, to* MRS. BERNICK*)* Oh, Mrs. Bernick, I feel most deeply sorry for you.

HILMAR: What an admission! Well, I must say—!

BERNICK: But you must not decide tonight. I beg each of you to return home to collect your thoughts and to look into your hearts. When you are calm again you will decide whether by speaking thus openly I have lost or won. Goodbye. I still have much to atone for; but that is between myself and my own conscience. Good night. Take away these trappings. This is not the time nor the place for them.

RŒRLUND: I should think not indeed! *(Softly, to* MRS. BERNICK*)* Run away! She was quite unworthy of me after all. *(Half-aloud to the* COMMITTEE*)* Well, gentlemen, after this I think we had better depart as quietly as we can.

HILMAR: How anyone is to wave the banner of ideals high after this I really—ugh!

The news meanwhile has been whispered from mouth to mouth. The CROWD *drifts away.* RUMMEL, SANDSTAD *and* VIGELAND *also go, arguing in subdued but vehement tones.* HILMAR *wanders out right. Silence.* BERNICK, MRS. BERNICK, MARTHA, MISS HESSEL *and* KRAP *are left in the room.*

BERNICK: Betty, can you forgive me?

MRS. BERNICK *(smiles):* Do you know, Karsten, this has been the happiest moment I have had for years?

BERNICK: What do you mean?

MRS. BERNICK: For years now I have believed that you were once mine, but I had lost you. Now I know you were never mine; but I shall win you.

BERNICK (*throws his arms round her*): Oh, Betty, you have won me! Lona has taught me to understand for the first time what kind of woman you really are. But Olaf—Olaf!

MRS. BERNICK: Yes, now you can see him. Mr. Krap—

She talks quietly to KRAP *upstage. He goes out through the verandah door. During the following, all the transparencies, and the lights in the houses outside, are gradually extinguished.*

BERNICK (*quietly*): Thank you, Lona. You have saved what was best in me—and for me.

MISS HESSEL: What else do you think I wanted?

BERNICK: Yes—was it this you came back for—or was it something else? I don't understand you, Lona.

MISS HESSEL: Hm—

BERNICK: It wasn't hatred, then? And it wasn't revenge? Then why did you come back here?

MISS HESSEL: Old friendship doesn't rust, Karsten.

BERNICK: Lona!

MISS HESSEL: When Johan told me about that lie, I vowed to myself: "The hero of my youth shall stand free and true."

BERNICK: Lona, Lona! How little I have deserved this from you!

MISS HESSEL: Ah, Karsten! If we women demanded our deserts—!

AUNE *enters from the garden with* OLAF.

BERNICK (*runs towards him*): Olaf!

OLAF: Father, I promise you I won't ever again—

BERNICK: Run away?

OLAF: Yes, yes, I promise, Father.

BERNICK: And I promise you, you shall never have cause to. From now on you shall be allowed to grow up, not as the heir to my life's work, but as one who has his own life's work awaiting him.

OLAF: And may I become anything I like?

BERNICK: Yes, you may.

OLAF: Thank you. Then I don't want to become a pillar of society.

BERNICK: Oh? Why not?

OLAF: I think it must be so dull.

BERNICK: You shall be yourself, Olaf. That is all that matters. As for you, Aune—

AUNE: I know, Mr. Bernick. I'm dismissed.

BERNICK: We'll stay together, Aune. And please forgive me.

AUNE: What! But the ship didn't sail this evening—

BERNICK: She shall not sail tomorrow, either. I gave you too little time. The work must be attended to more thoroughly.

AUNE: It will, Mr. Bernick. And with the new machines!

BERNICK: Good. But it must be done thoroughly and honestly. There is much in us which needs to be repaired thoroughly and honestly. Well, good night, Aune.

AUNE: Good night, Mr. Bernick—and thank you. Thank you!

He goes out right.

MRS. BERNICK: They have all gone now.

BERNICK: And we are alone. My name does not shine in letters of fire any longer. All the lights in the windows are out.

MISS HESSEL: Would you like them lit again?

BERNICK: Not for all the money in the world. Where have I been? You will be appalled when you know. I feel as though I had just returned to health and sanity after being poisoned. But I feel it—I *can* become young and strong again. Oh, come closer, come closer around me! Come, Betty! Come, Olaf, my son! And you, Martha. Oh, Martha! It's as though I had never seen you all these years.

MISS HESSEL: I can well believe that. Your society is a society of bachelors. You don't notice the women.

BERNICK: True, true. And because of that—now I don't want any arguing, Lona—you must not leave Betty and me.

MRS. BERNICK: No, Lona, you mustn't!

MISS HESSEL: How could I run away and abandon all you youngsters just when you're beginning to start a new life? Being a foster-mother is my job, isn't it? You and I, Martha—we two old maids—! What are you looking at?

MARTHA: How light the sky has grown! It's bright and calm over the sea. The *Palm Tree* has good luck in her sails.

MISS HESSEL: And good luck on board.

BERNICK: And we—we have a long, hard day ahead of us. I most of all. But let it come. Oh, gather close around me, you loyal and true women. That is something else I've learned in these past few days. It is you women who are the pillars of society.

MISS HESSEL: Then it's a poor wisdom you've learned, brother-in-law. (*Puts her hand firmly on his shoulder.*) No, Karsten. The spirit of truth and the spirit of freedom—they are the pillars of society.

Note on the Translation

The Pillars of Society is, like *A Doll's House* an *An Enemy of the People*, a fairly straightforward play to translate. The chief problems are Hilmar Tœnnesen and Lona Hessel. Hilmar talks in a fanciful manner, overloaded with adjectives and ridiculous flights of imagination, like Hjalmar Ekdal in *The Wild Duck*. Lona has a breezy, slangy way of speaking which contrasts markedly with the prim speech of the local stay-at-homes, and since she and Johan have spent the past fifteen years in America I have tried to make them talk like Americans.

The Norwegian word *samfund* can mean either society in general, or a specific community. Ibsen uses it in both senses, and I have translated it sometimes as society and sometimes as community, as the context demands.

The chief characters in *The Pillars of Society* are a good deal younger than they are generally played. The "incident" with Dina's mother took place fifteen years ago. Johan was then nineteen, so he is now thirty-four. Bernick was then four years older than Johan, so he is thirty-eight. Martha is the same age as Johan. Mrs. Bernick is older than her brother Johan, so is presumably in her middle to late thirties; and Lona Hessel is older than Mrs. Bernick and therefore presumably in her late thirties or early forties. She should not be more than a few years older than Bernick, if at all, since he nearly married her.

ABOUT THE AUTHOR

HENRIK IBSEN, widely regarded as the founder of modern drama, was born in Skien, Norway in 1828 into a family of prosperous merchants. His father's business failed suddenly while Ibsen was still a young boy, and Ibsen was forced to work as an apothecary's assistant. After six years of humiliating poverty, Ibsen entered the university, and in 1850 he was asked to join the new National Theater, where he wrote and directed plays and designed productions. His plays were not admired, the National Theater went bankrupt, and Ibsen, forced to live on the charity of friends and a government travel stipend, emigrated to Italy.

It was not until 1866, when *Brand* was published to critical acclaim and *Peer Gynt* to even greater praise, that Ibsen began to gain recognition as a playwright. The next decade was a fertile one. Ibsen's dramas of social and family life attracted more attention, and *A Doll's House* was produced to international admiration, though it aroused controversy for its unromantic portrayal of marriage and its realistic depiction of the tensions between husband and wife. Ibsen's next play, *Ghosts* (1881), which dealt frankly with free love and venereal disease, was violently attacked as indecent. His succeeding plays, among them such acknowledged masterpieces as *The Wild Duck* (1884) and *Hedda Gabler* (1890), were met with bafflement and disdain, the artistic establishment accusing Ibsen of being relentlessly pessimistic and unnecessarily obscure. In 1891, Ibsen returned to Norway, where he lived until his death from a stroke in 1906. He never lived to see the recognition that would one day place him among the greatest dramatists of Western Literature.

ABOUT THE TRANSLATOR

Michael Meyer is one of the leading Ibsen scholars of his generation. He was born in London in 1921 and educated at Oxford. He has lived extensively in the Scandinavian countries and taught English literature at Upsala University in Sweden. In addition to his translation of *The Plays of Ibsen,* available in four volumes from Washington Square Press, he has written a biography of Ibsen, translated the plays of Strindberg, and, most recently, written a biography of Strindberg. He currently resides in London.